DREAM
BUILD
BELIEVE

Love, Wine, Music and
the Founding of Notaviva Vineyards

STEPHEN W. MACKEY
Foreword By Shannon Mackey

www.mascotbooks.com

Dream, Build, Believe

For more information, please contact:
Mascot Books
560 Herndon Parkway #120
Herndon, VA 20170
info@mascotbooks.com

Library of Congress Control Number: 2016907720

CPSIA Code: PBANG0816A
ISBN-13: 978-1-63177-729-5

Printed in the United States

To Tristan, Duncan & Ronan

Bow your heads when you win.
Raise your heads when you lose.
Tell the truth.
Do your best.
Never give up.
Wherever your paths may lead, your stories began here.
We love you always.

To our parents

Thank you for your love, your faith, and your courage in
overcoming your doubts and fears to support our every endeavor.
As our lives have taken each of us down the paths less traveled,
you never questioned what we knew in our hearts.
You simply listened and loved and for that we are forever grateful.

To our family and friends

Thank you for your love, labors, generosity and enthusiasm.
We are indebted to you for the many times your words of
encouragement have inspired us through the many times we have
lost our way.

To Shannon

Thank you for the confidence and purpose you have bestowed upon my life. Thank you for the patience you have shown on so many occasions when I have come unraveled. Thank you for the encouragement you have given me during the darkest times. Most of all, thank you for just being you, for being the single brightest light in my entire universe. I once promised you a fairy tale, and regardless of what the world may hold in store for us in the years to come, whether the greatest achievements or the most dismal failures, I want you to know my life is complete because we have chosen to face the world together.

Forever yours,
Stephen

For Gram

Contents

FOREWORD
by Shannon Mackey

T. R. O. U. B. L. E.—that was the first word that popped into my head when I met Stephen. Oh my, did he make me nervous and excited the first time I laid eyes on him. He took my breath away. I'll never forget that image of him. I remember every detail of what he looked like—his bad boy long hair, tank top, running shorts, and work boots with white socks. It was the 90s—trust me, he looked good. Most of all, I remember his devilish smile and those bright blue eyes... picture a young Mel Gibson in *Lethal Weapon*. That was him. I also knew I wasn't ready for Stephen yet. At the time, I assumed he was a little too hot to handle. He still had plenty of wild oats to sow and stories to tell. I was satisfied with running into him over the years and wondering if the electricity between us was just my imagination or a harmless flirtation we rekindled each time he came through town. I casually kept tabs on him over the years. I remember hearing, at some point along our separate journeys, that he was engaged to someone else. I was heartbroken. Thankfully, that "grapevine" intel turned out to be false.

Then, one June day in the summer of 2002, he took my breath away for a second time, when I ran into him quite unexpectedly at an old friend's wedding and he was very much single. I gave him my number... then I gave it to him again about thirty minutes later, to make sure he hadn't lost it the first time. Real smooth. He simply said, "I'm coming to see you, and I think you know why." My answer was "Yes." That was all either one of us needed to say.

Now that I look back on those memories, I know what I truly wasn't ready for at the time was his energy and stamina. Stephen and I were not meant to be together when we first met because I had not yet discovered my sense of self. We both had a lot of growing up to do and separate heartaches to experience, and I needed to find my own inner strength before I could match wits and harden my gut to keep up with him. I had to become a very strong, confident, thick-skinned, gentle-souled person to keep up with Stephen, the same things he provides to me.

Stephen has never once made me feel insecure in his love for me and devotion to our family. I always describe him as being a true Gemini—two people locked in a body, who sometimes are diametrically opposed and other times are in perfect harmony. He can be a rugged warrior one minute and a graceful artist the next. He is the most dynamic and passionate person I have ever met, and yet he is the most secluded soul. Most people judge him without ever truly understanding him. He can be a bull in a china shop, but I wouldn't have it any other way. We have been partners in life every step of the way, whether personal or business. Although one person is usually out in front during that journey, they would not survive without the support from behind.

Our dream to build a winery was born on a romantic whim, and then fueled by pure grit and determination. It takes me by surprise sometimes, when I hear our story being retold. I think to myself that we must have been insane. On our first date at Breaux winery, I remember asking the question "Who gets to do this?" and him replying "Do you wanna?" It took my breath away for the third time... or was it the wine we were drinking? To be honest, I don't really remember how it all happened so quickly. The dream kind of found us, not the other way around. It took off from there like a rocket, and the dream soon owned us. Rather than taking our breath away, we would spend the next years of our lives simply holding our collective breath on our challenging journey.

Many parts of the original winery dream have come true over the years, but the highs have been much higher than we expected, and the lows, well, they have unfortunately been much lower. Ninety percent of the customers that walk through our tasting room doors have been delightful. Some have intentionally journeyed to our tasting room from all over the country because a piece of our story resonated with them. They may be searching out their own leap of faith, or perhaps they let one pass them by; either way, we provide them with evidence that the dream can come true. Other people are simply curious to check out a new venue. We love to see their mouths drop open when we tell them our story. The men usually give Stephen "Wow, I wish I had the guts" looks, and the women usually glance at me sideways, wondering "Are you nuts?" When they take that first sip of wine, they are almost always pleasantly surprised that these two "kids" can actually produce an amazing bottle of wine. Even the doubters, who walk into our tasting room to see if the notion of wine and music is a gimmick they can debunk, have been won over by the time they walk out the doors. We've provided them with a new way to think about wine and the entire experience surrounding it. Pairing wine and music is not a foreign concept; they've been doing it all along. They just didn't realize it.

In addition to the standard tasting room business, we've had the chance to host some of the most important events in people's lives, including birthdays, retirements, weddings, and births. Those events are what Notaviva was truly built for, and we love sharing our home with these people on their special days. That is what gives Notaviva its soul.

As with everything in life, the good must always come with the bad, and there are many tales of the remaining ten percent. Usually the worst stories become the best fodder, and at the very least, they provide us with a good laugh down the road, once the wounds to our pride have healed. It's unfortunate that those few highly disrespectful people who have no appreciation for backbreaking work can leave you feeling emotionally dejected or left picking up the literal pieces of property they destroyed at the end of a long day. Those are the people who have clearly never owned a business or created anything of any real substance with their own two hands; if they had, they would never be callous enough to shred your work for no reason other than to provide themselves with a selfish bit of humor. The winery business is not for the faint of heart, because at the end of the day you are mixing people with alcohol; it either brings out the best or the worst from them, once they let down their guard. Because this all takes place inside our home, with our children thankfully unaware downstairs, those wounds cut much deeper, and the notion that it's "just business" could not be further from the truth. Thankfully, Stephen and I have always found sanctuary in taking a drive with the boys to clear our heads. When we return, the customers are gone, and our home is once again revealed. Reading Stephen's recollections of the good times and the challenging experiences we have faced together on this journey, I could not be more proud of our accomplishments.

We're not good at listening to people's advice (don't mix business with pleasure, don't work with family, the list goes on). We're so good at not listening to that advice that we went ahead and founded two businesses together, on top of raising our family in one of them. Every day is a struggle to find the balance in our winery and multimedia businesses, but more importantly, to find the balance for our family and find our balance together. We are clearly insane, but it somehow works for us. We love working together, and we are able to provide equal support to each other. Somehow, through all of the stresses of building the house and the businesses, we were always able to work hand in hand. Now we have to find the balance of not always working, but living hand in hand. This memoir is a story of love and passion and constantly readjusting to find that perfect balance.

We are able to find some of the family balance by simply walking out the door and onto our land. Although I am proud of the structure we built, I am in awe of the natural land around it. I am truly at peace when I am working on our family garden, knowing that I can provide safe nourishment for my family; I know Stephen finds a similar solace when he is out hunting with the boys. The chickens and pigs have provided invaluable lessons to our entire family on the incredible circle of life, and an undeniable knowledge and responsibility for the food on our table. The one word that reigns loudly is RESPECT— respect for the natural world around us, not only it's beauty, but also its sheer power that we ultimately have no control over, respect for the land and the nutrients it provides to our family as long as we take care of it in return, and respect for the lives of the animals and the bounty they provide for our family.

Now that the boys are older, I think they are also finding more balance in their lives by connecting with the land, although their connections are far more creative. Boys will be boys, and they are given the freedom to express it. The giant mulch pile becomes the supreme fortress for epic Nerf war battles. Many an unsuspecting customer has narrowly escaped the whizzing of a Styrofoam dart behind their backs. The giant hill in the front of the tasting room becomes the Hoth scene from *Star Wars* and provides for supreme sledding rides. Whether it's camping in our field, racing with the dogs to round up the chickens, or mucking through the stream by the pond, they love to explore our land. One of the summertime favorites of our family and friends is "star club," which includes the boys hauling out every known blanket onto the front hill and dreaming under the stars that shine brightly in the open country.

Our family has also found an incredible balance and second home at Powhatan School. One drawback for the boys to living on the farm is that they don't have any close neighbors to play with, although they have learned to befriend the children of our customers quite quickly for a game of tag or fishing in the pond. Powhatan is far more than just a school. It is a strong community and a safe haven for our boys, and our family has been blessed by being a part of it. The boys are truly excited to go to school every day to spend time with their friends and mentors, and they love being given the opportunity to explore the campus and its surroundings. It's not often you find an educational environment that shares your same family values for learning and respect for the people and world around you.

When Stephen and I started down this path, we knew we wanted to build a family and provide a unique home, all while building a business that combined our passions. That was our dream, and we have succeeded in that undoubtedly. We were blessed with three amazing boys, all with very unique personalities. They are the center of our universe, and everything we do now is for them. We have learned, however, that dreams must remain flexible and be given a life of their own. What was once the dream for Stephen and Shannon must now include the personalities and desires of three young souls. Will they want to be involved in our businesses when they get older? Who knows; that will be their choice in the future. For now, they are beginning to experience the hard work of caring for the vines and tending to the farm. At the same time, they are reaping the rewards of fishing from the pond and hunting on our property. Watching them embrace those experiences makes the toil all worth it. They have been given a front row seat to learning the invaluable lessons of hard work and dedication, combined with equal part success and failure. It may not be a fairy tale, but it is our story.

Through it all, Stephen and I have created an amazing story that we hope has inspired others to take a chance and follow their dreams. Would we have done somethings differently over the years, now that we have the benefit of hindsight? Perhaps, but then that would not have been our story. We always seem to find the hardest path, but perhaps that is also the road less traveled for a reason. What's the point of taking the road if you don't have the bumps and bruises to prove it?

INTRODUCTION

I was born restless. Since early childhood, I have felt an incessant longing within—an urge to explore, to discover, to know. Coupled with that, to a fault, is a fierce, unyielding independence. I continually drive myself to the brink of physical, mental, and emotional exhaustion in defiance of my limits. So many have asked over the years, "Why? What drives you?"

I believe I am overly self-motivated out of a deep sense of obligation to my heritage, to my family, to my friends, to myself. While on tour as monitor engineer in 1994 with Tanya Tucker in New Orleans, my cousin Rusty told me, "Man, you just *have it*. You have *the gift*." It took me years to grasp his meaning. What did he mean by "the gift?"

Perhaps he meant creativity, the innate ability to conceive a vision, wholly new, original, and unproven. Perhaps he meant problem solving, the ability to work through a series of challenges to arrive at a solution, or maybe technical capabilities, being able to quickly grasp highly complex systems and equipment. Perhaps he meant artistic abilities, producing works in the visual and musical arts. It might simply be passion, the outwardly visible commitment of my emotions to whatever challenge I am undertaking. Perhaps all of these, coupled with a myriad of other talents, experiences, and skills, constitute "the gift."

As I navigated life's twists and turns in an effort to understand what "the gift" was, possessing it has instilled within me an enormous burden, a sense of responsibility. It weighs on me. In my view, being entrusted with such good fortune bears a cost—the continual expenditure of whichever abilities are being challenged is my obligation to those who have not been so blessed. In other words, *I believe I owe it to others to rise to my fullest potential.* Very often, however, this self-induced, overwhelming sense of responsibility negatively impacts my outward persona. As I continually fail at trying not to appear as a "know it all" while balancing my sincere desire to use my talents to make the world a better place, people find me driven, distracted, frustrated, antsy, or impatient. I often feel completely misunderstood; I am just trying each day to do my best with my given abilities, and therefore prefer the term "dynamic." I have been labeled much, much worse.

I came to believe at an early age that possessing talent alone achieves nothing. Take, for instance, any of my abilities, and I assure you, millions of people in this world possess talents far superior to my own. My differentiators, I believe, are my tenacity, drive, and work ethic, fundamentally grounded in my sense of obligation.

Possessing talent just happens, and I sincerely believe that everybody can be good at something. Work ethic, however, is learned, and it is hard-won. My independence and work ethic were simultaneously developed quite young, both out of observation as well as necessity.

My father, Mack, has had a long career in various intelligence agencies, and traveled often during my childhood. When he was home, he usually could be found building or fixing something—by himself, of course—a beer in one hand and a hammer in the other, in true Mackey fashion. While he was away, my curiosity and broken toys led me into the garage and to the toolbox. Early efforts adjusting bike chains quickly led to power tools and the soldering iron. I was quite the fix-it by sixth grade, although, on more than one occasion, I found myself running for cover after Dad ran the lawnmower over a crescent wrench I had left rusting in the front yard.

This pattern of self-reliance has followed me (haunted me...) throughout my various careers in audio engineering, information technology, business management, digital media, and agriculture. I have been continually employed since I was twelve years old, the legal age in Virginia at which one can get a worker's permit. Notwithstanding my entrepreneurial exploits occasionally shoveling driveways and mowing lawns for a few dollars prior to that, my entry into the American workforce began as a paperboy, carrying a heavy bag of *Loudoun Times Mirror* newspapers around the neighborhood.

To say that most of my mistakes, failures, injuries, and social gaffes have been caused by my independence and inability to ask for help would be the understatement of the century. It would also fair to say, however, that most of the men up the Mackey family tree, as far back as you would care to go, would echo that sentiment, assuming you could actually get one of us to admit we may have a chink in our armor.

Considering all of these complex elements of my persona, then, I suppose it is all the more improbable that on a planet of well over 7 billion beings, I happened to meet and marry the one person who is most capable of understanding and tolerating me—to the extent that I am understandable and tolerable. The joining of my life with Shannon's has bestowed upon me untold amounts of love, courage, inspiration, and confidence, driving me forward with the belief I can achieve anything. The births of our three sons has humbled me, and granted me a depth of love I had not thought possible. These four people are my inspiration, my driving force.

The pages that follow contain the honest, heartfelt, and often heart-wrenching story of our beautiful relationship and the founding of Notaviva Vineyards, our Virginia farm winery located in rural Loudoun County, about fifty minutes west of the small suburban town in which I was raised. Painful at times to write, hysterical at others, I have made every attempt to openly depict the dreams, fears, successes, and failures that have we have encountered along the way.

This book was written to show others the way; to prove that you are capable of rising to whatever challenges you might place upon yourselves. To let you know it is alright to be afraid; it is not alright to accept fear. To let you know it is alright to fail; it is not alright to accept failure.

Each of our lives is a journey comprised of a series of situations, obstacles, and choices. Simply by virtue of the mysteries of life, you are fortunate enough to have been endowed with intelligence, creativity, and the ability to make decisions not merely based on survival, but based on your own personal, subjective definition of a rich, rewarding life. Take a moment to close your eyes and ask yourself what you really want to do with the short amount of time you have been given. You chose to open this book—which path will you choose once you put it down?

PART ONE

Dream

CHAPTER 1

"Love at First Sight"

There were no fireworks. No cartoonish cacophony of crackles, whistles or explosions. No flashes of bright lights or colorful showers of sparks. For me, that moment went completely silent. It was as if all of my senses shut down, save my vision, as I struggled to comprehend the rush of emotion that had just overwhelmed me. As I regained my senses, I suddenly understood. It was an immediate transition from boy to man, triggered at last by the most mystical of human emotions. Although I did not even know her name, I knew with a glance that I loved Shannon deeply, and that this moment would forever change the course of my life.

Whenever I reflect on that scene, even though it occurred over twenty-three years ago, I am still amazed at how crystal clear the memory is. Perhaps even more incredible is the fact that, after decades of traveling around the world as a professional audio engineer, information technology developer, digital media producer, and now wine composer (with thousands upon thousands of experiences along the way), the moment I fell in love feels like it happened a mere heartbeat ago. My life has been a series of leaps of faith, where I have followed my heart to later discover how seemingly disparate events have come together to redefine my world. Though meeting Shannon in that place was a chance occurrence, the risks I had taken and choices I had made in the years leading up to that moment all paid off in the blink of an eye. Allow me to rewind the clock a bit, to shed some light on the events and characters involved in blessing me with my future wife.

In the winter of 1989, I was beginning my degree at the University of Miami in Music Engineering Technology after transferring from Virginia Tech, where I had studied Computer Engineering for three years before discovering the program at Miami. It was essentially a bachelor's of music with an intense focus in electrical engineering and physical science, designed to prepare students for careers in the audio engineering industry. Coursework included the core curriculum of music theory, orchestration, arranging, history, and instrumental performance. In addition to these courses were the technical ones— electrical engineering, physics of acoustics, digital audio theory, and architecture as it relates to recording studio design.

My principal instrument was saxophone, and throughout my three years at UM, I played the primary four (soprano, alto, tenor, and baritone) in various ensembles, small and large. Although not the worst saxophonist at UM (twenty-second out of twenty-four), I was still granted some leverage from my instructors due to being a MUE. It was understood that our career paths would not be performance-focused; although we were held to very high standards in our written coursework, we were not expected to compete for first chair in the world-renowned concert jazz band.

I established a name for myself in the live audio and production scene early, after seeing the band Bad English perform on the patio at UM. Being a die-hard Journey fan (Jonathan Cain and Neil Schon were in both bands), I was, of course, situated in the front row. After the show ended, I noticed several of my classmates rushing onto the stage to dismantle the audio gear. I called one over and asked how he got connected with it, and he told me to talk to Chris Bishop. Taking stock of my current bleak financial situation (delivering Herbie's Pizzas around Miami to scrape together my pickup truck payment, while other classmates were partying), I figured this looked a lot more interesting, and certainly more professionally relevant.

A few days later, I bumped into Bishop in the stairway leading up to the MUE recording studio. After a brief interview (during which he established I had a pickup truck and could be useful), he promised to give me a call. Two weeks after that, I was skipping class, unloading truckfuls of staging equipment into the sand on South Miami Beach. I was incredulous that I would be paid the princely sum of $75 for a mere six hours of backbreaking labor in the sun! I worked hard and passed my initiation load-in, and was asked to return that evening to dismantle the stage. Gladly accepting, I was informed I would be paid another $75 for the second shift. I would be making $150 in one day? I felt faint from this new goldmine of opportunity—working outdoors, physical challenges, high energy, punishing volume levels, and lots of bikini-clad women—live sound production was the Promised Land. I never slung another pizza again.

One gig led to another, and later that spring I was introduced to one of my many mentors, Antonio Parodi, who was widely recognized as a leader in live event production. In addition to his tour management with musicians, Tony was the production manager for all of the big Univision live television productions, including Carnival, Calle Ocho, and Nuestra Belleza. I recall Bishop introducing us at the Dania Jai Alai, where we were loading in for a twenty-four hour telethon production: "Tony, this is Steve Mackey, he is going to be one of your Marines." "Welcome to the team, a friend of Chris' is a friend of mine."

Instantly likeable, Tony was inspiring as well as nurturing. No matter how many hours we worked, no matter what time of day, no matter what conditions, Tony was always the first one awake and the last one asleep. I once worked forty-one hours continuously on the Calle Ocho production, and Tony was there when I showed up for load-in and still calculating expenses when I collapsed in bed two days later. He led by example, and gave us enormous flexibility to propose solutions and try our ideas, yet was always there to pick up the pieces when we made mistakes. He hired on promise—young, energetic go-getters who were short on experience but brimming with enthusiasm and can-do attitude always had a place on Tony's teams. I have subscribed his hiring philosophy to this day.

Two years later, in March of 1992, Tony introduced me to another of my long-time mentors, Chris Carlton, the technical director at the Dade County Youth Fair and Exposition. A widely respected touring audio engineer, Carlton was the front-of-house (FOH) engineer for Julio Iglesias. He was also very in-demand as FOH engineer for the large, live Univision television productions. Carlton had asked Tony if he had any talent who could operate mixing consoles as well as provide entry-level technical services. He was always in need of several dozen techs for all manner of positions in his shows.

The Fair is the largest fair in the state of Florida. Hundreds of thousands of visitors flock to the myriad of attractions over two and a half weeks from the end of March through April of each year. In addition to the wonderful rides, games, and other activities, there are a host of live productions, ranging from concerts and dancing to magic and ice shows. Internationally touring performers create unforgettable experiences for children and parents alike. Supporting these productions is a world-class technical team, comprised of full-time producers and directors, as well as a talented array of freelance and independent technicians.

Bishop and I landed senior roles at the Fair for the 1992 season, establishing a wonderful rapport with Carlton. Similar to Tony, Carlton was incredibly genial, nurturing, and patient, while encouraging us to try our hands at operating audio consoles, interfacing with the show talent, making production decisions, and learning the larger perspectives of the entertainment industry. His hiring philosophy also favored talent and enthusiasm over experience and chops.

Approaching graduation in a few months, I had begun to turn my attention to post-collegiate employment, which, given my experiences over the previous two years, was focused on live audio engineering. During several discussions with Carlton, he graciously promised to keep his ears open for positions. Sure enough, in May of 1992, he phoned to offer me a position on the Julio tour. A few weeks later, I departed my hometown of Sterling, Virginia for Cyprus, Greece, for the first gig of my professional career.

I toured with Julio for the rest of 1992 and much of 1993. In early March, Carlton turned his attention to the technical direction and staffing for the Fair. I was excited to return to Miami to work the shows, and Carlton placed me in charge of the Franz Harary magic show, where I would be lead audio engineer and production manager. Due to a last-minute scheduling change with a Julio concert, Carlton and I were delayed a few days, and missed rehearsals and the first two shows.

As Carlton and I were on tour with Julio—and I was being introduced to the wonders of Spanish wines—much of the staffing effort fell to Bishop, who recruited techs from the local pool of freelancers. In addition to the pros, Bishop also visited UM on a recruiting mission, seeking entry-level techs amongst the students. Each Friday morning, the music school hosted a forum for industry professionals to speak with the students, advising them on careers, technologies, and the like. One Friday morning, Bishop visited the campus and spoke at a MUE forum. Quickly briefing the students on the value of real-world employment in conjunction with a formal education, he inquired if any of the students would be interested in working on the technical crews at the Fair. He was quite surprised to see an eighteen-year old, six foot tall, fresh-faced beauty excitedly raise her hand. Having done some modeling in high school, Shannon did not exactly fit the stereotype of a "roadie."

Shannon's love of music and subsequent professional interest had taken flight when she took electric guitar lessons at the local music store while a freshman in high school. Her early influences were all the eighties big hair arena rock bands, and she must have looked pretty cool, rocking out with her black Ibanez guitar (which sported a pink volume knob), throwing the goat and blowing kisses to her Richie Sambora posters. During this time, a Christian rock band named Boundless played for her youth group, and she was instantly taken with live sound. Since it was a Christian band, her parents relented and allowed her to travel with them to run spotlight on weekends;

soon, she knew that live sound and music were her future. As she began to research colleges in her junior year, she learned about the program at the University of Miami and, realizing her chops would not gain her admission into the jazz guitar program, began taking classical guitar lessons.

Our paths converged in South Florida, two days after the start of the Fair. In an effort to get quickly up to speed on the status of the productions, I made the rounds to the various show sites, checking in on the crews and meeting each show's talent. As I approached the mix position in the show tent, the lead engineer walked up and began giving me the tech rundown and production schedules. It fell on deaf ears.

There she was, sitting at the mixing console, reviewing cues or something. She had turned around to see who had just arrived, and felt me staring at her—I was not known for my subtlety. Her face quickly drew a deep shade of red, and she immediately began inspecting her shoelaces, and continued to do so for the next five minutes while the lead engineer yammered on and on about some show-related nonsense.

"Huh? Did you say something? Who is THAT???" I asked, trying to recover and gather my wits.

"Sorry, buddy, that one is mine—looks like you got here a little late!" he replied.

Devastated, I could not believe that someone so beautiful, so instantly mesmerizing, could be mixed up in such a wolf's den of roadies, carnies, and other assorted scoundrels. I knew without question, however, that my life had been touched in a way I had never experienced before.

The lead engineer and Shannon began a rocky relationship that would last the next several years. I would see them often on my travels—staying with them the following year to work the Fair, stopping in as several of my rock tours traveled through South Florida, and even on occasion in D.C., where they ended up some years later. Each time, I always let her know how I felt about her. Long gazes, shameless flirtatious talk, and gentle touches—you name it, and I was guilty as charged.

The amazing thing was that we both always *knew* it. We knew it was real, we knew it was deep, and yet something always held us back. Although she often describes this time in her life as sitting on a shelf and miserable, she never cheated, and I never wanted her to. If it was going to happen, it had to be absolutely perfect. For two people who later would make their biggest life decision in the span of a heartbeat, this atypical self-restraint allowed us to grow as individuals. We learned life lessons, found our true selves, matured through various relationships, and suffered personal loss, all the while hoping that someday the stars would align and bring us together.

On June 8, 2002, they would do just that.

CHAPTER 2
"The End of the Road"

In the fall of 1998, four months after my thirtieth birthday, ten years of which I had spent in the professional audio industry, I was done. Toast. Fried. Cooked. Miserable. I recall lying in my hotel room in Panama City, staring at the ceiling fan. I had just gotten off the phone with my brother Jim, who was living in my Nashville home. He was also going through a rough phase of his life, soul-searching, trying to find his place in this world. After spending a year in a cage, bartending in a Nashville airport hotel, listening to drunk business travelers whine about their miserable lives, he had decided to head back home to Virginia. I simply told him to just lock the door, and I'd see him at Thanksgiving.

Pondering his situation and my own, I contemplated how my audio career had come full-circle. I had been shipped off to South America to work as the monitor engineer for the Reencuentro tour, which essentially was a Menudo reunion (minus Ricky Martin, who, in 1998, was doing just fine on his own). Interestingly enough, the other engineer on the tour was Chris Carlton, and the production manager was Tony Parodi. My two earliest influences and I, together again on a "reunion" tour—and here I was, pondering how this phase of my life could come to an end.

For a better insight into my frayed state of mind, a brief lesson in live audio and event production is in order. A typical production tour has two mixing audio engineers, plus additional support audio technicians (in addition to lighting crew, band crew, riggers, production assistants, accountants, wardrobe, catering, drivers, etc.). The front of house (FOH) engineer mixes the audio that the audience hears. That person is (usually) a safe distance from the stage, surrounded by a sea of partying people, being creative, mostly having a rather good time. The monitor engineer, on the other hand, is set up on the side of the stage (when not under it), and mixes audio so the band members can hear each other.

Some artists on stage are absolute professionals, and smooth communication between artist and engineer results in seamless mixing, happy bands, confident performers, and superior shows. Other artists, however, have been known to suffer from various forms of alcoholic and/or pharmaceutical stimuli, which can not only affect their ability to sing, but can also transform them into raving lunatics.

If you've ever been to a concert or watched one on TV, you've no doubt seen musicians communicating with their monitor engineer, whether you realized it or not. Sometimes it is as subtle as a glance over their left shoulder, pointing to their mouth and then pointing up, which translates to "I need my vocal a little louder." Oftentimes, the communication is made with the middle finger, however, and is intended to convey the artist's mortal hatred for the engineer and his burning desire to bludgeon him with a heavy piece of staging. Next is the inevitable launching of the microphone stand at the engineer's head.

You might think this gig sounds easy—just grab the little knob marked "VOX" and turn it to the right a few clicks, no problem. Unless you have actually stood at the lead vocal position on a rock tour, you do not understand the meaning of the word *loud*, much less the precise and delicate interaction of microphone rejection, loudspeaker placement, console gain structure, amplification technology, environmental factors, and a few hundred other factors that constantly keep a rock stage teetering on the brink of ear-splitting feedback.

Prior to mixing monitors for Reencuentro, I had just been out on tour with Ted Nugent for two months (who, incidentally, is a brilliant musician and an intelligent, amazing human being). Though some (most) people may find him a bit outspoken, I thoroughly enjoyed my time working with him. The volume level of that stage was second only to the volume level on the Bon Jovi "These Days" European stadium tour stage, which had a monitor rig for Jon that rivaled PA systems most concert tours could use *for the entire audience.*

So, here is my definition of loud: you walk up to the microphone, give a fine roadie "check one two," and your ears shut off—go completely quiet. Now, I am not an ear doctor, but it is my understanding that what happens is your eardrums get blasted with a sound pressure level (SPL) so great they get stretched to their limit, and can no longer vibrate. When they are not vibrating, they are not transmitting signals to your nerve endings, which means you hear nothing. You can feel the stage vibrating, and your head is physically vibrating, so you can hear low frequencies, but nothing above that. That's what "rock loud" means—so loud you hear nothing, sometimes referred to as "compression."

Please note, I am not advocating loud volume levels—quite the opposite. I strongly encourage the use of earplugs at concerts, and keeping your headphones and stereos turned down to a reasonable level at all times. Unless you want tinnitus or other permanent hearing damage, which I assure you is very real, unrecoverable, and becoming more of an annoyance in my everyday life, keep it turned down. I once worked with a monitor engineer who made me move a speaker from the left side of his rig to the right, because he had already lost the hearing in his left ear and needed the speaker on the other side in order to work. Seriously.

Back to being a monitor engineer, the person mixing so the band members can hear each other. On the Reencuentro tour, with a seven-piece band and six vocalists, not only did I have one person pointing at something and pointing up (they ALWAYS point up...), I had ten people pointing, while the other three were throwing gear at my head.

To make matters worse, on this particular tour, the budget only allowed us one small truck to carry band gear and my mixing console, which meant that in each city, we had to use whatever audio amplifiers and speakers the local sound company had. I'm pretty sure most of this gear came out of U.S. landfills when our regional companies had decided it was not fit for usage. I spent the better part of each day trying to deduce why knob #1 went to equalizer #7 then into amplifier #4 and sound came out of speaker #8.

The proverbial straw that broke the roadie's back was a five-day run in Venezuela. Normal touring, even in the U.S., is tough. Long hard days, multiple shows in a row, and long stretches away from home wear you down. Modern tours make sincere efforts to provide crews with comfortable accommodations—well-appointed buses, single hotel rooms, and adequate days off. Things do not always work out like that, though. In some South American countries, it is neither safe nor healthy to travel around in a well-appointed bus followed by a caravan of trucks with millions of dollars in audio gear in them. Hijacking is rampant, thus you typically have to fly from city to city.

This particular run went something like this:

7:00 A.M.	Arrive at the venue for load-in, discover the stage construction is about six hours behind schedule and half the stagehands are just a tad bit hungover from the party after the previous night's futbol match.
7:30 A.M.	Go in search of the equipment truck, which is likely on the wrong side of the stadium, still fully-loaded.
8:00 A.M.	Go in search of catering, which is likely in the back parking lot within scent of the stadium dumpster array—easy to find, just follow the flies.
8:30 A.M.	Find the stagehands and lead them to the truck and unload your gear.
9:30 A.M.	Go find your missing gear, which for some unknown reason has gone to the wrong end of the stadium.
10:00 A.M.	Reunited at last with your gear, begin unpacking consoles, power cables, signal interface cables, etc.

11:00 A.M.	Begin piecing together the shambles of the monitor rig in the grass behind where the staging technical area should have been set up three hours earlier, and should be setup sometime very soon (hopefully), but probably won't be for another few hours.
1:00 P.M.	Staging technical area is complete (only five hours late) and monitor equipment is rolled up the ramp into place, band gear rolls onto the stage to begin setup.
3:00 P.M.	Still trying to sort out equipment interface issues between our equipment and the local gear (same issues for the FOH engineer).
3:30 P.M.	Send a band gear tech to catering to bring back bananas or something edible—can't leave the stage, because if you take your eyes off the local crew to get something to eat, they will be gone when you return.
4:00 P.M.	Scheduled sound check time comes and goes; maybe half the local gear is working. Begin setting up microphones and patching stage input cables.
5:00 P.M.	Line check begins. Mic one goes into input 1 but shows up in monitor console channel 5 and FOH console channel 27. Begin troubleshooting.
5:30 P.M.	Repatch everything—band is pissed off and whining because they haven't sound checked yet.
6:00 P.M.	Repatch complete. Monitor console and FOH console have all inputs; bring on the band to sound check. Local systems starting to sound usable as adjustments continue.
6:30 P.M.	FOH engineer needs to hear a particular song chorus to check mix levels, but the horn section can't see the keyboard player and want to move, while the drummer and bassist are asking for more lead vocal, while the backup singers can't hear themselves because the local monitor speakers sound like shit, but the lead vocalists are happy because, thank goodness, we traveled with ear monitors. The promoter has already brought in a few dozen local model groupies for the rock stars to play with, but now they are getting more pissed off because the rhythm section needs to work out a part.
6:55 P.M.	Everybody hates everybody.
7:00 P.M.	Sound check finished. Band is happy again because the engineers and band gear techs have pulled off yet another technical miracle. Head to catering to find all the stage-hands and backstage ramp rats (second tier groupies) have eaten everything, leaving only a few cholera-laden vegeta-bles for the crew.

8:00 P.M.	Doors open, screaming dingbats flood the stadium, band is warming up.
9:00 P.M.	Showtime!
11:00 P.M.	Load-out begins. Disconnect interface cables to local gear, pack up microphones, cables, console, electronics racks.
12:00 A.M.	Stagehands are missing and need to be found (again). Gear is rolled down ramp, moved to truck to begin loading.
1:00 A.M.	Truck is loaded, leaves for next city.
1:30 A.M.	Crew heads to hotel.
2:00 A.M.	Crew arrives at hotel.
2:15 A.M.	Shower & quick nap (45 minutes).
3:30 A.M.	Lobby call for trip to airport.
4:30 A.M.	Arrive at airport.
5:30 A.M.	Wheels up—flight to next city (1 hour nap).
6:30 A.M.	Arrival—get luggage and meet crew bus at stadium (band heads to hotel to get some sleep—they've worked hard…).
7:00 A.M.	Arrive at the venue for load-in, discover the stage construction is about six hours behind schedule and half the stagehands are just a tad bit hung-over from the party after the previous night's futbol match.

I am not kidding when I say that this is an absolutely 100% accurate schedule of what a South American tour was like. And yes, we did five-in-a-row—Caracas, Maracaibo, Valencia, Maracay and Ciudad Guyana. We slept one hour at night, and maybe thirty minutes before or after sound check, but never more than two hours a day. Add on the very physical nature of assembling gear, running around a stage chasing down and patching problems, in 100-degree weather, and you begin to see what a miserable experience it could be—all for the love of the show.

Thus I found myself in a hotel in Panama, determined to change the course of my life. I picked up the phone and put in a call to the States, to my manager, Greg Hall at Clair Brothers Audio in Lititz, PA, and informed him that after this tour was over, I was done. He heard these sorts of rants a lot (road life really takes its toll on people's lives), and assured me that I could have some time off after the tour to rest, recharge, and be ready for the winter touring season.

Two months later, I sent in my official letter of resignation. It was Christmas 1998, and I was going home for the holidays at peace for the first time in years, knowing I was not getting on a tour bus ever again. I look back so fondly on those days now, grateful for the opportunities I had to travel and put together some of the biggest concert rigs to ever hit the road. It is incredibly rewarding to think you have played a role in putting smiles on millions of people's faces around the world. I'd had the privilege of meeting and working with some of the most intelligent, hardworking, and driven people I have ever known while in the pro audio industry. Several stood with me on my wedding day as groomsmen, and I shall always consider them brothers. The lessons learned on the road—namely those of diligence, tenacity, and never-say-die attitude—would play a much larger part in eventually founding a vineyard than I could have ever dreamed.

CHAPTER 3
"A Silly Little Word"

W hile I spent most of the nineties touring the world, living on tour buses and bumbling my way from one doomed relationship to the next, Shannon completed her degree and embarked upon a successful career in digital media business development. Upon graduation in 1996, she moved to Alexandria, Virginia (about forty-five minutes east of where I grew up), to begin working at the Advanced Television Technology Center. Though she had strayed from her first love of live sound, while at ATTC, she was involved in early HDTV and DTV equipment tests, including the first-ever HDTV broadcast from the Great Wall of China.

When Shannon left ATTC in 1998, she went to work for Comark Digital Services, where she developed products based on emerging DTV specifications. She quickly moved up the corporate ladder, landing a job as director of digital media at Discovery Communications, where she developed and managed global broadband and interactive television strategies. I moved back to Northern Virginia in early 2000, and a few months after I arrived, Shannon had already ended her relationship and taken a job as director of digital media business development, eventually reporting to Shane McMahon at World Wrestling Entertainment. She packed up and moved away from Virginia to Connecticut; once again, our paths had failed to cross.

My touring days were over, and I was determined to never go back. I was done, and I intended to make a living doing whatever else I had to. I had stayed completely clean and drug-free during all those years on the road. On my honor, I have never so much as smoked a single joint, much less chopped out a few rails of cocaine in the back lounge of a bus or shot anything into my arm. That actually led to quite bit of ostracization from other members of various crews, probably more than you might imagine. There were a few colleagues, however, who after I had refused a toke or a bump would kind of look at me with a great deal of respect, as if they wished they would have made a different choice at some point earlier in their lives. Oftentimes I would be the only person sitting in the front lounge reading, while the rest of the crew was in the back, partaking of various and sundry substances. I had been determined to protect my intellect, not endanger it with an addiction, and now that I was unemployed, I was extremely happy I did not have an expensive habit to support.

As my touring days had drawn to a close over the previous few years, I had begun to revisit my initial formal education in computer science at Virginia Tech as the most likely option for a new career. Dusting off my programming chops, I would write C++ programs for fun while sitting in my hotel room during days off on the road. I would have my laptop connected through the hotel phone lines so I could surf the Internet, and I had begun to develop a fascination for coding HTML, the underlying programming language of the world wide web. On a day off somewhere, I had grabbed a cab ride to the local mall, bought an HTML programmer's guide, and that was that. The first website I built was in winter 1998—a production guide for the Matchbox20 "Stole My Baby" world tour while I was touring with them as their FOH engineer. It was hideous, but I will never forget the feeling when I launched the site, and friends back home could read up on our gear list and tour schedule. I was hooked by the prospect of being able to exchange knowledge with people from around the world—an instant Internet fanatic.

Upon arriving home in Nashville in fall 1998, after the Reencuentro tour, I had formed my own small business, a web design company named Intertainment Technologies, Inc. A local lawyer helped me set it up, and I began landing some clients, mostly through networking and audio industry connections. Although I had no idea how to run a small business, I definitely knew I had no business sitting in a cube farm.

Every now and again, I would take a "one-off" audio gig. It became very surreal, running into former colleagues and hearing stories about new tours, new gear, and new opportunities. I had to talk myself down, reminding myself I was doing the right thing and reinventing myself for the long term, and some days it was harder to believe that than others.

Forming a home-based business gave me time to adjust to a much more stable way of life. I owned a single-family home in a Nashville suburb, and had converted one of the bedrooms into my office. I fell into a weird hybrid nocturnal development schedule, working until 2:00 A.M. each night, waking up at 10:00 A.M. and beginning the day.

Having no family in Nashville, and with my closest friends still on the road, I fell into a very isolated, lonely existence. There would be weeks at a time where my only contact with other people was asking someone for a spot at the gym, or giving my order to the person at a drive-thru window, or a quick phone call with a client for project clarification. After several months, I really began to enjoy the peace, the freedom, and the space.

I sat up late at night reading the industry news about all the newly created dot-com millionaires. Everywhere I looked, there was a story about some thirty-year old who had just struck it rich. I had just celebrated my thirty-first birthday in May 1999, and I was barely surviving with my own web design company, burning through my savings accounts—so I figured I was just as qualified as the next person to strike it rich during the Internet gold rush.

I began digging deeper into those stories, trying to understand how these businesses were succeeding, how people developed unique products, how they grew. I bought several books on writing business plans, and found myself at the Nashville public library, because most of the published industry data I needed for competitive analysis had not yet found its way online and was still in huge volumes of government hard copy.

One of the constants I discovered was that all of the people who were succeeding in business—not just online—were very passionate about their product and brand. I had taken a class at University of Miami on entrepreneurship, and clearly remembered this as a key lesson. So I began my own self-analysis, and it did not take long to realize my path would lead where it had always led, to the world of music.

This was the era of MP3.com, and I had several clients for whom I was posting original music on this and similar sites. The same fascination with art and technology that had steered me to audio engineering was now calling me online; but how, what, and why?

It was obvious that the consumption side of the industry was totally saturated. Well-funded venture capital-backed companies were furiously trying to figure out business models in hotly contested battles with the established music industry, and it was no place for a one-man startup. Weeks turned into months; although I had come up with a few promising ideas, I was fully aware I lacked the funding to bring any of them to fruition, nor did I possess the hardware or infrastructure to go at it alone. Then, one day in late summer 1999, the answer revealed itself as I looked within.

Passion—what was it about music that I was passionate about? Since childhood, I have always been curious about music's ability to affect a mood, to flip a bad day into good by changing the station. Thinking back to my music theory classes at UM, I recalled how much I absolutely loved theory, piecing together the analysis of notes and harmony, like some mystical puzzle whose real solution was different for everyone. I began to wonder, is the secret buried somewhere in those patterns of notes? There are infinite combinations, endless possibilities, available to anyone inspired to write a melody. Perhaps my answer was empowering and enabling people from all over the world to access, create, distribute, and share these complex and amazing little puzzles known as sheet music.

I had my direction; I would set out to build an online repository of sheet music, whereby people could either subscribe to the service or pay-per-download for individual works. With formal education in music business, I knew the complexities of licensing would have to be a second phase of the business. The first hurdle was building a proof of concept, a working model to pitch to potential investors. For this, I would need music in the public domain, the ability to transcribe sheet music into a downloadable online format, and an infrastructure upon which to build.

All those were relatively easy, affordable, and accessible, and in a few weeks I had figured out a process. I would take a digital camera into public music libraries, photograph works in the public domain (typically classical music from the 1800s), then print out the photos at home and transcribe the music from the photo into Overture (a composition software program), then create PDFs of the finished pieces for download. The business model was solid; the raw materials cost next to nothing, no royalties were involved, and the finished products were "build once, sell many"—which meant, over time, the production costs were paid in full, and the ongoing costs were merely storage and transfer bandwidth.

I quickly brought the working model to life, honing a lot of the production processes and evolving the business plan. The whole point was to get this idea funded quickly, because in fall of 1999, venture capitalists seemed to be giving away millions of dollars to anyone who could scribble a business plan on a napkin. I spent months drafting and re-drafting a very comprehensive business plan, complete with competitive analysis, growth projections, P&Ls, balance sheets, marketing strategy—just about everything except a name.

What would it be called? What word existed that could convey my passion for the seemingly magical power that music possessed? I spent days at the library, researching musical terminology, foreign languages, technology terms, and every time I thought I had come up with the perfect name, I always found that .COM name was already taken.

Thus began the quest for the perfect word, a simple way to describe the impact that music has on human emotion, that rush that you feel when you hear your favorite song, or the emotion that overcomes you when you hear a sad song. Turning to Italian, the language of music, I filled up page after page with various word snippets and combinations. Everything was way too long, or flowery, or just plain ridiculous. The answer was found in the smallest, simplest little package—a music note.

Just one music note, all by itself, without melody, harmony, progressions, the most basic building block of every song ever sung, the atom of the musical universe, in Italian is known as a "nota." Found within every note which has ever been played is a kind of magic, the spirit of the composer connecting with the dreams of the listener, full of life—"pieno di vita." Playing on the alliteration of the two words, the aggregation became "Notavita," meaning the life within music or the music of life.

Eureka! That .COM name was available! The United States Trademark Search was clean as well. I needed one more gut check, to make absolutely sure the name would work internationally. Having taken a marketing class at UM, I was keenly aware of how brand names could fail overseas. Everyone has learned of the "Nova" car debacle in South America—having a car named "no go" did not exactly work out as planned.

So I rang up a very dear friend, Patricia Santostefano. Her family owned a villa in Italy and it was her second language; given her love of music and her fluency in Italian, I knew she would be the perfect person to validate. I explained, and she immediately loved the idea, but told me straight away it was a little off. Even though it was technically grammatically correct, a real Italian would never say it that way. She said a more appropriate way would be to say "Nota Viva" and I instantly recognized the beauty of the word and was now even more excited.

I spent the afternoon conducting due diligence and clearing the word for usage, found it available everywhere. By that evening, I had reserved www.Notaviva.com and was drinking a bottle of wine, toasting my forthcoming global domination of the music publishing business.

A few weeks later, I had finished writing the business plan for the project, and decided to take it to the local Small Business Administration office to review it with a counselor. As we discussed various forms of funding, the conversation turned to grants. The counselor, a wily retiree who had founded a series of successful businesses, looked me right in the eye and said, "Listen to me, young man, forget about applying for any kind of grant. You're white, you're male, you've never served in the military, and you have nothing physically wrong with you. Nobody is going to grant you a dime." Seemed pretty clear to me that trying to secure some venture capital funding was the only option to get this initiative off the ground.

I began submitting the business plan to various venture capital companies and decided to move back to Northern Virginia to be close to family. My grandfather had recently passed away, and my grandmother was moving down from Pennsylvania to split time between my mother's home and my Aunt Gin's home. Mom was still working, and this was going to be a very tough adjustment for everyone—thus, the realization that I needed to head home to help out really tipped the scales. I had a standing job offer as the Webmaster at the National Renewable Energy Lab (NREL) in Golden, CO, but declined the offer in favor of moving back home to Virginia.

It was winter 2000, and some VCs were responding to the business plan submission with various degrees of interest. A month later, the Internet bubble burst, the stock market crashed, VC money dried up, and it was over. The business plan for www.Notaviva.com went in my memory box for good. That vision for fame, fortune, and untold wealth was simply not meant to be.

I took a job with a company called Luminant, consulting on a big IT project for RJ Reynolds. I had to get on a plane every Sunday night and fly down to North Carolina, live in a hotel for five days, and fly home on Friday night. I was back on the road again and miserable. That lasted a whole two months, after which I found a great position as a webmaster for an Internet security firm called TruSecure. The next two and a half years would be some of the most memorable times of my life; to this day, I still count the colleagues from my small development group among my dearest friends. I had made it to all fifty states and forty-two countries on six continents by the time I was thirty, and ended up right back in the town and house where I grew up, living with my mother and grandmother, commuting in Northern Virginia traffic to work in a cube farm as a junior-level IT geek.

CHAPTER 4
"Love at Second Sight"

After a few months living at home, it was obvious that I needed a place of my own. I had decided to keep my options open and chose not to sell my home in Nashville, instead renting it to Scott Savage, previously the drummer for Jars of Clay. The rent almost covered the mortgage, and I continued to build a little equity. Purchasing another home while still owning in Nashville was not going to work out, so renting became the only option.

I was fortunate to work out an arrangement with my cousin Tom, his wife Beth and son Camden, whereby I rented out their finished basement. Camden is a special needs child, and I found the daily exposure to the challenges they faced as a family to be both humbling and inspirational. No matter what difficulties I may have been having at work or in my personal life, all quickly vanished in the presence of their strength and deep love for their little boy. I recall one evening when Tom, Camden, and I were sitting on the front porch, and Camden suddenly had a seizure. Tom gently held him and talked him through it until he came around. Terrified, I turned my head and wept. They were wonderful housemates, and we often had Sunday dinner together, dining on fresh vegetables Tom had grown in his backyard garden. I treasured those moments, and promised myself that someday I would share similar dinners with my family, eating our own homegrown produce.

Summer faded to fall, and although I was content in my career and accommodations, I kept an eye on the real estate market. One day, my coworker Rob Klause brought in the Loudoun Times Mirror real estate insert. He had stumbled upon a rather odd advertisement, and had thought of me. Seems people often think of me when they see oddities.

The ad simply showed a photo of a wood stove, and the copy read, "25 acres—woods—hunting cabin—$116,500," with a phone number and street. It was way out in northwest Loudoun, in an area I had never even been to, though I had spent most of my life in the county.

Camden's birthday was that weekend, a beautiful October Sunday with the leaves in full color. I spent some time celebrating with the family, and then decided to take a drive to check out the property. The drive westward through Loudoun is one of the most serene and beautiful landscapes in the country. I found the street, but since the property did not have a real address (how cool was that!), I had to make a guess as to which was actually for sale. After a few tries, I was unable to find a plot matching the description, and continued way up to the top of Short Hill Mountain.

My 1992 Camaro was definitely not suited for the drive up the rocky, washed out road, but (as I often do) I decided to keep moving no matter what. Suddenly, coming around a bend, I saw a partially hidden gravel path. Driving through some overgrown weeds and underbrush, I emerged in a small clearing next to a small in-earth lodge. The cabin was hideous—run-down, overgrown, and moldy. I had never seen anything like it, though; the back wall was completely underground, built into the mountainside for thermal efficiency.

Next to "the shack" (as we would come to call it) was a clearing cut into the trees, about one acre in size. The view from the top of that mountain out over the valley was breathtaking. I stood there, breathing in the crisp mountain air, took another look at the shack, and decided on the spot that it was mine.

I was so thrilled at my discovery that I had to share it with someone, so I drove back to the birthday party and convinced my mom to come back out with me and have a look. My mother has always been my biggest fan and supporter. I sensed in her the usual motherly reservation and concern, but also a tone of excitement; this was so completely whacked, so far out of the ordinary, that it might just be worth doing. Looking back, perhaps she realized I had left home, traveled the world with rock stars and scoundrels for ten years, and managed to come home in one piece; maybe this was not so crazy after all.

A real trooper, she closed her eyes and held on tight as we headed back up the mountain (neither a fan of heights nor windy roads) and onto the property. A simple, soft "wow" as she took in the view, and I knew she understood. The living conditions were well below her comfort level (the shack was only 600 square feet and had a small generator for power), but the serenity of the location was immediately evident. We stood there for a while, taking in the sunset.

That night, I called the real estate agent and set up an appointment to come in the next day. I asked if anyone else was interested in the property, and learned that an attorney who owned several adjoining pieces of land was trying to low-ball them. Resolved that the property was mine, I showed up with earnest money in hand and made an offer for the full asking price. An hour later, the contract was signed.

I had to sell the Nashville home, but as luck would have it, Scott and his wife Kim had been looking for another place closer to friends and family and were ready to move. A few days later it was listed, and the market was hot in the fall of 2000; the house went quickly, and the $20,000 in equity went right into closing on the shack. A few days later, I was the proud owner of a dilapidated hovel that even drunk hunters thought was a dump, and twenty-five acres of the most beautiful forested land I had ever set foot upon, with spectacular sunsets above the Blue Ridge Mountains.

As I was settling into my mountain shack, Shannon was settling into a rental house on the beach in Milford, Connecticut with her dog Tamra. Since the house sat right on the beach, Shannon could only rent it from late fall through the end of winter. In early 2001, she began looking for a home to buy as Tamra recovered from a surprise attack by a neighborhood pit bull. Though her new circle of friends at WWE kept her out late in New York City, she wanted something in a quieter neighborhood, and found a fixer-upper in New Haven, about an hour's commute from her office (on a really good day). As Tamra recovered, Shannon realized she was very lonely and needed a playmate; Shannon adopted her second rescue, and in May 2001, moved in with her two dogs and got to work renovating her upstairs master suite.

Over the next eighteen months, I settled into a great routine, making the long drive from my mountaintop hideaway into the Dulles Technology Corridor, working hard with a talented team of great people, and reigniting my passion for composing music. Many evenings in the shack were spent writing and recording original songs, as well as transcribing orchestral film soundtracks to learn more about orchestration, arranging and scoring for visual media. I was so inspired by the music of James Horner, and set out to transcribe the entire Braveheart soundtrack, re-arranging many of the songs within my Reason software composition suite. I found studying, transcribing, and writing music to be the most rewarding pursuit I had ever tried.

I was in and out of a few relationships, but beginning to wonder if perhaps I was just too damaged, or just plain weird. I suppose I was a bit of an enigma—by day an upwardly mobile IT professional whose back-stage and tour bus stories could shock anyone into mortified silence, by night an aspiring film composer working from a remote mountain lair to the hum of a gas generator and heat from a wood stove.

Sometime in the winter of 2002, I happened to exchange emails and phone calls with my college friend, Shannon's ex, and we caught up on many lost years. During our first call, he mentioned that I had to meet his fiancée, which I was shocked and secretly elated to realize was NOT Shannon. Apparently they had parted ways a couple years earlier, around the time we all had fallen out of touch.

A few weeks later, I took a week of vacation time from TruSecure to join forces with Bishop and Carlton out in Las Vegas, working audio production for a large Coors corporate event. After one of the shows, we were enjoying ourselves at the cigar bar, and I asked Carlton if he knew where Shannon was, what she was doing. Maddening thoughts of the one who got away were tormenting me—how was I going to get in touch with her?

A couple of months later—June 8, 2002—fate delivered, and we were reunited in the most unlikely place, her ex's wedding. Having recently rekindled the friendship, I had received an invite, and having just ended a relationship, had decided to go solo.

The wedding was in the atrium of the Reagan Building in Washington, D.C., and I will never forget coming off the elevator, looking around at all the guests, and just like that—there she was. It was the same exact feeling as the first moment we met. I could see the shock in her face when she saw me; clearly she had no idea I would be there either. A huge hug that made my knees go weak, and I knew that this was it—a second chance at love at first sight. We chatted for a few minutes, getting caught up, and I learned she was there with a date, though she quickly clarified it was not that kind of date—not that I cared, anyway. The look in my eye, lingering gazes, flirtatious talk, and the sheer electricity between us made it obvious that there was magic in the air.

Later at the reception I asked Shannon for her number, and as she gave it to me, I just came right out with everything that had been locked in my heart for so many years: "I'm coming up to Connecticut to see you, and I think you know why," to which she simply smiled and replied "Yes..." The reception went late, and then turned into a University of Miami alumni trip to a local dance club; somewhere around 4:00 A.M., we all decided it was time to call it a night. I was in no shape to drive home to the shack, so I bummed a couple hours of sleep from our friend Bruno in his hotel room down the street. As we were leaving the club, Shannon gave me her number again (just to make sure I had it). For the next hour, poor Bruno was subjected to the inebriated ramblings of a lovesick idiot as he tried to get some sleep.

"I LOVE her, Bruno, I mean I am totally in love, done, married, she is perfect! PERFECT!!! I love you too, Bruno—I love everybody."

"I'm happy for you, Mackey, now shut the hell up and go to sleep or I'm going to throw you out of my room."

Later that morning, I made the hour drive back to the shack, and upon arriving, subjected Bobby Simmons, my Nashville buddy who was spending the weekend, to the same lovesick ramblings. Bobby would tell me years later he remembered that conversation for the sincere happiness in my voice and the outpouring of emotion—love and loneliness were topics we had discussed often—and he could tell right away something was different. He had been out late the night before as well, so we grabbed a quick nap and then went into the town of Leesburg to attend the annual Potomac Celtic Festival. Having just experienced the most incredible night of my life, I wanted something to symbolize that moment. I bought myself a silver Celtic knot band and placed it on the ring finger of my right hand. In my heart, I knew it was just a matter of time before another band would be placed upon the same finger of my left hand.

I have worn that ring to this day.

CHAPTER 5

"First Date"

I called Shannon a few days later, and we talked for hours. We chose the weekend after July 4th for my first visit to Connecticut. The next few weeks were agonizing, waiting, wondering, and planning. What was I going to put together for our first date?

By the time I left for Connecticut, I had decided that the best plan was no plan. Other than a day in the city and a show on Broadway, the rest would be left to total spontaneity. I was so nervous on the drive up, I could barely focus on driving, which can be problematic on the New Jersey Turnpike. At least I had someone to talk to—Seamus, my recently adopted stray kitten, had been invited along on the trip and proved to be a good listener.

As I neared New York, I gave Shannon a call to let her know I was getting close. She had gone into the city for the evening with her crew, and they were all doing their part to lessen the burden of apple martini inventory in Manhattan. We had pre-arranged that when I hit a certain bridge she would head out of the city. Completely unexpectedly (it was midnight!), as I came around the north side of the city, I ran into bumper-to-bumper traffic. I called Shannon and told her I was stuck, and she said she was as well. In this traffic jam of thousands of cars on a hot New York City summer night, she had gotten onto the interstate two cars behind me. As the traffic began to move, I slowed down and let her pass, and I will never forget that smile she flashed me as she sped past, waving and laughing. It was going to be a great weekend.

We arrived at her home in New Haven, an adorable 1920s fixer-upper with great New England character, and Seamus and I settled in to the spare room. Shannon had an early morning appointment to take her very naughty mutt Gypsie to obedience school. One look into that dog's eyes and I knew she was wasting her time, but at least Seamus and I got to sleep in.

Later that morning, we got ready and made the drive down to the city, parked near Times Square, and got in line for Broadway show tickets. Shannon looked amazing in her purple flower print sundress, and my head was already spinning. As luck would have it, we were able to get two tickets to *Phantom of the Opera*, and were thrilled, as we had both always wanted to see it.

We chose a nearby deli for some huge sandwiches—nothing beats a good NY deli! After lunch, we decided to head down to Ground Zero and see the progress on the World Trade Center work, walking the sidewalks and seeing the various posters, photos, flowers, and shrines commemorating lost loved ones, looking down into the pit from the observation platform. Although a very sobering experience, we felt it was important to share that together. After Ground Zero, we both felt like we needed a coffee, so we headed over to Greenwich Village to visit some shops, see the sights, and spend the afternoon talking over cappuccinos.

I had made the conscious decision in the weeks prior to visiting that I would not make any physical advances. That choice was becoming agonizing! Sitting there talking, enjoying the afternoon, falling fast, I wanted so badly to reach across the table and take her hand. Yet I was reveling in the fact that we were connecting intellectually, and somehow that felt even more incredible than the chemistry we had experienced over the years. Our conversations were delving deeper into all facets of life, and as the afternoon quickly passed, we found ourselves closer than ever.

It was time to head back to Times Square for a quick dinner before the show, and we enjoyed some wonderful Vietnamese food. The conversations continued, and we laughed over crazy umbrella drinks. We arrived at the Majestic Theatre, and I quickly ducked into the men's room to change. Shannon would later tell me that when I went around the corner, she was struck with this terrible, inexplicable fear that I might not return. When I got back, she appeared a little rattled yet relieved, and when I asked if she was alright, she just smiled.

The show was sold out and the theatre was brimming with anticipation. We took our seats just as the house lights went down, and let ourselves get carried away by the magic of the production. As the story unfolded, I was finding it more and more challenging not to take her hand, yet remained determined to be a perfect gentleman. Anyone who has seen *Phantom* will tell you it is a moving experience, and to see it as the pinnacle of the ultimate first date—words cannot describe.

We left the theatre and treated ourselves to a Starbucks coffee and pastry for the road, got into my truck, and began the drive back to New Haven. Lost in our own thoughts, I turned on the CD player and we quietly listed to Dar Williams' *The Green World* album. I glanced over at Shannon, and she almost appeared to be having a conversation with herself. Later she would tell me she was telling herself that this was really happening, and it was time to let down her guard and let it happen. As Dar sang us the final verses of "After All," I finally reached over and took her hand, and gently held it as we drove home.

We cuddled on the couch late into the night, until we could no longer keep our eyes open. Determined to keep my promise to myself, I headed upstairs and straight into the spare room. Shannon stood in the doorway looking at me, and said, "I don't want our date to be over yet. Can you behave yourself?" I replied yes, and we went into her room and crawled under the covers. She was lying in my arms, and I staring at the ceiling fan, afraid to move or breathe. Then it happened—she sat up, leaned over, and kissed me. It was the most gentle kiss that has ever been, soft as the touch of a down feather, lingering a few moments, carried away into a dream as we fell asleep in each other's arms.

We awoke late on Sunday, made each other breakfast, and just talked the day away. Shannon showed me her garden; she was very proud of the vegetables and herbs she had grown. I promised her that someday I would build her the biggest garden she had ever seen.

That afternoon, we sat out in the backyard in the sun, and delved deeply into conversations about family, spirituality, career goals, interests, and dreams. I was terrified that this might all be too good to be true, so we really opened up to each other, seemingly trying to find incompatibilities. Perhaps in my mind I was thinking that either this was going to last forever or I wanted it to end that day, because I knew that I had fallen faster than I would have ever thought possible. Every stone overturned revealed a new depth to our shared visions and philosophies, bringing us closer and closer together.

I left New Haven that afternoon, both of us emotionally promising that this relationship was already a commitment, that the long distance would not keep us from each other. Not even an hour from New Haven, my cell phone rang and Shannon was there, the deep sadness in her voice barely concealing the tremors of excitement we were both feeling. I had already promised to return in two weeks, and so began the waiting and wanting we would have to endure over the next several months.

CHAPTER 6
"A Romantic Whim"

Through July, August, and September, we saw each other almost every weekend. In early August, I had the opportunity to mix a concert for Jars of Clay at the Mohegan Sun Casino in Uncasville, Connecticut. My mom, Aunt Gin, and Aunt Debbie seized the opportunity to come see the show and wear out a few slot machines. Shannon was set to meet the family in our hotel room at Mohegan Sun.

I remember hopping in the shower before heading down to rehearsals, Shannon nervously pacing the room, awaiting their arrival. As I pulled the shower curtain shut, there was a knock at the door. Shannon rushed into the bathroom saying, "They're here—you need to come out here and help me!" to which I responded, "Good luck," and shut the door. The cacophony that ensued as they burst into the room was hysterical; I do not think Shannon got a word in edgewise. As I knew she would, she won them over instantly, and before I could towel off, they were pulling her downstairs to the casino.

This was an amazing time for us—falling in love, discovering each other's dreams, and exploring wonderful places. We enjoyed dinners in New York City, a weekend rendezvous at a bed and breakfast in New Hope, Pennsylvania, meeting each other's families, making romantic dinners, and lying awake late at night, talking about the future.

The first time Shannon visited the shack was the weekend she came down for my sister's twenty-third birthday party, held at my brother Jim's townhouse. This party introduced her to the rest of the Mackey friend and family clan. Everyone fell in love with her right away, and before the night was over, the ladies were talking about weddings and babies. The next morning, we began the long drive out to the shack, about fifty minutes from Jim's place. I wanted to do something special for our first day together on the mountain, so we stopped at a landscape nursery along the way and bought an Autumn Blaze maple tree, which we planted together in front of the shack.

The road up was washed-out gravel, which only led to my property and a communications tower on top of the mountain. Unbelievably, as we were driving up, Shannon turned to me and said, "I've been up this road before." Impossible, no one had been up this road before—but sure enough, during her stint in HDTV, she had been up to the tower site, evaluating its potential. Seriously, what were the odds of that?

As we pulled up to the shack, the sun was setting over our valley, and the scenery captured her immediately. We watched the sunset, and planted the maple tree. I showed her the notebook of log home designs I had been putting together, with photos out of magazines, floor plans from the Internet, kitchen and bathroom ideas—everything. Earlier that year, I had made the trip down to Charlotte, North Carolina to attend the Log and Timber Frame Home Expo, and had already begun researching log home producers. She fell in love with the idea of building a custom home on the property, and we began to dream about raising a family in our own log home, watching the sunset over our valley.

Late in September 2002, Shannon was coming down for the weekend, and I had put together our plans for her visit. Each weekday, along my drive out of the valley to my IT job, I would pass Loudoun's largest winery, Breaux Vineyards. It was a magnificent 400-acre farm with 100 acres of vineyards and a beautiful Tuscan-décor winery and tasting room. I had never been to any of the wineries in Loudoun (numbering thirteen at that time), but had seen a sign in front of Breaux advertising their forthcoming Harvest Festival that Saturday.

Having visited Sonoma Valley during my audio career, I thought that a winery date might be a lot of fun.

The day dawned, a perfect fall Saturday, beautiful skies and ideal temperatures. We slept in, enjoyed a late breakfast, and made our way the few miles up the road to Breaux. After purchasing our tickets, we made our way over to the vineyard entrance, where they were offering hayrides through the varietals of vines. As we sat back and enjoyed the ride, Shannon became increasingly quiet and introspective, with a curious look on her face. The grounds were beautiful, the vineyard immaculately maintained, and the impact on both of us was deep and immediate.

After the hayride, we wandered over to the outdoor tasting tent, where we enjoyed sampling their wide variety of wines. At this point Shannon was utterly silent, and I began to worry she was not feeling well, or perhaps was not enjoying the outing. We finished the tasting and bought a bottle of wine to enjoy later, and walked out to the picnic area. Just as we exited the tent, Shannon stopped short, turned to me and asked "Do people really get to do this for a living?" I replied, "Do you want to?" to which she immediately said, "Yes!" I just looked at her and said, "Okay," and that was that. In an instant, we had changed the course of our lives.

We spent the rest of the afternoon enjoying the scenery at Breaux, and made dinner at the shack, but the conversation never left how we were going to do something like that. It seemed to us that owning a winery would be the perfect pursuit to convene all of our various interests and passions: family values, agriculture, environment, wine, art, music, entrepreneurship, and freedom. Not that we knew anything about making wine, or the wine industry, or farming, but we knew that it did not involve cube farms, IPOs, quarterly sales quotas, or any of the other corporate rat race elements that we had come to despise as impediments to real creativity and an honest family-focused lifestyle.

That Monday, upon arriving at work, I immediately began a Google search on how to grow wine grapevines in Virginia. Interestingly, someone at Virginia Tech had completed a research project on viticulture business plans, and had published a comprehensive work called "The Economics of Winegrape Production in Virginia," which I immediately downloaded and absorbed. The depth was superb, and I was quite impressed by the detail and clarity. When my co-workers asked how the weekend went, I told them we were founding a vineyard. I received a chorus of "Awesome," and found it interesting that not one of them said anything like "You're crazy," or "Sure you are"—they just seemed to totally support the idea right from its inception.

As we continued our research (I am pretty sure neither of us accomplished any of our salaried tasks that day), we uncovered a wealth of information on viticulture and winery business plans, and began to learn more about the Virginia wine industry. We talked for hours that night, brimming with excitement about the prospect of this new direction in life, yet we had absolutely no idea how to make it happen financially.

The next day, I began searching Loudoun realtor websites, seeking land for sale. From my whole one day of research, I knew topography was critical in locating a vineyard, and that we would be looking for land with rolling hills or situated on the slope of a mountainside. That mitigated cold air masses (late spring frosts) and allowed proper water drainage. Armed with that "wealth of information," the search was on.

Having become quite fond of the Between the Hills Valley where the shack was located, I discovered another established vineyard nearby (currently named Doukénie), and it seemed to me a logical area to begin looking for land. Using the Coldwell Banker site, I found a few small plots, about twelve acres, at the southwestern end of the valley. Arising early the next day, I went to have a look at the various parcels. The first property I looked at was tucked away along Sagle Road; it was just over twelve acres, had a great slope, and was nice, but looking at it did not really move me. For some instinctive reason, I checked it off the list. I continued down Sagle towards the next property, and coming around a bend, I saw a "For Sale" sign that had not appeared on any of the online listings. Apparently it had just been listed a few days before, and had not yet been entered into the MLS database—42.25 acres listed at $590,000.

The sign hung in front of a decrepit old house, covered in mildew, with broken windows, rusted roof, overgrown brush, a broken refrigerator and minivan in the front yard, plaster peeling off the sides, and stray cats moving freely in and out. There was an outhouse to the left, and a junk shed with all manner of rusted tools inside, over a goat and sheep pen knee-deep in manure and wool. The house sat on a hill overlooking a farm pond and grazing pastures, complete with rusting farm implements and broken barbed wire fence. To the right of the house sat a pitiful barn, waist-deep in manure, with a few ragged sheep running around and two old horses. It was the second property I looked at, it was the coolest place I had ever seen, and it was perfect.

I saw right through the junk and the overgrowth, and could envision a beautiful restored tasting room looking out over the pond to the vineyards in the distance. The topography was ideal, the character immense, and the potential vast. I hurried off to work and called Shannon, telling her I found it, and somehow made it through the day. I told my coworkers at lunch that day about the discovery, and we resolved to visit it during lunch the following day. When we rode out to have a look, they all pretty much agreed that the place was a total dump, but very cool with huge potential.

After work that Friday, I made the trip up to Connecticut. We spent the whole weekend discussing finances, trying to figure out a way to make this happen. Shannon had about $70,000 in her 401(k) and I had about $10,000 in mine. She had about $30,000 in her checking account, and I about $10,000. Land purchases are quite different than home purchases, as there is an absolute requirement for a 20% deposit (no "zero money down" deals for land). We had to come up with $100,000, as we figured we could make an offer in the low $500s. Although we were making decisions fast based on a romantic whim, we realized we did not want to tap into our retirement accounts yet.

The grim truth emerged that our only option was to leverage the equity in one of our homes. Although both of us had fallen in love with the mountain property and the dream of raising a family in a log home, it made sense to sell my beloved property. In the two years I had owned the land, it had appreciated from $116,500 to $220,000, an incredible amount of equity. Shannon was well established in her field and made almost double what I made. Since I had just begun a career in a new industry two and a half years earlier, it would likely be easier for me to relocate. We could sell the shack, put all the equity into this new piece of property, and move in together up in New Haven, seven hours away from our farm. Though an emotionally difficult decision for me, the logic was clear and the financial plan sound (enough). By the time I left on Sunday, we had charted a new course in our lives. We decided to make an offer immediately, and Shannon wrote a check for $5,000 for the earnest money.

The next day, I contacted the listing agent, and met with them on Tuesday to drive the actual property lines. On Wednesday, October 9, 2002, we made an offer of $500,000 and signed the contract. Shannon signed via fax, having never even seen a picture of the land. At the meeting with Coldwell Banker, after signing the offer, I officially listed my land for $220,000. The next day at work, I submitted my letter of resignation to Pat Cross, our VP of development. A dear and trusted friend to this day, Pat was incredibly supportive, outwardly positive, and made a very emotional decision much easier.

During my last days at TruSecure, I had a number of conversations with my colleagues about the future prospects of vineyard ownership. Shannon and I had been discussing ideas for brand identities, and I shared them with the dev team. I had been knocking around the idea of using my funny little word in the branding; it had great alliteration with "vineyard" and had an awesome backstory, but for some reason I had not been totally convinced yet. Out of the blue, Korte walked into my cube one afternoon, and said, "Hey, why don't you call it Notaviva Vineyards?" Something about the way he said it, or the fact that someone else thought it was cool, or maybe just hearing someone else say it out loud for the first time—who knows—but I knew in an instant that the name would resonate. I called to tell Shannon immediately, and she loved it, and Notaviva Vineyards was born.

Pat was incredibly tolerant that last week, as our dev enology team lunch meetings stretched into two-hour excursions, helping me work out business plans. My co-workers threw me a fantastic going-away party. After all of the road tours I had been through, as well as various other careers and pursuits, this departure was by far the most difficult. Our group had a camaraderie not typically found amongst professional colleagues, and I had leaned on them heavily during my transition from road life to corporate life. Though I would miss their companionship greatly, I knew these relationships would continue to grow well into the future. They all adored Shannon, and I was leaving with many blessings.

Saturday, October 26th, I awoke and began packing for my final drive to New Haven. I believe it was at that moment I realized I was on the hook for three mortgages, and I was unemployed.

CHAPTER 7

"New Haven"

Even before I had handed in my letter of resignation, I had begun to seek jobs in the New Haven area. I had sent out a few dozen resumes, and the response had been positive. I had received an offer from a small IT firm in New Haven, and another from Greenfield Online, a marketing firm specializing in Internet survey development and panel management. Neither seemed especially engaging, nor the salaries great, but at least I knew that I was marketable. I sat on the offers, as I really had my hopes set on the webmaster position at the Juilliard School of Music in New York City. Although it would have been an asinine commute and a lower salary, the exposure to the world of elite music education would have been fantastic. Since departing the pro audio industry, I had really missed the daily close contact with music and musicians, and knew working in that environment would have so many added benefits and interests.

After the last in the series of Juilliard interviews, I made the drive up to Boston for a few days to work a corporate gig for Chris Bishop. It always felt great to be back in action, setting up the gear, making all the necessary adjustments, working through rehearsals, and executing the shows. During afternoon rehearsals, I received a call on my cell phone from Juilliard, and was getting ready to jump for joy at the job offer. My contact broke the news that it had come down to me and one other person, and the opportunity was lost. I was devastated.

At the next break in rehearsals, I went upstairs to my hotel room, took the Greenfield Online offer letter out of my suitcase, called Jenni Cahalan, director of operations and said, "I'll take the job and can start Monday." By now she had figured I was not interested, and was very glad to hear from me. The company had embarked on the migration of all their survey systems to a new platform, Confirmit, and the onsite training was to begin Monday as well. I called Shannon and told her the news, and although she was just as sad as I was about the Juilliard gig, we both realized the commute would have seriously impacted our time together. Although Greenfield was not my lifelong dream job, we would be able to float all three mortgages until my land sold, for a while, anyway.

The biggest benefit in taking that position was that we were now able to commute together. We would take the back roads from New Haven to Wilton, an hour trip, and then Shannon would continue on another thirty minutes to Stamford, headquarters for WWE. I had so much to discover in Connecticut, and we had some wonderful times visiting places, dining out, attending shows, and meeting new friends. Still, our hearts and minds were now firmly set on our farm in Virginia, and we continued our research into viticulture and enology.

When we had made the offer and signed the contract, we inserted a contingency clause for forty-five days to conduct a feasibility study on the land, to ensure it was viable for viticulture. Our online research led us again to Virginia Tech, who had created the "Virginia Viticultural Suitability Map," a color-coded map of the entire state. The various color codes were created by a complex computer model, whose variables included prevailing soil composition (texture, drainage, depth, pH) as well as slope (fall and azimuth), maximums, minimums and averages for temperature and rainfall, among a host of other computations. We learned, through their study as well as the Loudoun County soil maps, that our property fell in the 99th percentile for viticultural suitability. We felt we had as good a chance as anyone for farming world-class winegrapes.

Having decided to go through with the contract, we began forming financial backup plans in case my property didn't flip right away. Plan one was known as the "parental bridge loan," where we each got to place a phone call to our possible future in-laws to try and come up with $80,000. We asked for $20,000 each from Sue and Roger (Shannon's mother and father), $20,000 from my mother, and the last $20,000 from my grandmother. I was so nauseous I do not remember many of the details, but the first conversation went something like, "Hi Roger—umm no, your daughter does not yet have a ring on her finger—can we borrow twenty grand?" I thought I was going to pass out. Ever the pragmatist, Roger wanted to be sure BOTH names would be on the deed (50/50), while Sue and Mickey wanted to ensure they were buying into a lifetime supply of free wine. My grandmother, who had been suffering from TIAs and the onset of Alzheimer's, thought it all sounded like a "lovely idea." In the end, they were all very supportive, all agreeing they were proud to play a part in giving us a shot, though Shannon and I were now operating about four light-years outside of their collective comfort zones.

Now that we had spent half a million dollars on land and were telling everyone we were starting a vineyard, we figured it was high time to try and actually make a bottle of wine. Being December, neither fresh fruit nor juice was an option, so I purchased a home wine kit online, a Merlot. We went through all the sanitization, followed all the steps, carefully added yeast and chemicals, and were thrilled over the next few days as the fermentation filled the house with the most wonderful aromas. While in Nashville, I had actually begun home-brewing beer, so I was familiar with the basic processes of fermentation, and many of the techniques were very similar.

I had stayed in close contact with my friends from TruSecure, and as I sent them updates via ICQ and email, Korte suggested I start my own blog about our vineyard adventure. I had enjoyed reading his blog since moving north, as it kept me in close touch with everyone. He assured me I would be glad someday that I had taken the time to write everything down. In fact, this memoir would not have been possible had it not been for the blog—I would have never been able to unweave this story from memory.

Shannon and I had the most incredible first Christmas together, showering each other with fun and romantic gifts, and then making the long drive down to Virginia to enjoy an evening gift exchange and dinner with my family. As a stocking stuffer, I had bought Shannon a copy of the Great Big Sea "Road Rage" concert CD, and she was in love with the wit of their lyrics and energy of their live performance as we went rocking down the interstate. I will never forget her saying, "Now this is the kind of wedding reception music we need to have!"

Along with the excitement and happiness of the holiday season came the creeping realization that we were already getting into financial trouble. My mountain property had been viewed by a few curious people, but for some reason, the notion of living hermit-like with no electricity on top of a mountain did not have such wide appeal. We did receive an offer from an adjoining landowner; it was far below our asking price, so we passed and decided to wait it out. Our original closing date of December 27th had to be rescheduled for late January, in the hopes that the land would sell, but we knew that the middle of winter would be the last season anyone would be looking for that type of property.

As January slipped by, we knew we were out of time, and that my land was going to sit until spring. We were really going to be in a dire financial mess in a few months. Still, the excitement of closing kept our spirits high, and we were in constant contact with Farm Credit, our lender. Closing was set for 9:00 A.M. on January 31st, and a mere one week out, I received a call from our loan officer, saying their regional officer was reviewing the load prior to closing, and had decided to balk at the loan. I was fit to be tied—was this not something that should have been decided three months ago? No matter how I pleaded, they stuck to their decision that the home to land value (because the house was such a dump) was outside their acceptable ratios, and they would not approve the financing.

Making a panicked call to our Coldwell Banker agent to explain the situation, I thought she was going to faint. She rallied quickly and told me to call a friend of hers, Vince Tricarico, VP for First Savings Mortgage. I called Vince the next day, and caught him at home on a Saturday morning. He said the timing was really tight, but he was interested and wanted me to fill out his online loan application. Given that I had everything in a folder for our closing, it was a simple matter to run through the form. Vince called me that night, having already pulled our credit report, and told me no problem. Our credit was immaculate, and even though the ratios and numbers were bizarre, he felt we could do business. I promised him that if he made this happen for us, I would give him right of first refusal on our future construction loan package. We both laughed, believing that day to be decades in the future.

Sure enough, Vince came through. That Thursday night, Shannon and I made the drive back down to Virginia, and spent the night in the shack. We tried to get some sleep, but the excitement was just too much. Closing went relatively smoothly, and we signed our way through a foot-high stack of papers. They handed us the key, which, according to all the papers we just signed, was worth more than the house it unlocked.

After closing, we went for a late breakfast and headed out to see the land and the beautiful castle I had picked out for my princess. Although I had previously taken Shannon around the entire property, she had never actually set foot inside the house (which, at the time, we believed would be our future tasting room) until the day she put her name on our loan for half a million dollars.

CHAPTER 8

"The Engagement"

I had known by the end of our first date that I had found the love of my life, and every decision made from that point on brought me closer to marrying Shannon. Upon arriving back in Connecticut after the land closing, I started to piece together the framework of my marriage proposal.

Shannon had wanted us to take a trip to South Florida so I could meet her extended family. Having been raised in Palm Beach Gardens, many of her aunts, uncles, and cousins were still in the area, and her father Roger was retired and lived in PGA National. As I pondered the trip south, it dawned on me that we were approaching the tenth anniversary of the year we met at the Dade County Youth Fair, and the plan began to take shape.

The Fair runs from the end of March through the beginning of April, so I suggested that we go down on vacation after WWE's "Wrestlemania," held in mid-March, to relieve the stress after her busy season. She bought into that, and we set our travel for Friday, March 28th.

Though neither of us is materialistic, I wanted her diamond to be perfect. Luckily, we had not yet merged all of our financial accounts, so I still had a personal VISA card with a zero balance and a $15k limit. I made a phone call to VISA to prepare them for an upcoming big purchase, which they thanked me for, indicating a five-figure purchase at a jewelry store on a zero balance credit card would definitely have been rejected!

I began doing research into the four Cs and pricing out some stones online, but knew I would have to hold it in my hand prior to purchasing. Calling local jewelers, I found a great little shop with a superb reputation, Valentine's Diamond Center in Milford, Connecticut. I met with the owner and his mother, who showed me two stones "around" my budget, and after viewing them, the choice was simple—1.25 carat, D color, VVS1 clarity, and an ideal cut. The stone was to be placed in a platinum solitaire setting, unadorned by other stones, simple yet perfect—like the hand that would bear it.

A few days later I got the call that the ring was ready, snuck a drive to Milford, and sat in stunned amazement. I had never seen anything like it, and the sudden realization set in that I had to keep track of this ring for the next couple weeks until our Florida trip. That made me dizzy; I think I drove fifteen miles per hour with my hazard lights on the whole way home. I stashed the ring down in the basement, in about four layers of locked boxes—mouse-proof, dog-proof, Shannon-proof. Coming in from work in the evenings, I would race downstairs as soon as I could to check that it was safe and still sparkling brilliantly.

That weekend, we made a trip down to Virginia for a family gathering. As my brother Jim had gotten engaged to his girlfriend Shayna a few months prior, the ladies' talk eventually turned to wedding plans, which eventually turned to the ladies asking Shannon (well within earshot of me, of course) "So, when are you going to get engaged? Well?" I looked over at these expectant, staring, clucking hens, and taking my life into my own hands, replied, "No ring for a year—you have to be dating *at least* a year before you can think about getting engaged." Their outcry was deafening, and I was lucky to escape the room unscathed. Shannon was upon me instantly, asking "What? What kind of stupid rule is that?"

Little did they know that the travel dates had been a scam, the diamond had been secretly procured, the Miami conspirators had been mobilized, and the proposal was being written.

During this time I had been in touch with Chris Carlton down in Miami, who was again working as technical director for the Fair. As Chris had some travel commitments during the Fair run, I would later learn that his wife Caroline would also be instrumental in making my proposal possible. I told Chris that I wanted to get engaged at the Fair, in one of the tents where we used to work as technicians so many years earlier. It seemed to me that since this was the place we first met, and we had missed the opportunity then to join our lives together, it was the ideal place to right that wrong and close that chapter.

Chris put me in touch with his lighting director, Roland Tapia, whom I had known from my time at the Fair, and we began to put together the design of the evening. Shannon and I would arrive at the Fair late in the evening, Chris would have our names at the employee entrance security gate, and we would stroll the fairgrounds while Roland finished up his last ice show, cleared the tent, and moved security personnel outside. Essentially we would have the entire place to ourselves, with Roland standing by at the lighting console. I trusted his instincts, and just told him wash the ice with a warm romantic lighting look. The rough details set, all that was left now was the travel to Florida.

As the trip neared, I had to put together a fake itinerary of our outings while we were in town. It was a simple matter to type up a phony hotel confirmation receipt for a place in the Florida Keys, and Shannon believed that after spending time with her dad at his place on Friday night and Saturday morning, we were going to visit the University of Miami campus then head down to the Keys for a romantic getaway. Though we both had graduated from UM, we had never actually been there together.

Shannon had decided to travel down one day before me so she could spend time with Roger. He and Sue had divorced several years earlier, and Roger had mentioned to Shannon he had been seeing someone, though Shannon (who does not miss a trick) had detected something different in Roger's mood lately and was already hot on the trail. I dropped her off at the airport with a gentle nudge to take it easy on this woman. Shannon called me immediately after their breakfast date the next morning, giddy with excitement. Vivacious and lovely with Midwestern sensibilities, Beverly Peetz had passed her audition with flying colors.

I was worried sick about traveling with the ring. I decided that a ring box would be way too obvious, should my bag be opened at Roger's. I removed the ring from the box and taped it to the center of a CD, with the stone in the center hole. The CD was one of her favorites, and Colombian artist Soraya would watch over the ring while we traveled.

Shannon has a very close relationship with her father, and I knew it would be very important to ask his blessing prior to proposing. As we were staying at Roger's place the first night in town, I planned to corner him at some moment to ask. Much to my horror, as we were leaving for the airport that morning, Roger called Shannon to let her know his mother was ill, and that he had to rush up to Superior, Wisconsin. Thinking quickly, I told Shannon, "Give your dad my cell phone number in case he needs to reach us, and while you're at it, let's program his number into my phone."

We arrived safely at Palm Beach International, took a cab to Roger's place and spent the night. We slept in the next morning, had breakfast, and began getting ready for a big day out. Shannon hopped in the shower, and I realized this was probably my one chance to sneak in a conversation with Roger. Quickly dialing, the phone seemed to ring forever before he picked up. Stammering like a fifteen year old, I began with an apology that I had not been able to ask this in person, and I told him how much Shannon had meant to me, how I felt our lives were meant to be joined together, and asked for his blessing. I will never forget his response—"oh, Oh, OH!!!" a crescendo of surprise, realization, and excitement. He was incredibly complimentary and supportive, and by the time he gave me his blessing, I was crying uncontrollably. I heard the shower shut off, thanked Roger, hung up the phone, and pulled myself together.

We hopped in Roger's car and began the drive south, stopping along the way so Shannon could show me the old home of her maternal grandparents, Momsabelle and Charlie Pops. We left there and visited their resting place, a serene memorial garden overlooking the Little League baseball field where he used to love to coach. Shannon would tell me later that she whispered a prayer to them while we were there, telling him she had found the one.

After some excursions around Miami and UM, I revealed we were not heading towards the Keys, which was on our fake itinerary. She looked at me in amazement, now trying to get me to spill the beans as to what our real plans were. No response was forthcoming as we headed deeper into Coral Gables.

I had reserved us a room at the beautiful Biltmore Hotel, and upon checking in, Shannon was getting increasingly excited, nervous, and anxious. I told her we needed to have a light meal and get a quick nap, as we had a long night of fun ahead of us. Neither of us slept, but lying down for a bit helped to restore our energy after the long day of sightseeing. We showered and got back in the car. Shannon had no idea where we were going at first, but as we got closer to the Fair, she began to recognize the landmarks, and by the time the rollercoasters were visible, she at least knew where we were going, yet still had no idea why. Stopped at a red light, I told her, "We're going into the Fair so I can kiss you, which I wish I had done ten years ago."

As we pulled up to the security gate, I spoke to the guard on duty, telling him our names and that Chris Carlton had set up our entries. Just then my phone rang; it was Roland, telling me the last show was over and that he needed about an hour to prep the tent. Shannon got very suspicious during the phone call, and then began getting very nervous. She told me that while she was working the Fair the year after I had left, she organized a stripper for Carlton's fortieth birthday party, and he swore he would get even with her someday. By this point she was freaking out, thinking that I was now part of some Carlton scheme to embarrass her as payback. She was asking constant questions, getting nothing from me except fibs and misdirection, keeping her totally off balance. She was getting a little pale.

We took the long way around the fairgrounds. When the final call came from Roland, indicating it was go-time, Shannon so nervous I could barely keep her moving. Half-leading, half-pulling her in the direction of the ice tent, we made our way through the tens of thousands of visitors. Arriving at the tent, a security guard posted outside let us in; it was a beautiful, almost magical scene inside.

Roland had designed soft lighting upon the ice, with slowly rotating lights in warm colors. Taking Shannon by the hand, I walked her over to the front, and told her wait right there. I quickly checked in with Roland, and he said he had made one small cue for when I actually popped the question, so he would be watching closely. He showed me where the audio console was, and I moved down to put in some music for the moment. This entire time, poor Shannon was convinced that Carlton and some Chippendale's dancers were going to pop out of the ice, and she would die of embarrassment.

I reached the audio console, and put in one of Shannon's favorite songs, Frank Sinatra singing "Someone to Watch Over Me," and pushed up the faders. As Old Blue Eyes came through the audio system, Shannon began to relax. I pulled the Soraya CD from the case and struggled with removing the ring from my heavy-duty tape job. It was held fast; as I pulled at the tape, I looked down and realized I was standing on top of a drainage grate. Knowing that if the ring popped out of the CD, out of my hands, and down that grate, it was lost forever, I made the quick decision to leave it on the CD and put it back in my pocket.

Taking Shannon by the hand, we walked out onto the ice, where Roland had place a small carpet so we could dance. I held her close and we danced a few verses in silence, then I began. I had written the proposal out and memorized every word, because I knew when the moment arrived, I would be overcome with emotion. Having that mental picture of the paper, it came out easily. As I spoke, I could feel her pulling me closer, and she began to realize what I was saying, what we were doing here, what was happening. I reached down into my pocket, pulled out the ring, dropped to one knee, and proposed. At that same moment, Roland slowly moved the lights to the center of the rink, and there we were—Shannon crying, saying, "Yes! Yes!" and I on one knee, both bathed in moving lights shimmering off of the ice.

I stood and held her and she was in an absolute state of shock. "How did you...? Who is up there...? How long...? Oh, please tell me you asked my dad!?" The questions were coming faster than I could answer, we were both crying and laughing and reveling in the pure joy of the moment. Though the band was a little big, the ring looked perfect on her finger and she was delighted with the setting. "How did you know that is exactly what I wanted? We never even discussed it!"

Slowly we walked from the ice, Roland coming down from the booth to congratulate us, and Caroline meeting us at the side of the tent to congratulate us as well. We realized that the security guards who were supposed to be waiting outside had all snuck in to watch, and they gave us tearful hugs. Thanking Roland and Caroline, the ultimate proposal now behind me, I felt elated, like I was walking on air.

Shannon could hardly speak coherently, she was sputtering out question after question so fast, trying to piece together the long chain of events that led up to this moment. I told her everything, every detail, every fib, every level of misdirection, not missing a thing. At some point during our walk back to the car, she looked down and said, "Holy crap, that is a ROCK, baby!" and suddenly got nervous and turned the stone down to her palm, already feeling protective of it.

By the time we left, we were caught in exit traffic, so we started making phone calls from the car. We called her dad first, since he was the only one who had known what was happening and had been a nervous wreck all day, hoping that everything was unfolding well. Next we called my mom, then Shannon's mom, then my dad, then my brother and sister, then Shannon's brother, and then we were calling everybody. There were well wishes and tears of joy on both sides of the phone, Shannon with her phone in her right hand, and her left hand held out in front of her, staring at her ring in amazement. We got back to the Biltmore well after midnight, totally drained but still riding a complete adrenaline rush. We ordered room service while we continued to call people and wake them up. We finished dinner, decided that 2:00 A.M. would be a good time to stop calling people, turned out the lights and then, well, you know...

CHAPTER 9
"Wine and Music"

The people from whom Shannon had purchased her house had painted every single room but one salmon pink. The kitchen even had pink laminate cabinets and countertops. The one room that was not pink had frightful white wallpaper with little blue flowers. Immediately after she bought the home, she converted two upstairs bedrooms into a master suite; however, the rest of the house was still in definite need of a makeover.

At some point that winter, just after the closing, we arrived home after a long commute and winemaking discussion. As we walked into the den at the rear of the house, I saw a Sharpie pen lying on the floor. I reached down, picked it up, and (knowing this room was getting painted) drew a picture of two wine bottles on the wall. They were situated so they would be the first thing we would see, coming into the house. On one of the bottles, I wrote "Adagio Merlot." There was no real thought behind it, it was just a spur-of-the-moment scribble to give us a daily reminder of where our futures lay.

I called Shannon over to have a look; she laughed and thought the idea could be a lot of fun. Just like that, we decided to name all our wines after a musical term, the notion being that each wine would have a personality similar to a musical instruction, for example

"Vivace," meaning "lively," or "Cantabile," meaning "graceful, or full of expression."

We spent the next several months focusing on our careers, enduring the strain of three mortgages. As spring rolled around, we began to get emails and phone calls from the adjoining landowner, reminding us that his earlier low-ball offer still stood. By this point we were near desperate, as our savings were almost gone and our incomes barely covered the mortgages and living expenses. Shannon was beginning to push for considering the low offer; even though we would have come up short on what we owed our parents, we would be able to pay them back over the next year and get out of this mess. We had just returned from Florida, and I was able to convince her to wait three more weeks. The first two weeks would be the end of our listing contract with the realtor, after which we would be able to do a "for sale by owner" (FSBO) for a week. The weather was beginning to warm up, and the property did not look as dismal as it could under a blanket of snow.

Two weeks later, when our listing agreement expired without so much as a phone call from any prospective buyers, I had my sister put out the FSBO signs along Harpers Ferry Road. Two days later, I received a call from a young lady, a ranger for the National Park Service who worked in Harpers Ferry. She was looking for something secluded and unusual, and the shack fit the bill perfectly. She made us an offer just a bit below our asking price. As a gentleman's agreement, I had promised the interested neighbor I would let him know if we received another offer, so I gave him a call.

The next day we received his fax for a cash offer at full asking price. Since technically our listing agreement had expired and this was a new offer, I was able to negotiate a much lower flat-rate set-tlement fee with our previous listing agent, so she could conduct the closing on our behalf through power of attorney. Since it was a cash deal, closing happened in a matter of days, and Shannon and I cut checks to our parents (happily, with interest), I paid off the ring, and we put the rest in savings. Although my beloved mountain property was now gone, I could smile, knowing it had provided us the opportunity of a lifetime.

We were immersing ourselves in viticulture and enology research. We attended our first Wineries Unlimited, the largest winery trade show on the East Coast. We scheduled a vacation in late May to attend a winery planning seminar hosted by Dr. Bruce Zoecklein, professor of enology at Virginia Tech. We eagerly anticipated spending a week on the new property, sleeping in the dump. I recall my dad's comment when first seeing the place—"Son, I've seen foxholes in 'Nam nicer than this place." Our intent was to take the entire week and begin cleaning up the grounds and working on the house. We hadn't intended to begin a restoration with hand tools, but we really felt we needed to connect with our farm, and nothing achieves that better than some sweat equity.

Family and friends came out at various times during the week to help out, cutting down brush, tearing down partition walls, just getting dirty and having fun. By the end of the week, a few of us had world-class cases of poison ivy, sore muscles, and cuts and bruises, and though we had accomplished very little, we felt a great glow of satisfaction that yes, this was ours and we could do whatever we wanted to it.

We believed we were beginning renovations on our future tasting room. About a mile south of our place, on Sagle Road, sits a beautiful restored stone home, same floor plan, built the same time as ours. Though our place was covered in plaster, much of it had peeled away from the chimney, revealing the stone underneath. It was the assumption of the real estate agent, and subsequently us, that the remainder of the main structure was stone as well, though we knew the addition was early twentieth century wood frame.

On our last day of vacation before heading home to Connecticut, Jim and Shayna had stopped by to visit, and Jim wondered what condition the stone would be in, after sitting beneath the stucco covering for so many years. I was determined to find out, so I took a sledgehammer around the side of the house and attempted to knock off a bit of the plaster from the stone. Imagine my shock when the sledgehammer went right through the plaster, punching a hole through the lathe. Removing the hammer, decaying bits of termite-infested wood began pouring out the hole like corn flakes from a cereal box. Sure enough, we realized at that moment that our gorgeous stone house fixer-upper had just revealed itself to be a decaying log home, only held upright by the plaster and lathe that covered the decomposing wood. Shannon and Shayna were inside when I had hit the wall, and thought the place was going to collapse.

Shayna went pale and decided it would be a good time to say goodbye. I settled into a broken lawn chair with a beer and the realization that our future renovation project had just turned into a razing and new construction. Not that we had the money for either, but it pushed the whole timeline back that much farther. I wished I had figured that out at the beginning of the week, but we all had fun, bonded with the land, and just endured the first in a long line of bone-headed sweat equity disasters yet to come.

We had also spent some time evaluating potential wedding sites. Even before we left Florida, Shannon had decided she wanted to get married outside, somewhere on the property. Although much of the land is visible from the road, there is a completely secluded area at the rear, and we decided to be married somewhere in this peaceful meadow. We settled on a small glade at the edge of the forest, right at the back edge of the property. It would require the removal of about four trees and untold amounts of dead underbrush and some stump grinding, but in the end would look like a completely natural amphitheater, which we decided we would outline with a stone wall. My sister has a degree in horticulture, and she was very excited to help us design and create the site.

We returned to Connecticut, determined to turn the house setback into an opportunity. Whether we liked it or not, we knew we were going to have to build something from scratch. That began to be very inspiring, and I still had my binders and magazines from all my log home research. Though a log home tasting room did not really seem to fit the setting, we began to think more about timber frame structures. We settled into a very focused routine, concentrating hard on our jobs, staying late at work, and making aggressive career choices, knowing that the sooner we were able to pay down our debts, the closer we were to making the vineyard dream possible.

I was still dabbling with my home-based web design business, and had developed some new technologies for survey respondents to participate in research studies via their handheld devices. Taking a huge risk, I invited each of a dozen senior Greenfield executives to a demo luncheon, and shopped the technology to them. Although they felt the technology was solid, they believed that wide acceptance of the model was still a few years away and passed. They were very impressed, however, by my entrepreneurial spirit and the initiative I had shown in calling them together. They decided to offer me a promotion to head up a new business unit, and a week later I went from a developer salary to six figures with commissions. Although I continued to be the de-facto Confirmit programming expert within Greenfield, I was now deeply immersed in client and project management.

Just goes to show you that opportunity is all around us, and that if you never challenge yourself or choose to rise above your norm, rarely will anything special ever "just happen." I spent many hours in the basement of the Connecticut house writing code and debugging applications, and although that proposal was passed over, I was still presented with a unique opportunity, which I seized and grew to substantial reward. In fact, I used my first commission check to purchase our first tractor, a used John Deere 850, and my second commission check to purchase a bush hog. The salesman at Browning Equipment asked, "You know how to drive one of these things?" and I responded, "Absolutely," though I had never even sat on one in my entire life. After a jolting ride around the building, I found myself fumbling to get the tractor back in gear as it slowly rolled backwards down the hill, out of the parking lot and into oncoming traffic on Main Street. The salesman slowly reached over and covered Shannon's eyes, drawling, "Don't watch this part, darlin'—this ain't gonna end good..."

Now part of the core middle management team, I would subsequently be granted a stock option package. As Greenfield was heading toward an IPO, I knew there would be some future payoff; though it would not nearly be enough to fund an entire winery startup, it would be critical for funding the establishment of the vineyard. Shannon was receiving superior reviews from her WWE management team, and later that year received a substantial bonus, on the order of tens of thousands of dollars, much of which funded our wedding, and the rest was put into the vineyard accounts. Each night, arriving home from work, we would gaze at the Adagio Merlot drawing, and though we were tired from long hours at the office, knew we were moving in the right direction with a sound financial plan of debt reduction, credit monitoring, and salary increases.

We settled into a regular routine of making the trip down to Virginia every other weekend. These began with Shannon leaving work and driving up to Wilton, picking me up by 6 P.M. We would head north to pick up Interstate 84, which we would take west to Wilkes-Barre, Pennsylvania, catch Interstate 81 down to Harrisburg, loop around Harrisburg on the PA Turnpike, then head south on Route 15 through Gettysburg, then Frederick, Maryland, and home to the farm. Very early on, we abandoned the absurdity of the Interstate 95 "experience" through New York and New Jersey, and though this route took about forty-five minutes longer, it was a much more pleasant drive, taking about six and a half hours depending on traffic leaving Connecticut.

We actually began to look forward to these drives, as they were such a departure from the hectic schedules and frantic paces we kept both kept at work. Half of our wedding creative design was conceived while traveling, and much of the Notaviva Vineyards brand essence. We continually challenged ourselves to explore what we wanted it to be from all perspectives: the customers', the employees', and ours. Time and again, we arrived at the conclusion that we wanted it to feel less like an upscale winery and more like a coffee shop. We wanted it to be hospitable, a sizeable space that still felt cozy, with a welcoming aura of craftsmanship and family values.

About this time, I happened to be reading a *USA Today* article while sitting in the Wilton Starbucks, which conveniently sat directly below the Greenfield Online headquarters. Interestingly, the article was about Starbucks' brand identity, and their notion of a "third place," i.e. 1) home 2) work and 3) your "third place." Thinking fondly back to my times with the dev team at the Clubhouse (or "Clubbaggio," as it became to be known) I realized that this philosophy was one we would espouse for Notaviva.

Late one night, somewhere on Route 15 in Maryland—I know this because I still have a crystal clear image of that moment in my mind—Shannon was sleeping and I was rolling around musical terms in my head for wine brand names. It occurred to me that not only should our wines be named after musical terms, but that we should actually pair each wine with a different genre of music. Why put on a wine label, "Best paired with chicken," when we could say, "Best paired with acoustic guitar rock"? We do this all the time anyway, most of the time not even realizing it. You likely have a different "favorite party song" for an evening out with friends, yet is that the same music you play for a romantic moment? Music has the intrinsic ability to alter human emotion—ever been sad and then heard your favorite song on the radio? What happened? Lifted your spirits, did it not? So, then, I rationalized, why not take an "upbeat" wine and pair it with "upbeat" music? And why not take a "serene" wine and pair it with "serene" music?

Research has proven that the human brain works differently in altered environments; when people are removed from their day-to-day rush and stress and allowed to meditate or break a continuous chain of thought, new thought processes and creativity emerge. I have always felt more creative while driving at night, watching the white lines rush by, focusing on the taillights ahead. Somehow all of these stimuli, coupled with a varied mix of CDs and moods, allowed that idea to come to light. When Shannon awoke, her response was beyond enthusiastic. We laughed and immediately fell in love with the idea, and Shannon made me promise we would make a wine that was "Best paired with 80s metal" that she could drink while throwing the goat.

Reflecting on that moment today, there is no way we could have known the joy and excitement that this concept would bring to our customers. We will never tire of seeing the light in people's eyes when they first visit and we explain the notion of pairing wine and music together, hearing them excitedly say, "That is amazing! I LOVE that idea!" Nor will we ever tire of seeing those same people return with a new group of friends, proudly saying, "This is the place I told you about, where they pair their wines with music!"

To create an identity that is wholly unique, relevant, and legitimate, which puts smiles on the faces of thousands of people from all walks of life, while earning an honest dollar selling a locally grown, hand-made, artisanal product, in an atmosphere of hospitality, local art, music, craftsmanship, and family values would come to define our vision of success. Though the road ahead would be fraught with setbacks, that vision has certainly come to pass.

CHAPTER 10
"Building the Wedding Site"

My brother Jim and Shayna were married the evening of Friday, October 10, 2003, and both Shannon and I were blessed to be in the wedding party, I as best man. Their ceremony was held at the Meadowlark Botanical Gardens, a stunning outdoor site overlooking the grounds, with a beautiful reception hall.

About a month before, they were thrown a couples' wedding shower at Tom and Beth's place. Everyone was there, friends and family alike, and all enjoyed a very loud time. The invitation was graciously extended to Shannon's parents, who, though divorced several years earlier, still maintained a cordial relationship. Sue was unable to attend, as she traveled extensively in her position with Pratt and Whitney, as well as in her role at the time as president of the American Society of Mechanical Engineers (ASME). Roger's relationship with Bev had been progressing and she would also attend; this was to be my first meeting with her. We hit it off right away, and spent the afternoon getting better acquainted while indoctrinating Roger and Bev in the ways of Clan Mackey. They survived it pretty well.

While they were in town, we had the opportunity to take Roger and Bev out to see the land for the first time. The look on his face was classic—the same look you see when someone takes a bite of some bad seafood. If he had cell phone coverage, he probably would have called his financial advisor just to double-check his twenty grand was still back where it belonged. I seriously cannot say I blame him; driving up to that old farmhouse for the first time was a shock to everybody (you paid WHAT for this?). As with everyone else, the rolling beauty of the surrounding meadows, forests, and mountains quickly brought a hush to their doubts.

Having just purchased our tractor a few weeks prior, I'd only had an opportunity to bush hog a few access trails back to the rear part of the property, where our own wedding was to be held the next summer. Roger is a graduate of Harvard University, who did a stint in the Army (quarterbacking their European football team), and had a very successful decades-long career in business development for Pratt and Whitney. So picture me and my bride-to-be, taking her father back to this secluded meadow where we had decided to get married. In our minds, we saw romance, beauty, and an opportunity to bring a creative vision to life. In his mind, however, he saw an overgrown disaster, and a daughter (whom he put through private school alongside the sons of wealthy PGA professionals) who would be getting married in muddy bare feet with dandelions in her hair—to a roadie. He was probably thinking, "Why don't you just elope to Haight-Ashbury in a VW bus with the rest of the hippies and save everyone the trouble of tromping through these waist-high briar patches—I'll buy the gas and dandelions..."

Daddies love their daughters, however, and the excitement in Shannon's voice as she told him our plans must have captured his imagination. Even though he could not envision what we were planning, neither his support nor his faith in us ever waivered. He did an amazing job of remaining upright, even after Shannon delivered the final blow—he would be wearing a kilt when he walked her out of the woods. If we were four light-years outside of Roger's comfort zone when we bought this place, we were in another galaxy now.

Our one guiding principle in the design of our wedding was that if we had seen it at another wedding, we would not do it in ours. We wanted everything to be completely original. The core vision for the design was the secret night wedding scene from one of our favorite movies, *Braveheart*. No blaring trumpets, grandiose pomp and circumstance would distract from the true meaning of the moment. The tone of the ceremony would be serene and peaceful, with a focus on the vows, each other, and the love between us. The reception was to be held under a tent a short walk up the hill through the meadow, and extravagant decorations were unnecessary; we knew we would rather spend the money on great food, great wine, and great music.

Influenced by our backgrounds in event and television production, we wanted the guests to feel like they were watching a magical story unfold. The setting of the site was key to achieving that effect; we decided to place it at the edge of the woods, looking out at a meadow of two gently rolling hills. The site was to be a huge semicircle cut into the tree line, rimmed with a rock wall and natural landscape elements. The rock wall would have a gap just off center, framed by two large trees, and we would have to clear a path back into the woods for the bridal party staging area. At the center of the clearing, we would build a triangular platform (the number three being central to Celtic lore), upon which we would stand. The guests would sit in the meadow, facing this platform and clearing, and the wedding party processional would come out of the hidden woods, taking the guests by surprise and drawing them into the scene.

We had Rebecca come up with a landscape design for the foliage. Step one was the clearing of some dead trees to create the basic shape of the semicircle. Using the front-end loader on the tractor and the bush hog, we slowly began to reclaim the forest from the underbrush and hunter campsite garbage that had accumulated over the decades. We also cleaned out the entire tree line on either side of the site, as we knew it would be seen by guests and captured in photos. Jim and I spent a few miserable hours with a stump grinder to finish up the clearing, leveled a few high spots with the tractor, and we had the blank canvas we needed to begin.

At the top of the meadow we have several old rock walls, mostly falling apart, which we dismantled into the front-end loader and bed of Rebecca's pickup truck. These were relocated down to the wedding site to begin the rock wall installation. We hand-stacked the wall one at a time to ensure it was solid and stable. The look was natural and unassuming. Rebecca was on-hand to help us install the landscape plan she had designed. When spring came and the meadow began to green, buds emerged on the trees and newly installed foliage; we got our first glimpse of the natural beauty of the meadow and forest.

Work was also underway to clear brush from the entry to the property from Sagle Road. The half-mile path to the parking area was in dire need of widening and stabilization—there was a creek just behind our pond and the culvert crossing was washed out. Using the loader on the tractor, I relocated a few dozen large rocks to ensure this crossing would be able to handle the one hundred plus cars we were expecting. We had a local contractor come in with some three-inch stone to shore up the meadow entrance from Sagle, as well as a few other trouble spots along the road back to the site.

The effort was not without its share of debacles, and I often tell these tales at the tasting bar to guests interested in our backgrounds. I laugh at their incredulous stares as they come to grips with the fact that this beautiful structure, with its stunning views and fine wines, is not the result of a dot-com-millionaire success story, but rather hundreds of sweat equity projects, most gone awry. During all this preparation, Seamus the cat battled a snake in our living room (where Shannon had just been walking in bare feet); the porcelain tank of the toilet froze and fell apart in the unheated house (it was eighteen degrees inside one night). I was bush hogging some brush up a hillside when the brakes on the tractor went out, and I found myself rolling backwards down a hill unable to stop. When I finally ran into a boulder (stopping rather suddenly), I was nearly thrown right off the back onto the rotating tractor PTO, where I would have been shredded into unrecognizable bits.

I caught the tractor on fire. I ran over an overgrown barbed wire fence with the bush hog and spent three hours unraveling the mess. Shannon was mowing, hit a rock, and broke the driveshaft because I had installed the wrong shear bolt. I was using the chainsaw to clear limbs and nearly fell off the ladder with the chainsaw throttle locked in place. We had raccoons move into the basement. The house was broken into and a thousand dollars' worth of tools were stolen. Countless mashed fingers, twisted ankles, strains and sprains, cuts and bruises followed us every step of the way. It was awesome.

During this time, we were still hard at work in our vineyard research. We had subscribed to numerous industry periodicals, bought dozens of vineyard and winemaking books, and visited local vineyards. We had narrowed our varietal selection to a dozen or so that we believed would thrive in our site. We learned about rootstock selection, and how the proper choice was critical in ensuring long term viability of the vine as well as the proper amount of de-vigor potential. It turned out the challenge in Virginia was not in getting vines to grow, it was keeping them from growing too vigorously. We decided to plant a small research vineyard to evaluate nine different varietals—Viognier, Cabernet Franc, Petit Manseng, Tempranillo, Cabernet Sauvignon, Sauvignon Blanc, Seyval Blanc, Traminette, and Chambourcin—using three different rootstocks (3309, 101-14, and Riparia Gloire). On March 24, I used the bush hog to clear a site and lime the rows, and on April 10, Rebecca, Jim, and Shayna came out and we hand-dug seventy-two vines, put in a small trellis, and added bamboo stakes and Snap-Max vine shelters. We knew all along these were just test vines and that they would likely be dug up at some point, but even more than the actual research aspects, this project felt important. It was another tangible step in the pursuit of the bigger picture. We found you need to have something real to hold on to when faced with the inevitable challenges and seemingly impossible situations that arise along the way. Like the cartoon bottle of wine on the wall in New Haven, those vines became a source of inspiration for us, allowing us to stay focused.

All of these projects culminated (so we thought) the weekend prior to the wedding, with a daylong gathering of family and friends pitching in to finish up the preparations. Everyone rolled up their sleeves and worked on last minute details. If I had to guess at a number, I would say Shannon and I put in a combined 600 hours of sweat equity into building our wedding site, plus another 100 combined man-hours contributed by family and friends. At least every other weekend for eight months—and every now and then with a three-in-a-row—each weekend working all day Saturday and Sunday, toiling to complete the project. Now we found ourselves enjoying a cookout with everyone who had taken the time to help out. It was our first experience in hosting a family farm dinner gathering, and seeing my little cousins running around the property, throwing rocks in the pond, adults enjoying drinks as the sun set over the valley, we finally let ourselves begin to believe that this might really happen for us. Deeply grateful to all who pitched in, we were overcome with emotion watching everyone enjoy this vineyard dream that had already tested our resolve many times.

All that was left to do now was put the finishing touches on the ceremony plans, though as we had already learned during the previous year and would be reminded of numerous times in the future, Mother Nature yet had a part to play. The last stretch before the ceremony would prove to be the most challenging yet.

CHAPTER 11
"The Wedding"

Although I had spent a decade on the road, and we both had been involved in all manner of live productions both large and small, the design, planning, and execution of our wedding was likely the most challenging project we had ever set our minds to because we fretted over every detail. We both had a very deep-seated belief that the effort we put into our wedding would be a reflection of the love and commitment we shared for each other. We also believed that planning and sharing every detail together would not only make the ceremony special for each of us, but would bring us closer together as a couple.

During the winter of 2004, we began to research locations for our rehearsal dinner. Since no one in either of our families had any experience with the wine industry—it was not like we were fourth-generations farmers or anything—we thought it would be a great time to introduce them all to a farm winery setting. We researched the local vineyards and settled on nearby Doukénie (at the time known as Windham Winery). That winter, we had taken a lunch break from our site projects and had gone over to visit with Nicki Bazaco, who, along with her husband George, had founded their winery in the late 1990s.

We talked at the bar, discussing details about the rehearsal dinner, and at some point Nicki asked why we wanted our event at a winery.

We filled her in on our land purchase and dream of founding our own winery, and a small group, who was meeting in the tasting room, overheard our conversation. One member of the group was their winemaker, Doug Fabbioli, who approached us and introduced himself. Gregarious, eccentric, and an immediately likeable Italian "hand talker," Doug chatted with us for a few minutes, and offered up his assistance as we moved forward. He handed me a card for his consulting business, Bella Luna Winery, and said, "Don't get into this business, but if you do, call me first and I'll help you get sorted out."

As I often do when instinct dictates, I put his card in my wallet—a wallet I found when cleaning out my grandfather's desk in 1999 while staying with my grandmother as he lay in a Harrisburg hospital, the victim of a stroke—and would place a call to Doug later that fall. All these years later I still have that card in the same wallet, though the card, wallet, and hands that carry them all look quite a bit worse for the wear.

I am of Scottish descent, and since we were both inspired by the *Braveheart* secret night wedding sequence, we had decided early on that the ceremony would have a Celtic theme. Since we began dating, Shannon had also come to love Celtic music, everything from the raucous pub favorites to mystical New Age styles. Music would, of course, play a huge role in the ceremony, and we spent countless hours reviewing CDs, deciding which piece would complement which element.

We decided to have different themes for each segment: a somber yet hopeful theme for the remembrance of lost loved ones at the beginning of the ceremony, followed by a "leaving home" theme for our mothers' entrances, a warlike drum-heavy theme would bring in the black-kilted groomsmen, followed by an ethereal tone for the bridesmaids, then a sweet melody for the ring-bearer and flower girl, and a mystical yet inspiring piece for Shannon's entrance. Like watching a movie, each piece created a unique atmosphere and complemented each moment as it unfolded.

We wanted live music in the wedding, and wanted to ensure the performers were of the highest caliber. We knew we would spend a large portion of our budget on a band, but felt it had to be perfect. After searching and searching, we reached out to Cherish the Ladies (CTL), world-famous as America's most beloved and successful all-women Celtic group, fronted by the incredible Joanie Madden on flute and whistles. After some negotiating with their booking agent, we were able to lock in the full band with two dancers for the reception, and a smaller trio playing live during the wedding. At $7,000 for world-class talent, we felt it was a bargain.

Certainly the most personal musical element was the song I wrote for Shannon. I had performed in two of my cousin's weddings many years earlier, and though I knew I would not be able to perform at our wedding, I wanted to create something special for Shannon. In the discussions with CTL, I had asked if they would perform the song for me, and Joanie, Heidi, and Mary were delighted. We all realized it would be very difficult, because there would be no way for us to connect for a rehearsal. I asked them to sing live to track, so that I could send them the sheet music, melodies, and backing tracks ahead of time, so they could rehearse on their own.

Over the course of several weeks leading up to the wedding, I worked late at night composing the piano, string, and horn arrangements (very much influenced by James Horner's *Braveheart* soundtrack to fit with the rest of the ceremony), writing and re-writing the lyrics and sheet music, until it all came together. The lyrics were based on the period of my life when Shannon and I were reunited, an otherwise somber and lonely time spent soul-searching atop the mountain.

"Shannon"

Once he walked alone in darkness
Under cold and moonless nights
Seeking solace from the forest
Yet the hope waned in his eyes

Shannon came to him one summer
Brought the dawn of a new day
Clearly now he sees before him
Strength renewed shall never stray

All she is he will be
Dreams become reality
Cast away all he knew
So true, Shannon shall light the way

Light the way...

Obviously the most important part of any ceremony is the vows, and we were determined to write every word, making it completely unique, special, and reflective of our relationship. We spent hours upon hours researching, reading, writing and re-writing the vows. It was far more challenging that we realized, yet also far more rewarding. In the end the vows were a beautiful array of readings drawn from various cultures, our personal promises, commitments from family, remembrance for those lost, and a look to the future.

Selecting the wedding party was another introspective process. We looked back over our lives, taking stock of all the various friends and family who have impacted not only each of us personally, but our relationship together. We wanted the ring-bearer and flower girl to be chosen from either side of the family, and with a plethora of adorable cousins, the choice was quite challenging. Shannon's cousin Bennett Robelia would be ring-bearer, and my cousin Marissa Croson would be flower girl. Shannon chose her friend Alexis Pearce to be her matron of honor, and her cousin Jessica Hill as maid of honor. Bridesmaids were her cousins Allison Robelia, Ashleigh Hill, Kristin Hill, my sister Rebecca, and my sister-in-law Shayna. Coming through the trees in their aubergine dresses, these beautiful ladies would look like fairy-tale princesses. I chose my brother Jim as best man, and my groomsmen were childhood friends David Hibberd and Ken Wright, road warriors Shane Hamill, Bobby Simmons, and Chris Bishop, and Shannon's brother, Steve Skemp. A finer group of gentlemen and scholars has never been assembled (rogues, the lot of 'em).

Our mothers would start the ceremony by walking through the trees to light floating oil lamps in front of the wedding platform. My father would walk with Jim and me, and Roger—in his kilt—would give Shannon away. My aunt, Debbie Hartwick, and Shannon's godfather, Dave Hymer, would give readings. To draw our extended families together, and since the groomsmen were not to be seen by the guests prior to the ceremony, we asked four of our uncles to serve as ushers. Sue's brothers, Jeff and Buzz and my uncles Bob Madden and Russell Dennis rounded out the attendants (rogues, the lot of 'em).

Whittling down the guest list was another major challenge, as our first pass through a list of invitees numbered well over five hundred! We knew we'd never be able to fund a gathering of that size, but really wanted to have a huge wedding reception. In the end, three hundred and sixty invitations went out, and well over three hundred would attend.

The wedding site was ready, vows were written, music prepared, and attendants and guests were beginning to travel to northern Virginia as we kept a close watch on the weather forecasts. Things were beginning to look grim, as thunderstorms were expected to roll into the area Friday morning and stay through the weekend, but we kept our hopes high and had a backup plan of conducting the entire ceremony in the tent. Though our hearts would have been broken to not use the site we worked so hard to build, we were not in danger of being rained out completely.

As a surprise wedding gift to Shannon, I purchased a 19' Tahoe Q4 bow rider boat. Living in South Florida, Shannon had always enjoyed spending time on a boat, waterskiing, fishing, or just enjoying being on the water. While at University of Miami and working the Fair in the following years, I had also come to love boating. As there were numerous lakes near our home in Connecticut, as well as our future home in Virginia, I knew we would create some of our own great memories. Thursday morning, while Shannon and her mother were running errands, I ran down to Winchester to pick up the boat, taking it back to Doukénie, where I would surprise her with it when we arrived for the rehearsal dinner.

Most of the wedding party who had traveled from outside the area stayed at the Bavarian Inn, a romantic country chalet in nearby Shepherdstown, West Virginia. Shannon and I also had reserved a suite there. On Thursday evening, after showing the wedding party and traveling family the shack and the site, then setting up the tables and chairs, we all headed back over to the Bavarian for dinner and drinks. Though exhausted, with a full day ahead, we stayed at the bar late into the night.

We awoke Friday with a long list of last-minute preparations and errands, and split up right after breakfast to begin the day. The rain began by late morning, and by noon it was absolutely pouring. Looking at the weather report, we knew that our afternoon rehearsal would be held in the reception tent. Worst of all, the quarter-mile road leading back to the wedding site was completely waterlogged, and as dozens of cars made their way back to the site for the reception, it became impassable by anything other than four-wheel drive vehicles.

The reception went smoothly, though Shannon was an emotional wreck, fearing that we would have to hold the ceremony in the tent. I did my best to console her, yet I could tell she was heartbroken. With the rehearsal completed, it was time to head over to Doukénie for dinner. Shannon and I went in separate cars so I would have a chance to uncover the boat before she arrived, and I told her I needed fifteen minutes to prepare the surprise. We all made our way through the deluge, and I took the boat cover off and set up the Bimini top as a rain cover. By the time she arrived, Shannon was so distraught about the rain and condition of the road, she barely grasped the situation. I helped her up into the boat and we took a few pictures; I remember her face, so sad that the weather had turned out so horribly.

The rehearsal dinner was a fantastic time, our families mingling, wandering around the tasting room and winery, learning about the winemaking processes. We handed out our handmade gifts to the bridal party, and took a moment to introduce each one to the group, telling everyone what was special about these relationships. By 10:00 P.M. it was time to call it an evening, and everyone ran to their cars, Shannon heading to our suite at the Bavarian and I to the Hibberd's home in nearby Charles Town, WV. As we kissed each other good-night, I promised her that everything would be fine in the morning.

I awoke the next morning to bright sunshine streaming through the window. It was a perfect summer morning, temperature in the low 70s with no humidity. I had resolved that I would not go over to the wedding site, though I knew there were about 100 projects going on. I went through all the projects one by one, and wrote out details on everything I knew remained to be completed, and sent them over to the site with David. Chris Carlton, who had recently finished up the Barbra Streisand tour, would be running sound for both the ceremony and reception with his son Nick; Chris Bishop and a local sound company tech would be working on setting up the PA systems (one for the ceremony in the woods, another for the reception). Bobby would get the alcohol from my brother Jim's house and run some other errands, and my older brother Brian, brother-in-law Bob, and a host of other friends and family would be working on the site.

My phone began ringing early, and it became apparent that although the weather was turning out to be perfect for the ceremony, the damage to the road and site had been considerable, and everyone worked incredibly hard to repair it. Shannon and I had spent eighteen months building this site, and I knew that my role was to rest and focus on the true meaning of the day, not to be moving mud. In fact, it never even crossed my mind that it would be anything less than perfect; I had total confidence that our friends and family would pull it off.

Around 1:00 P.M., the groomsmen and I began getting dressed. We had lunch, enjoyed a few beers, and got into our kilts and clansmen shirts. It was really amazing seeing the guys dressed in kilts for the first time! The visions that we had for the day were now becoming real, my excitement was mounting, and I could not wait to see Shannon.

As we drove in I was shocked to see several of my family members still working on the road—they had been out in the sun for over seven hours and were still going strong! As I knew it would, the place looked amazing, and the several spots that were nearly impassable earlier that morning were now accessible even by two-wheel drive vehicles. We drove around to the rear meadow, checked in with Nancy Craun, a wedding coordinator we hired to handle day-of communications, and made our way into the woods behind the site. Our photographer, Rodney Gibbons, took some incredible shots, my favorite being all the groomsmen lined up atop a rock wall amidst the trees. As we were taking photographs, I heard Carlton EQ'ing out the PA, and I heard Heidi Talbot of CTL singing "Shannon" as she practiced walking through the woods. I was so moved I had to take a break from the pictures, and just stood there listening to her perfect voice drifting through the trees. We finished up the grooms-men photos just as the ladies were arriving, so we moved off so that I would not see Shannon.

At 6:00 P.M., it was time to begin. Mary Coogan, guitarist for CTL, was seated on a bench in the woods behind the ceremony site and began with a soft introduction, while Joanie Madden, flutist, came walking through the woods playing "The Waves of Kilkee," followed by our mothers. Once our mothers lit the floating oil candles in front of the platform and were seated, Mary and Joanie began the Loreen McKennitt tune "Dante's Prayer" while Heidi came up through the woods, singing the haunting lyrics. Our handmade programs listed the names of our deceased friends and relatives, and this short re-membrance ceremony to honor them was very moving.

Without warning, the Celtic drums began as Tannas' "Mairead Nan Cuiread" played through the forest, setting the stage for the groomsmen's entrance. The guests were on the edges of their seats, waiting and wondering what would happen next; a few moments later, they began to catch glimpses of Hibberd coming through the trees. At 6'4", wearing a black kilt and a clansmen's top, he was a for-midable sight to say the least. The groomsmen entered and arranged themselves around the perimeter of the wedding site, standing watch over the ceremony, followed by our officiant, Tony Hileman. I then entered with my father on one side and my brother Jim as best man on the other. Shannon and I had never seen a groom escorted by his father, and thought it would be a wonderful way to thank him for the great influence he has been in my life. All carefully timed out to the length of the music, the last drumbeats faded into the woods just as I stepped atop the wedding platform.

Next was the entrance of the bridesmaids to the hauntingly beautiful "Ubi Caritas" by Connie Dover. It was incredible to see the ladies coming through the woods in their shimmering aubergine dresses, baskets of flowers in hand, perfectly complementing the colors of the forest. Led by Matron of Honor Lexi and Maid of Honor Jessie, the ladies joined the groomsmen around the perimeter of the circle.

The bride's processions began as Kim Robertson's "Labyrinth Waltz" played softly, accompanying Bennett and Marissa as they slowly made their way up the path. Bennett, in a black children's kilt (holding the rings in his sporran), was incredibly attentive as he escorted Marissa (wearing a dress handmade by Debbie) up the path, watching her every step as she dropped flower petals along the way. Marissa was the epitome of grace, even flashing a sweet grin to the guests as she entered the wedding circle, taking a seat with Ben on a small bench behind Jim, where they would occupy themselves during the ceremony by pulling the wings off of the cicadas.

I knew Roger and Shannon would be close behind, so I closed my eyes and lowered my head. I did not want to see her until she was just at the edge of the forest. Carlton and his son Nick were smoothly navigating all the transitions from the audio console, and slowly faded out the procession theme. We all paused a moment, listening to the sounds of the forest.

The bridal party and guests were all gazing at Shannon when her entrance theme began. We chose "Gift of a Thistle" by James Horner from *Braveheart*, which anyone who has seen the movie will recognize from the scene where the young William Wallace is given a thistle by the girl Murron at his father's graveside, signifying the beginning of their relationship together. I opened my eyes, looked up, and there she was, holding Roger's arm, slowly moving into the wedding circle. If I thought I had been stunned when I first saw her so many years before, this was a true emotional revelation. Many men dream of marrying a princess; I was actually going to. We whispered, "I love you" to each other several times as she came forward, Roger looking so proud, enjoying this moment that he had likely pondered since first holding his baby girl.

Tony began the ceremony, and we proceeded through the declaration of intent and our hand ceremony, a very moving exchange describing how each of us would support the other through the joys and challenges ahead. David read the "Apache Wedding Prayer," followed by our vows. Debbie then read, "We May Live Together" by Anne Bradstreet. We lit the unity candle, while Heidi sang "Shannon," accompanied by the music backing tracks and Joanie playing live flute.

Next was the ring exchange, which also had its own thematic background, "For Love of a Princess" by James Horner. As the music began to crescendo, Tony completed his words and said, "Stephen, you may now kiss your bride." Not wanting that moment to ever end, I just held Shannon and gazed at her for a moment as she whispered, "Kiss me," and slowly I pulled her closer. In those few seconds, it was as if all of my life experiences came together with a renewed reason for being—to share that moment with her, and to begin our lives together. We kissed, a long, beautiful kiss. We included our family in our vows, and as Tony asked everyone if they would support our progeny and us in the years ahead, they all gladly responded, "We will." Tony then presented us as Mr. and Mrs. Stephen Mackey to thundering applause, laughter, and shouts. It was the happiest moment of our lives.

The reception lasted long into the evening, with Cherish the Ladies raising the roof with the finest Celtic music, accompanied by their Irish dancers. We ate, drank, laughed, hugged, took thousands of pictures, and partied the night away, while the kids played flashlight tag and chased each other around the meadow. It was the perfect ending to years of hard work, and we were so proud to be able to share it all with the multitude of people who had encouraged us along the way, and worked so hard to make it all possible. As we drove away to our hotel near Dulles Airport to prepare for our long flight to Tahiti the next morning, we paused a moment to look back at our families, the site, the tent, and this beautiful property upon which we were going to build our home, our family, and our lives. Moments like that are precious, and unforgettable.

The next morning as our shuttle picked us up from the hotel, it began to rain again. By the time our plane taxied out onto the tarmac, it was pouring, and would be for the next several days. Somehow Mother Nature decided to give us a break, placing two weeks of solid rain around one perfect summer day.

Our honeymoon was idyllic, on the romantic Tahitian atoll of Manihi, in a raised hut with glass floors looking down into the water. Breakfast served by canoe, scuba diving with sharks, sailing the South Pacific, and lazing in the sun provided a much-needed mental and physical break. The atoll had a black pearl farm on the other shore, which we visited for an amazing tour, watching the locals pry apart the oysters to retrieve the gorgeous pearls. We would name our boat the "Manihi Pearl" to commemorate the experience.

Although we had achieved so much in such a short time, we knew the greatest obstacles still lay ahead. The dream had come to pass. It was time to build.

PART TWO
Build

CHAPTER 12
"Going Home"

The first several weeks after we returned to New Haven were spent in typical post-wedding bliss. Phone calls from family and friends, who had been at the wedding, re-living the events of the day, were a favorite of ours. We also began spending weekends out on the boat on nearby Candlewood Lake. One time we just anchored out in the lake, lowered the Bimini top like a tent, and spent the night sleeping in the boat with our two dogs. Several other times, we enjoyed camping on a small island in the middle of the lake. It was so peaceful, just mooring to a tree, setting up our tent, building a campfire, and cooking out under the stars.

We also made two trips up to Lake Winnipesaukee in New Hampshire, an incredibly beautiful classic New England setting. Boating to the surrounding towns, walking their charming waterfronts, visiting shops and cafés, and anchoring in the secluded coves, lazing in the sun were some of our most memorable moments that entire summer. We talked for hours on end about the wedding, the honeymoon, and our future. These were beautiful times, and during many of the struggles we would face in the years ahead, we would look back upon them with a wistful nostalgia.

Always the talk turned to our vineyard plans. Throughout the summer, we began to feel increasingly restless, drawn to Virginia, knowing our future would be there. We still had no real business plan, and though we had acquired several examples through the seminars we had been attending, and found many others online (Virginia Tech and University of Washington, among others), we had not yet begun to derive our own. Even with two six-figure incomes, we did not yet have the financial resources to embark upon the winery path. We were able to float two mortgages, pay off all our debt, and build our retirement accounts, but by now we knew that founding a 5,000 case winery would cost a million dollars. That figure did not include the land or a house, so of the million we needed, we were short, oh, about a million.

About this time, we had a very unique and chance meeting with a renowned leader of the Spanish wine industry. Shannon and I had decided to take the long way home from work one Friday evening, and chose the vibrant town of Norwalk for dinner. We wandered the streets, debating which restaurant to go to, when we happened upon the Spanish-themed Barcelona having a wine tasting event. Always looking to learn something new about wines, and not knowing anything about the event, we chatted with other guests and enjoyed the amazing selection of olives and cheeses; Manchego has been a favorite ever since.

As dinner finished up, we were introduced to the guest speaker, Juan Torres, fourth-generation owner of the famed Torres brand. After giving a short presentation, he visited tables. After we informed him of our plans, he ended up sitting with us for nearly thirty minutes—trying to talk us out of it! He told us that to make a small fortune in the wine industry, you have to start with a large one. He was delightful and very gracious with his advice and his time, and we knew we were very lucky to have the opportunity to learn from him. As all dreamers do, we clung to his stories of Spanish sunsets and fine wine. Somehow, the horror stories of bad harvests, huge barrel invoices, and razor-thin profit margins seemed to go in one ear and out the other.

As fall approached, we realized there was no point in remaining in Connecticut any longer. Though we were both making great salaries, our hearts just were not in it, and each trip back to Virginia made it harder. Though I was sitting on a stock option package that would have likely funded the entire winery startup within ten years, we knew we would never survive away from the farm that long. Shannon's career, though lucrative, began to take its toll on her, mentally and physically, with its aggressive corporate culture and high burnout and turnover rates.

We had known early in our relationship that we wanted to have children right away. Given our ages and the fact that we both had our hearts set on four children, we felt it would be safest and healthiest to not wait too long. Right after we returned from our honeymoon, we felt it was time to let nature take over; with all the stresses Shannon was enduring at work, we were having no success. That was really the tipping point in the decision to leave Connecticut, and given that as our rationale, there was never a second thought about leaving the salaries, big bonuses, and stock options behind—we have never been motivated by those "incentives" (or "vices," depending on your perspective).

Shannon began shopping around, and within a few weeks, she had secured an interview with AOL. Several weeks later she received an offer letter, which she happily accepted. The effect of her resignation from WWE was instantaneous; she was absolutely glowing, and I was so happy for her. Rather than beginning a job search and resigning from Greenfield, I informed them I was moving to Virginia. As Greenfield was expanding to be a global company, they were already operating with remote development capabilities. It took a few days of apparently heated discussion between the executives, but they approved me to relocate to Virginia and work remotely from our home office there. Both of our salaries secured, it was time to plan the move.

We had been scanning the house-for-rent sections of the Loudoun newspapers, believing at the time (naively) that we would only be in the rental for a year or so while we constructed the new house. Our rental recon team (my mom and Aunt Gin) went out to investigate a quaint one-bedroom home, somewhat isolated, on seven acres of land at the southern end of Short Hill Mountain, about a ten-minute drive from the farm. We signed the lease and were set to move in the second week of November.

Since resigning from WWE, Shannon's spirits had been totally renewed, and she was thrilled to be moving to Virginia, and for the new career that awaited her there. Though not her lifelong dream job, she had an instant connection with her new boss, Geno Yoham, whose great management style and fun personality were such a departure from the position she was leaving. He was also quite the wine aficionado and was completely taken with our plans for the vineyard. In the years ahead, Geno would work for wine during several harvests.

November 4th was the night before Shannon was to leave New Haven, and we had some very emotional moments walking through the house together, stopping in each room to recount the memories. Shannon had been feeling a little funny for a few days, so she bought a pregnancy test (actually she bought three, all different brands, just to be sure), and four months after our wedding, we learned she was pregnant with our first baby. The body is amazing, and it was almost as if hers knew the time was not right while she had been in such an anxious mental state. As soon as she had cast off the weight of that career, and renewed vigor with our approaching opportunities, her body welcomed a pregnancy. The body and mind are indelibly linked, and when we have met people who have asked us about pregnancy challenges, our first questions have always been, "Where is your head? Where is your heart?"

As we prepared to leave the next morning, we took the long way around so we could pass in front of the house and pause for a few minutes to give Shannon one last look. We had decided to sell the New Haven house as a FSBO, and began posting "Open House" signs throughout the neighborhood and on the nearby main intersections. The house looked great, and though we had priced it about 10% higher than recent comps, we were hopeful that all our sweat equity projects would justify the higher asking price.

When I finally left for Virginia in early December, we had some solid inquiries but still no offers. Going into the winter, we realized we were now on the hook again for three big monthly payments—two mortgages and a rental home. Even with those pressures, we were glowing with the feeling of finally coming home. We had a great little hideaway shack, two secure careers, a blank canvas property, and a healthy pregnancy. We purchased a 3D home architect software package and began designing floor plans; date night would be dinner in and hours lying in bed, drafting our dream house. At long last, we began putting together budgets for building a home; though a full-fledged winery startup was still not a remote possibility, we knew with the equity in the New Haven home, our perfect credit, minimal debt, and professional salaries, a construction loan would now be within reach.

We just needed to sell the house...

CHAPTER 13

"First Planting"

By mid-September 2004, we had made the decision to move forward with our vineyard planting. We had met the winemaker Doug Fabbioli sixteen months earlier at Doukénie, and I had carried his business card in my wallet ever since. He was pleased when I called to tell him we were ready to move forward in some small capacity. We were confident we could establish at least an acre of vines, possibly two, in the spring of 2005.

Just about every resource we could find indicated that planting an acre of vines cost roughly $15,000 for marking the rows, preparing the soil, planting labor, and trellis installation, among a host of other costs (not including the land or any required equipment). We knew we could bring the costs way down, likely under $10,000 per acre, by doing much of the work ourselves; sweat equity labor would be the primary factor in all of our planning moving forward. Vines, chemicals, trellis and fencing supplies cost what they cost, but great savings would be possible by eliminating consultant fees.

We pored over the budget, salary, and savings figures, and knew we did not have the capital to plant the entire vineyard, but realized we could afford two acres. Our research and conversations with Doug and other area growers all pointed to Viognier (vee-ohn-yay) as the up-and-coming white varietal, and Cabernet Franc as a red varietal well-suited for Virginia's climate. Viognier, originally from the Rhone Valley in France and the only permitted grape in the French wine Condrieu, had shown great promise in Virginia's challenging viticulture climate, and we were hopeful it could someday put Virginia on the international stage. On October 1st, we placed our order with Vintage Nurseries in California for an acre each, signed the contract, and sent in our deposit.

Half an acre of this first planting was funded by wedding gifts from our family and friends. We were so moved when we sent this money to the nursery, knowing that all the love and support of each of these people would go into something real, tangible, and long lasting.

We scheduled an onsite meeting for Doug, after which we would decide how (or even whether or not) to proceed. We met on November 6th, and, as great advisors should do, Doug challenged us during that first conversation, really digging in deep to understand our motivations. He made it abundantly clear that this was not the path for huge financial rewards.

Doug gained reassurance as our conversation continued from the fact that we had both come from a live event production background. Those experiences instilled within us a mindset that would be critical for our sweat equity approach to the wine industry. He agreed wholeheartedly that there would be numerous times we would be faced with impossible odds, forces of nature, and overwhelming budget shortfalls. Having the courage to keep moving forward, no matter the obstacles, would be the key to launching this business.

He did support our decision to move forward, because we all had a clear understanding that this initiative would be scalable; we did not have to come up with the capital for a complete startup on day one. We could plant an acre, then a few years later plant another, then begin making a little wine, and so on. We knew we would be starting small and working our way up. The big question was at what point would the demands of a winery startup make it impossible to hold down full-time corporate careers. Satisfied that we would be able to make an honest go at it, Doug excitedly jumped from his chair and said, "Let's set up a date to mark out your field!" We scheduled

Friday, November 26th (the day after Thanksgiving) as our first day of vineyard preparation.

I spent Thanksgiving morning bush hogging the meadow so we would have an easier time marking the field. Step one of any vineyard installation is an analysis of the layout. We had determined during our feasibility study that both the front meadow (around ten acres) and rear meadow (another ten) would be suitable for winegrapes. We also knew that there were some low spots at the boundaries that would not be suitable, and we looked to Doug to help us determine where to place the boundaries, to ensure we would not face topography issues later.

We spent about an hour walking the front meadow, and Doug was pleased with the topography of the two primary hills. As we had anticipated, he advised we stay well away from some low-lying areas closer to the pond. We established a perimeter of about seven acres enclosing both hilltops, directly in view of where the tasting room would sit. In our minds, we could already fast-forward five years and envision serving wine at the tasting bar, looking out through the picture windows at the perfect rows of vines. I believe this ability has been one of our greatest assets, to not allow ourselves to be limited by "what is" but to expand our vision and stay focused on "what could be."

One of the funding challenges in establishing a vineyard is determining from the outset the maximum outer perimeter for fencing requirements. It would neither be cost-effective nor efficient to move fencing as the vineyard expanded, thus we had to budget for deer fencing around the entire seven-acre perimeter, even if we would only be planting one acre. The white-tailed deer population in Northern Virginia is enormous. Shannon, Doug, and I marched through the thigh-high grass, placing bamboo stakes with colored flags on top to outline the site.

It was then time to establish the orientation of the rows. There are a myriad of considerations to be weighed in determining how to orient rows of vines: the widths between rows, vine-to-vine spacing, hill slope and aspect, equipment size, anticipated yields and trellis design are just a few of the variables. We had determined that we were interested in either a vertical-shoot-positioned (VSP) trellis or a Smart-Dyson trellis configuration. We had also learned that eight-foot wide rows and five-foot vine spacing presented a suitable density to achieve a four to five ton per acre yield.

As we discussed this design with Doug, he expressed concern that the eight-foot rows would be a little tight for maneuvering equipment. Eight-foot rows look plenty large when they are just bamboo stakes in the ground, but Doug's experienced eye knew they would look quite different in a few years, with a full canopy of foliage. His reasoning sounded logical to us, because at this point, even though we were now planting our own vineyard, we had never actually even picked a grape, much less driven a tractor down a row of fully canopied vines. We expanded our row spacing to nine feet.

The other major consideration was the row orientation as it relates to compass direction and hill aspect. Most schools of thought prefer vineyard rows to be oriented in a north-south configuration; however, this has to be weighed against the safety factors inherent in the prevailing hill slope aspect. For example, if you have an east-west hill slope and you install north-south rows, your tractor will always be riding at an angle. This is both a safety concern (tractor rollovers are the number one cause of death in Virginia agriculture) and efficiency concern for sprayer usage. There is give-and-take between optimal and reasonable when it comes to making the final determination.

We decided to let the hill aspect guide the decision, to ensure the tractor and sprayer would always sit most upright when working within the rows, our rows set in a northwest-southeast orientation. This did create a slightly precarious situation, in that the tractor would always be at uncomfortable sideways angles when maneuvering at the ends of the rows. We felt this would be manageable, though to date I am the only person who has ever sprayed or mowed the vineyard due to this safety concern. Tractors have an hour meter for the engine (rather than an odometer), and at this writing, I have spent nearly one thousand hours mowing and spraying.

We began marking out the rows, Doug giving us instruction on layout and marking techniques. We decided to mark out the entire front portion of the vineyard, just over three acres, regardless of whether we would be planting one or two acres. It would save time in the long run, allowing us to keep the weeds down in the future planting rows with the regular herbicide applications required under the vines. Each row would be four hundred feet long, and we set out bamboo stakes every one hundred feet. Our small research vineyard was not in alignment with the new row configuration, and we made the decision to pull it out. Doug helped us mark out the first two hundred feet across forty-two rows, and when he was confident we had the task under control, he bid us farewell for the day. Shannon and I called it quits by late afternoon. My mom came out to help two days later, and we finished up the layout that Sunday.

Once the marking was complete, it was time to sub-soil the rows, which is essentially driving the length of the row with an implement that cuts a deep slice in the ground. This allows the soil amendments to penetrate the hardpan and work their way down into the ground over the winter. Doug had pulled soil samples and sent them off to the lab, and we had a custom fertilizer mix created, which I applied on December 11th, along with a ton and a half of lime per acre. The vineyard rows were finally prepped and ready for the spring planting.

We spent that Christmas in Florida, reveling in the joy of telling people our first baby was on the way. We had fun giving Roger a diaper changing kit, complete with tool belt, hard-hat, goggles, and rubber gloves. Everyone was so excited to hear the news of the upcoming vineyard planting in April, though with a baby due in July, they were beginning to wonder how on earth we were going to manage it all.

Amazingly, we had been able to keep the news from my mother, who had (often quite dramatically) longed for grandchildren for years. We flew home from Florida in time for my annual family Christmas gathering with mom's side of the family. Knowing this would be a momentous occasion, I went inside and asked mom if she could come help us bring in some gifts. When she got to the car, I told her I had a special gift for her. She opened it up, and saw a doormat that read "Grammy's House." She screamed with delight, and asked if she could go in to tell everyone. She flew through the door, and the chorus of congratulations and hugs was overwhelming. We were on top of the world.

We spent the rest of the holidays and the early part of winter 2005 cuddled up in front of our woodstove, eating ice cream, watching movies, and reading books about parenthood. I was beginning to feel the additional strain of working remotely. I often found myself on conference calls to India at 2:00 A.M., helping the developers sort out issues. I needed to head back to India (third trip in two years) , and spending two weeks in New Delhi, plus my scheduled trips to Wilton, Connecticut made it clear to me that I could no longer bear the travel with a baby on the way. I had walked away from a travel-based career in pro audio, and there was no way I was going to resume one now.

I began submitting resumes to area companies, seeking digital media product development and management positions. I stumbled upon an opportunity with comScore, a leading online market research firm, submitted my resume, and shortly thereafter was called in for an interview. I was intrigued by the opportunity, and I was savvy enough to pick up on the conversational undertones and knew they would be driving for an IPO in the very near future. This was somewhat reassuring, as I would be walking away from a very large unvested portion of my stock options from Greenfield. I discussed the opportunity with Shannon, and she was all for it. I handed in my resignation on February 10th, and quietly walked away from the corporate nirvana of a six-figure salary and vested pre-IPO stock options.

I was now well into the deer fence preparations. I would spend each weekend bush hogging brush, removing old rusty barbed wire, pulling rotting fence posts, and burning piles of debris to clear the perimeter of the vineyard. Rising at 6:00 A.M., I would don my coveralls, prepare a lunch, and head over to the vineyard. I would swing through the local gas station for a giant cup of coffee (which usually tasted more like a tall cup of warm axle grease). From 7:00 A.M. to 7:00 P.M., Saturday and Sunday, I would toil in the meadow. This is when I began my overuse of Ibuprofen (which would become a serious issue later) and got to the point of taking four pills (800 mg) three times daily on Sunday, Monday, and Tuesday. Some mornings

I would be sitting in my cube so sore and stiff I could barely focus on reading an email, and the reality of the underfunded sweat equity model was beginning to take hold.

Some days Shannon would bring lunch over, and we would sit in the grass looking at the progress, knowing that each day was bringing us closer to the goal. One day, she came by to show me some new baby outfits she had just bought for our boy (we had recently had the first sonogram on March 2nd), and we laughed and enjoyed looking at the adorable tiny outfits.

Prior to having the sonogram, we had settled on names for a baby girl; for some reason, we were just sure that is what we would be having. Shannon had visions of a little girl in a sundress and dirty bare feet chasing a puppy through the meadow, and I loved the notion of raising a daddy's girl tomboy. Unable to find a first name we liked, I decided to create my own (it's what I do). While researching music for the wedding, I fell in love with a song called "Ailein Duin," a haunting Celtic melody. I worked with the spelling and came up with "Ailyn," though I later found out the name did already exist as an obscure variant of "Aileen," which was why we had never seen it in any of the baby name books. Shannon loved the name "Skye," so we were all set to name our baby girl Ailyn Skye Mackey. Those plans were put on hold two seconds into the sonogram, when the first image—a picture between the legs—revealed quite a different situation. Not to worry, we thought, there would be plenty of other babies coming, so we would just have to wait to meet Little Miss Mackey in a few years.

Typical of new parents, we had whittled a list of fifty boy names down to zero, and were back at square one. One morning at comScore, I was downloading some classical music to ease my grumpy joints (and demeanor) and stumbled upon the Wagner opera *Tristan and Isolde*. I thought it was a cool name, and sent it to Shannon via instant messenger, and she responded, "THAT'S IT!!!" We both instantly loved it, and pulled a top contender from the previous list for his middle name; our little boy would be Tristan Connor Mackey.

Somewhere around this time we decided to cash in my vested stock options from Greenfield, which we were going to use to fund the initial planting as well as make some equipment purchases. The post-IPO lockout period had ended in January, and we were now able to sell the shares. Since I had resigned with only a small portion of my options vested, I had sacrificed quite a large payout; however, even with the minimal options I acquired and Greenfield's trading price, we still walked with nearly $50,000. This would completely cover the first two acres of vines, labor, and trellis installation, as well as all the supplies for the deer fence that would surround the entire vineyard. We also treated ourselves to a new digital SLR camera for Tristan's arrival.

It is likely that this was the very same day I made another frustrating phone call to our deer fencepost supplier near Pittsburgh, inquiring to the status of our delivery. Apparently my 125 ten-foot posts and ten twelve-foot posts, weighing in at a mere 11,000 pounds, were too small of an order for a freight company to take the job and make the delivery. Most of the truckers they used only wanted to deal with the massive orders to cattle ranches and the like, not some silly vineyard in Virginia. The weeks passed, and with our April planting fast approaching, it became clear that I would have to rent a truck to go retrieve my posts.

I went to Rentals Unlimited to pick up a flatbed truck and left for Blairsville, Pennsylvania. I slept in the truck in the lumberyard parking lot overnight, so when they opened at 7:00 A.M., I could be the first truck loaded and home by noon to unload and begin the installation. As I watched the all-terrain forklift load up the flatbed with over five tons of lumber, I realized there was no way a truck this heavy would be able to make it out into a soggy meadow to offload the posts. I called ahead to my crew of volunteers, a mix of family and friends, and advised them that we would need to use Rebecca's pickup truck in 4WD and do small transfer loads to get the posts distributed. We loaded about ten or so posts into her pickup, drove them out to the vineyard, and then hand-carried to their respective holes. It was a very long afternoon, but the crew was awesome. We made the best of a very messy situation and enjoyed a few beers afterwards.

The next day, we began the actual installation of the posts. The postholes were now filled to the top with water. Putting a few inches of gravel in the bottom of the hole for drainage, then using the post to splash out the water, we could backfill the dirt around the post to set it firmly in place. We worked through the day, and by late afternoon we had set about seventy-five of the 125 posts. The following weekend I continued the fence post installation by myself, which was considerably more difficult without the help of the lads.

Saturday, April 16th, dawned clear and beautiful, and I was up at five in the morning, dizzy with anticipation. Laying my hand on Shannon's belly while she slept, Tristan woke her with a big kick, I suppose to wish me good luck. I arrived at the vineyard a little after six and checked the vines, which had been soaking in water all night to swell the roots. The vineyard was prepared, the materials were all on site, equipment was ready, and I was as excited as a five-year old on Christmas morning.

Doug had urged us to hire a vineyard consultant to help out with the planting, and we had met Mike Newland a few months earlier at a Loudoun Winegrower's Association meeting. Our tractor was neither large enough nor powerful enough to mount the tree planter that we would use for the vine installation, and we hired Mike for his expertise and use of his equipment.

Mike introduced us to his crew chief, Quentin Garcia. Watching Quentin and his crew work that day was unbelievable; their dedication, work ethic, and attention to detail were superb. Quentin was accustomed to having his men do all the work themselves, and seemed quite surprised when I told him I would sit upon the tree planter and plant every vine myself.

A tree planter is essentially a seat on a plow; an installer sits on a seat a few inches off the ground, with a plow blade between your legs that cuts a groove into the ground, and two wheels under your butt that pinch the earth back together after you drop in your seedling, or, in our case, vine stock. Like most farm implements, it pretty much looks like a rusty pile of junk that will tear off any human appendage it can get its teeth into and unmercifully spit out an unrecognizable pile of ground meat. I could not wait to get onboard, and I believe the rusty tree planting implement was salivating at the thought of its forthcoming meal of roadie-turned-vintner hands.

We lined up the tractor at the top of the first row, Quentin driving, me on the tree planter, Mike handing me the vines, and three crewmen behind me with shovels to tidy up the planting. Quentin hit the gas and away we went. As the plow edge opened up the groove in the soil, I placed the first vine, let go way too early, and watched it fall over as the two wheels buried it underground. Quentin stopped the tractor to a laughing chorus, Mike rolled his eyes, gave me a few more pointers, and away we went again. The second try went much better, and in a few minutes I had the hang of it.

It took several hours to complete the Cabernet Franc planting, after which we took a break for lunch. Shannon had come over by mid-morning and was visibly disappointed she would be unable to ride the tree planter; it was not a job for someone who was five months pregnant. She was able to dig a hole with a shovel though and planted a vine the old-fashioned way. After lunch we commenced the Viognier planting, and finished up by mid-afternoon.

Once the tractor starts rolling, you do not even have a chance to think about the enormity of what is happening. You just stay focused on the task at hand, trying to ensure that each vine goes into the ground perfectly. It was only later, after the equipment was put on the trailer and the crew had left, that we took a moment to look out over our two newly planted acres. It was an incredible feeling, taking stock of the new vineyard, thinking back to the romantic whim that had set this story in motion.

The following weekend, we scheduled the installation of the bamboo stakes and grow tubes that accompany a new vineyard. Each new vine receives a five-foot bamboo stake, pressed into the ground about a foot, which will support the shoots as they begin to grow. Set around this stake is a plastic grow tube, which has to be assembled from two halves, and is placed over top of the stake and vine to provide a kind of miniature greenhouse, protecting the vine from the elements and critters wishing to make a meal of the tasty new shoots.

Grow tube installation is one of the few working days in a vineyard that is well suited for children wishing to participate in farm activities. No chemicals have yet been sprayed upon the vines, it is not one hundred degrees outside, and the grow tubes are not heavy. It is one of the more pleasant days involved in the establishment of a vineyard. We had a crew of about fifteen friends and family members come out for the day, and many of my younger cousins (ages two through seven) were amazing little helpers. It was such a fun day, and although everyone was totally wiped out by mid-afternoon as we were chased out by some impending thunderstorms, we had installed over half an acre of grow tubes, and all two acres had bamboo stakes in place.

The other major installation that was underway was the trellis posts. With the vines spaced five feet apart, an eight-foot tall line post would need to be pounded two feet into the ground at every fourth vine, or twenty feet apart. At either end of each row, a thicker end post was pounded deeper into the ground, and would become the key to the end-brace construction, which would eventually support the weight of the fruit and the vine canopy. As I researched this process, it became clear to me that this was one of those tasks best left to a professional with the proper equipment. I had made some inquiries to local equipment rental places, and learned that they no longer rented post-pounding equipment, due to the large number of horrific accidents. A post-pounder is a huge hydraulic ram, which uses a heavy tower to pound a pressure-treated pine post into the ground. The hydraulic power raises the tower, and when the lever is released, a set of enormous springs brings it crashing down onto the top of the upright post. A person needs to steady the post and hold it upright for the first few strikes, and many people had inadvertently had their hands atop the post at the moment the ram came down, instantly smashing their hand and typically removing it from the rest of the arm.

I contacted a local fencing pro, Donnie Ulmer of Milcreek Fencing. The skill and experience of his crew made for short work, and they distributed and pounded the two acres of posts in just a couple days. Without a doubt, that was the best money we spent.

Although I had made great progress on the deer fence installation, I had come to a dead-end digging some of the postholes. The rear section of the vineyard is incredibly rocky, and much of it had a layer of rock. The auger on the rear of the tractor was just not able to punch through this layer, and using a digging bar was not an option. I went back to Rentals Unlimited to get a pneumatic jackhammer, a large tow-behind compressor complete with air hoses and an extremely heavy hammer with various cutting implements. I spent May 7th pounding down through the rock layer, trying to reach a depth of thirty inches to ensure a proper setting for the post and enough height to attach the deer netting. This was a horrible, abysmal process and incredibly exhausting. Once the rock was broken down into small pieces, I had to dig it out by hand. With nearly thirty holes to do, it became clear I was not going to finish in one day.

Over the previous few weeks, my beloved grandmother, Mary Lightner, had fallen ill, eventually settling into a coma. For several days, many of my cousins and siblings took turns staying with her in the hospital, as no one wanted her to be alone when she passed. When I arrived home that evening, my mom called to let me know she was gone. Although we'd had time to prepare ourselves for that call, Shannon and I were both overcome with grief. My head had already been pounding from the physical abuse of eight hours of smashing rocks with a jackhammer, and now was even worse from crying my eyes out. I awoke late that night with feelings of nausea, dizziness and pupil dilation. Dehydration, coupled with a slight concussion and the emotional stress of losing Gram, had certainly taken its toll. I was a physical and emotional mess, and was completely miserable.

Sunday morning, I got off to a much-needed slow start. Shannon made me a big breakfast, as there was no way she was going to let me out of the house without eating properly. I knew I needed to get back out to the vineyard and finish the rock pounding, as the equipment rental fees would add up quickly. I followed breakfast with a handful of Ibuprofen, dragged myself out the door, drove to the vineyard, and fired up the jackhammer. Another six hours of pounding and it was over; all the deer fence post holes had been dug, and now it was just a matter of setting the posts over the next few weeks. I returned the equipment, got home late that night, showered, and settled into bed with my head against Shannon's tummy and fell asleep curled up next to my wife and little boy.

Our dream of establishing a vineyard had come to fruition years ahead of any previously foreseeable (or rational) timetable. We said we were going to do it, and we just went ahead and made good on that promise, without even pausing to ask how or why. I was now in a critical race against time to finish the deer fence before the vines grew out of the top of the grow tubes, or it would all be for nothing. I began to feel the intense weight of the pressure we had placed upon ourselves. Between the tractor, equipment, supplies and labor, nearly fifty thousand dollars in cash was spent; it was in the ground and gone. Would it have gone to college educations? Retirement accounts? Family vacations? None of that mattered now, that decision was behind us. This was a milestone in so many different regards; we now knew there was no turning back. Although I did not fully grasp it at that moment, the timing of this realization, coupled with Gram's passing, had impacted me so greatly that it would soon forever change the course of Notaviva Vineyards.

CHAPTER 14

"New Parents"

Right from the beginning, Shannon had committed herself to a natural childbirth, as she wanted to be aware of every sensation and wanted no risk of drug effects on the baby. After researching the various techniques and methods available, she settled on the Bradley Method of husband-coached natural childbirth and we registered for classes. I was incredibly excited about Tristan's forthcoming birth, and wanted to be as much a part of it as I could. We chose a midwife delivery in a state-of-the-art birthing facility. Loudoun County has many of the finest healthcare professionals and facilities in the country, and we settled on the Birthing Inn, which hosted two telemetry rooms complete with large tubs and roaming vital monitoring.

The classes were held each Tuesday over an eight-week period. They began with some background into Dr. Bradley, his research and teachings, and how the methodology evolved. We learned about the various stages of labor, with the husbands being instructed on various techniques to reduce stress and pain as the labor intensified. As the course progressed, we began to get into more detailed and graphic descriptions and visuals. Not only were we being instructed on a textbook delivery, but also on the myriad of issues and dangers that can arise during any labor. Then came the videos. It was comical watching everyone's reactions during the showing of the birth videos. Essentially, all the women were cooing and blubbering in their Kleenexes, and the men were all white as sheets, doing their best not to throw up.

We decided very early on that the only person who was going to determine when Tristan would be born would be Tristan. As long as neither Shannon nor he was in any imminent danger, then there was no way we wanted any kind of intervention for the sake of con-venience, either ours or a healthcare practitioner's. It was critical, then, that Shannon find someone who supported, encouraged, and understood her commitment to natural childbirth. Shannon had spent countless hours researching practitioners and methodologies, and had settled on the Loudoun Community Midwives, a practice comprised (at the time) of Margie Brandquist, Wendy Dotson, and Paula Senner. These three ladies were impressive in their dedication to prenatal care, their knowledge of and commitment to natural childbirth, and their perfect blend of genuine caring and absolute professionalism. Shannon loved their philosophy of around-the-clock on-call, whereby any one of the three could deliver our baby, no matter when he decided to arrive. They made it clear that they were there to provide for Shannon and Tristan's health and safety, not the other way around. There would never be any "hurry up Tristan, we have other plans" mindset or similar artificial birth parameters.

As a father, I also felt they did a wonderful job of keeping me engaged in both the prenatal process as well as the birth training. Childbirth is naturally a very woman-centric experience, and I will admit there are magical bonds created between mother, child, and midwife that do not involve the father. Those bonds develop very early in the process, well before the actual delivery, and one aspect of the Bradley training I am grateful for is the knowledge that those bonds must be honored and not resented. In the end, from my perspective, the health of both mother and child are the only things that matter; nurturing and supporting those bonds is a key role of the father for the positive mental, emotional and spiritual well-being of his wife.

Not only did parental planning and vineyard startup tasks consume us, but also another career change came calling. During April, I interviewed with America Online for a director position overseeing the Winamp digital media player. During the career search that led me a few months earlier to comScore, I had submitted resumes for several positions at AOL and TimeWarner. Apparently, since I did not deactivate my account, my resume was still live in their database, and when the position opened up, they contacted me. Though comScore was on the fast track to an IPO (and no one in their right mind would walk away from a second stock option package), the reality of my day-to-day situation was beginning to take its toll. I had been trying in vain to work my way into the programming and product development unit, however those teams were being run out of the Chicago and recently acquired Toronto offices, thus it was clear I was going to be stuck in panel management. I figured it could not hurt to take an afternoon off to hear what the folks at AOL had to say.

The interviews went very well (I was interviewed by four people) and I was immediately intrigued by the possibility of returning to my musical and audio engineering roots. A Winamp user for several years, I was very familiar with the product. The additional benefit of being able to work at the same company as Shannon and our ability to commute together made it an obvious choice for me. When the job offer came a week later, I accepted immediately, tendered my resignation from comScore, and walked away with just two months of a forty-eight month options package. When comScore went public in June 2007, I lamented yet another "would have had a half million dollars" moment that was simply not meant to be.

I allowed myself a week and a half off before starting at AOL in mid-June and spent the entire week finishing up the deer fence—so much for resting up before the new gig. Much of the efficacy of a deer fence is behavioral; a deer can jump right over a 7'6" fence if they are motivated enough to do so. If the fence is up before they know a tasty meal waits inside, they will not bother. Working eleven consecutive twelve-hour days, with only a brief afternoon break for Shannon's baby shower on June 11th, I completed the 11,000' deer fence project on the 12th, our one-year anniversary and the evening before my first day at AOL. The vines were safe, and though there were still numerous vine training and trellis construction tasks needed, the pressure of the vineyard's potential demise had lessened considerably.

We enjoyed a relatively peaceful few weeks leading up to Tristan's birth. I spent most evenings and each weekend working out in the vineyard, running trellis wire, spraying herbicide in the rows, tying vines, and pulling off the grow tubes to train the vines and allow them to more fully develop. Just about all of the vines were now about waist-high, with a few nearly six feet tall!

Preparations for the baby's arrival continued back at the house. Since we were in a one-room rental, Tristan would be joining us in our bedroom. I was very disappointed I would not be able to build and decorate a cute nursery, but we made the best of the situation by purchasing a matching set of farm-themed baby décor to liven up the room. Shannon spent most of this time rearranging all the baby clothes and supplies into the limited space. When she got it just like she wanted it, she pulled it all apart, I moved the furniture, and she reconfigured it all over again. Like most new fathers, I watched in awe as the room came apart and was reassembled nearly a dozen times. Apparently organizing a baby's room is not as simple as organizing a tool cabinet; who knew? For those men who have not yet experienced this, the process is known as "nesting," and is a very natural impulse of an expecting woman. As a courtesy to first time fathers-to-be, here are a few questions to be avoided:

Q) "Don't you think the dresser is fine right here?"

A) "It's too far from the crib!" Sniffling.

Q) "Didn't the bassinette look better over there?"

A) "It's too close to the window, it might be drafty!" Crying.

Q) "Do you really need 12,000 baby wipes for one little ass?"

A) "It's called a tushy and it's going to be so cute!" Sobbing.

It was a fascinating time, and I was trying my best not to appear as an insensitive brute, working hard to be both supportive and attentive. Especially fun were the many circular conversations, for example:

"What do you think about this baby outfit?" she asks.

"I like it," I respond.

"Well, what about this outfit?" she asks.

"I like it just as well," I respond, careful to not imply anything negative.

"You have to pick one," she insists. This is known as "the setup," and dark clouds appear on the horizon.

Trying hard to read her eyes to find the right answer, I moronically respond, "The first one." BUZZ—wrong answer.

"I liked the second one, why don't you like it?" Sniffling. Insensitive brute.

We weathered the experience as well as any new parents, though to this day, I contend the room ended up exactly as she had arranged it the first time.

We had been unable to sell the New Haven house, and the burden of two mortgages and a rental payment had taken its toll, eating away at the remainder of my Greenfield option cash. As Tristan's due date approached, Shannon became increasingly adamant she wanted the house gone before the birth, as she did not want to contend with the financial worries once the baby arrived. As luck would have it, the second week of July, an offer came in. Though it was well under our original asking price, we decided to make a small counter offer, which was accepted, and we were relieved that chapter in our lives was finally closed. Until that house was sold, we were not in a position to begin interviewing builders for the new home, and now that burden had been lifted. Once Tristan was born and safely home, we could begin the search for a general contractor.

On July 17th, Shannon awoke at 5:30 A.M. with mild contractions, and by 7:30 A.M. they had intensified to the point that we were quite certain this was the day. Shannon called the midwives to let them know, and since she was comfortable and relaxed, we decided to spend the morning at home. I loaded the SUV, we both showered and got ready to go, and by late morning she was eager to move to the Birthing Inn. We checked in at 1:30 P.M., and when our nurse walked in to introduce herself, I almost fell over in shock to see my sixth grade girlfriend standing there, Laura (Wilson) Frazier. She would be assisting Paula Senner, our midwife, throughout the birth.

Shannon changed into her gown, had an exam, and was fitted with the telemetry monitoring equipment. We walked the halls and stood together rocking back and forth, while her contractions increased in intensity and regularity. I had brought some sports drinks and fresh fruit in our bags for Shannon, and she continued to eat and drink until the nausea got too bad. We both believe that keeping her hydrated and nourished was a huge help during the exertions that would soon follow. Her progress was slow throughout the afternoon, and I did my best with massages to keep her relaxed and confident. By early evening, she told us she was ready for the tub, a pain management and relaxation technique often used in natural childbirth.

I can remember clearly how intense her contractions were becoming once she was in the tub, and we settled into a groove whereby I would countdown the contractions (amazed that each one was exactly sixty seconds long, no more, no less), and in between contractions we would give her water to keep her hydrated, wipe her face with cool water, and try to keep her comfortable. However, the moment a contraction started, she would push everyone away, telling us that when a contraction was occurring every touch felt like it weighed a hundred pounds. She got out of the tub a few times so Paula could give her an exam to gauge her progress. After eight hours in the Birthing Inn, her cervix had not budged at all, and her frustration was mounting and evident. Back to the tub; now the contractions were clearly becoming unbearable, and there moments when Shannon was in the middle of a contraction and I could tell she barely recognized me. I was in awe of her strength and commitment, and encouraged her by keeping her focused on her love for her baby. "You are doing this for Tristan, you are a strong woman, a dedicated mother and you love your baby boy."

Watching her labor in the tub was one of the most emotionally trying experiences of my life. I would have given anything to take some of that pain away, but childbirth is a woman's burden. That she chose to submit herself to that experience for the health of our baby is a gift I can never repay. Around midnight, Shannon was shaking uncontrollably in desperation, crying aloud, "I can't do it anymore, I don't want to feel like this anymore, please, please make it stop!" Our Bradley training taught us that when a woman feels she can longer go on and is ready to give up it is a sure sign of transition, the passage of the baby's head through the cervix. Through my tears, I whispered to Paula, "I think she is in transition," to which Paula smiled warmly and replied, "She did it, she is there." I kept encouraging her by keeping her focused on Tristan, telling her, "You're there, baby, we're going to meet out little boy very soon."

At 1:00 A.M. Shannon knew it was time to push, and we rushed her out of the tub and onto the bed. Paula checked her, felt the top of the head, knew the birth was imminent, and advised Laura to assemble the team. Three additional nurses silently rushed into the room, configuring the equipment, assisting Paula, and preparing for Tristan's arrival. Their well-rehearsed protocols were incredible to observe; they were seamlessly perfect. Shannon sensed the moment was upon her, and was pushing with renewed spirit. I was holding her left leg up, and Paula was coaching her, keeping her focused. After what seemed like an eternity, I could see the top of Tristan's head emerging and began screaming, "I see him! He's almost here! You're really doing it, baby!" Shannon was now pushing with everything she had left, Paula was guiding Tristan, and suddenly the head was out, followed in an instant by the rest of him. Like throwing a switch, Shannon felt the pain ease, and began crying and screaming, "Is it over? Is he really here?" Paula, visibly proud of Shannon for her incredible effort, simply replied, "Yes, he is, here is your baby boy," and laid Tristan upon her chest. I was laughing and sobbing uncontrollably, kissing them both, so proud of Shannon for enduring all that pain, her commitment to our baby unwavering. Twenty hours of labor, just under an hour of pushing, and Tristan Connor Mackey was born 9 pounds 8 ounces, 21 inches long, at 1:46 A.M. on July 18th, 2005.

CHAPTER 15

"Plans & Permits"

S hannon was famished after her labor and delivery, and even hospital food sounded delicious, so the nurses had dinner brought in. We spent the rest of the morning visiting with family, sharing our baby, and reveling in the excitement of the moment. Tristan was taken to the nursery for a bath and a nap while we were moved to the postpartum side of the Birthing Inn. We had chosen to room in with Tristan, so once we were settled, he was brought over in the rolling bassinette. Shannon snatched him up right away, and began her first true attempts at breastfeeding. She is a natural mother with keen instincts, and all of her reading and preparation allowed it to go very well.

We only had a little time to cuddle before all our friends and extended family came rolling in. The day was spent recounting the labor and delivery, and thank goodness I was keeping notes, because apparently it is critical to get the times and metrics absolutely perfect for the ladies. Centimeters, positions, locations, time stamps; you would have thought I was preparing for a rebuttal in the Supreme Court. Men are satisfied with "healthy boy," but the ladies, not so much. Details please, and you better get it right because what the hell else were you doing in there anyway...?

By evening, everybody had gone; we had dinner and finally settled in with Tristan and began another once-over, taking our time looking at his fingers and toes, nuzzling his face, all the blissful new parent moments that we had awaited. He was here, mother and child were healthy and safe, and we finally fell into a deep sleep.

We had decided to only spend one night in the Birthing Inn, and on the 19th, it was time to head home. I was a nervous wreck driving Tristan home for the first time, and probably did ten miles under the speed limit the whole way. We took the phone off the hook and tried to get some sleep; for the most part, Tristan cooperated. He was a very easy baby, nursed well, and settled into a pretty regular schedule right away.

After another day of taking it easy, it was time to head back out to the vineyard to continue the trellis construction and vine tying, as well as apply some insecticide for the Japanese beetles. I was shocked at the condition of the vineyard when I arrived. Although I had only been away for two weeks, it looked like it had been abandoned. The weed growth around the vines was astonishing, and I had to do some hand weeding to get the huge ones out before applying more herbicide to the smaller ones. The reality of working outside in the summer heat had definitely set in; a few 100-degree days in a row made for some pretty exhausting work.

We immediately began contacting general contractors in the area. We had decided early on, while still living in Connecticut, that we were going to design our own home. We knew there would be no way we would be able to afford a house, a tasting room, and a winery all at once, so we designed the house so that it could also serve as the tasting room. With extensive experience in computer aided design (CAD) software from my audio production days, we purchased a "prosumer" version of an architectural design software package. In the months following our wedding, we had begun laying out the floor plans for the home. Date night while Shannon was pregnant with Tristan was lying in bed with the laptop, coming up with new floor plans and designs.

The original design concept was based around a large open floor plan on the main (second) floor, living quarters downstairs, with an upstairs loft. The first loft design was simple, essentially taking half of the main floor and raising it up so it looked like a big square. Functional yet unappealing, that design never really felt right. Sometime around the wedding, I showed our designs to my aunt Debbie. Though she loved the open floor plan, she agreed the loft design was too basic, and suggested we expand the space by extending two catwalks down each side of the building. These would overlook the downstairs tasting area, allow people closer access to the picture windows, and help create several cozy sitting areas on the catwalk and underneath. We loved the idea, and immediately incorporated it into the design.

During the summer of 2004, we had visited two of the timber framing companies we had been researching who maintained model homes. The Yankee Barn Homes timber frame, even though it was used as a model home, was actually a second residence for a nearby family. As we pulled up, we were giddy with excitement and immediately realized that timber frame homes are even more alluring in person than in pictures. We were greeted warmly by the sales rep, who showed us around the house, answering questions, pointing out interesting architectural elements, and giving us deeper insight into this time-honored craft. Interestingly, the home featured extended catwalks on the second floor, exactly like the ones we had just incorporated into our own plans. Seeing them in person cemented the design.

The owners of this home had also created a small confined play space above the loft for their grandchildren. Tucked way up in the rafters, it was almost like a loft above a loft. It struck me that creating such a space above our loft, though removing the walls to open the space, would create a perfect elevated stage for our musicians for their live performances. I mentioned it to Shannon, who loved the idea right away, and we could not wait to get back to New Haven to add this extra element to the CAD program. One other change that was conceived during this trip was to cut out the front edge of the loft, so that it did not extend too far over the tasting bar, to make the bar more airy and allow people to stand above and look out over the tasting area activities. With the key architectural features of the tasting room in place, it only took a few tries to get the bathrooms and storage area figured out, though the design of the tasting bar and kitchen would prove to be much more complicated, and completing it would take us well into the next year.

The most challenging aspect of our home design was actually the living quarters on the ground floor. We spend countless hours configuring and re-configuring the layout of the bedrooms, bathrooms, mechanical spaces, play area, and nursery. When designing living quarters, you learn to do a deep analysis of your living habits, deriving goals that the space will support. One added challenge of a timber frame structure is the downstairs support for the load of the massive timbers sitting above the sub-floor. Many of the point loads beneath the timbers would be well over seven tons in a one-foot by one-foot square, and steel beam supports would have to be hidden in the walls of the basement. In a sense, the wall locations in the basement are dictated by the placement of the posts upstairs, and defined the layout of the bedrooms.

We knew we would need an outside entrance into a mudroom and adjoining shower, to ensure the grime of farm life did not encroach too much into the house. We were also determined to separate the children's rooms from the playroom, to ensure they could be quiet spaces for homework and creative thought. The playroom would double as a kitchenette, as one aspect of our tasting room vision was to host weddings and special events. The downstairs living area would have to be wholly self-contained for when the upstairs was being used for an event. Finally, we wanted our master suite to be a special place, fostering serenity and relaxation. Early in my audio career, I had the opportunity to stay in a magnificent suite at a hotel in Las Vegas, which had a Jacuzzi tub adjoining the bed. We figured we owed it to ourselves to recreate this design, given the intense physical nature of farming, and budgeted for such a tub in our room. Above the tub would be a gas fireplace and high-definition widescreen television, complete with surround sound home theater. It seemed quite appropriate for two degreed audio engineers designing their love nest.

With just about everything figured out, the upstairs kitchen and tasting bar continued to be a problem. Shannon was insistent that each design I concocted did not have enough counter space. Her vision was for long stretches of countertops with bowls and bowls of cookie dough, jars of sprinkles, and little children with flour in their hair sneaking oven-fresh Christmas cookies. My vision was for as much floor space and operational efficiency as possible in the tasting bar. I was also set on using the bar as the central hub of the floor space, yet leveraging its design to offset and complement the timber frame style. Bringing these two visions together was quite challenging.

I realized that it would be helpful to build a life-size model of the kitchen, and actually play house within the space. Measuring tape in hand, I determined that the width of our rental house galley kitchen was nearly the exact width of the planned kitchen. Taking some scraps of cardboard, sawhorses, and marking tape, I began to lay out different configurations of a virtual kitchen in the rental. After a few iterations of this process, we arrived at the final design, essentially based on two intertwined L-shaped work areas. This allowed for plenty of workspace near the stoves, as well as a large tasting bar area for future guests. We also opted for two of everything, to ensure operational efficiency during busy hours: two dishwashers, two ovens, and two sinks. As a complementary design element, I decided to create a curved bar to offset the numerous ninety-degree and forty-five-degree angles typical of timber framing. Making a round bar out of square stones would prove to be a complex challenge down the road.

The last design element that would later prove to be a concern was the structure of the roof. The initial plan called for a large open gable on the front of the house, complete with an inside sitting area adjoining the catwalk, so guests could look out onto the front lawn through large picture windows. We wanted the front of the home to have an open, inviting look, with plenty of space for a full-length covered porch. This design was well liked by everyone, but much later on in the process, this aspect of the home would have to be modified at considerable expense.

One of the timber frame companies we had been researching was Lancaster County Timber Frames, or LCTF. I have a very special affinity for Lancaster County, Pennsylvania, as it is the area where my grandparents, Mary and Walter Lightner, lived. It is also home to Clair, my former audio employer, the world leader in professional touring and system installations. Many people found it odd that the world's largest sound reinforcement company would be located in Pennsylvania, in the middle of Amish country. Once you met the people, it became easier to understand. This region is filled with hard-working, creative people with an innate sense of craftsmanship and quality.

This philosophy is evident in all aspects of Lancaster County life. Attending the open house in the mid-1990s for the new Clair headquarters, I had never seen a more eclectic group of people— road-hardened audio engineers, tattooed guitar techs, small children, grandmas and grandpas, and traditional Amish families. Everyone got along famously, and these small groups of people from completely disparate walks of life happily chatted about their role in the company. This scene moved me deeply, and I had vowed to someday also run a business that would bring communities closer together.

Given my history and experiences in Lancaster County, LCTF definitely had an edge in the recruiting phase, though I would not just give them the business if I were not absolutely confident in their capabilities. During my initial phone conversation with Tony Zaya, president of LCTF, I learned he had gone to college with Roy Clair, co-founder of Clair Brothers. To me it was a sign, and I sent over our initial floor plans for LCTF to prepare a rough quote. On October 11th, 2004, one month before leaving New Haven, we had our first frame quote in hand. I assured Tony I would be in touch when the time came to move the project forward in a more formal manner.

Over a year later, as our conversations progressed, it became clear that LCTF represented everything we had hoped for in a timber frame manufacturer. On August 18th, we went to the county offices to apply for our well and septic permits, and on the 26th, we received the formal proposal from LCTF:

$158,500 for a Douglas Fir frame (vs. $144,250 for white pine)

$34,500 for structural insulated panel (SIP) walls

$24,750 for the roof (minus plywood and shingles)

$9,650 for the loft

The quote was very much in line with our expectations—not the cheapest timber frame, not the most expensive, but likely the highest craftsmanship. The last piece of the puzzle was LCTF's construction process, which ensured Josh Coleman, our frame designer, would accompany the frame to the site to participate in its assembly.

We still had not selected a general contractor, and were becoming increasingly frustrated. It was challenging to get people to return our inquiry phone calls. I had met with two, and had toured a few homes they currently had underway in our area. Both were competent builders, and the homes were spectacular, though a bit more formal than the style we had envisioned. During each meeting we discussed budgets, and as I disclosed what we had hoped to pay for the home, they advised it was simply not possible.

One of the biggest myths we uncovered about building a custom home was that all of the financial estimates we had researched were completely incorrect. In any timber frame magazine or home building book, we saw article after article claiming that a timber frame home could be built for about $125 per square foot. We even spoke to some builders at a home expo who claimed this was possible. As we learned, nothing could be further from the truth. For years, we had been working based on the assumption that Shannon could possibly be a stay-at-home mom or perhaps become a teacher, so her schedule would align with the children and she could have summers off to focus on our winery. We knew that building prices in Northern Virginia would be more expensive, given the regional economics, but we were confident we could hit the number with our sweat equity contributions. After disclosing this figure to the first two contractors, they apparently decided we were not worth the trouble and stopped returning my phone calls. Two more phone calls with contractors ended up in the same dead end.

I stumbled across an advertisement in a local magazine from Ron Hawes, a long-time Loudoun builder with expertise in heavy timber construction, so I placed a call to his office. I spoke with Ron's daughter Shawn, who put me on the phone with Richard Darr, Ron's project manager. We talked for a while, and as I gave him the overview of the project, I could tell he was interested. He was open to the idea of LCTF as the timber frame subcontractor, even though Hawes specializes in heavy timber structures.

As we came to the inevitable subject of budget, he simply asked, "So, what do you think you can build this for?" I responded $650,000, figuring a 4,500 square foot home at $125 per square foot, with just under $100,000 of sweat equity and materials savings. Then came the polite pregnant pause, followed by, "Well, you can't do it for that." Frustrated, I advised Richard of all the research we had done on building. He was the first to tell me openly, "All that stuff you read in books and magazines is bullshit. There are only two numbers that matter: the one your lender gives you as to what you can afford, and the one your builder gives you as to what you can build."

Still intrigued by the project, Richard asked me to send over a copy of our plans anyway, and he would take the time and put together an actual estimate for us. I figured I had nothing to lose, and that we needed to see the number to decide once and for all whether or not this dream had come to a screeching halt. A few days later Richard sent over their proposal, and I was in shock. The estimate to build our home was $900,000 (including the quote from LCTF), or basically $200 per square foot. The news was devastating.

After some serious soul searching, we decided that there was only one direction we could move—forward. Gone was the notion of Shannon pulling back; we were both fully committed to professional careers for as long as it took to build our winery. There was no business plan, just an unwavering faith in one another that we could do it, somehow, someday. Greater still was the desire to build it together while raising a family. We both wanted our children to be part of the process, as we knew some of life's greatest lessons would be learned along the way. We did not care if we built a five hundred case winery or a twenty thousand case winery; simply selling a bunch of wine was never the objective, nor was huge financial rewards. It was all about our lifestyle—family-centric, agricultural, environmental stewardship, arts, culture, retail, and special events—these were our objectives.

I called Richard back the next day, told him we had accepted the fact that our original financial plan was not viable, and that we were committed to ensuring we would remain professionally employed for as long as it took. He seemed relieved, and the conversation moved forward to my sweat equity initiatives. Our plan from the beginning had been to build as large of a structure as our budget would allow, with minimal focus on elaborate and expensive accessories. Every line item in a contractor's bid has materials with a considerable markup, and I knew full well I could shave tens of thousands of dollars off his estimate by purchasing and transporting many of the materials myself. Though it cut into their profit margin, he and Ron were both open to this.

Richard advised me that the bank would need to use his figure for financing, as their risk assessment typically assumes that the homeowner will be in over their head and the contractor will have to bail them out. The bank needed to ensure they were paying for a completed home, not one that had a punch list a mile long because the sweat equity guy could not complete his tasks. We agreed that the proposal would likely get volleyed back and forth several more times, but that we had a good basis to begin a relationship. We made a verbal commitment to Ron Hawes that he would be our general contractor, and began discussing securing financing. I told them I would keep them apprised of our progress as we worked through the loan application process, and that I had no intention of interviewing any more contractors. On November 4th, 2005, we signed the timber frame contract with LCTF, which we would need to secure financing, in addition to the forthcoming Hawes contract.

I had interviewed several of Ron's references, and had come to gain solid confidence in his experience, capabilities, and craftsmanship. In a nutshell, however, Ron Hawes won our business because his was the only company that called us back.

A few days later, I met my friend Rob Klause for lunch, and we ended up (where else) at the Clubhouse, back in our favorite chairs, drinking coffee and telling stories. I filled him in on all the latest challenges with the budget and contractor selection. While we were talking, I happened to glance down at my left calf and noticed a tiny black dot in the middle of a small red circle. Leaning down, I could see it was a tiny tick, perhaps the size of a pinhead, which I pulled off and held up for a closer look. Sure enough, it was a deer tick, and both Rob and I knew that I would have to get that looked at by a doctor. I returned to work that afternoon, where one crisis led to another, followed by more phone calls and emails about the house project, all of which derailed my attention to that tick bite. By the next day, I had forgotten about it completely. I will regret that little oversight for the rest of my life.

CHAPTER 16

"Dream House"

It was time to secure a lender. True to my word, my first phone call was to Vince Tricarico at First Savings Mortgage, the lender who had bailed us out at the last minute during the land purchase. Vince was thrilled to hear all the news and that we had already progressed so far. He gave me a link to his website so I could begin downloading all the forms that would need to be filled out, as well as numerous checklists of items the bank would need. Applications, financial documents, contracts, blueprints, and permits were among the items, and I realized it was going to take several months to pull everything together.

Since we had chosen LCTF through a series of phone calls and emails and signed the contract through the mail, we figured it was time to actually go and meet the team. The floor plans that we had created were a very solid foundation for them to work from, but did not include any of the actual post and beam design or engineering. It would be up to Josh to use his expertise and really turn our concept into a structural work of art.

We left for Pennsylvania after work on Friday, November 18th, and narrowly avoided a disastrous accident. Charles Town Pike (Route 9) is a two-lane highway that runs northwest southeast through our region of Loudoun. Filled with blind curves and hills as well as limited passing areas, there are numerous fatal accidents along this road. We had pulled out onto the highway and had gone about four miles. As we approached a blind curve, I noticed there was an oncoming car in the other lane. Driving these kinds of roads as often as I have, I made a mental note of a safety zone on our shoulder, in case he swerved into our lane. No sooner had I glanced at the shoulder then another car shot out from behind him, crossing the double line while trying to pass too early, and was speeding right at us for a head-on collision. Without even thinking or braking, I spun the wheel to the right and drove right onto the shoulder. As I glanced out my side window, I noticed that for a split second, we were perfectly aligned, three abreast—the first car in his lane, the second speeding car in our lane where we should have been, and us on the shoulder.

As soon as the car had passed, I spun the wheel back to the left and put us back on the road, just as the shoulder dropped off into a creek. We were so rattled by the experience that we could not even speak for about five minutes, when finally I asked Shannon if she was alright. Realizing we had narrowly escaped a high-speed head-on collision by a matter of inches, it took a long time for us to regain our senses. Tristan, just four months old, just played with his toys the whole time. The entire incident maybe lasted one second, but remains vividly imprinted in my memory; to this day, I slow down approaching blind curves and always have an escape route planned from any driving situation. You never know.

When we arrived, we were met by Amy Weaver in contracts, our frame designer Josh Coleman, and Tony Zaya. We toured the facility for a couple hours, and then Josh took us up to the design studio, where we were able to see wireframe CAD drawings of our frame. It was an unbelievably inspirational moment, actually seeing the detail of the joinery and some of the creative elements Josh was working on. I filled everyone in on where we were in the financing process, and promised them we were moving forward as quickly as we could pull it all together.

Once our shop tour was over, it was time to head out and see two of LCTF's recently completed projects. The first was a residence sitting high on a hill overlooking the Susquehanna River. The frame was Douglas fir and the ceiling was a white pine tongue and groove. We instantly fell in love with the color combination of the two different types of wood, and knew these would be our choice as well. Next we went to a restaurant at a local golf course, which contained some design elements similar to those in our plan, namely a catwalk loft encircling the main floor. We enjoyed lunch with Josh, discussed the many perils and complexities of building a home, and became more and more excited about the project. We knew we were going to have a great relationship, building something very special for everyone involved.

We received a new set of renderings from Josh on December 21st, and were beyond impressed at some of the upgrades he had made. Our original front door plan was offset from the center of the home because we thought the center bent post had to go down to the subfloor. A bent is a framework composed of several structural members that defines the cross-section of the timber frame. Josh engineered a solution using a header beam (actually the largest piece of timber in the frame, at 8" x 12" x 32' long) sitting upon two smaller posts, with the door in between. He also designed two amazing three-way joints, which framed out the tasting bar. Other detail work and highlights were also included, though one aspect of our original floor plan was beginning to concern me.

Originally we had wanted a large gable on the front of the house, to create a welcoming covered porch. However, in this last round of wireframe drawings, Josh had included a rendering of how a guest would view the music loft. I noticed how lopsided the interior ceiling would be due to the large gable, and became seriously concerned about the acoustics. Though we were not building a performing arts center, the acoustics of the space and eventual translation of music and spoken word performances was of the highest concern. From our studies of recording studio design and acoustics at University of Miami, we now realized that the roofline was going to be a major problem.

Since a roof does not fall into the category of "we can fix that later," we knew it was going to have to change now—otherwise, we would end up regretting the decision forever. Going back into our CAD program, we altered both the front and rear rooflines. In the front, we removed the large gable and added four dormers, equally spaced along the house in between the five bents. In the rear, where there was simply a flat ceiling, we added in another four dormers, so that the front and rear were identical. I sent the updated plans along to LCTF, and about a week later received the updated contract reflecting the roof modifications. We would end up paying nearly $14,000 more for the new roofline, but were convinced in the long run it would be money well spent, ensuring the best possible live performance quality. We were also excited about the additional light that the rear southern-facing dormers would let into the space.

In the middle of all this designing and construction planning, we enjoyed baby's first Christmas in our small rental home. Although we had already cut way back on expenses in preparation for the construction, we did allow ourselves to treat Tristan to some wonderful gifts. Shannon found an adorable handmade rocking horse at a local craft show, and I found a fabulous little green riding tractor at Tractor Supply, our most-visited establishment for vineyard supplies. We spent the morning playing with Tristan in front of the tree, and he had no problem tearing through the wrapping paper. Later that afternoon, we enjoyed a big family Christmas at my mother's. Although we were exhausted from the construction process preparations and all the late nights finalizing the floor plan and gathering financial records, we let it all wash away for the day, surrounded by loved ones. It was a much-needed respite, however brief.

By the first week of 2006, we had put the finishing touches on the basement floor plan and printed a series of rough blueprints and renderings to send to the Hawes team. It had been a long road getting to this point, dating back to the days before Shannon and I began dating, when I had begun researching custom log homes. To actually hold a set of plans that we had developed ourselves felt very fulfilling. As we sent them off to Ron for development into proper blueprints by his architect at Munsey Log Homes, we knew we had given it our all.

Throughout January, we continued to deliver additional financial documentation to Vince, and at last he felt he had everything he needed to begin the approval process. This was an especially trying waiting period, given all the work we had put in. We had received positive feedback from Vince on our income-to-debt ratios once the construction loan was rolled into a mortgage, but that still did not constitute a loan approval. It was still very possible that the bank could come back and deny the loan, and everything to this point would have been for nothing. Once he had all the documentation in place, it was time to get the final approval from his senior management. Days turned into weeks, and we began having trouble eating and sleeping.

The call came at the end of January, and it was hard to say who was more excited, Vince or me. He was genuinely happy for us, and advised that we had been approved for a construction loan of $1.2 million dollars. Although he referred to the eventual mortgage as creative financing, he was very complimentary of our credit ratings and the diligence of our documentation and applications. He faxed over the loan approval letter, which I needed to send to both Hawes and LCTF. I was so excited to tell Shannon that I walked over to her building and told her in person. We hugged and cried together right there in the middle of her cube. The last piece of the puzzle had fallen into place.

In our years poring over timber frame books and magazine, we often wondered how homes were selected as features, and we began reading the fine print, where we found addresses, phone numbers, and email addresses for the editors and publishers. We knew our home would be different from most in these books, in that people would actually be able to come visit the finished structure. We thought having our home appear in one of the magazines would be mutually beneficial in terms of marketing our winery and for readers who wanted to see a frame in person.

We emailed all of the popular timber frame magazines, as well as other industry publications: construction, rural life, decorating, and the like. With no response, we began to think there must be some other way of attracting interest from these publications. We considered having Tony Zaya from LCTF reach out, as his credibility in the industry would likely at least garner a response, and the visibility for LCTF would have been fantastic.

By the end of February there had still been no interest in the story, and we decided to put off any more inquiries until the house was actually built. We figured sending photos of the completed structure would have more weight. One night, as we lay in bed pondering interior decorating ideas, we happened upon the Home and Garden Television (HGTV) website. It had a fantastic repository of decorating ideas, categorized by style, and we surfed the galleries for hours. At some point, we asked ourselves how people ended up on HGTV. Looking around the site, we noticed a small link in the footer at the bottom of the page that simply said, "Be on TV."

I clicked the link, and we were taken to a page that listed all the shows that were slated for production in the months ahead. Each listing had a brief synopsis, and the idea was to match your upcoming project with the most compatible show. As we read down through the list, we came across a show called *Dream House*, a documentary series following homeowners throughout the entire process of building a home. Since we were both long-time fans of HGTV, we figured that being on one of their shows would be the coolest thing ever.

The form on the website was incredibly short, consisting of name, phone, email, subject, and brief commentary. My subject line read "Virginia Farm Winery Owner Sweat Equity Custom Timber Frame Project with Babies and Professional Careers," or something to that effect. I am actually surprised that they did not write us off immediately as psychopaths, but I suppose it was catchy.

We hit the "Submit" button on the form with a chuckle, and faded off to sleep. We awoke the next day and went through our morning routine of dropping Tristan off at daycare and making our way through the typically absurd Northern Virginia congestion to work. Later that afternoon, I was checking our Notaviva Vineyards email account to see if any contractor or financial information was being requested, and noticed an email from High Noon Entertainment, entitled, "*Dream House* Questionnaire."

Incredulously, I read the email from Lauren Kotlen, a production assistant who had received our form information. I gave Shannon a quick call, and she was similarly incredulous. The questionnaire was looking into our background, our inspiration for building a home, why we thought our story was special, and how we could convey that to a television audience. Most of the information was easy to retrieve, as I had been keeping dates and photographs in my blog entries. I filled out the questionnaire that evening and sent it back, amazed that we had even made it this far.

Two days later Shannon got a call from Lauren, and had a brief interview over the phone. I was in a meeting, and Shannon messaged me I had to call Lauren ASAP, which I did immediately afterwards. Lauren was fantastic to speak with; having been in the entertainment industry, we connected on many levels, and I was able to anticipate many of her questions.

Over the next several days, we sent them dozens of pictures and stories from the blog. Eventually, Lauren told us that the executive producer of the show, Debra Koehler, would like to do a phone interview as well. Shannon and I each talked to Deb individually, and part of the reason for that was that Deb would ask us both the same question, trying to see where there might be tension, disagreement, and discord, which make for good television. Through the whole process, we made it clear that not only was the house a dream, but the whole idea of founding a vineyard was as well, for us, our children, family, and friends.

After weeks of information gathering, Lauren and Deb put the final touches on the pitch to HGTV. Shannon and I were sure the bottom was going to fall out at any moment, but we kept doing our best to provide any info they asked for; the requests seemed endless. A few days after they made the pitch, we got the news that the network was interested and they were going to fly Deb out from Colorado to spend a day with us, filming Shannon, Tristan and I, as well as our contractor Ron Hawes and footage of the old house, the property, and the vineyard.

Deb was fantastic to work with. We were so at ease with her, and never felt awkward in front of the camera. No matter how great our story sounded on paper, we had to be able to convey our emotions with the camera rolling. Deb took the footage back and worked with her editor to create a seven-minute pitch for HGTV, known as a "sizzle reel." At 5:00 P.M. on April 11th, Shannon got the call that we had been selected.

We later learned over six thousand people had applied for that season of *Dream House* and it is overwhelming to consider the amount of work that High Noon undertook during the selection process. Vetting that many applicants down to a handful to shoot for demo reels must have been an exhaustive process, and we knew better than most the level of effort involved. That said, we were also keenly aware what the impact of being selected for a reality television production would mean for our construction project. As complicated as our lives had been, nothing could have prepared us for the challenges ahead.

CHAPTER 17

"Second Planting"

Amidst all of this were the ever-present needs of a first-year vineyard. Winter is the time for equipment maintenance, trellis repair, pruning, planning, and upgrades. The winter of 2006 was very busy with the tasks required to manage our newly established vineyard.

We knew that our first tractor would not be big enough to carry or tow a sprayer around the vineyard. We purchased a new CIMA P50 sprayer for $9,500. The P50 is capable of holding 165 gallons of water, which at 8.33 pounds per gallon plus pesticide weight is over 1,400 pounds. Add that to the 600 pounds that the sprayer weighs, and the tractor has a one-ton dead load attached to the three-point hitch when you begin spraying.

After exhaustive research, we decided to purchase a new John Deere 5425 81-horsepower tractor from nearby Carlyle and Anderson. Given the amount of hauling and lifting we would be doing, we opted for the front-end loader as well. Saving our cash for the home construction, we put $2,000 down and chose a five-year loan for the remaining $40,000. We were three months away from signing a construction loan for $1.2 million, and had just spent another $52,500, also upgrading to a six-foot wide bush hog.

On March 5th, I headed out to the vineyard to begin our first pruning. Every winter, all the vines must be pruned and trained to ensure optimal growth and spacing during the upcoming season. Given that these were just second-year vines, the main concern was ensuring the trunks were nice and straight, the cordons were trained down to the cordon wire, and that we were not over-developing the vine by trying to leave too much growth. The key to any new vineyard is to ensure long-term viability, healthy vines and quality fruit. It is not a yield race, in the sense that you are not trying to maximize short-term fruit yields, but rather ensure the highest quality fruit.

To that end, pruning is always a backwards process. Our cordon wire is at a height of 42" inches above the ground, and each vine runs alongside the bamboo stake placed next to it when it was planted. If a shoot had grown six feet the previous season, we would tie it at the cordon wire and stake intersection, lay it down horizontally, and cut it eighteen inches from the stake. This is now referred to as a cordon. Our vines are five feet apart, so many ask, "Why not extend the cordon thirty inches, since you had all that growth? Wouldn't you get more fruit sooner?"

A young vine is not capable of supporting that extra growth, and exhibits what is known as "apical dominance," where the last eighteen inches of cordon have healthy growth, while the portion in the center has weak growth. The vine would not be optimized for long-term quality production. Given that our two-acre vineyard with 1,920 vines was, by most industry metrics, rather tiny, we were committed to doing it right. You cannot make great wine from poor fruit.

The best-case scenario for each vine would be establishing two strong trunks, bent sideways at the cordon wire into two healthy cordons. It was obvious that the acre of Cabernet Franc was much more vigorous than the acre of Viognier, and about 80% of the Cabernet Franc was pruned and trained in this manner. The Viognier, on the other hand, required a lot more pruning back. Working backwards along each shoot, I tried to establish an eighteen-inch cordon. If the shoot had not reached that length, or was dead at that point, I would cut it back to the cordon wire and stake intersection. If it was dead at that point, it got cut back down to the ground to three buds, to start all over again. Beneath the ground, the vine now had a much more developed root system. Even a vine with only three buds above the graft union will develop more quickly in the second year.

Later that afternoon, Shannon and our two dogs joined me, and we enjoyed a brisk afternoon of pruning the vineyard together while her mom watched Tristan back at the house. Days like this are peaceful and romantic, and working the land together creates special bonds. There is an honest simplicity in caring for crops that is at once both tangible and mystical. We talked and dreamt about the days when our children would join us in this endeavor.

I spent the entire following weekend pruning vines. The weekend after that, I completed the last four rows and began installing the trellis catch wires. Catch wires are the support structure for the vine canopy, and their layout varies with the type of trellis support system you are creating. Our trellis is a Smart-Dyson configuration, a form of vertically-divided canopy where the vine shoots are trained both upwards and downwards from the cordon, allowing for optimal fruit-to-foliage balance.

With the Smart-Dyson configuration, our cordon wire is place at 42" inches above the ground, and the catch wires are placed on either side of every post, spaced above the cordon wire at increments of eight inches, ten inches, and ten inches. Each April, the vines undergo "bud break," when each bud swells before pushing out a tiny shoot. Each shoot quickly grows upward between the pairs of catch wires, which help support the delicate young foliage from wind and rain. The catch wires are the key vine training mechanism, which opens up the fruiting zone, allowing the grapes to hang unobstructed near the cordon wire, while the foliage canopy is held in place above. Installing catch wires is a tedious process, whereby the six wires are paid out along the rows, lifted into place at the proper height, then nailed to the line posts with U-shaped fencing staples. Though I somehow managed to survive the day with all ten fingers somewhat intact, I realized my rate of progress was abysmal.

The following day I was able to hone my processes and complete two rows, and though I was still figuring out efficiencies, things were going more smoothly. I timed my progress and realized I could bring the time down to just under three hours to complete each row. Doing the math and looking ahead, it was obvious I would not be able to finish the remaining twenty-one rows before the shoots emerged, so I tapped the family and friend network. The following Saturday, my sister Rebecca, her fiancé Dan and my friend Rob Klause hammered trellis nails while I drove up and down the rows, laying out wire. We had a lot of fun that day, though by late afternoon, everyone was a little sore. The next day I was out in the vineyard again by 8:00 A.M., and by late afternoon, all twelve 400 foot Viognier rows had wire laid out, and ten of the rows had been hammered and tensioned.

When we got the call about being selected for *Dream House* a few weeks later, Deb immediately asked if there was anything happening in the coming weeks. We were scheduled to plant another 1.25 acres of vines on Saturday, April 22nd, just eleven days away. The vines were scheduled for delivery, and the labor crew and consultant Mike Newland were scheduled as well. Deb recognized the opportunity for a video shoot and essentially decided on the spot to send a field crew out for a few days to capture the planting. Just like that, our television series production began.

On Tuesday the 18th, it was obvious that the planting day schedule was in jeopardy due to the weather forecast. Major storms were moving across the Midwest and were projected to hit our area on Saturday, making the vineyard installation a muddy, dangerous mess. I frantically began making calls trying to determine if everyone could change their schedules and move the planting up one day to Friday. Everyone could, and everything was in place, except for having no vines to plant. The vines were already on a UPS truck somewhere in the Midwest, and were not scheduled to arrive until Friday afternoon. A UPS representative helped me understand their routing procedures, and advised that the boxes of vines would be at the local distribution center near Dulles Airport sometime in the overnight hours, and that they would be transferred to the local delivery truck sometime that morning. They indicated that they could tag the boxes to be set aside, and that I could pick them up at the distribution center.

I awoke at 5:00 A.M. on Friday and made my way down to the UPS center. I had my tracking numbers in hand, and explained the situation to the counter representative. She called in a warehouse employee to help search out the boxes, though it was apparent something was amiss. It seemed that all four boxes had been checked into the distribution center, and were quickly and efficiently already packed onto the local truck, scheduled for a 3:00 P.M. delivery—disaster. The warehouse kid decided to go have a look for himself, because even though the computer thought the truck had left, it might still be sitting in the lot.

About thirty minutes later, he came through the swinging doors with a dolly containing three boxes. The local truck had just been getting ready to leave, and he was able to pull three boxes off the rear; the fourth was buried. We had enough to begin the day, so I thanked them for their efforts and began the trip back to the vineyard.

I arrived at the vineyard right around ten, and was met by Chris Barrett, the High Noon field producer, who introduced me to the director of photography (DP) George Patterson and his wife Pam, who would be the audio engineer. Chris began instructing us on how the video shoot would proceed. George would capture interesting activities on tape from various angles, while Chris would take notes and begin framing out questions to follow up on later, during soundbite interviews. Everyone was clear that we were not actors. We walked the crew through the planting process. Once Chris and George knew what was going to unfold, they were able to plan out their camera shots. Pam wired Mike and me up with our wireless lavaliere microphones (lavs), and we did a quick sound check. We got right to work.

When we broke for lunch around 1:00 P.M., Shannon called to say she was on her way to meet the UPS truck to get the last box of vines. She arrived about an hour later, just as we had run out of vines to plant, and as she was pulling in, so was the High Noon producer, Sean McLaughlin, who had just flown in from Colorado. Once she had changed into her work clothes, it was her turn to ride the tree planter and place the vines. She had been looking forward to this for the entire year, as she had missed it the previous year with the pregnancy. Shannon planted several rows of Viognier until her hands got too cold, so I finished up the last two rows. As the tractor slowed to a halt after the last vine was in the ground, the sky opened up and the rain came down.

Tristan had us up early the next morning, and we had a full day of television production ahead. Chris, George, and Pam arrived at 9:00 A.M., secured our lavs, and we began taping. George captured footage of the outside of the rental, the beautiful view of the valley, and shots of the interior. We began our interviews in the office, using our guitars and keyboards as background. We took a quick break for lunch so Shannon could nurse, then we moved to the living room for more interviews. Tristan was included this time, and was adorable and quite accommodating. It definitely took a while for us to relax, and just get comfortable being in front of the camera. Taping ended about 6:00 P.M., and although we were wiped out, we spent the evening at Jim and Shayna's, recounting the events of planting day and the videotaping to everyone.

We awoke Sunday morning and enjoyed a big breakfast, knowing we had yet another full day of taping ahead of us. We made our way over to the vineyard, and another production team was already on site, filming more footage of the home exterior and the landscape. I unlocked the house and showed them around while they filmed the dilapidated interior. We filmed all morning, until it was time to break for lunch. After the break, we reconvened at Doug Fabbioli's newly opened tasting room in the basement of his home.

Doug was hosting a release party for his new "Fratelli" red wine, and a crowd of about eighty people was gathered on the crush pad, enjoying the beautiful spring day. After filming at Doug's for a few hours, we went back to the vineyard again for some more footage. I was just playing along by now, and was so completely exhausted I could not even think straight. Filming wrapped at 6:00 P.M., and since Sean had to fly back to Colorado the next morning, he talked us into dinner. Although he was the show producer, he would be coordinating everything from Colorado—watching the tapes, organizing the crews, and unraveling the storylines.

Finally, after three long days of working and filming, we lay in bed, recounting the events. Though exhausted, we were still buzzing with excitement over the new planting, the exposure to the filming process, and the realization that this was all really happening. Drifting off to sleep, it was time to put the weekend behind us; tomorrow it was back to work.

The weekend after our second planting, it was time to host another grow tube party. Our friends and family would have the opportunity to participate in the television production, which they all found very exciting. Chris, George, and Pam were on hand early to have everybody sign their releases, install microphones on Shannon and me, and begin capturing the footage. The day started with Shannon and Shayna erecting a sun canopy for the playpen, as Tristan and our new niece Makenzie would be spending most of the day outside with us under my mom's watchful eye.

The guys placed bamboo stakes next to each vine, while Shannon, Rebecca, and Dan worked on de-suckering the year-old Viognier and Cabernet Franc. The vines had undergone bud break the previous week, and de-suckering is when you remove unwanted growth from areas of the vine that are not supposed to have shoots, namely the trunk, so that the vine will focus its resources on healthy canopy growth upward from the cordon.

The vineyard was abuzz with activity, and it was a sight to see! The camera crew found it all fascinating, and was very impressed to see so many people pitching in, reminiscent of colonial barn-raisings, when family and neighbors would gather together to help each other build their farms. Many of the vineyards in the area rely on volunteer help for planting, pruning, bottling, and all kinds of tasks.

After a long day in the field, we had installed all the Viognier grow tubes, completed the trellis catch wire hammering, and begun installing the catch wire tensioners. It was an incredibly successful day, and everyone felt a real sense of accomplishment. For those who were still standing, we had dinner under the canopy. As we watched the setting sun drop behind the mountain, we celebrated with a few bottles of wine, recounting the stories of the day and dreaming of the wines that these vines would bear.

Shannon and I celebrated in other ways later that night, the results of which would be realized a month later.

CHAPTER 18

"Signing the Loan"

Early Monday morning, April 24th, we met at Ron's office in Lovettsville to walk through the construction estimate and identify which aspects of the project would be Hawes' responsibility and which would be ours. We also worked out the draw schedule with Shawn Hawes, who would coordinate with Vince and the bank. They handed us our $3,000 bill for the blueprints. The next day, I faxed over several documents Ron needed to apply for the building demolition permit, such as the well digging permit, well abandonment permit, septic abandonment permit, property plat, building layout, Dominion Electric demolition letter, and temporary electric panel work order. I also faxed Vince the last mortgage statement from the land loan.

Both Shannon and I had been speaking to a friend about positions with a startup creative agency in Rockville, Maryland, and realized it was a viable opportunity. Closing was just over a week away when we made the call to Vince that we were changing careers. I thought he was going to pass out. Quickly regaining his composure, he advised that we ran a high risk of not qualifying for the loan due to the timing, the size of the company, and its few years in business. We decided that it was in our best interest to hold on taking the new positions until after all the paperwork was signed and the deal was done.

During that phone call, I told Vince of the HGTV show, and that they were keen on filming the signing of the loan. He must have questioned his sanity at this point, wondering how a seasoned banking professional like himself could possibly have gotten involved with such a band of screwballs. He graciously agreed to run it by his executive management. He phoned the next day to let us know the filming had been approved, though we would have to move the signing to a boardroom rather than his office, to ensure no sensitive documents were caught on camera.

On April 26th, we signed the construction contract. The home price had crept up slightly to $717,467.72 due to some of the clarifications we made on Monday, though much of that would be lessened by our sweat equity projects. We wrote a check for $22,036.70 to secure the schedule and begin the permit application processes. Ron would counter-sign the contract that night, and Shawn faxed it to Vince so he could begin drawing up the loan. With all the Hawes paperwork in place, Richard scheduled the house demolition for the week of May 22nd. He also advised that the foundation and sub-floor would be ready for the timber frame installation the second week of July, and Josh at LCTF confirmed the timber frame construction would commence on July 17th.

HGTV was interested in installing a time-lapse camera on a large pole right in front of the house to capture footage of the demolition as well as the construction. We contacted Dominion Power to see if they would allow us to mount the camera on the pole directly in front of the house, but they refused, citing safety concerns. Now I had to find a contractor who could install another pole so the camera crew could install their gear.

We scheduled the loan signing for May 3rd, and loan closing of May 9th. We awoke at 4:00 A.M. on the day of the signing well before the alarm was to go off. Our dog Tamra was clearly suffering from an unknown eye malady. We called the 24-hour veterinarian and they asked we bring her in right away. During a brief examination, the assistants advised that the condition looked serious, and that we needed to leave her there until the veterinarian arrived later that morning.

Shannon had raised Tamra from a puppy, having snuck her in and out of her dorm room at the University of Miami in her backpack. They had been everywhere, from Florida to Washington, D.C., Connecticut and back to Virginia. Tamra was smart, sassy, protective, and very intelligent. Shannon was a mess, but we knew there was no way to reschedule the loan signing.

We were at the bank headquarters by 8:00 A.M. George and Pam met us there, got our microphones in place, and then we all reviewed the filming. It all went smoothly, but was very overwhelming; we had just signed a construction loan for $1.2 million dollars in front of television cameras. When we had been approved for the loan a few months earlier, we were elated, filled with the hope of this new adventure and all the promise it held. Signing the timber frame and construction contracts seemed a very natural progression, exciting yet not daunting. Signing the construction loan however, suddenly made everything seem very real. We were no longer two kids acting out a romantic whim; there was other people's money involved, and lots of it. Failure now would mean financial ruin.

Shannon's thoughts turned immediately to Tamra, so she placed a call to the veterinarian to check her status. We learned that they had to do an exploratory surgery, and had discovered a tumor growing between her eye and brain. There were basically two options: put her down or remove the eye and tumor, hoping it was benign and that she could recover. Shannon approved the surgery, and an already emotionally taxing day hit rock bottom.

Long before we had scheduled the closings and resignations, we had scheduled a long weekend trip down to see Shannon's family in Florida. Even though we had so many things happening, we still figured it would be our last chance for a quick escape prior to beginning the actual construction process. It turned out to be a wonderful trip, with many memorable moments. We enjoyed Tristan's first visit to a beach, his first ride on a carousel, and an afternoon spent on Chris and Sharon Bishop's yacht watching the Lauderdale Air Show from the water. We had several family dinners, and were able to forget about the anxiety of the upcoming year for a few days. It was the last time we would be able to relax like that for a very long time.

On May 9th, we went to closing on the loan. We plowed through the pile of papers in just under an hour, putting dozens of signatures on financial statements, deeds, and the like. As we were leaving, I got a call from the Loudoun County health inspector, who was on site confirming the well abandonment. The well drilling company had pulled up the old hose, wiring, and pump from the existing well and filled the entire thing with concrete. I then got confirmation from a local utility subcontractor that they were coming in the next day to install the power pole for the time-lapse camera, and that the High Noon crew would be in the following week to install the camera and recording hard drive.

The next day was my last at AOL; Shannon would continue on for another week. I spent the 11th working in the vineyard. On the 12th, I sprayed the vines with an application of fungicide so they would remain healthy and clean, and packed my suitcase and computer gear. The next day I was on a plane to Sun City, South Africa, for an eight day trip for our new company, leaving Shannon to tend to the television production scheduling, career transitions, a ten-month old baby, and a one-eyed dog wearing a veterinarian's head collar.

CHAPTER 19
"Demolition"

The gig in South Africa was a success, and we knew our career leap of faith was going to work out. Although I had a lot of experience flying internationally, for some reason I was having a lot of trouble adjusting to the time difference. I had never felt so exhausted on any previous trips, and was also having a lot of joint pain that was very unusual. I attributed it all to the travel and recent pace of our lives, and just figured I could live with it for a few days.

I kept in close contact with Shannon through instant messaging, and also stayed on top of the email from bankers, contractors, and television producers. One evening during a break in rehearsals, I was messaging with Shannon, and she told me to call her. I borrowed a satellite phone, wandered out to the lobby, and called home. She had taken three home pregnancy tests—all were positive. We were giddy with excitement, even though we worried about the timing and the unnatural level of concurrent major life changes we had underway. We laughed and cried together, seven time zones apart, and agreed to keep it our secret for the first trimester.

I flew in late the evening of the 20th, and could not wait to see Shannon and Tristan; it had been my longest time away from them since he was born. We awoke early the next morning, and I was excited to go by the vineyard to see the old house for the last time. Demolition was scheduled to begin the following morning, my thirty-eighth birthday.

May 22nd dawned bright and beautiful, a perfect day for the demolition. We arrived at the site early, got our microphones in place and shot a few scenes in front of the house. Then it was time to pull out the last few remnants worth keeping. We pulled apart the fireplace and salvaged an old painting that had been put in place to cover up the opening, likely dating back to the late 1800s. We also pulled out the hearthstone, capstone, and other pieces, so we could use them later, either in the new house or landscaping projects. Then it was time to get out of the way and let the track hoe operator, a neighbor nicknamed Dozer, get busy.

First to go was the small outbuilding next to the house. Dozer just reached out with the bucket, curled it under, and pulled the roof off like tearing the top off a cardboard box. A few more swipes took care of the walls, and the building was gone; it took about twenty minutes. Next he positioned the track hoe on top of that building to begin tearing apart the house addition, a section added to the original structure sometime in the early 1900s. By lunch the addition was gone, and we took a break to enjoy the gorgeous day. When work began again, it was time to begin on the main house; first to go was the roof. When it was gone, we stopped for a few minutes to have another look inside the attic. You never know what you might find hidden in the attic of a two hundred year-old building. Ron had told us of a story of another project where the homeowners found a Civil War officer's sword behind the fireplace, valued at several thousand dollars. I had delusions of finding enough artifacts in a secret room to fund the entire project. We found junk.

Once the demolition was finished and the dust cleared, we looked through the debris pile for interesting items. We found numerous hand-forged nails and other construction items; all were kept. We were really able to see the terrible condition of the original logs. It was amazing the building was still standing at all, and Ron speculated that the only thing holding it together was the plaster and wire lathe covering the inside and outside. It helped reassure us that the structure was beyond salvage, and that we had made the right decision in not attempting to restore it. The bad news was that there was not a single piece of usable timber that could be resourced for the new home. We had a vision of building the tasting bar from this lumber, but everyone advised us not to bring this wood anywhere near the new house, given the likelihood of termite eggs. It would all have to be burned.

Day two of demolition began with salvaging an old corncrib, which had been used by previous residents as a granary to dry and store corn. Though quite weathered, it was structurally sound with a decent roof. We felt it could someday be an interesting addition to the winery experience, perhaps used as an outside tasting bar. The building was about fifteen feet long, four feet wide, and ten feet high, so Ron strapped it to the forks of his John Deere skid steer. The building was too top-heavy to move without help, so Dozer positioned the track hoe next to the corncrib and steadied it on the forks as Ron lifted it. They inched across the field in tandem to the edge of our property and gently set the building down on a makeshift foundation of cinder blocks to keep it up out of the mud. The corncrib survived the operation with only a few scratches, which Ron quickly educated us, were defined as "character." The rest of the day brought the end of the old barn and remaining outbuildings.

Late that afternoon, the well drilling team arrived to set up their rig in preparation for the next day. The well location was somewhat limited by county regulations, as the well site had to be at least fifty feet from any nearby property line, water feature, and structures, either existing or planned. We were limited to a small plot just behind the planned parking lot and winery building; however, since there were three known springs within one hundred yards and a nearby creek, the drillers indicated they were optimistic about the potential for finding water.

The following morning we made the ninety-minute drive to Rockville to meet our future colleagues. We stayed for about two hours, and then headed back to the construction site, where Dozer had dug an enormous burn pit in the field adjacent to the vineyard.

It was large enough that a six-wheel dump truck could drive right in, dump a load of debris, and drive back out. They had been busy all morning using the track hoe to pick up debris, load it into the dump truck, and then transport it down to the burn pit. The entire building site was looking more and more like a blank canvas as the debris, junk, and underbrush was cleared away.

I checked in with the well drillers and was shocked to learn they had dug down to six hundred feet and were barely getting a one-gallon per minute refresh rate. To put that in perspective, several of our neighbors have wells about fifty feet deep with thirty gallon per minute refresh rates. Loudoun County had a minimum refresh rate that was required for a well to pass inspection, and one gallon per minute was the absolute minimum. We ran the risk of not passing inspection, and we had already dug past the budgeted depth. I was presented with two options: abandon this well and dig another, or keep going deeper to try and hit water. Both choices had cost ramifications. Abandoning the well meant it would have to be filled in, and there was no reimbursement for the digging. Digging deeper now meant we would have to upgrade the well pump and electrical system, because pumping water up from such great depths meant a heavy-duty pump. I opted to continue digging, hoping we would increase the refresh rate.

The next day, we were relieved to achieve a one and a half gallon per minute refresh rate at a depth of seven hundred seventy feet, just thirty feet before our agreed upon limit. Though that refresh rate was above the county code minimum, we knew it would not support the operational needs of a winery. A hole of that depth held about one thousand gallons of water, which was fine for bathroom usage, but would have to be carefully calculated when swelling barrels during winemaking. Swelling barrels is the process by which barrels are filled with water, allowing the oak to draw in water and expand the wood, sealing it tightly. Some production runs would require the concurrent swelling of dozens of barrels at a time, each with a volume of either two hundred twenty five or two hundred twenty eight liters, nearly sixty gallons each. Sometime in the early afternoon, the count health inspector came out to perform a percolation test on the new drain field site, and it passed with excellent metrics.

The burn pit was to be lit at 4:00 P.M. that afternoon. There are a lot of safety preparations that have to be in place before lighting a fire of that size. The local fire department had to be notified, and the contractor had to secure a tank of water large enough to extinguish the entire fire if something went awry. With all the equipment in place, we held a safety meeting with Ron, Dozer, and the television crew. Once the fire was large enough and camera-worthy, Shannon and I would have a seat in the field to be filmed watching the burn. We were wired with our microphones, and watched as the fire slowly built in intensity. The sun was setting as the fire reached its peak and the camera started rolling. Approaching the fire pit about one hundred feet away, even at that distance, the heat was extreme, as the burn pit was nearly eighty feet long and about twenty feet wide. As the fire raged, Dozer was in the track hoe manipulating it, and adding additional tree limbs that had been staged on the sides of the pit to ensure the fire kept going at a controlled rate.

Though the demolition burn closed one chapter in our construction project and began another, it was a very emotional experience. Two hundred years ago, that pile of smoldering timber had been someone else's dream house. It was difficult to ponder the number of joyous life experiences that likely occurred in that place. How many family holidays, birthdays, and special events happened here?

It was also hard to accept destroying a structure that had witnessed so much in terms of American and Virginian history. That log home had witnessed and survived our Civil War. In fact, there are documented tales from the war of encounters in that old house. It had seen the evolution of farming from horse-drawn plows to modern farming equipment, and from horse and buggy transportation to modern automobiles. Though we had no choice but to accept the unsalvageable state of that building, we were resolved to honor its memory by creating a place of such timeless beauty people could believe it had stood for two centuries, with all the spirit that amount of history engendered.

CHAPTER 20
"Breaking Ground"

The fire burned for four days, and even after Dozer backfilled the burn pit, you could still see some steam and smoke rising up out of the ground. The home site had been smoothed over in preparation for grading, and the parking lot site where the outbuildings had stood had been smoothed over as well. The site was now a blank canvas.

On June 2nd, we met with Ron to determine the placement of the new house. This is definitely not as trivial a process as one might think. You have to consider setbacks, yard space, driveways, utilities access, and the views through the picture windows. These decisions were further complicated by the fact that none of the grading had been done, and we had to envision things like hills being moved.

Once we had determined where the house was going to sit, we had to decide its orientation. We explained to Ron our vision of customers standing at the tasting bar, looking out through the picture windows at the views of the vineyard and Short Hill mountain in the distance. Ron suggested that rather than standing down in the basement trying to decide, he could put us at the bar. We grabbed a tape measure and figured out roughly where the tasting bar would be. Then one of Ron's crew, Trevor, drove his skid steer over to the center of the pit, and Shannon and I stepped into the bucket. Trevor lifted us up in the air about twelve feet, and we were suspended in mid-air, right where customers would be standing at the bar. We gazed out over the landscape, amazed at how beautiful it was going to be.

Ron grabbed a tape measure and pounded a stake in the ground directly beneath us. He then pulled the tape out towards the vineyard. I directed him to the proper angle, and he pounded in another stake delineating the centerline of the house. Once those were in the ground, Trevor lowered us back down and Ron squared off and pounded in another stake, representing the front corner of the house. Just like that, the house was sited. Shannon and I talked through a few more items with Ron, then hopped in the truck for our ninety-minute commute to Rockville.

While the demolition was taking place, Josh at LCTF had been trying to make contact with the blueprint engineer to begin the engineering approval and get the final blueprints created. Shannon and I designed the floor plans and basic frame concept and handed those plans off to Josh, who created the actual frame design and made upgrades and enhancements. Then his timber frame design had to be reviewed and approved by a structural engineer, to ensure the loads on all the posts, beams, and supporting structures conform to building codes. Once an engineer reviewed the frame, his notations go to an architect, who actually draws up the official blueprints. Once the architect's work is complete, the plans go back to the engineer for his seal of approval, at which point they are ready to go to the county in the permit application. A complicated process with many points of failure, this would prove to be one of the most frustrating aspects of the whole project.

Our entire summer schedule and frame delivery date hinged on having the engineer's seal on the final blueprints. Without that seal, Ron would not be able to apply for our building permit and begin the first phase of construction; our site would sit empty, and our frame would sit in the LCTF warehouse. Even allowing ample time for delays in both the engineering and permitting processes, the original schedule had Ron completing the foundation, basement walls, rough framing and sub-floor construction from mid-June through mid-July. The original frame delivery date had been July 17th, but with the extensive delays in the engineering process, that date was now in jeopardy. In late June, we rescheduled the frame delivery for August 14th.

I still had a vineyard to manage, so any spare time I had in the evenings and weekends were dedicated to chores. The vineyard required regular fungicide sprays to prevent outbreaks of downy and powdery mildews, as well as black rot and a whole host of issues that plague vineyards in Virginia. Our new $10,000 CIMA P-50 vineyard sprayer was delayed, so the first few months I had to spray the vineyard using my little handheld wand and tow-behind mini-sprayer. When the CIMA finally arrived, I couldn't believe the difference in the rate of application and the incredibly fine dispersion deep inside the vine canopy. A quality sprayer is one of those purchases that pays for itself pretty much instantly. Poor spray applications can result in the loss of an entire crop. In addition to spraying fungicides for the mildews, I also had to apply an insecticide to ward off hungry Japanese beetles, as well as a foliar fertilizer to compensate for a magnesium deficiency in the vines.

Doug paid me a visit to give me some pointers on dropping fruit, a process that involves analyzing each vine, evaluating the shoots, and determining how much fruit load to leave on each vine. Any excess is cut off and dropped to the ground, to ensure the vine is not over-cropped, which results in poor quality fruit and weak wines. The HGTV crew was on hand several times to capture footage of spraying, vine training and mowing. To a person, they all told me that any notions they ever had of someday owning a vineyard were now a distant memory—a person would have to be crazy to want to do this the way we were going at it. Some days it would be so hot outside and I was so tired from all the demands on my time, I would drive my truck under a tree, crack the windows, recline the seat and nap with the engine running and air conditioning on during the hottest period of the day. In addition to all the physical labor in the vineyard, I was also taking a distance learning course from UC Davis, "Introduction to Winemaking," and had hours of DVD lectures to watch. We settled into a routine where Shannon would drive us home in the evenings while I would watch my lectures and listen via headphones.

While I was spending every available spare moment in the vineyard, Shannon was taking care of Tristan back at the shack, running the household, and taking care of herself with her Bradley exercises. In addition, she was online doing design research for the house, working late at night on sales contracts and event planning, and trying to spend time with our families so the pressures of all our various commitments would not too adversely impact Tristan. We looked forward to reconnecting late in the evening to discuss the details of the day, and tried our best to stay awake and talk, but most nights we just collapsed from exhaustion.

On July 5th, we finally got word from the engineer that he had completed his preliminary review of the plans, and had sent them along with his data to the architect. A process that normally takes two weeks had taken nine, and we still had weeks ahead of us before we could actually begin the construction. The architect, understanding the pressure this process, had put on all the crews. On July 11th, Tony Zaya at LCTF phoned to say they had begun laying out and carving our frame the day before.

The following day we made our first draw request for $50,000 to cover Ron's deposit, the demolition invoice, and the frame deposit. With all the checks in the mail, and the architect's revised plans re-submitted to the engineer, all we needed was the final seal on the plans and we were ready to apply for our permit. We learned that the engineer had left town for a week on summer vacation, and that another several days would be lost, as well as our schedule—again. We set the new frame delivery for September 11th, 2006.

On July 15th, we awoke in excited anticipation for Tristan's first birthday party; his actual birthday was just a few days away. We knew that our shack was far too small to have any number of guests over, so Ken and Kim Wright, Tristan's godparents, had offered to host his party at their place in nearby Leesburg. Enjoying a much-needed break from the pressures of work and the construction delays, Shannon and I were glowing watching Tristan open his gifts and spending time with friends and family. Tristan's favorite cartoon was now "Bob the Builder," and his cake had a bulldozer pushing gumdrops down a chocolate road. We were thoroughly exhausted by the time we returned home, and enjoyed a quiet evening reminiscing about the day and rubbing Shannon's belly, hoping that baby number two had fun at the party as well.

On the 19th, Ron called to advise us he had received the final plans and was on his way to the county building to apply for the construction permit. Loudoun County did a wonderful job of turning around our application, and on August 1st, Ron had our building permit in hand. We were elated, though I knew there was an enormous amount of work that had to happen in order for the site to be ready for the arrival of the frame on September 11th. I phoned Josh to give him the good news, and he was excited to know we would now be rapidly moving forward.

August 9th, Ron arrived early with his loader to begin cutting away the hillside to prepare the site for the footers. He moved the dirt from the hillside around to the rear of the house and created a new backyard for us. In addition, he also created a temporary access road for the cement truck, as well as another access road and a delivery pad for the timber frame flatbed. I found the whole process very fascinating, and was grateful for Ron's experience. During our research process, we would often read stories of "do-it-yourselfers" who had tried to be their own general contractors on large-scale projects, only to end up creating vast fields of mud, inaccessible by equipment or crew. Ron was able to see the entire process, knowing that these temporary access points would later be rebuilt for other purposes.

Now that construction had begun, the project took off at a furious pace. By the end of the next day, the footers had been sited, measured, dug and poured, along with the enormous concrete piers that would support the point loads of the timber frame within the slab. On Friday, August 11th, the large aluminum forms that would create the basement walls were assembled, and we had our first serious construction mishap. While the concrete truck was pouring the walls, the weight broke one of the aluminum panels, and concrete began pouring out all over the backyard. Luckily, no one was injured. It was a very tense moment with a lot of shouting and running, but everyone was all right. Ron assured me there would be no issues with the wall, as once they repaired the forms, they would continue the pour so that the concrete would be well integrated. The only real damage was to the concrete subcontractor's wallet, as all the concrete on the ground was a total loss.

Ron organized a meeting with the HVAC contractor and the plumber to discuss final locations for all the major systems. We had to make a change to the location of the washer and dryer, as their antici-pated location did not have enough room for the enormous HVAC unit that would heat and cool the house, along with the huge ductwork that would be required to move all the air. Over the next several days, the plumber installed all the drain work underneath where the slab would be poured. The foundation was sealed with a thick coating of spray-on rubber, and Ron backfilled the gaps between the hill and the foundation. The morning of Friday, August 18th, Shannon, Tristan, and I were on site to watch the pouring of the slab. I pushed one of Tristan's plastic building blocks down into the concrete for good luck.

By this time, our Cabernet Franc grapes had completed the process known as veraison, when they turn color from green to purple. The variations in color in each cluster as the berries transform are beau-tiful. Somehow keeping up with my vineyard chores, I had managed to install all the new cordon wires, maintain my spray program, and destroy two more sprayers in a long series of asinine, expensive, and painful debacles known as "learning to farm the hard way." Founding a vineyard, having children, building a massive home while filming a television show, and commuting long distances to a travel-intensive professional career was a little overwhelming.

The next week, Ron and his crew installed the wooden I-beams that would span the twenty-eight foot width of the home and create the base of the subfloor. Once the beams were in place, work began on framing the basement walls. The enormous point-loads of the timber frame would have to be supported by steel posts and concrete piers, and much work was required to incorporate these additional structural components into the walls of the downstairs living areas. On August 29th, Ron called to give us the good news that the subfloor was complete, and the site and foundation were ready to receive the timber frame just less than two weeks away.

The following week, on September 5th, we arrived for Shannon's ultrasound. It took just a few seconds to reveal that Shannon was carrying a healthy baby boy, and that he looked wonderful. We lay awake that night cuddling Tristan, telling him all about his baby brother and the wonderful times they were going to have together, chasing puppies around the vineyard, exploring the woods, fishing in the pond, building campfires, and starting their own band. We were exhausted but elated, hopeful yet terrified, and anxious but committed. So many things had been set in motion, and though it sometimes felt we had little control over any of them, we knew we had to stay focused, otherwise everything would completely unravel in an instant. The pressure was intense and mounting daily, yet we held on to one another tightly and forged ahead, always believing in the dream for our babies and ourselves.

CHAPTER 21

"Meeting the Frame"

P rogress on carving our frame at LCTF was rapid. Coordinating with the HGTV crew, LCTF, and our work schedules, we planned a visit to York, Pennsylvania on Saturday, July 29th to see the work in action.

We arrived at the shop early and met the camera crew. Everyone was in high spirits; though we were used to being in front of the cameras, it was a new experience for the LCTF team, who took it in stride and settled right in.

Tony was visibly excited to show us his handiwork, a custom carving that would adorn the main beam on the wall overlooking the vineyard. He had hand-carved the word "NOTAVIVA" using a set of carving tools created by a master Japanese craftsman who also made samurai swords. The work was stunning, and we were very moved to see this beam coming to life in the hands of the company founder. One of Tony's colleagues was carving two grape clusters, which would be installed on either side of the word.

As we entered the shop, we saw the second bent already assembled on the floor. We immediately realized how deceiving the size of the frame is when it is lying down; it looks very small. Shannon asked Josh, "What does it sit on?" to which he replied, "Nothing, it just sits on the subfloor." To get a better sense of how tall it would be, Shannon walked over and laid down on the ground with her feet at the base of the frame and "looked up" towards the peak of the rafter. I joined her, and as we lay in the sawdust looking at our rafters, Tony commented, "No one has EVER done that before!" We could have cared less that the television cameras were rolling; we were enjoying exploring our future home together.

Tony continued showing us around the shop, and watching the craftsmen using the chain mortisers, chamfering routers, and augers was incredibly intriguing. Thinking back to our decision to engage LCTF on this project, I was reminded of Tony's assurance that they hand-cut every joint; here we were, watching it unfold before our very eyes. They asked me if I would like to drill one of the peg holes that would be used to hold the frame together, and I jumped at the chance. Shannon looked a little sad, so the crew asked her if she would like to drill a hole as well. She stepped up onto the beam, held the massive drill, and began to auger another hole. I thought Tony was going to pass out, watching a pregnant client using power tools in his shop.

Meeting the frame was the highlight of the entire project. Years of dreaming, planning, saving, and hard work had brought us to this day, with this wonderful group of people who were pouring their hearts into our home. I believe that timber frames are living beings, which have souls comprised of the gifts from the forest as well as all the people who work on them. I captured a photograph of Shannon holding Tristan's hands as he stood on the beam bearing the NOTAVIVA carving, and we could not help but hope that he might be married below this beam one day. We were in a dreamy state the entire ride home, wistfully pondering all the wonderful times that were yet to come in our beautiful home.

On our ride home, we also decided what to do with any fruit we might be able to harvest. Though most vines take three years to produce any sort of usable crop, a few vines do produce nice clusters of fruit in year two. Talking to Doug about this a few days earlier, he encouraged us to pick the fruit and make some wine. "Better to make mistakes on 15 gallons rather than 1,500 gallons!" We settled on picking whatever Viognier and Cabernet Franc the vineyard would provide and making wine as Christmas gifts. We would have to spend about $2,000 to acquire some small home winemaking equipment, a press, and 70-gallon stainless steel variable top tank.

I began tracking the Brix levels in the fruit in early August and plotting their development on a harvest chart. Degrees Brix is the sugar content of an aqueous solution, and is used to approximate the sugar levels in grape juice. Since grapes have other dissolved solids in the juice, the degrees Brix is not an entirely accurate representation, but it is considered close enough to make an intelligent decision on harvesting. It is a common misconception that degrees Brix is an indication of ripeness; the only thing it really tells you is a rough indication of potential alcohol in the finished wine. Ripeness is actually a subjective term, defined by a winemaker depending on his or her vision for the finished wine. One winemaker's definition of ripe may be another's definition of over-extracted mush worthy of mass-market jam.

As I walked the Viognier block, I found it fascinating to see the diversity in fruit ripeness between the interior of the canopy, the eastern side of the canopy, and clusters that may have been exposed to the afternoon sun on the western side of the canopy. Canopy management is critical in ensuring consistent fruit development, and I began to appreciate very early on that wine is not made—it is grown. Popping a few berries into my mouth from the shaded interior of the canopy revealed nice tart acidity, while the berries on the outside of the canopy revealed complex fruit flavors, most notably apricot and pink grapefruit. Tasting the two together was an interesting combination, and I began to understand the delicate balance of sugar levels, acidity, and flavor composition.

We planned our first-ever harvest for Saturday, August 26th. Since we anticipated only picking a few hundred pounds of grapes, we only had to enlist two volunteers: Ken and my brother Jim. The television producers insisted that the camera crew follow us when they learned we were planning to pick some fruit and make some wine. Our first Viognier harvest and crush provided some of the most memorable footage of the entire series, and by the time it was over, we had succeeded in convincing the camera crew that we had about as much business making wine as a room full of chimpanzees.

The morning dawned bright and clear, and we all met at the vineyard. Shannon was thrilled to be able to participate, since all of the pesticide residues had worn away and she was able to get into the vineyard to help pick grapes. My mom stayed at the shack to watch Tristan so Shannon could join us for the day. We used Ken's pickup truck and harvested about 400 pounds of grapes. A week before, I was despondent, thinking that there would not be anything left to pick. We learned the hard way that the local bird population was enjoying our ripe delicious fruit, and we quickly realized we would need bird prevention measures for the following season.

It only took a couple hours to pick all the fruit, load it into the truck, and head back to the shack to process it. Having never processed grapes before, and not having an outside area to crush the fruit, we made the ill-fated decision to process the fruit in the kitchen. Neither Shannon nor I had ever even seen this process done, much less participated.

I had hoped to perform a "whole cluster" press, where the complete fruit clusters are loaded into the press without having to pass through a crusher/de-stemmer. Our little home basket press was simply not up to the task, and could not apply enough pressure to burst the berries and press out the juice. It was becoming increasingly clear that we had no idea what we were doing. As the winemaker, it was my job to figure it out, and I knew I had to make some fast decisions. Since we did not own a crusher/de-stemmer and you can not exactly run down to the store to buy one, I decided that we would crush by hand. Most people have a large tub on hand to crush by foot; however, having been in our work boots all morning, we not only didn't have a suitable vessel to crush in, we didn't have suitable feet to crush with. Doing it by hand was actually not too bad, and we were able to load the press basket full and were getting some delicious juice out of the bottom.

Next, we realized that we could not get a hard enough press because we could not hold the press still while we were cranking down the lever. With grape juice everywhere, we were sliding around the kitchen, making a mockery of modern winemaking. Frustrated and exhausted, I went into the garage to retrieve my drill and some screws. Shannon's eyes went wide as she realized what I was about to do; the look on my face made it clear that objections would not be entertained, so she quietly went back to sorting the fruit. Moving the press into the position I needed, I screwed it to the kitchen floor, right through the linoleum. Once the screws were in place, we were able to get a tighter press, but then we broke the screws. I ran over to Nichol's Hardware to purchase some lag bolts. I drilled three pilot holes and ratcheted the lag screws into the kitchen floor. With the press now immobile, a tight press in the basket and juice flowing freely out the bottom into pails for collection, I was confident we had succeeded in making complete jackasses of ourselves on national television. The crunching sound that was heard in the show was not the press breaking apart; it was the floor being destroyed. That said, the juice we extracted from those grapes was delicious, and I knew I had fifteen gallons of Viognier and a great winemaking project ahead of me.

Without a proper winery and chilling equipment, I had no way to settle the juice, which is the first step in making a white wine. Improvising, I moved the three pails into our second bathroom and installed a window air conditioner. I turned the thermostat down to fifty-five degrees and chilled the juice overnight. The following afternoon, I racked (transferred) the clarified juice to three carboys and pitched my yeast. Keeping the bathroom at a chilly fifty-five degrees actually kept the fermentation temperature in check, and the wine slowly began to ferment over the next few weeks. The aromas were so superior to any of the kit wines I had made previously, and we were thrilled that the wine was turning out so well.

Weeks later, when fermentation finished, the living room and kitchen were still sticky from the harvest and crush. The kitchen floor was ruined, with three giant holes right in front of the sink and imprints of the press feet gouged into the linoleum. I was too tired to care, and too enamored with my three carboys of juice that we harvested from our own land to even worry about the $1,500 rental security deposit I had just sacrificed.

As the frame delivery day drew near, I realized that our Cabernet Franc would also be ready for harvest. Normally red vinifera grapes are harvested in mid- to late-October, though this timing is dependent on a wide variety of factors. Young vines ripen their fruit much more quickly than established vines, so our vines were ready almost a month earlier than they would be in years to come. On Sunday, September 10th, we harvested our grapes and brought them back to the shack for round two.

We quickly sorted much of the fruit by hand, pulling out mummies, which are small, shriveled berries that had been killed earlier in the season by an outbreak of black rot. Having learned our lesson from the disastrous Viognier processing, we crushed the Cabernet Franc outside the garage alongside the rear of the house. My crop estimate for the Cabernet Franc was as terrible as my estimate for the Viognier, though in the other direction. Where my Viognier estimate was far too high, it was far too low for the Cabernet Franc, and we had much more fruit than I had anticipated. We filled the seventy-gallon tank, along with six winemaking pails, and still had fruit left over; Shannon decided to make Cabernet Franc jelly for Christmas gifts as well. In filling the fermentation vessels, I did not leave enough headspace in the tank nor pails for the expansion of the grape cap. A few days later, I went into the garage to find grapes spilling out of the large tank; the pressure in the pails (even with an airlock in place) was so great that it had blown the tops off with such force that there were grape skins stuck to the ceiling of the garage.

Monday morning, September 11th, started off dreary with a constant drizzle that slowly turned to rain over the course of the day. We arrived at the job site early just to meet the crew and take a few pictures. Joe McCarthy, LCTF founding partner and site foreman, was on hand to welcome us and show us around the numerous stacks of well-marked timbers that would slowly become our home over the next few days. It looked like an enormous Erector set waiting to be put together. A large crane had been situated in front of the foundation, which would be used to lift the heavy beams and frame pieces into place. We visited with Josh for a few moments, and then got out of the way and let the crew get to work.

The LCTF crew was experienced and professional, and right away established a covered work area in the rear of the house. Using tarps and temporary bracing, they created a large shop so they could stay productive even if they had to take a rain delay. Since the LCTF crew would be covering the frame with the structural insulated panels (SIPs), they could be working on customizing those pieces if the weather was not cooperating for frame building. They advised that the first day was typically just an organizational day, and that if any work was done on the frame, it would likely just be a couple of posts to get started. Sure enough, when we stopped by the job site that evening, we could see that four posts with connecting beams from bent number one were standing in place, held together with temporary bracing attached to the subfloor. We just sat in our truck holding hands, looking out at the beginning of our house.

The following day dawned bright and clear, and we made our way over to the construction site. We had taken the remainder of the week off of work in order to be on site as much as possible for the assembly of the frame. It was fascinating watching the crew work on assembling small sections of the frame on the ground, then seeing the crane lift them into place. I found it interesting that at the bottom of each twenty-four foot tall post, they had inserted one of the Ash pegs that would hold the joints together. Josh explained that these pegs helped align the frame to the exact spot on the subfloor where they were intended to sit, and kept the frame from shifting during the construction process.

As we learned by watching the assembly, each section of the frame is created with very specific joinery, designed in advance not only for structural integrity and aesthetic beauty, but to allow for the seamless connection of the timbers. The frame assembly is already thought out well ahead of the carving process, essentially in Josh's frame design software. Given the complexity of the joinery, the weight of the timbers, and the costs that would be incurred if the job did not go smoothly, it is imperative for the frame designer to accurately specify which kind of joint will connect each timber. Whether a dovetail, bird's mouth, mortise and tenon, or other complex hidden joint, every single connection is designed specifically to not only have great structural integrity and aesthetic value, but also work in concert with the assembly process. Once we knew which kinds of joints were assembled in what manner, observing the crew select which sections were next made a lot more sense. Though timber framing has always been considered an art, the modern industry leverages the finest in emerging technological capabilities and operational processes to push the design envelope.

Once the posts for bents one and two were in place and standing upright, they were connected with the large beams, known as girts, that would form the supports for the interior catwalk. As soon as those were secured, it was time to lift the roof truss rafter assembly into place. Watching that big triangle soar into the air as the crane lifted it higher and higher was enough to take our breath away. As the truss was slowly lowered into place, the crew was in position high above the subfloor on scaffolding, ready to guide it onto the posts. I was stunned to see such a complex piece of trussing and joinery slide seamlessly into place atop six connections, four posts, and two knee braces. A few firm taps with their rubber mallets, and the truss was fully seated in place, then secured with the ash pegs. Less than an hour later, the rafters for bent number two were in place, then the connecting purlins and eave plates were installed. Constantly checking the frame for structural integrity, Joe, Josh, and the team used ample band clamps and temporary bracing to ensure the frame was safe and solid, even though it was only partially assembled. There are so many horror stories about people getting seriously injured during frame assembly due to missing pegs, insufficient bracing, or any number of unfortunate mishaps; safety must always be a top concern.

Although they took it in stride, it was obvious that having a television crew on site during frame construction was slowing down the process and making certain aspects of the assembly more challenging. The LCTF crew hung in there, however, and made sure that they communicated each step to the field producer to ensure the camera would be in the appropriate spot to capture each move from the best angle. By the end of day two, the third bent had been erected and connected to the second bent, though once the third rafter assembly was set in place, the crew realized that one of the joints had not been cut at the shop. One of the field crew, Chuck, had to climb up to the third truss and sit atop the ridge beam, over 28 feet in the air, and hand-cut the next ridge beam joint with a hammer and chisel. Though the work took about an hour, the joint was perfectly cut, and when the next ridge beam was set in place the connection was seamless.

By late afternoon the crew called it quits for the day, and Shannon, Tristan, and I spent about an hour taking pictures and gawking at the frame. It was so strange that these exact same pieces of wood had looked so small when we first met them several weeks earlier at the shop. Now that we were standing under them, it did not seem possible that they could reach so far into the sky. I could not resist climbing up the scaffolding and standing upon the catwalk beam to gaze out over the vineyard. Shannon and I held each other while Tristan watched us from his stroller, content that the day was a great success and that the assembly was going as planned.

The next day was essentially rained out, but the LCTF crew made the most of the day by working under the tarp behind the house, pre-assembling the eight dormers that would sit atop the house. There were a few breaks in the rain, which allowed the crew to assemble and erect bent four. The area between bents three and four would eventually house the main tasting bar, and was comprised of the most complex of all the joinery in the house. A fascinating three-beam joint would form an opening in the catwalk above, allowing people to stand at the railing and gaze out over the main tasting room floor through the windows to the vineyard beyond.

Thursday, with only one bent to go, the crew was eager to get moving. Though the joinery between bents three and four was more complex, assembling the joinery between bents four and five was more complicated, as this is where the structural components for the music performance loft were located. With additional bracing in place to hold the music loft beams, the remaining four posts were lifted into place. Adding complication was the fact that there was no longer any open floor space. The first four bents were simplified, in that the pieces on the ground could just be stood up, but by the time the last bent was ready to go, there was a house in the way. We learned that the joinery for the last bent was different than the previous four for this very reason. By the end of the day the frame was essentially done, with only one piece remaining to be put in place. This was purposely delayed so that we could participate in the placing the following morning, accompanied by a bit of ceremony.

Friday, September 15, 2006 was a perfect day, from the weather to the homebuilding events. Traditionally in timber framing, the crew signs the top of the last piece, and Shannon and I watched as each member of the team signed the final ridge beam that would be situated above the music loft. We held each other closely as the crane lifted the beam high into the bright morning sky, and I choked up as I watched it lowered into place. With the last beam installed, there was just one more piece left; the crew had saved the last peg for Shannon and me to hammer in place. The last peg in the home is located right at the tasting bar, and when Chuck handed me the peg and hammer, I decided that we needed to sign it. I signed our three names, but felt it needed something more special. Remembering the inscription on the inside of our wedding bands, I quickly removed my ring and wrote, "Is thu m'annsachd" on the peg, Gaelic for "Thou art my most beloved." From our love for each other as well as for our children, our home and our family, it seemed the perfect blessing upon the frame.

I hammered the peg in place, then Shannon gave it a few taps, and Tristan had his little toy hammer in his stroller, so he took a few whacks as well. His laughter as he pounded the peg in place captured everyone's heart. We all laughed together, and with the last peg in place, we moved on to the dedication ceremony.

The placing of the "whetting bush" is a time-honored tradition, whereby an evergreen bough is nailed to the highest point of the frame. Though people may have different interpretation of this ceremony, most everyone agrees that it is intended to pay homage to the trees that were felled for the timbers used in the frame. For the builders, it signifies the end of another successful project. For the homeowner, it signifies the completion of the most important phase in the construction of a new home. For everyone present, it is a moment of celebration. We watched as the crane lifted the bough up to the crew, sitting high above us on the last ridge beam. As they nailed the bough into place, a great cheer went up from everyone; we knew that our frame was complete, everyone was safe and sound, and we were moving forward to closing it in. Having experienced so many heart-warming moments already that morning, it did not seem possible that the best was yet to come.

During the entire week of construction, the NOTAVIVA carving and grape clusters had remained hidden behind a wrapping of plastic. The crew had planned all along that the removal of the plastic would be a special moment, and had taken the time to build a small section of scaffolding for Shannon, Tristan, and me to climb so we could remove the plastic ourselves. With George behind us capturing every-thing for the television show, I slowly began to pull away the plastic, handing it to Tristan so he could help me. As I turned to look at the beam, I could not hold back the flood of emotion that overtook me. I bowed my head and placed it against the beam. The years of dreaming, toiling, risk taking, and persistence had come to this moment. It was beyond fulfilling; it was a defining moment in my life. I could feel Shannon's hand on my arm, and could hear Tristan cooing next to me, and for a brief moment, I was utterly at peace.

It was time to reveal the grape cluster carvings. I slowly removed the box covering the first one, holding it in front of my face and enjoying the suspense, and then lowered it to catch my first glimpse of the carving. It was spectacular, the perfect complement to the carving of the word. The frame itself is a work of art, but to have these carvings incorporated into it takes it to a higher level. For the first time, I felt the magic of our timber frame.

Many times since that day, I have longed to return to that moment when I saw the NOTAVIVA carving for the first time, just to bask in the serenity of those few seconds. Quite often, it has felt as if the entire world has conspired to destroy our dreams, and we have lost hope in the face of seemingly insurmountable obstacles. It is in those times, when we have felt like giving up, that the frame speaks to us. It stands over us, reassuring and inspiring, giving us hope that we can prevail. At night when the world has gone still, I have placed my hands upon these timbers, feeling its life, seeking its advice and listening to its guidance. I know in my heart the wisdom of the forest and the power of the earth lie within this work of art; I need only open my mind to their truths. I am a husband, I am a father, and this is the home I have built to raise my family and serve my one true love. Together, we will never fail.

CHAPTER 22

"A Star to Watch Over Us"

I t took the LCTF crew another week to finish up the sides of the house, requiring the customization of dozens of 4' by 8' SIPs. They had developed custom tools to streamline the process, which allowed them to quickly carve out the internal Styrofoam insulation. Each window and door opening required additional lumber support, so the crew created channels in the insulation, which were reinforced with framing. Though the frame itself is incredibly sturdy, the manner in which the SIPs were attached both to each other as well as the frame created a solid skin the whole way around the house.

We received another hit to the budget in the form of an additional septic system pump. Though our system was designed for gravity-flow, the septic subcontractors advised us that there was a low spot in the field between the septic tank and the junction box, which fed the drain field. There were really only two options; the first was to raise the field and eliminate the low spot, creating a 300 foot long hump across the meadow. The other option was to install a pump in the tank, which would force the waste through the low spot and back up to the junction box. We figured having to explain to thousands of curious customers that the hump running across the meadow was a septic line did not really play well into our romantic vision of a bucolic vineyard view.

Shortly after the walls were completed, the LCTF crew had installed the knotty pine tongue and groove ceiling and the base of the roof. The roof is comprised of overlapping layers of the tongue and groove ceiling, then nine inches of solid Styrofoam, then sleepers for air circulation, then plywood sheathing, then the shingles. Carefully scheduled in the midst of all of this roofing work was some preliminary electrical wiring. One of the major considerations in a vaulted ceiling timber frame is that the home has no attic; there can be no wiring relocation after the roofing is complete. Before any of the roofing could be installed, I had a walkthrough with Richard and the electricians to show them my electrical plan and point to the specific locations where they would have to bring wiring through the ridge beams and purlins. Once the electricians finished the installation of the wiring, the LCTF crew was able to move forward with the base roofing.

On Wednesday, October 4th, I left for New Orleans for nine days. Working on a sales conference, this would be my longest trip yet away from Shannon and Tristan. I knew that I would be working a long string of twenty-hour days, but I also knew that Shannon would be just as exhausted. Taking care of Tristan and heading into the office each day, as well as working with the construction crew and the camera crew to keep the scheduling moving forward was a lot to ask of someone who was six months pregnant.

She kept it all together, however, and when I landed late in the evening on Thursday, October 12th, we went straight to bed. Though I had a lot of post-show work to complete, as well as pre-production work on our next show in Houston the following week, I was able to work from the shack and finish up by early afternoon. We spent that evening and most of the next day trying to decide what color our siding, trim, and roof were going to be. We finally narrowed it down to two choices: light grey siding with white trim, or dark blue siding with light grey trim. We went to the store and bought pieces of pine shelving and different shades of dark blue and light grey and white paint, and made little houses. Once we had created all of the miniatures, we were able to decide on the dark blue with light grey trim option.

We also had to decide on a siding material. The original budget was based on a wooden material known as T1-11, though Richard had suggested we upgrade to a board and batten material for a more traditional barn look. We had fallen in love with metal roofing, but the cost to complete the entire roof in metal was well beyond our budget. I asked what it would cost to just complete the front porch in a brushed silver metal, with the dormers and roof in shingles, and learned it was $5,000 more. Feeling it would be a great look for approaching visitors, we decided to move forward with that option. That $5,000, plus the $1,200 upgrade for the board and batten siding, meant that more interior pieces had left the budget. We were quickly working our way toward a beautiful new home that would sit completely empty.

As soon as the house was closed in, work began on the interior partition walls and the catwalk flooring. From here on out we would be working only with Ron's team, and it was time to say goodbye to the crew from LCTF. We had grown so close; it seemed hard to believe that over two years had passed since we had first contacted Tony. Joe treated everyone to a wonderful celebratory dinner, and the crew confided that although our project was not nearly their largest, nor their most complicated, it was everyone's favorite. It seemed that our story and our vision for our home and business had touched each of them, and they assured us that they would continue to visit in the years to come. Many hugs were traded as we left that night, and everyone knew we had all participated in something very special.

Friday morning, October 20th, I was scrambling to pick up samples for the metal available for the covered porch roof. I had to hurry, because my sister Rebecca's wedding was that evening at a botanical garden about an hour away. Both Shannon and I were in the wedding party, and needed to put the construction project out of our minds to focus on the importance of the day. Worse than chasing a roofing sample book, my crew was loading in a show down in Houston, Texas, and I was taking calls from my stage manager, trying to sort out production issues, in the midst of our wedding preparations. Though I was able to excuse myself for load-in, I was to be on a flight early the next morning, scheduled to arrive in Houston in time for lighting focus and scenic installation.

The wedding was perfect, and I just could not get over how beautiful my baby sister looked as my parents walked her down the aisle. I was eleven when she was born, and distinctly remember sitting in the backseat when we drove her home from the hospital. The years of fond memories all came flooding back, and though I cry at every wedding I attend, I was a particular mess that evening. Shannon was stunning in her royal blue bridesmaid dress, made even more beautiful by her pregnancy. It was becoming quite obvious that she would be having another large baby, as many people asked during the reception if she was due any day. When they learned that she still had eleven weeks to go, most people just stared in shocked disbelief. Pregnant as she was, nothing could keep her off of the dance floor, and we held each other closely as we swayed to the music.

I was out the door the next morning and on a plane to Houston at 6:00 A.M., arriving on time and heading straight to the venue to oversee the production load-in. Shannon and Tristan attended the morning-after brunch traditional for our family weddings, and afterwards took curious family members out to the construction site. Most of them had not been to the land since our wedding, and were shocked to see the progress. My cousin's husband Gary helped chase out two woodpeckers who had moved in through the openings, who were particularly unwelcome in our timber frame home.

I flew back in from Houston late on Tuesday, October 24th, and after getting a few hours of sleep, had to be at the construction site for a 7:00 A.M. interview with the Loudoun Times Mirror newspaper. Word was spreading quickly that Loudoun's newest winery-in-progress was being filmed for a national television audience, and they were keen to do an article. We figured the press would be great and could help start building some excitement about both the winery and the eventual airing of the television series. The interview went well, and was followed by back-to-back meetings with the plumber, electrician, HVAC team, and Richard. This last meeting was to discuss the incorrect installation of the music loft floor, which was supposed to be installed on joist hangers between the timbers, but had been set on top. Given our knowledge of music events, audiences, and sight-lines, we were very concerned that having the stage too high would be problematic. The camera crew was all over these conversations, hoping to film some good tension. To some extent they were not disappointed; although Richard agreed that re-doing the floor would be a challenge, he and the team acknowledged a mistake had been made and they were willing to make it right.

Ron's team had made great progress on finishing the outside of the house, installing the board and batten siding, adding the trim work, and completing the various roof sections. We were thrilled with the look of the board and batten, and were glad we made the choice to upgrade from the T1-11, which would have given the house a much flatter look.

In early November work commenced on the interior systems, with the plumber beginning his work on the drain lines. Most of the interior framing had been completed at this point, and given Shannon's due date in early January, she began asking about likely move-in dates. We knew at this point that it was impossible to be in the house by the time the baby arrived, but we were hopeful we could still be in by mid-winter. Richard indicated that once all the systems were in place behind the walls, the drywall would go very quickly, as would the subsequent finishing; it might be possible for us to be in the house by late February.

The coordination of the various systems throughout the house is easily the most complicated puzzle that has to be solved during the construction process. Without clear communication, a subcontractor might end up putting a line (plumbing, HVAC, or electrical) right in the way of where another system has to pass. One of Richard's main jobs was to ensure that not only were the various systems physically located in the proper place, but that the scheduling of the subcontractors was coordinated in such a way that as soon as one subcontractor was finished, the next subcontractor could come in right away. Due to the complexities of the systems, it never happens that way. Delays, mishaps, and schedule conflicts are part of the construction process.

In our world, if twenty thousand people are expecting a concert on a Friday night at 8:00 P.M. then there will a concert—period. It does not matter what piece of gear is not working; it will get fixed. It does not matter how sick, hurt, or tired the crew is during the load-in; the show will happen on time and you will do your job, no matter how miserable you feel. That same mindset does not apply to home construction. If a day's tasks are not completed or an issue has arisen, well, then too bad, the subcontractor will usually just head out at normal quitting time and everything just shifts back a day or two. Hopefully the issue would at least be reported back to Richard so he could plan accordingly, but as we would see, that was not always the case.

I give Ron and his team a lot of credit, because after seeing some of the issues that arose during our project, I am rather amazed that any home has ever been built anywhere. Even allotting extra time in the schedule sometimes never seemed enough, as there were situations when a subcontractor faced a problem that could not be quickly resolved, requiring the subsequent subcontractor to be pushed back a day or two. However, each subcontractor was typically working on multiple concurrent jobs, and most of the time each delay would conflict with another commitment, requiring them to push back even additional days. Losing a day here, three days there, was really going to add up over the next several months, and considering how late we got started, I was already starting to get nervous about finishing the house within the one year deadline the bank imposed at our loan signing.

The trim carpenters, Vernon and Tim, were busy with the siding and trim work outside, as well as the music loft repair upstairs. Their most important task, and arguably their most complicated, was the installation of our signature five-pointed star window at the peak of the wall overlooking the vineyard. The original design of the home featured a semicircle window, but when my grandmother had passed away in May 2005, I began contemplating some way of honoring her memory in the design of the house. Shannon's grandmother had passed away just two months before our wedding, and she was still feeling her loss as well. We had decided that our home would somehow incorporate the spirit of all of our lost loved ones in its design.

As children riding in the car to visit my grandmother at her home in Pennsylvania, we would pass the famous Star Barn sitting on the south side of route 283. Built in 1872, this barn is listed as a National Historic Landmark with the National Register of Historic Places. Seeing that landmark, my brother and I would know Grandma's house was just a short distance away. On the one-year anniversary of her death, just a few days after we signed our construction loan, I had found myself recalling those fond memories of trips to her house, and all the wonderful excitement that she brought to our family gatherings. Though our home plans were complete and on their way to the architect, I began to ponder a window in the shape of a star. I sent Josh at LCTF an email explaining the concept, and he said that since the window did not have any structural significance, it would not affect the engineering phase of the project and that he would be happy to update our drawings with a four-foot wide star window. As soon as I saw his rendering of the vineyard wall incorporating the star window, I was committed to changing the design and making it happen.

Placing a call to Andersen's custom windows division, I explained to the sales representative what I had in mind. Though she was unaware if they had actually ever constructed such a window, I could tell she was fascinated by the story behind the design, as well as the opportunity to deliver such a piece. Sending over the plans that Josh had created, she assured me she would have a quote in a few days. When she called and advised that the window would cost $1,900, I locked in the project right on the phone, and called Ron to tell him that I had just made a major change to the plans.

When the window arrived at the local lumber store, it was apparently greeted with a great deal of curiosity and intrigue. The store employees could not help but open the package and take pictures of the window; as it turned out, it was the only five-pointed star that Andersen had made at the time. When I picked it up on October 30th and drove it over to the job site to show the crew, their reaction was a little less than enthusiastic. They knew immediately that framing in this window, with all its various trim carpentry angles, right up near the peak of the roof (with completely different angles) would be incredibly challenging. Having seen Vernon and Tim's attention to detail on the other elements of the siding and trim construction, I had the utmost confidence that the star window would be installed perfectly, and when we got our first glimpse of the window in place on November 6th, it took our breath away. One of the more comical scenes in the television series is the conversation between Vernon and Tim as they discuss the installation. Their matter-of-fact exchange belied the complexity of the actual work, and their fun banter truly conveyed their genial mannerisms.

Sitting proudly at the peak of the roof, overlooking the vineyard and greeting visitors heading southwest on Sagle road, the window is a unique, instantly recognizable icon, defining our personal and business philosophies. Historically, people have put symbols on homes and barns for a myriad of reasons; some were placed to ward off evil spirits, some for good luck, others as a symbol of welcome. Given that our window was placed to symbolize and honor family, we feel that the star window represents all of the above. As a window, it looks both outward as a symbol of welcome, and inward as a symbol of protection and good luck. Through the years, it would watch over us in ways we never imagined.

Perhaps the most mystifying aspect of the star goes back to a poem I penned for my grandmother while still attending the University of Miami in 1989. While studying for midterm exams, with not a dime to my name, I found myself daydreaming about Christmas presents. With no way to purchase gifts for anyone, I decided to write a Christmas poem for my grandmother. We celebrated each Christmas Eve with my cousins, and this large family gathering has become the hallmark of our holiday traditions. Exchanging gifts with each other, telling stories of past holidays and family events, feasting and laughing has provided some of our most cherished memories. During that gift exchange, when it was time for me to give Gram her present, I simply walked over and handed her a simple $2 frame holding the poem I had written. Though not my intention, she asked if she could read it aloud. Somewhat embarrassed, I responded, "Of course, Gram, it is your poem..." As she read, a hush came over the room, and when she got to the last line, her tears were echoed by each of us.

I include the poem below to illustrate that, even in this day and age, there is magic all around us. Small acts of kindness and genuine displays of affection can reap rewards far beyond their intended circumstances. Nearly seventeen years after my grandmother read my simple Christmas poem aloud to our family, the significance of that story would be forever impressed upon each of us, as well as upon every visitor to our winery.

"Three Christmas Wishes"

I remember Christmases that have gone before
grandchildren gathered 'round
Their bright-eye innocence and impish grins
where love and laughter abound

If I could have but a single wish
in my memories it would be
To add each year more joyous thoughts
of Christmas with my family

I see the Christmases we share today
our family draws closer together
More precious than the gifts we give
are the feelings we have for each other

If I could have but a single wish
in my lifetime it would be
For the world to share a peaceful night
on Christmas with my Family

I dream of Christmases that have yet to come
when our grandchildren's grandchildren appear
In the light of the dawn 'round the tree they will scurry
the beauty from my eye draws a tear

If I could have but a single wish
in my passing it would be
To become a star and forever shine
at Christmas upon my family

Copyright © 1989 Stephen W. Mackey

CHAPTER 23
"Sweat Equity"

There was still plenty of work to do in the vineyard. I spent each weekend building the trellis for the newly planted Viognier that we had installed in the spring. Running catch wires and building end braces for an acre of vines is pretty exhausting, particularly when you have to keep taking breaks to give quick sound bite interviews for a television crew. I kept at it, however, and finished the end brace construction the day after Thanksgiving. I kept moving forward with cordon and catch wire installation through early December, with the knowledge that once I began working in the house, it would be very difficult to find vineyard time.

From the first moment Shannon and I decided to build a home, we were committed to performing as many of the construction tasks as time would allow. Regardless of whether or not we had experience in any particular aspect of the project, we wanted to do as much of the work as possible ourselves. We both knew that it was essential we build as large of a structure as our budget would allow, and that we could continue to work on both interior and exterior upgrades in the years to come. We figured we could paint, plant, and finesse the home as the business grew, but that stretching walls would never be an option.

In the summer of 1986, just after I finished high school, I worked for my cousin Bill Madden in his new startup, Tops of the Town, his countertop design and manufacturing business. At first, like many small business startups, we would take on any job just to provide cash flow; several of our first projects were abysmally miserable, but kept us busy. For the next several summers, I worked with Bill, learning carpentry in the shop. In addition, perhaps providing some of the greatest learning experiences of my life, we would go into customer's homes and install the new countertops. I was exposed to all facets of running a small business: marketing, writing bids, meeting with customers, designing, manufacturing, and installing.

We also installed ceramic tile, plumbing fixtures, and appliances. On several occasions, we completed entire bathroom renovations, tearing out existing bathrooms down to the studs and rebuilding everything. In the middle of all of that hustling, working, and learning the trades, we would drink beer, lift weights, and play golf, sometimes all in one day and often in that order. I was in love with the self-discipline and sense of freedom that comes with being an entrepreneur, and these experiences were some of the most formative of my late teens and early twenties. I applied these skills often to upgrading my parent's home as well as my own homes through the years, gaining in skill and competency along the way.

Shannon also had practical experience in home construction, having undertaken a major renovation project in her Connecticut home prior to our relationship. Working hard to remove existing walls, open up two bedrooms into one, and renovate a master bath, she also had a do-it-yourself attitude, and had been looking forward to working through many of the sweat equity projects we had anticipated in our own home. Our surprise pregnancy had definitely changed our capacity to complete all those projects, and her disappointment at being left out of many of the early projects was matched by my anxiety of losing half of our two-person workforce.

December 16th was day one of our sweat equity involvement in the construction of our home. From my perspective, it was a comical and painful disaster, however, through the show producer's lens, it was "great television." I had taken the previous day off from work and done a walkthrough of the home, taking measurements (though most were committed to memory at this point). I went on the first of dozens of trips to the local Lowe's to purchase supplies, this time for the installation of audiovisual and data cabling. In addition, I bought some new tools—including my first laser level—which would later provide a rather comical moment for the cameras when it was revealed to Shannon for the first time. I was so excited that night I could barely sleep, and could not wait to arrive at the job site the next morning to begin work.

The camera crew was waiting for me when I arrived the next morning, and before I could get to work I had a quick interview to walk the viewers through the tasks of the day. Once that was done, it was time to start installing conduit and wall boxes, and pulling audiovisual cables. I began in our master suite, punching out pre-cut knockout holes in the wooden I-beams. I realized pretty quickly that not only had I completely underestimated the enormity of the tasks, but that having a camera pointed at me for the majority of the projects was going to be one of the most annoying aspects of the whole experience.

Most of my home improvement projects over the years had been completed in relative isolation, as I typically preferred working alone so I could contemplate different options, move through some trial-and-error tests, and make decisions quickly. Now I found myself having to take frequent breaks to explain what task I was about to tackle, how much each supply and tool cost, and what was likely to go wrong. Then the crew would move into place while I waited for them to frame the shot, then I would commence. After about five hours of trying to work in this fashion, I told the crew they just had to keep up and capture me in real-time. Moving through the next several months in that manner would have easily added 25% more time to my already over-committed time frame, not to mention the physical threat to the crew's safety from my inevitable temper tantrums. They took the news in stride, understanding that they did not really have a choice; I believe they also understood they were likely to get more realistic footage this way.

The follies of the day included a smashed thumb, a gash in the back of my leg from a still-spinning drill, a few falls from the ladder, and a twisted ankle. Most were actually filmed in real time.

While I fumbled around inside, the painters arrived and began work on the siding. I went outside to have a look at their technique, expecting to see a couple articulated bucket lifts taking the painters up to the upper reaches of the house. I was stunned to see a painter carrying a paint bucket in one hand and a brush in his teeth, scurrying up a fifty-foot ladder. This fellow shot up that ladder without a care in the world, standing near the top without any sort of safety gear in place, painting away. I decided to head back inside, embarrassed, knowing he would spend the entire day on that ladder without incurring a scratch, while I had managed to stick a drill bit in my leg standing on the third rung.

By the end of the day the crew had captured some great footage, and though I was a physical mess, I had managed to install all of the home theater conduit and wiring in the master suite, as well as half of the security system video and power cables, plus some other data and video cables. Though the day had gotten off to a rough start, I settled into a good groove by late afternoon, and the crew had worked out their strategies as well. By the time they left I was still going strong, and worked well into the evening. I decided that no matter how tired I was, I would keep an accurate journal of each day's tasks, a daily and running tally of hours worked, plus progress photos. When I got home late that night, I quickly created a blog entry and downloaded the photos. Including the planning hours from the previous day and the fourteen hours I had just completed, twenty hours had been already been spent; the tally would be over one thousand by that time the following year.

Early the next morning I was back on the site, installing subwoofers in the music loft floor for the main tasting room PA system. George was on-hand solo to capture the action. The subwoofers were actually designed to fit between the floor joists with the speaker cone pointing up through the floor, and had to be installed upwards from underneath. I was standing atop some scaffolding, trying to hold the speaker up while screwing in a support bracket. The screw gun slipped off the screw head and the bit tore right through my left thumbnail, the same one I had smashed with the hammer the previous day. In a fit of searing pain, I launched the screw gun, and George barely got his head out of the way in time to avoid a broken nose. It went right down the basement stairs, bounced across the floor, and skidded to a stop about twenty feet down the hall. George chided, "Nice distance..." as I clutched my mangled thumb and counted the stars I was seeing. After a few minutes, I regained my senses, climbed down from the scaffolding, and found the first aid kit. Once the thumb had been tended to, I went down to the basement, recovered the drill, and went right back up the scaffolding to where I had left off.

It is hard to describe the working conditions; it was like working in a silent, deserted refrigerator. The house had no power yet, and my only source of electricity was a temporary circuit box installed on the power pole in front of the house. I ran long extension cords in through the front door. Out of that I ran two work lights, which I would reposition around the house depending on where I was working. Being the middle of December, it was usually in the twenties and thirties inside the house, and when George left, I was completely alone, working in the cold. In a pitiful attempt to enjoy what holiday spirit I could, I had a portable CD player and a few Christmas CDs that I would play as I pulled cable around the house. That was another miserable aspect of the sweat equity process; whenever the camera was rolling we had to turn off all the radios, because the producers refused to pay any music licensing royalties; not only was it cold and dim, it was also eerily silent. The best part about having the television crew depart for the day was firing up the music and elevating the mood.

The following Saturday, December 23rd, I was back on site very early in the morning. The painters had been very busy during the week, and the entire house had been stained with the exception of the rear dormers. The HVAC team had also been busy during the week, installing a lot of duct work. In addition, the plumber had begun running supply lines throughout the basement. I spent some time reviewing their work, impressed at the evident attention to detail. I enjoyed an injury-free, productive day, installing several runs of conduit between the master suite and the electronics hub near the bar on the main floor. I ran several thousand feet of video and data cables as well.

Since we were so tied up with the construction, our careers, and Shannon's pregnancy, we had decided several weeks earlier that there would be no Christmas decorations this year. Not that we had anywhere to put them, since the rental house was filled to the eaves with audiovisual equipment, tools, and construction supplies. Still, with the following day being Christmas Eve, I just could not accept waking up on Christmas morning without a tree. Though Tristan was just eighteen months old, he was old enough to appreciate the thrill of seeing presents under a tree. Looking at the clock, I realized I would barely make it into town in time to buy a tree before the lots closed for the season. Hurrying into Purcellville, I was devastated to find the only place in town with any trees left had already closed for the day. Not to be denied, I cut down and loaded a tree into my truck, and slipped twenty dollars through the mail slot.

I had no idea where to even begin looking for our tree lights, so I quickly swung by Nichol's hardware store, a historical institution in town. Just as they were turning the "open" sign to "closed," I squeezed through the door, asking if they had any decorations left. Grabbing two strands of lights and a couple boxes of glass balls, I paid the clerk and made my way home. Luckily, the tree stand was sitting on a shelf, and Shannon was delighted. The thought of no tree for our baby boy hadn't been sitting well with her either.

We enjoyed a peaceful Christmas Eve with family, and settled into bed late that evening, Tristan snuggled up between us. On Christmas morning, he awoke early and we told him that Santa had come during the night. He shot into his bedroom where we had placed the tree, and squealed with delight when he saw the presents. Shannon and I were both so exhausted we could barely shuffle across the tiny house, but seeing his little face light up is one of our fondest memories of that time. Sipping coffee, watching him open his gifts, we both dreamed of all the big family Christmases that were yet to come in our new home—little ones gathered around the tree, overlooking the vineyard.

Later, we headed over to my mom's place to spend the afternoon with family. One of the high points of the day was handing everybody their very own first bottle of Notaviva Vineyards wine, our Viognier that I had bottled a week earlier one evening at the shack. In addition to the wine, Shannon had made some Cabernet Franc jelly, and both the wine and the jelly had branded labels that I had printed up and affixed. We had a laugh as we opened up a jar of jelly. Shannon had used a normal table grape jelly recipe, however the amounts of pectin (much less) and sugar (much more) in winegrapes prevented the jelly from completely firming. Who knew? Though it was more the consistency of super-heavy syrup, it was absolutely delicious, and we emptied the jar in no time.

We had decided to let everyone know the baby's name by way of our family Christmas card. It occurred to me that we had a complete John Deere family we could use to represent ourselves. The big tractor would be me, the riding mower would be Shannon, Tristan's little riding tractor would be him, and a small toy tractor sitting atop the riding mower would be the baby. I staged the photo by moving the machines into place in the vineyard. Using photo-editing software, I was able to retouch the shot and add in a "zoom" bubble so people could see the small toy on the riding mower. Inside the card, it simply read, "Happy Holidays from Stephen, Shannon & Tristan (and introducing Duncan Gregor!)."

We slept in the next morning, had a big breakfast, and then I made my way over to the site to put in a full day pulling more video and data cable bundles. In addition, I installed the five-wire HDTV cabling from the electronics closet out to the two flat-panel televisions on either side of the tasting room. George was on-hand solo to capture some footage, and we got some really cool shots of me working late into the evening. At one point, George actually set up outside the house, filming through the windows at me pulling cable in the tasting room. Since the big picture windows still had their protective plastic film affixed, it gave this eerie blurred glowing effect as I moved back and forth in front of my single work light. By 9:00 P.M., we had both had enough and decided to call it a day.

The next three days were spent in the office, making preparations for a show that would be happening while I was away on paternity leave. I was working hard to ensure that every aspect that could be planned out in advance was detailed and transferred to the team that would be on site. These days were long, with early starts and late evenings, though the holiday break made the commute much more bearable.

Saturday, December 30th, was only a half-day of construction, since our extended family holiday party was being held that afternoon. Not having the luxury of a day off, I did some quick framing and drywall work in order to mount the network hub panels for the video and data connections. I went home, took a quick shower, and loaded Tristan and a few gifts into the truck. Poor Shannon was really having a hard time getting around now. The weight of the baby, plus the aggravation of heavy winter clothing and coats, had made travelling around very cumbersome. Once we were at my cousin's place, Shannon quickly settled into the couch to enjoy the day, and I chased Tristan around.

These holiday parties have been a family tradition for as long as I can remember. My family, Grandma and Grandpa, Aunt Gin and all of her kids (my five cousins), plus associated boyfriends and girlfriends, close child and adult friends, and on and on would turn into a gathering of nearly fifty people. Squeezed into our house or Aunt Gin's house on alternating years, these parties started in mid-afternoon and often culminated at midnight mass. As my siblings, cousins, and I grew and started families of our own, the gatherings grew as well, and moved to my cousin Julie's place in nearby Purcellville. It was one of our most cherished days of the year, and was easily the most visible hourglass of our generational transition. Seeing the younger cousins grow from babies to kids, while watching our parents get a "little better" each year was like adding a page to a holiday memory album that we put on the shelf for a year, only to dust off next season.

I clearly remember staring out the living room window in anticipation of Gram's arrival when I was little, knowing that the entire trunk and backseat would be stuffed with presents for all the grandchildren. Seeing them pull in front of the house, we would rush out and meet them at the car. Gram would have her scarf tied neatly about her head to ensure her hair would not get blown out of place on the walk up the driveway, and Grandpa would be left to shuttle the bags of presents into the house, with his little elves trying to catch a glimpse of the name on each present. On this day, so many years later, I could not help but think about Gram as my mom pulled up and we helped her unload her truck full of presents for all of the little ones.

The following day was New Year's Eve, and for me was just another day at the construction site. We had already decided that we were too burned out (and too pregnant) to attempt making it to any kind of party that night. Our plan was to try our best to simply stay awake until the ball dropped, though that was really a stretch goal.

Although the day was productive, I was so completely exhausted it was hard to feel good about the progress. I had spent the entire day working up in the music loft, and since neither the catwalk nor the loft had staircases installed yet, I must have made about fifty trips up and down two ladders, several times carrying tools. I had worked well into the evening, and it was pitch black outside, as the nearly full moon was hidden behind the clouds. I was missing Shannon and Tristan terribly, and felt bad that another day had gone by leaving them on their own. I knew how much trouble Shannon was having getting around, and at eighteen months old, Tristan was an absolute busy body.

Feeling completely dejected, I knew it was time to head home to enjoy a few hours of family time before the ball dropped and we rang in 2007. Looking out the window, I could see the valley begin to brighten as the clouds parted. As I unplugged the second of my two work lights, throwing the house into total darkness, I experienced one of the most magical moments of my life.

There, on the floor of the kitchen, was a glowing white star. Puzzled, I looked up, and lo and behold, the moon was shining through the star window, casting this shape into the house. For the next half hour, I watched the star slowly drift across the floor, moving out toward the tasting room as the moon rose high above the valley. I simply could not believe this was happening.

We all have moments in our lives when we are shown a sign, and it is up to us to ensure our minds and our hearts are open enough to accept the truth and beauty of such a gift. I knew my grandmother was shining down on me through her memorial window, watching over me as I worked late into the night. It was pure chance that our house faces due east; we pointed it in that direction because we liked the view. The star window was a last minute decision, and almost did not happen due to complexity and cost. Why was I working late on New Year's Eve, when I should have been home with my wife and son, on a night with a nearly full moon?

It is easy for pessimists to pass these off as happenstance; perhaps that is all they are. Just maybe, however, it is possible to wonder what truly is the deeper meaning of each of our lives. The impact that Gram had on everyone that knew her was palpable. She never had a bad word to say about anybody, and outwardly loved each of us with an honesty that was utterly genuine. You simply just felt better for spending a few moments with her, and you could see in her eyes she cherished every second. Such a love never dies; it follows you through life, guiding you and protecting you. It is that love, shown to me that night, which has helped keep me on this path.

If you really want to live forever, love deeply and unreservedly. Show it through good times when it is easy, and show it even more during challenging times when it is difficult. That kind of uninhibited love will inspire and endure long after you are gone.

Love is the only sweat equity that lasts.

CHAPTER 24
"Taking a Baby Break"

I completely subscribe to the theory that unborn babies are fully in tune with their mother's physiological and emotional states. It seems sensible to me that the external and internal stresses affecting a pregnant woman's state of mind, hormones, and metabolism would naturally impact the baby, during the time they are physically connected as well as the months beyond. It was no wonder, then, that Duncan Gregor Mackey would be born with an anxious look on his face, an unsettled tummy, and sleepless nights for the first six months of his life.

On New Year's Day 2007, I was back out on the job site after sleeping in and enjoying a big breakfast with Shannon and Tristan. She had reached the point that most women do at the end of their pregnancy, when they just want it over. She was so big, much bigger than she had been with Tristan, and he was born at nine pounds eight ounces, so she was already preparing herself for an even bigger baby boy coming in a couple weeks. She was having regular weekly visits with the midwives, and they had determined that she was experiencing polyhydramnios, a medical condition indicative of an excess of amniotic fluid.

Even though I was able to sleep in that morning, I still awoke feeling completely exhausted. I could not even remember the last time that I felt rested, and the nagging pain in my joints was becoming very problematic. Most mornings I needed to pull myself out of bed using the bedpost, and the joints in my legs took nearly an hour to loosen up before the pain went away. I just upped my dosage of anti-inflammatory pills and attributed it all to the ongoing sweat equity projects and lack of proper rest.

I spent eight hours on the site repairing the floor that was cut for the subwoofer, installing more audiovisual conduit between the electronics room and the music loft, and installing another cabling bundle. I called it quits in order to make it home by early evening, and Shannon had somehow found the energy to make us dinner.

The next day we were back in the office; things had become so challenging for Shannon that the midwives directed her to work from home until Duncan arrived. I dropped Tristan off at daycare to give her the peace and quiet she needed to focus on her contract reviews and business development tasks, and she was able to stay on top of her job while avoiding moving around too much.

On Wednesday, January 3rd, I stopped by the site to review the exterior painting and was disappointed to discover an error made by the painters. It seems they had ordered two different kinds of stain, and now the front and back were a different finish than the two sides. Apparently someone bought a batch of acrylic-based semi-transparent stain, and another person bought a batch of oil-based semi-transparent stain, and now the house was completely mismatched. I pointed out the issue to Richard and he called the owner of the painting company out for an inspection. Sure enough, the owner saw the issue and assured us they would rectify the situation at their own cost. Two days later, they had me review a small test area where they had re-applied the oil-based stain on top of the previous application, and the transparencies now matched up. I agreed that this would be an acceptable fix, and they painters were scrambling up their fifty-foot ladders as I headed off to the office.

On Saturday the 6th, I arrived on the site early in the morning to review the work done that week by the subcontractors. The HGTV crew was on hand to do the walkthrough with me. I was very pleased with the work that had been accomplished, and after fidgeting through what seemed like an endless array of questions for the camera, I was finally able to get to work.

Prior to installing the fireplace in our master suite, I had installed a grand total of zero fireplaces. I had downloaded and read all the installation manuals from the Heat & Glo website and figured it really did not look all that complicated. The challenge as I could see it was not installing the fireplace, but rather the ductwork for the exterior vent. Shannon was more than a little suspicious about this operation; she feared any leaks in the ductwork would allow exhaust gases to enter the bedroom. I figured I could pack enough sealant into each joint to make the installation completely safe and leak-proof. Of course, the television crew loved the tension, and filmed the entire installation.

After the fireplace was installed, and measurements taken for the ductwork, it was back to the audiovisual and security camera cabling installation. I had a horrible time installing the front porch security cameras, as I had to use a six-foot long drill bit to snake the cabling back into the house through several joists. Seriously, it took me over two hours to drill a few holes and feed the cable through, and as if that was not stressful enough, I had to work in front of the camera the whole time. By the time I finally got it installed, I was ready to smash the drill, the security camera, the television camera, and the next person who asked, "That looked like it was harder than you expected, can you tell me about it...?"

By that point, the crew could sense the danger they were in and scooted off to lunch; the film crew would pay Shannon a visit at the rental shack to capture some footage of her and Tristan. Shannon got her microphone on and answered the usual barrage of questions, describing the last days of her pregnancy, the challenges of chasing Tristan around, and the misery of living in an over-crowded rental shack. Though we were now in the sweat equity phase and each day I headed to the job site meant another box was leaving with me, it was still a complete disaster inside that place. In fact, it was hard for George to even get some of the shots, because there was nowhere to stand.

The sad thing about many of these interviews was how clearly it was conveyed that neither Shannon nor I were as completely tuned into this pregnancy as we had been with Tristan. Although her first pregnancy was rife with major life changes as well, those paled in comparison to the issues we were faced with during the last months before Duncan's arrival. There was no sense of preparing the home for the arrival of our new baby. Everything was in damage control mode, and we were just struggling to keep our heads above water. Although she tried hard to voice a positive outlook during these interviews, the strain and exhaustion were evident in her face, and it showed for the camera.

The following day I installed cabling for the security system. Since the exterior cameras were positioned high above the ground overlooking the rear and sides of the house, Ron allowed me to use his all-terrain man lift. I drove it around the house and positioned the bucket. Since I could not drive from the bucket, I had to put it into position, go into the house, and climb out a window into the bucket to get myself in place to do the work. The camera crew was now completely convinced that I had something wrong inside my head, but the work had to get done, and I had limited time to make it happen.

The next two days at the office were long and arduous, preparing for the show that would happen while we were home with Duncan, as well as four more events coming up in February and March. Working on scenic design, drafting audiovisual RFPs, evaluating proposals, coordinating crew travel, negotiating deals, and keeping the creative team engaged in the office kept me busy late into the evenings. I was now taking eight hundred milligrams of an anti-inflammatory three times every day to combat the physical toll I was inflicting on my body, which was beginning to cause me chronic stomach discomfort. I was terribly worried about Shannon, Tristan, and the baby, and had to manage it all on top of coordinating schedules with the subcontractors and television crew.

I took Wednesday, January 10th, off from work in order to be on site for the delivery and installation of our large propane tank in the front yard. I completed the installation of the fireplace ductwork, and sealed (and sealed and sealed) the joints. I was anxious to hear from Shannon, who had gone to her weekly appointment with the midwives. Although Duncan's due date was still a week away, I had trouble believing he was going to wait that long, given Shannon's size.

She called me around lunchtime and was crying and laughing with excitement. Due to her polyhydramnios and estimated birth weight, Paula had decided to break her water the next morning. Duncan was coming! I was overcome by emotion and exhaustion and wished I had been holding her in my arms. I promised to get home as quickly as I could so we could get some rest and get completely prepared for the day.

I quickly called Ron and told him the news. I had conferred with him some weeks earlier, and had decided that on the day Shannon went into labor, all work would cease on the house. Shannon and I wanted total focus on this baby, and felt we needed everyone's assurance that there would be only one thing happening in our lives on that day. Ron agreed, and began calling the subcontractors to advise them of the schedule change. I then called a meeting with the television crew and we began to discuss the plan for the following morning. We had known for some time that the crew wanted to capture footage of us leaving for the Birthing Inn, and now that we had a day's notice, it actually made scheduling the crew much easier.

Paula wanted Shannon to check in at 8:00 A.M., so we decided they would arrive at the rental at 6:00 A.M. to film us getting into our truck and driving away. We dropped Tristan off at my mom's house, and made our way to the Birthing Inn. As we approached the hospital, we paused and let the crew get into place to capture a shot of us driving up. We had requested and were granted permission to film inside the telemetry room, but no medical procedures could be taped. We had no intention of allowing any personal moments to be filmed, and the crew was completely respectful. In many ways, they had become like our extended family, and we could see the joy in their eyes as they got a few shots of Paula discussing the plan with Shannon. Once it was time to begin, they took one last shot from the hallway as I closed the door. We all hugged and they wished us well, and I assured them I would call as soon as I was able.

At 9:40 A.M., Paula broke Shannon's water, and she was on her way. By 10:00 A.M. we were up and moving, walking the halls. As with Tristan, I had snuck in some sports drinks and fresh fruit so Shannon could have some small snacks while she still had an appetite. At 11:00 A.M., she was hit with her first really big contraction.

At noon, Paula checked her and was amazed at how quickly things were progressing. Shannon decided to spend some time on the yoga ball, propping it on the bed and leaning over it to take some pressure off her lower back. By 2:30 P.M., she told us she needed to get into the tub. By 3:45 P.M., we saw the telltale signs that she was in transition. At 4:15 P.M., we got her into bed and onto her side. Four big pushes, and Duncan Gregor Mackey was born, 10 pounds 6 ounces, 22 inches long with a 15 inch head and 14-½ inch chest, at 4:35 P.M. on January 11th, 2007. He just missed Paula's record by two ounces, and as with Tristan, Shannon did not have so much as an aspirin the entire delivery.

Paula laid Duncan on Shannon's chest and we hugged and cried together while looking at this amazing, enormous baby boy. To this day, we laugh when we look at pictures of his foot card; the first foot they stamped hung off the edge, so the second one was stamped diagonally to fit on the paper. Once all the "weights and measures" procedures were complete, they gave him a quick wipe-down, wrapped him up like a burrito, and popped a hat on him, then gave him back to Shannon. All at once, she was overcome with emotion and burst into tears as she held our new baby boy. In no time, both grandmothers swooped in for a proper inspection, just about bumping foreheads as they leant in to get a look at "Moose," as the nurses had dubbed him. We spent the next hour with family as they all took turns holding Duncan.

George, Pam, and field producer Clai Lashley stopped by after breakfast the next day, and amidst hugs and tears, got to meet the new star of the show. He was great on camera, just cuddling and yawning, a natural born talent. Unbeknownst to us, that morning, before coming out to the Birthing Inn, George had stopped by the construction site to film the sun coming up over the mountain. The editors used that shot to create a beautiful transition, showing the peace and serenity of our home site covered in a silent dusting of snow, along with the metaphor of a new beginning. We were so in love with this new baby and his very proud and curious big brother, but in the back of both our minds we knew that the next few months would be the most trying of all. As if it had not been difficult enough up to this point, now we had a newborn in the mix.

As we lay there late that night cuddling Duncan, we talked out the last phase of the construction and how hard it would be on everyone, perhaps our boys most of all. To prove to us he was listening and understanding, Duncan started screaming and then threw up. Looking down at Shannon holding our newborn baby boy, I felt like I was going to do the same.

CHAPTER 25

"Long Cold Winter"

Not only did we feel like we had missed the joy and anticipation of Shannon's pregnancy, we now felt like we were missing the most precious times with a newborn, those first few weeks at home. There would be no time for sleeping in, no time for lazy afternoons cuddling with the baby, and no time curled up on the couch watching movies and eating ice cream. Duncan had arrived; he and Shannon were healthy and safe, and it was time to get back to work.

At three days old, Duncan made his first visit to the construction site so Shannon and I could assess the progress the crew made. We had known for weeks now that my sweat equity tasks were intertwined with the tasks and progress of the subcontractors, so I resolved to be back on the site the next day to continue installing cable bundles. On January 15th, I put in a couple hours of time to keep on schedule, and headed back to the rental shack to spend time with family and friends who were visiting Duncan.

Now that the baby was here and we could get our heads totally focused on the construction project, we realized that we were in very serious danger of not finishing the house by the one-year deadline that the bank had stipulated at closing. We had less than four months left on our construction loan, by which time we needed to have our certificate of occupancy (CO). Analyzing all the remaining aspects of construction, plumbing, electrical, drywall, painting, floors, appliances, and landscaping, it felt like we had to complete two-thirds of the entire project in one-third of the project timeline. Feeling that pressure, with the exhaustion of tending to a new baby and an eighteen-month old and knowing I had to be back in the office in a few days, was really taking a toll on me.

The following day, January 16th, I was on site before the subcontractors arrived. Roger and Bev were in town visiting the baby, and Shannon brought them over so they could check out the construction. The film crew captured their whole visit, and it was invigorating to see their reaction to all the progress we had made since their last visit.

January 17th was my last day of paternity leave, and I was determined to enjoy a few fleeting moments at home with Shannon and the boys, as well as our family and friends who were stopping by. Tired beyond belief, we tried our best not to talk about the project plan and the challenges of the coming months, but that was proving nearly impossible. The construction was controlling every aspect of our lives, and as we looked ahead over the mountain of work yet to be completed, coupled with busy travel schedules for our upcoming event productions, it began to look more and more like the entire disastrous mess was soon going to implode.

To make matters worse, we were starting to wonder if we had forgotten how to care for a newborn. Even though Duncan was only a week old, it was clear that he had his own unique personality, completely different than Tristan's had been. Every technique that used to work so well with Tristan when he was crying had little (or an adverse) effect on Duncan. We could not figure this new baby out, and he was not able to sleep longer than about ninety minutes at a stretch before his belly started to bother him. He had an anxious look about him all the time, and we felt horrible that our situation might be causing him such distress.

Shannon was amazing as she did her best to deal with the baby while still tending to Tristan. We figured that Duncan's birth would be the perfect opportunity to keep Tristan at home for a few weeks, and then switch him into a daycare closer to our future home. At the time, he was still in daycare in Ashburn, Virginia, completely the wrong direction from our office in Rockville, Maryland. When we would tell people that we did a daycare drop-off in Ashburn, then had to navigate the Capital Beltway on our way to work in Rockville (and then back again in the evenings), they would look at us like we were completely daft. They were so right.

The night before my one-week paternity leave ended, I got two hours of sleep while trying to help Shannon with the baby, answering emails about upcoming shows, and fending off an anxiety attack about the construction progress. Shannon was in an exhausted daze, trying to nurse Duncan in between screaming fits. The rental shack was a complete wreck, with Tristan's toys strewn about and construction materials piled to the ceiling. We were both absolute zombies.

The next day at the office was a blur. We had landed a new client and had a show in less than six weeks in Florida that I was going to produce. While that show was in pre-production, the rest of the team was preparing for an enormous show at the Washington Convention Center that would be occurring the same week in March. It was a first for the growing company, having two major productions happening simultaneously in different cities, with all the associated advance processes taking place in tandem.

Thankfully my paternity leave did not count against vacation time, but I would still have to carefully manage taking time away from the office to work on my sweat equity commitments. Certainly every weekend from now through May would be dedicated to the construction, and if I needed to be on site for a few hours in the morning, then I would have to make up the time by staying late into the evenings.

Saturday, January 20th, I was in the house for ten hours working on the audiovisual and data cabling; it was a peaceful day because there were no subcontractors on hand and no television crew. I was able to actually have my CD player on, and having music playing throughout the house felt wonderful. The following day I was able to complete the last of the cabling installations and was elated to be finished with that phase. It took me over an hour to scour the house for spare parts and tools, which I sorted and stored outside in the shipping container.

On Wednesday, I was working the morning at the job site before heading to the office to work late, and was talking to the head electrician. He asked me when I planned to frame in the tasting bar; since we were not planning on being open to the public for quite some time, I said I planned on tackling that project in the summer. He informed me that was not possible; since the bar had several electrical circuits running through it that were on the approved plans, it would have to be constructed in order for the house to pass inspection. Just like that, a critical new project dropped into my lap.

Late that night I got to work in TurboCAD, the program we used to design scenic pieces and ballroom layouts. We wanted a curved bar to complement the straight lines and mitered corners of the timber frame. I created a 3D plan for the tasting bar skeleton, which was essentially a series of two-feet by six-feet pieces of lumber standing on end, each ten degrees apart from the next around a 180 degree arc. By having each piece fall exactly on ten degree increments, I knew the edges of the braces in between each one would be cut at five degrees on each side. The key to the whole structure, however, would be the subtle curve of the braces. For these, I used TurboCAD to create and print out a life-size template that I would use to custom cut each brace on my band saw.

Saturday, January 27th, I was up early and over at the job site by 8:00 A.M. Yet another sleep-deprived night with little Duncan tucked in between Shannon and me, in an upright vibrating seat that actually seemed to give him some comfort. He was able to sleep for almost three hours at a stretch, which although not great, was still better than where we were the previous week. Friends and family would tell us that their kids were sleeping from 9:00 P.M. until 7:00 A.M. when they were that age. Wonderful, thanks for that tidbit of information; it really helped.

Given the complexity of my tasting bar project and the high likelihood that I was about to make a complete idiot of myself, the HGTV crew was on-hand early to capture all the action. Due to the manner in which I was intending to cut the bracing, I had to bring my band saw over to the job site. I had printed out enough of the paper templates so that I could lay out the entire project before committing to driving nails into the subfloor. When the crew saw the paper templates curving around from one large beam and meeting perfectly on the other side, they were visibly surprised by my CAD and carpentry skills, though equally disappointed that my plan actually worked properly the first time.

Knowing how complex the construction would be, I had invested in a new pancake air compressor and set of nail guns to aid the process. Using a combination of a mitre saw and band saw, I pre-cut all the curved bracing, then cut the series of uprights that would hold up the bar. Beginning at the main kitchen post, I installed two braces and an upright in a continuous sequence, using temporary shims and braces to hold everything in place while continuing around the curve. It was very challenging keeping it all level, but with the extra temporary bracing and several bar clamps, it was really starting to feel very solid. After putting in a ten-hour day, I decided to call it quits to head home for the evening. The television crew had called it a day around mid-afternoon, and though usually I would fire up the music when they left, for some reason I just wanted some peace and quiet. There was something very satisfying about working on the bar, envisioning the thousands of people who would someday enjoy a glass of wine standing in this very spot, the wonderful family events. It was in those moments of solitude I would find myself rejuvenated and re-inspired, just by pondering the fun times that lay ahead.

The following day I was back on site for another ten-hour workday, and began building out the bar structure from the other side, the intent to have each side meet in the middle, so that even if any adjustments had to be made, it would stay symmetrical. The process went very smoothly.

During the week, the electricians kept moving forward with wire installation, and on Tuesday, January 30th, the HVAC team fired up the furnace. I swung by late that night after work and was thrilled to see that system finally working; over the next few days, we slowly brought up the temperature so the frame could adjust to the change. My hands would definitely not miss working in the sub-freezing temperatures.

After an incredibly busy week at work planning the upcoming shows, I was right back in the house the following weekend to start reinforcing the bathroom floors for tiling. By the end of the day Saturday, both bathrooms were ready for tile, and on Sunday I finished the last of the audiovisual cabling installation for the tasting room televisions. Another weekend gone, another eighteen hours of sweat equity on the books.

The following day, on February 5th, the electricians finished roughing-in all the remaining wire, and the next day we passed our first electrical inspection. Although our first inspection went well, the second one did not, as we failed our preliminary framing inspection. Ron was not concerned in the least, and after the carpenters installed a few more firestops, we passed our framing inspection and were cleared to begin installing the insulation on Monday.

Saturday, February 10th, was another day spent working in the house, but with one significant difference: Shannon was able to join! My mom was watching the boys back at the rental shack, which allowed Shannon to come out and help install additional subflooring in the kitchen. She was thrilled to spend a day working in the house, and the television crew was on hand to capture her return. We completed most of the subfloor installation, and then took a break to have dinner over at my brother's place. The following day was the last of the subfloor installations. Another weekend faded into the past, and another eighteen hours of sweat equity along with it.

Monday, February 12th, the construction crew started and actually finished installing all the insulation in the basement. Since the upper portions of the home were all created from structural insulated panels, they needed no additional insulation. The next day we passed our close-in inspection, and the house was approved to begin drywall installation.

Valentine's Day was a complete disaster on so many levels. The drywall had been scheduled for delivery, but due to ice and snow, the entire job site was inaccessible. Worse, my plans for a Valentine's Day escape were completely derailed. I had thought it would be great idea to surprise Shannon with a romantic getaway package at the Ritz-Carlton in Tyson's Corner, and I had coordinated with my mom to take Tristan for the night so Shannon, Duncan, and I could spend an evening away from it all. Given the nasty weather, I asked Shannon whether we should scrap the plans. She was hesitant, but the thought of getting out of the shack for a night proved too tempting, so we all met at a restaurant adjoining the hotel for dinner.

As my mom and Tristan walked away, Shannon just started crying, terrified of being separated from him in such bad weather. Duncan screamed, nursed, and threw up in thirty-minute intervals throughout the night. I felt lower than dirt that I had dragged everyone into such a disaster. Although she would never say anything, I could tell that Shannon would have been much happier enjoying a movie rental on the couch at home, with the boys tucked safely away from the winter weather.

On Saturday, February 17th, I decided to go ahead and begin tiling the tasting room bathrooms, even though the drywall was not yet installed. Typically you would wait until the walls were done and do the flooring last, but given the continually slipping timelines, I had to go ahead and begin. I was at Home Depot right when it opened to purchase a wet tile saw to speed up the installation of the ceramic tile. Shannon and I headed to the job site to begin tiling while her mom watched the boys. It took a while to get the tile unloaded into the house, which was filmed by the television crew. Once that was done, we all took a break for lunch, then filmed a few sound bites about the state of the project and our anxiety over the schedule.

Finally, it was time to begin laying out the tile to create a cut plan, placing dry tiles on the floor to determine where to begin to ensure the most sensible placement of cuts down the line. After an hour of dry-fitting, I arrived at a strategy for placement. I took the new wet saw out of the box and assembled it while Shannon mixed the tiling mortar. I fired up the saw, and was shocked to hear the incredible racket that came from the motor housing. The unit sounded like someone had filled the motor with gravel. Our brand new saw was completely shot, and our one day together this week working on the house went up in smoke.

Shannon was visibly upset, realizing that she was not going to get to spend any time on actual construction. We packed up the saw, took off our microphones, and bid the crew farewell as we headed back out to Home Depot. They had another unit in stock and happily made the exchange with no questions, but by now it was time to get Shannon home to the boys. I dropped her off and grabbed a quick dinner, then turned right back around to the job site. Arriving there around 7:00 P.M., I assembled the new saw, filled it with water, and turned it on. Even a ship-shape tile saw is deafening, but this unit was obviously in proper working order, with no gravel clogging its innards.

I began tiling the ladies' bathroom. Working late into the night, hoping that the cacophony of the saw would not irritate the neighbors, I was able to finish the entire bathroom by 11:00 P.M. before calling it a day. As the house still did not have the lights installed (just a few working outlets for tools), it was yet another late night with just a couple of work lights. Though not as creepy as being in the house when it was as cold and dark as a closed meat locker, it still felt a little weird unplugging the last light and walking out alone into the icy winter night.

Even though the failure of the tile saw and the unforeseen change of plans had ruined our day together, I somehow felt different, even enlightened. I was starting to feel more resilient, as if each successive debacle that we faced together had less of an impact. It seemed I was able to stay focused, accept the situation at hand, and quickly determine the best course of action to keep the project moving without getting emotional or distracted.

The following day was devoted to audiovisual component installation, the equipment high above the tasting room in the music loft. Ken was on hand to help out with the installation; I believe he was somehow drawn to the more ridiculous projects. The thought of missing the chance to stand atop scaffolding three stories in the air while holding a drop-down projection screen was more than he could take; he had to be there. Since we had heat in the house and there would be no loud noises and sawdust, Shannon brought the boys over to check out the progress, and make sure I had my safety harness on while climbing.

Once the screen was complete, Ken had to head home and our friends Rob and Tonya Klause came by to meet Duncan and bring us lunch, which we enjoyed while our kids played together. It was nerve-wracking, chasing toddlers around a construction zone, trying to keep them from picking up stray nails and finding every splinter in the place. We visited for a while and enjoyed the much-needed social break.

That evening I offloaded my photos and updated the blog, along with my hours. Since mid-December, I had already put in nearly two hundred hours of sweat equity, and knew that several hundred more lay ahead. With our two big productions drawing closer, the pace at work was picking up rapidly and I was working later and later into the evenings.

On Wednesday, February 21st, I stopped by the construction site after work to check out the drywall progress. It was great to see the walls finally coming together in the basement. Outside, the crew had been able to dig the trench from the house to the well, and we were scheduled to have running water in the house within a week. That would be very helpful for the tiling projects, since I had been shuttling water over to the job site in five gallon water jugs to mix mortar and fill the tile saw. We were still using the portable rental toilets outside, delightfully crisp in the sub-freezing temperatures.

On Saturday, February 24th, once the bathroom was finished, I began immediately laying out the tile in the kitchen. It was going to be an incredibly challenging project, since I wanted to lay all the tiles at a forty-five degree angle to the room. Those angles, coupled with the large curve of the tasting bar and the internal bracing, would make for some complex cuts. Given that the tiles we were using were porcelain, they were extremely tough to cut and very hard on the wet saw blade. May as well make everything as complicated as possible, I always say. It took all afternoon just to measure, cut, and install the tiles within the bar curve, and I called it a day late that night.

Returning to the site the next day, I continued along with the kitchen tiling. Progress was incredibly slow, and again I worked well into the evening. Driving back that night, I could not wait to get a hot shower and hopefully play with the boys, if either of them was still awake. Suddenly, along a dark stretch of road, a doe jumped right out in front of me. Though I tried to swerve, it was no use; I hit the deer right in the middle of my front bumper, knocking it underneath the truck. Fearing that someone else would run it over and damage their car, I pulled over, went back, and dragged it off to the side of the road. Definitely not how I had hoped to end the day; as my last night of sweat equity in the month of February drew to a close, I just stood on the side of that dark, cold country road, staring at the stars, wondering how on earth I was going to get this house finished in time.

CHAPTER 26

"Race to the Finish"

March began exactly like February ended, with a series of crises piled upon each other. Saturday the 3rd would be our last day working in the house for almost two weeks, as our two big shows were upon us and it was time to travel. Shannon came off of maternity leave a week early in order to stage manage the event in Key Biscayne that I was producing. Given that she was still nursing, we would have to bring the boys along with us, along with some grandparent support. Roger and Bev agreed to stay the week with us in an adjoining room, so they could watch the boys while we were in the ballroom of the Ritz-Carlton.

I had a serious conversation with Ron and Richard about the project timeline, and about my concerns for getting the occupancy permit by May 9th. They conceded that we were running short on time and agreed to schedule the subcontractors in parallel. We brought in several members of the crew to hang drywall upstairs on a Saturday, while a finisher was working on mud and tape downstairs. The television crew filmed everything, enjoying capturing the mounting tension, knowing that it would make for some great footage.

My mom agreed to watch the boys so Shannon could join me at the house; we had to turn our attention to the vineyard for a few hours. We spent the morning pruning Cabernet Franc vines. After lunch, Shannon began painting some test patches of drywall with our color samples. I continued tiling the kitchen floor, and after painting, she joined me until she had to head home to relieve Mom. Working late into the night, I was able to install the final pieces of kitchen tile.

The following day, Sunday, March 4th, I had to spend the entire day in the office with final preparations for my Miami show. Working on client presentations, guiding production assistants through last-minute details, and sending dozens and dozens of emails to the client and technical crews, it was a full, busy day. By now I was consistently having trouble getting around, as the continual abuse to my muscles and joints was really taking a toll. I simply could not get comfortable in a chair, and if I sat for too long, had great difficulty getting up and moving again. I was actually looking forward to a couple weeks of sixteen-hour days working on the back-to-back shows, so I could take it easy for a while.

While I was at the office, Shannon was home tending to Tristan, who was very sick and needed regular nebulizer treatments. He was so upset due to being sick that he would not let himself go to sleep as long as he knew Shannon was in the house. He could see her through the glass doors to his room, and hear her walking around the house. So in order to let Tristan get some sleep, Shannon took Duncan outside into the truck. As she came back inside to change Duncan, her cell phone rang; it was the delivery truck with all of our appliances, letting her know they would be at the house between 1:00 P.M. and 5:00 P.M. Tristan was not pleased with being woken up from his nap, and screamed the whole ride over to the house to make sure Shannon was aware of his displeasure. The camera crew had been filming Shannon that day, and also followed her over to the house, where Shannon, the two boys, and the three-person crew waited until 4:47 P.M., when the delivery truck finally showed up.

That Tuesday, Shannon and I awoke at 4:00 A.M., packed up the boys, and headed to Reagan National Airport for our trip to Miami. The flight went very smoothly, and once we were safely on the ground, Shannon's spirits lifted immediately. The weather was perfect, and for a few fleeting moments, we were able to leave the worries of the construction project behind us.

The next few days were a blur; everything went superbly, our crew did an amazing job, and the client was thrilled with the results. Roger and Bev brought the boys by to check out the production before rehearsals began, and it was a special moment to have them see what Mommy and Papa do.

Late Friday night, after the show was finished and the crews had completed load-out, we had a wonderful family dinner at the hotel restaurant. Shannon and I were able to live in the moment for a much-needed recharge. Holding hands and watching the boys making friends with adjoining tables, it dawned on us that this was what the journey was all about. Our endeavors would make possible such incredible, unique opportunities and experiences for our boys. Although we had dreamed about moments like this for years, taking stock of that moment was very inspirational. Our love for each other and for these two amazing little boys reignited our commitment, and we knew without saying a word that no matter what might lie ahead between then and May 9th, we would overcome. We knew we would not fail.

Arriving back at Reagan National the next afternoon, Shannon and the boys headed back to the rental shack, while I stayed in Washington, D.C. to join the rest of the team at the Washington Convention Center for the next several days. The next day, Shannon and her mom pruned the one-year old Viognier vines that we had planted the previous spring, while my mom watched the boys. Shannon felt sad; the next day was the first day of daycare. It would be her first back in the office, looking ahead to the next several productions coming later in the spring.

The Washington show was a resounding success. Shannon and I immediately dove back into construction mode, and were on site early the morning of Saturday, March 17th. Shannon began applying primer to the ceilings of the bathrooms, bedrooms, and hallway. I laid the tile in the boys' bathroom. The television crew was on hand to film everything, and everyone was in good spirits, telling jokes and making each other laugh. Once the boys' bathroom was complete, I moved the wet saw into our bedroom and began laying the tile in our bathroom. After several frustrating failures with the tile nibbler, I got so irritated I removed the guard from the tile saw and used the side of the blade, my bare fingers just a few millimeters from the spinning blade. The television crew was just waiting to see a finger come flying off. Of course, right in the middle of this debacle, in walks Shannon; realizing that it was hopeless to say anything resembling good sense, she just turned around and went back to painting.

The following day I completed the floor tiling in the master bathroom, and my friend Brian Korte stopped by for a few hours to help out. We enjoyed catching up, and after I showed him around for a bit, he pitched in and applied some more primer in the rest of the hallway and the downstairs kitchenette. I actually left for the day by early afternoon, as Shannon and I were taking my mom out to a concert as a thank you for all the babysitting she had done over the past months. We went to an amazing local venue, the Barns at Wolf Trap, to see George Winston perform. We all had a wonderful time.

It was that evening that I began to think about my earliest memories with my grandmother, and I wondered which moment in the years ahead would be Tristan's or Duncan's first memory of theirs. I found myself pondering our successive generations, and the influence that each one has upon the next. What would be my grandchildren's first memory of Shannon and me? What would their first memory be of Notaviva Vineyards? Something was changing inside me, and though I could not put my finger on it, I knew it was real, it was significant, and it was happening fast.

Four days later, on March 22nd, I began using my saved vacation time to work on the house. I was not checked out from work—quite the opposite. Our next big show was just three weeks away in Houston, and the advance work was in full swing. In order for me to make it all happen, we had to have our Internet installed at the vineyard, so I could stay abreast of emails during the day while taking breaks from construction.

It was incredible being on site during the week! I had gotten used to working at night and on the weekends, usually by myself. The house was now abuzz with activity, and members of the crew were everywhere. The painters were working in the catwalk and loft areas, and the carpenters were hanging doors and installing trim in the basement. Ron and Trevor were outside using the Bobcat to install huge landscape boulders, and it seemed like everyone needed me to answer questions. By the end of the day, I had sorted out dozens of issues for everyone, both at the house and the office, and had actually managed to hang several pieces of backer board for the wall tile in the master bathroom. It was a great day, and even though I knew I was going to be sore and miserable the following morning it felt good to see all the progress.

Two days later, Shannon surprised me with a wonderful treat; she dressed both boys up in their matching Virginia Tech Hokies sweat suits. We played in the living room for a while and took some adorable family photos. It was the perfect way to lift my mood, as I was really feeling the strain of being away from the boys so often. After such a beautiful morning it was very hard to leave, but I had to get back over to the house. I was able to make great progress on several fronts, completing the grout for the boys' bathroom floor, installing the base cove in the master bathroom, and grouting the kitchen floor. All that kneeling and standing and running up and down stairs made for a miserable evening and even worse morning, but after Shannon made a big breakfast, we both headed back to the house while my mom settled in with the boys.

I got right back to tiling, and through the morning I was able to finish the wall tile in the boys' bathroom. In my exhausted state I was not thinking so clearly, and when I showed Shannon the finished tile, she gently pointed out that I had forgotten to install the soap dish and towel rack. Thank goodness she caught that, as the mastic had not yet set up, and I was able to remove a few tiles, make the cuts, and install the other pieces without too much trouble. Shannon was applying more primer around the basement, and after we took a break for lunch, we both went out to the vineyard to run trellis wire in the new

Viognier block for the rest of the afternoon. Being outside together have always been some of the most special times we have shared; working the land with someone you love connects you in a unique way. It is real and tangible, and knowing that each young vine could be with us for decades to come gives us a true sense of fulfillment. The afternoon passed by far too quickly, and though we were sad to leave the land, we were eager to get home and get our hands on the boys.

Shannon and I had been analyzing our construction budget, and had come to the realization that we were still within the extra amount that the bank had allotted for the project. We felt we had a good handle on the expenses that we would incur over the next two months as the project neared completion, and decided to commit some of the excess loan to the construction of a winery building.

Early on in our planning, we had attended several log and timber frame home shows, and had become acquainted with Conestoga builders, who specialize in pole barns and metal buildings. I reached out to them in early March to discuss the project, and they indicated they could begin construction by the end of the month. We budgeted $40,000 for the building, which we would roll into the mortgage. For that money, Conestoga could build the shell of the 1400 square foot building, and install the slab inside so that it could be used for storage upon completion. Although we did not feel we had enough money to install electricity, water, and insulation in the building, we knew that we had to take this opportunity to get it erected, and that we would outfit it for winery operations at some point in the future.

As we were discussing the winery with Conestoga, we were also discussing the site preparation with Ron, since we actually did not have an area to put the building. Ron was happy to help building up the pad. As it turned out, he had a friend in the business that was in the process of excavating a road in nearby Leesburg, and needed a place to dump a large amount of rock and fill dirt. We ended up with about thirty dump trucks of red shale rock and clay fill dirt.

On Tuesday, March 27th, I was again using vacation time to work on the house, and while Trevor was outside moving dirt from the dump trucks onto the winery pad, I was inside grouting. Incredibly, the electricians also decided to show up, and were switching and plugging in the basement and connecting circuit breakers into the fuse box. Since the house was so big, we had two separate 200 amp panels that all needed to be connected. Knowing quite a bit about electrical installation from my audio days with Clair Brothers, I simply did not feel that they had an appropriate sense of urgency about their work, and it was making me very nervous. Upstairs, however, Vernon and Tim were making great progress installing trim in the tasting room, and seeing the perfection of their trim work made me feel like a complete hack. That said, they were very complimentary of the tile work as well as the complexity of the bar structure, which made me feel pretty awesome.

Two days later, both Shannon and I were on site for the entire day, and began the morning by cleaning the basement in preparation for the flooring installation. It was definitely not a fun task, given the amount of drywall mud, construction adhesive, dirt, and debris that was scattered everywhere. Since the carpet was going to be coming in soon, we had to get each of the boy's bedrooms cleaned out, though we were hoping to get each one painted before the installers arrived.

Trevor had completed the work on the winery pad the previous day, and Conestoga arrived in the morning to drop off all of their building materials. They were set to begin drilling holes for the installation of the winery the following day. It was a bit overwhelming to see how quickly everything moved. The only setback was getting a release from the county zoning office, indicating that since it was simply an agricultural building, no additional permits or inspections were required. Conestoga had a policy that prevented them from doing any work until they had a copy of all permits, or a copy of the release. During my first call to the county, I was passed around to several different people in various departments, then incorrectly advised that we needed to provide blueprints and a site plan in order to get our permits, and that we had several other applications to fill out. I told Ron about the call, and he indicated that information was completely incorrect. I called again and got another representative on the phone. After explaining the situation, the representative simply asked, "Is this an agricultural building that will not have any customers inside?" I told him that was correct, and he faxed over a release to Conestoga. We were on our way.

After lunch, Shannon got to work priming the walls in the boys' bedrooms, and I began the installation of the laminate floor in the kitchenette. After quite a few mistakes, I fell into a good rhythm and finished the entire room in a few hours. By dinnertime we called it a day, and headed back to the shack to see the boys.

The next day, our project manager from Conestoga called me at work to advise that the crew was having a terrible time digging the holes for the poles due to the amount of rock in our fill dirt. We discussed the situation (and the fine print in the contract) and it was resolved that we would have to pay another $1,000 for the additional crew and machine time necessary to complete the job. So much for free fill dirt.

Saturday morning began with a road trip up to the Lancaster County Timber Frame shop for a lumber pickup. Since I would be building all the newel posts and railings for the tasting room catwalk, I wanted the lumber to match the timber frame. My plan was to rent a flatbed truck, drive to York, Pennsylvania to get the lumber, return home and unload the Douglas fir, then use the truck to get all the flooring materials from a supply house in nearby Martinsburg, West Virginia.

It was great to see some members of the LCTF crew, whom I filled in on all the progress. Looking at my watch, I realized that time was running short, so I was on my way back to Virginia. Using our master bedroom as a temporary storage location, so as not to clutter up the upstairs as it awaited flooring installation, I moved quickly through the unloading and was off again to the next stop for flooring. Unbelievably, when I arrived at 3:20 P.M., I found the doors locked and the place closed. It turned out the store closed just a few minutes earlier at 3:00 P.M. I could not believe my luck; why did I not think to check their hours while I was planning the day? Dejected, I drove the whole way back to Frederick, Maryland to return the rental flatbed, which I now had to reserve for later in the week.

When I arrived back at the job site late that afternoon, Shannon was finishing up priming the walls in the kitchenette. Since the plan for the day had gone off the rails, I decided to try and make the most of the situation. As Shannon headed back to the rental to relieve my mom and take care of the boys, I began hanging cabinets in the kitchenette.

Having installed hundreds of cabinets during my years working at Tops of the Town, I knew that hanging wall cabinets single-handedly would not be fun. However, using a series of temporary braces in combination with my new (and highly ridiculed) laser level, I was able to get them up without too much difficulty. Once they were all in place, I realized that I was not really happy with the layout, and resolved to discuss moving one of them with Shannon the following morning. Sometimes things that make a lot of sense on paper make no sense at all in the real world. Like starting a winery, building a custom home, raising babies, and filming a television show all at once. Actually, that does not even make sense on paper.

The following day, we swapped out my mom for Shannon's mom to handle babysitting duties, and we both got an early start at the job site. Shannon agreed that one of the kitchenette cabinets had to move, so we took care of that first before moving all the tools—and my beautiful laser level—up to the tasting bar to begin installation of the kitchen cabinets. With Shannon helping, the installation of the first set of wall cabinets went so much more smoothly than in the downstairs, and in a couple of hours, we had one side all hung. The base cabinets, however, would prove to be much more challenging.

Using the laser, I determined that the floor of the tasting bar sloped downward ever so slightly, about a quarter of an inch from one end of the bar to the other. I decided to mount the first cabinet on the high side and then add shims to the rest of the cabinets as I worked my way down along the wall and around the curve of the bar. Beginning with the cabinet next to the refrigerator, I was incredulous when I realized the HVAC crew had placed a floor register right where two cabinets met. I had to custom cut the bottom of the cabinets so that they would fit properly around the angled register. That could have been easily avoided with a quick glance at the blueprint, but such are the challenges of multiple crews working at various times around a home.

Shannon was eager to see how some of the appliances would look once they were set in place, so we unpacked both dishwashers and the dual wine coolers and put them in their positions. Again, we found an HVAC register right where the white wine cooler was supposed to be located, so we had to custom cut some more cabinets and relocate the cooler, but it all worked out in the end. By mid-afternoon, Shannon had to head back to relieve her mom, while I stayed on to place the remaining base cabinets and peninsula.

Working late into the night, I was delirious with exhaustion as I drove home, but I was determined to keep the blog updated with the daily photos and share the progress with our growing number of friends and potential customers. The word had been spreading like wildfire through the local communities and in the media that one of Loudoun's upcoming wineries was under construction, and we had begun to have visitors coming by to check out the progress. In fact, we were having people drop in on Saturdays wondering if they could do a wine tasting! Although we took that as a positive sign of good things to come, and we were still quite some ways off from offering wine tastings to the public, we knew that it was time to start building the buzz about our future plans.

Two days later, after an incredibly busy day in the office preparing for our upcoming Houston show, I was back at the construction site to check out the previous day's progress before heading up to re-rent the flatbed truck. I was thrilled to see that Conestoga had completed not only the installation of the main posts for the walls, but had also installed most of the wall supports as well. By the time I snapped a few progress pictures for the blog, they were already starting on the installation of the roof trusses. We had chosen an attic truss option, a style that would allow for the later installation of an office space high above the floor of the winery. We knew at some point that would come in very handy, as once the winery was up and running, we would need the space for administrative operations.

I arrived at the Lumber Liquidators warehouse by 10:00 A.M. and had a great conversation with the manager about the complexities of the wood we had selected. Several months earlier, Shannon and I had attended the Dulles Home Show, a large expo where construction vendors gather to display their products. As we were walking through, we happened upon a flooring display, where various samples were assembled in a large checkerboard fashion. Right in the middle of the display was the most beautiful section of flooring I had ever seen, a completely unique deep burgundy wood. The representative advised it was called "Bloodwood," and we knew right then that we had found our flooring. Speaking with the manager at the warehouse, I learned that it is one of the most difficult hardwoods to work with, due to its incredibly high density. I had still hoped to install all the hardwood flooring myself, though as we spoke, I began to realize that was looking more and more unlikely. As a backup plan, I got the name and phone number for one of their recommended installers. Packing up, I paid special attention to every strap on that truck; since I had just loaded over $12,000 dollars of flooring, I did not need that spilling out on the road.

When I arrived home, I was even more shocked at Conestoga then when I had left. In the four hours it took me to purchase, load, and return with the flooring, they had completed the installation of the roof trusses. I snapped a few more progress photos, then began the miserable chore of unloading all the flooring. The first part of the truck was not so bad, as I had selected a red oak floor for the gift shop, and each one of those boxes only weighed fifty pounds. After moving all twenty-two boxes, I began the difficult part, unloading the Bloodwood. Due to its incredibly dense structure, each piece weighs twice what a similarly sized piece of red oak would weigh. Given the amount of Bloodwood flooring we were going to install, over 1,800 square feet, I had purchased eighty-four boxes to ensure enough overage, all of which had to be distributed over the three stories of the tasting room. I knew I was in for a rough time.

I began taking boxes up to the music loft, then up to the catwalk; after the first twenty boxes, the first ton of flooring, I was beginning to tire quickly. By this point, George, who had been filming the entire debacle, could not take it anymore, and put his camera in the case and began to carry the boxes with me. We got several more unloaded, and then I realized that a few of the Conestoga crew were still putting their tools away down at the winery site. I ran down to meet them and asked if anybody was interested in making a quick $100. My offer was well received, and in under an hour, we had the rest of the truck unloaded and the flooring stored safely inside the house. It was all I could do to make the forty-minute drive back to Frederick to return the flatbed before returning home to Shannon and the boys for some quiet time before getting some sleep in anticipation of a long day at the office.

The next Saturday dawned a beautiful spring day, and I took advantage of the weather to tackle some vineyard tasks. I spent most of the day running catch wires along the trellis, and then nailing the fencing staples in place to hold them. The trick with the curved fencing staples is not to bang them in too tight, otherwise the catch wires will not be able to slide through them freely as the tensioners are tightened, and also as the vine canopy blows in the wind and the trellis wires expand and contract throughout the seasons. Once I ran out of wire, I decided to head back into the house to continue installing cabinets.

Sunday, April 8th, we returned to the music loft to complete the installation of the audiovisual equipment. Finishing up the speaker installation, I began working on the LED stage lights. For future upgrade purposes, I installed a few extra runs of control cable, which would allow us to eventually control each lighting instrument's color from a remote console. Although sound guys typically do not do lights, I thought it was coming along pretty well. Shannon joined me for the afternoon and brushed off her audio engineer skills, assembling the Neutrik speaker connectors required to attach the cabling from the amplifiers to the hanging speakers. By the time we called it a day and headed back to the shack, we had crossed over the 400 hour mark of sweat equity.

With our Houston show approaching, I had more and more tasks to complete and meetings to attend in order to ensure the show was coming together properly. Staying late at the office both Monday and Tuesday nights, I wondered while driving home why I did not just set up a cot in my office and sleep there. In my physically exhausted and sleep-deprived state, the extra several hours of sleep would have been welcomed; however, I could never bring myself to spend a night away from Shannon and boys unless it was an absolute necessity. As more and more building materials moved from the shack to the construction site, our rental was actually starting to look like a real place again, and not a storage warehouse.

Wednesday, April 11th, my brother Jim took a day off of work to help me move all the remaining appliances into place and construct a template for the curved countertop. It was a huge help having him work with me to move everything, as I was worried that the heavy appliances would damage the new tile. We started in the kitchen, moving both ovens into place, and then the over-sized refrigerator. Once those were safely in place, we went downstairs to install both sets of stackable washers and dryers. Since the entire building would be supporting both a family and a business, we needed to ensure maximum capacity for all aspects of each. When it was complete, our house would have two ovens with stoves, two refrigerators, two freezers, three dishwashers, two washers, two dryers, four wine coolers, and an icemaker. The appliance bill was staggering.

The following day I was back on site early in the morning to get right into more grouting. I had purchased some used wine barrels that I had cut into custom vanities for the men's and ladies' restrooms in the bar area, and it was time for Fred to install the fixtures. In order to do that, the vanities had to be set, but in order for that to happen, the floors had to be grouted.

People were everywhere, and I enjoyed touring through each room, looking at all of the new items. The house was really showing signs of progress—except for the electricians' tasks, since they had not bothered to show up again. Even though they had installed some lighting fixtures and we were able to use the overheads in a few areas, they still had a long way to go. On the days they did manage to show up, it was just two junior members of the company. It was obvious that all the other trades understood the time crunch and were sending extra crew along, but not so with the electricians. I was furious. I called Ron and told him that if the electricians were not on the job site the next morning, I was firing them, taking the remainder of their allocated funds, and giving it to the first electrician who stepped through the front door. The camera crew was eating it up.

I needed something to lighten my mood, and decided at that very second that it was time to pull all the protective plastic sheeting off of the windows. I was sick of looking at the blurry view through the plastic film, and since all of the window casings had been installed, I figured it could not hurt. What a huge difference that made; the house seemed to instantly transform. Everyone stopped what they were doing and just stared for a minute out the big picture windows that overlooked the vineyard; the view was stunning. It was just the attitude adjustment that I needed, and I was ready to dive into the next task.

Downstairs in the master bedroom, I had set up a workshop to produce the newel posts that would surround the catwalk and music loft. Shannon and I had looked at hundreds of magazines and website design galleries, but one of the elements that eluded us was the design of the catwalk railing. We knew an overly elaborate, Victorian railing style wasn't going to fit the style of the home. The wrought iron railings that caught our eye were far beyond our budget, so eventually I had just decided to make my own. It seemed to me that hand-crafting the newel posts to look like miniature versions of the timber frame posts would be the way to go, and simple black balusters would provide the necessary strength to ensure safety for the boys and customers, without distracting from the appeal of the Douglas fir.

I scratched out a rough design on a piece of paper, using height dimensions based on county code and newel posts available in the stores. Then, referring the style of the posts, I began cutting the first post as a proof of concept. It took quite a while, since I was figuring out the best way to make each cut, but after a few attempts, I found a method that seemed to work well. Taking the first newel post up to the catwalk along with a temporary railing, I installed a few test pieces along with the balusters. Sure enough, the simplicity of the

Conducting a wine tasting, January 2010

Duncan and Tristan washing harvest lugs, September 2010

Eight-point buck taken on first hunt, November 2010

Celebrating Mother's Day with family and friends, May 2013

railing style looked great against the frame, and I knew I could now move into production mode. With twenty-seven newel posts to build from scratch, I had to quickly establish a few economies of scale. I decided to end the night on a positive note, and headed back to the shack to spend some time with Shannon and boys.

The next morning before heading in to the office, I went by the house to see if the electrical crew was on site. Sure enough, not a single person was there, and true to my word, I called Ron and fired the electrical company. Ron was furious with them and assured me he would get to the bottom of the situation, but I told him it was too late, that I would be making calls throughout the day trying to find a new subcontractor. Though not a pleasant conversation, I knew the costs we would be facing if we had to refinance the construction loan. What a few unprofessional electricians thought of me did not hold a candle to the check I was going to have to write. That contentious situation made for a miserable day at the office, as I pulled together final preparations for the trip to Houston in two days while trying to find electricians to salvage our project.

Saturday, April 14th, I made my way to the house, where Shannon had been busy painting two of the three downstairs bedrooms. The colors were great, and though each of the rooms had some difficult angled corners, she was doing an amazing job. Much to my surprise, I was greeted by the electricians I had fired; apparently Ron had gotten directly in touch with the owner of the company. The difference in their attitudes and work ethic was palpable. I was completely forthright, telling them that I had fired them, but was very appreciative to see them back on the job. I got to work right away on producing newel posts, and spent the rest of the day working on them until it was time to get home, enjoy dinner together, and pack for the quick trip to Houston. On Sunday, as I was leaving for the airport, my mom arrived to watch the boys for a few hours while Shannon headed over to the house to put the second coats of paint on the boys' rooms.

The Houston show was a relatively small industry analyst event; the load-in only took one day, and rehearsals went off without a hitch on Sunday evening. We had more rehearsals on Monday morning, then the show on Monday afternoon, and finished loading out by late evening. Tuesday morning, I flew home from Houston and drove straight out to the construction site. While Shannon continued with the basement cleanup, I was completely focused on creating the newel posts. We were both completely exhausted, and decided to head home in time to get showered and have dinner with the boys before my mom headed home to get some much needed rest before work the next morning.

Throughout all of this babysitting coverage provided by both of our mothers, they each continued to hold full-time jobs. They graciously used their own vacation time and sacrificed their weekends to help us find the time to work on the house. Without their help, we would have been completely lost, and there is no way we would have been able to finish all the tasks to which we had committed ourselves.

On Thursday, April 19th, I finished cutting the last of the newel posts, and took a much-needed break from carpentry. A few weeks earlier, I had attempted to activate the security cameras to no avail. After spending an hour on the phone with tech support, they realized that they had installed the incorrect video card before it shipped from their warehouse. The new video card had arrived earlier in the week; I installed it and the cameras and software recognized each other instantly. Our security system was finally up and running, without any further crises. I turned my attention back to finishing the newel posts, beginning the long process of sanding and oiling each one. Using the same Danish oil that the Lancaster crew used on the timber frame, the whole house filled with the smell of the freshly applied oil.

While I was working in the master bedroom, the Hawes team had been busy finishing up several other tasks around the house. The carpenters completed the interior trim around the star window, an incredibly complex task that turned out perfectly. They also completed the front porch railings, which used the same design as the interior railings I had created, though with silver balusters to match the silver metal porch roof. Their work was outstanding, and I found myself daydreaming of customers sitting on the front porch, enjoying glasses of wine on a warm summer evening. Throughout the project we would get those little glimpses of the future, those brief moments when a small fragment of the dream would suddenly be brought to life by the completion of a task. Now that the tangible tasks were coming together so quickly, those moments were also happening more often.

Sunday I awoke early, to begin a fourteen-hour day of construction and vineyard tasks. I began with the installation of the custom newel posts, and as with all tasks, the first few took much longer than expected. My newel post project was now a dependency for the flooring installation, which was scheduled to begin in just three days. Given the fast-approaching May deadline, and our limited days off from work, we had realized that there was no way I would be able to get all the hardwood installed, so we had decided to engage the subcontractor recommended by Lumber Liquidators. That would prove to be one of the best decisions we made on the whole project.

By early afternoon I had figured out an efficient process for installing the posts, and after a quick lunch, made my way out to the vineyard to take advantage of the remaining daylight. My brother Jim joined me for the afternoon, which we spent hammering more catch wires to the vine trellising.

Monday, April 23rd, the Hawes crew focused on their grading tasks, both around the new winery as well as around the house. As Ron was working on those, Trevor began cutting in the base for the new driveway. After discussing the options with the Hawes team, Richard suggested having the driveway make a loop in front of the house, so that limos would be able to drop visitors off right in front and then pull straight through, rather than having to back out. As we would later learn, no matter how much planning you put into a driveway, and how obvious you believe you have made the path, a limo driver will still manage to do the exact opposite and crunch their undercarriage on a landscape boulder.

Tuesday would prove to be a marathon fifteen-hour day, beginning at the Tops of the Town manufacturing shop in nearby Vienna, Virginia. I had not been to the shop in years (Jim had dropped off the template earlier), so it was great to visit and see dozens of photos from the old days stapled to the walls under a thick layer of shop dust. After discussing the countertop template and installation plan with lead carpenter Douglas, I made my way out of Vienna through Northern Virginia rush hour traffic and headed west to our beautiful scenic Western Loudoun countryside. Driving out Route 9 through the little town of Hillsboro, I could see Hillsborough Vineyards' tiny buds swelling to life, with a few small shoots of bright green gleaming in the morning sun. Knowing that our own three acres of vines were also emerging from dormancy, I felt a sudden exhilaration, knowing that this fall would bring our first commercial harvest. Somehow, someway, we had to get this house finished without losing focus of that important fact. Our Cabernet Franc and the first acre of Viognier plantings would soon yield several tons of fruit, assuming I could keep them tended over the next few weeks and through the summer, amidst the insanity of finishing the construction.

Once I arrived at the house, I immediately began working on the newel posts, knowing that I was out of time and that Tom Daniels, our flooring installer, would arrive early the next morning. Hustling through the installations, I finished the ones in the music loft up by mid-afternoon, leaving just a few more in the catwalk for the next day. Reviewing my ongoing checklist, I realized that I had not yet created the custom bullnose flooring pieces that Tom would need for the catwalk and music loft perimeters. A bullnose flooring piece has a rounded edge on both the top and bottom, so that it can be used as a border piece that extends out into space. Since those pieces are not commercially available, they have to be carved from one of the stock pieces. After routing the newel posts in the soft Douglas fir, the Bloodwood felt like routing pieces of granite. I was shocked at how difficult that wood was to work with.

I stopped by the house on my way into work the next morning to visit with Tom and his son Lance, who would be assisting him on the project. A quiet, mild-mannered man with a soft-spoken West Virginia drawl, Tom was instantly likeable and clearly experienced in his craft. As soon as we met I could tell he was troubled about the project, and right away showed me the reason for his concern. The

Bloodwood was so dense that he was not able to use his flooring nailer on it; the tongue of the wood just split off from the impact of the nail being driven through it. Typically the nail just penetrates through the wood into the subfloor below. Tom had read about the installation, but had not really believed that wood could be that hard; he was a believer now. Tom and Lance would have to pre-drill every single nail hole before driving each nail, a time-consuming and laborious process that would significantly cut their progress time from 400 square feet per day down to 150. When I returned to the site late that evening to check their progress, I was stunned at how beautiful the flooring was, but knew that they were facing a very difficult road ahead. Worse, I knew that our flooring installation budget had just doubled.

Thursday morning I was out on the job site bright and early, and shortly after, Tom arrived to finish the flooring in the music loft. That only took them a couple hours, then they moved down to the main level to install the red oak in the gift shop area. What a difference the materials can make when it comes to installation times! Using their regular flooring nailer, they were able to progress through the gift shop in just under five hours, and the work was spectacular. After watching them for two days, I was relieved I had not tried to install all the flooring myself.

Outside, the Hawes crew was installing the first layer of the new driveway, a huge dump truck slowly releasing several tons of base stone along the curved path with the precision of a small riding mower. A few quick passes with the skid steer, and the base layer was complete. Once that was done, Ron spent a few hours fine-tuning the front yard grading. Just like that, we had a front yard, though at the moment it was nothing more than hard Virginia clay.

Two days later, after another long day and late night at the office preparing for our next event, both Shannon and I were at the house while my mom came over to watch the boys. Shannon immediately started painting the downstairs trim, while I worked on the final installation of the fireplace in the master suite. Since we now had running water and the water heater had been connected, we ran the tub while testing out the fireplace. It would have been tempting to jump right in, but we had a television camera recording our every move. After a quick break with the television crew, Shannon had to head back to the rental to relieve Mom, so I took advantage of the nice weather to work out in the vineyard. I was able to nail up four more rows of trellis catch wires before running out of daylight.

Sunday, April 29th, both Shannon and I were right back where we left off the preceding day, her painting trim and me working on sinks. Part of our upcoming final inspection would necessitate finished surfaces around every sink and the top of the tub surround. We took a quick break for lunch, then she returned to painting and I went upstairs to the tasting bar to install the range hood above the dual stoves. I had opted for a sleek contemporary design, and the professional range hood looked great. I made my way back out to the vineyard to continue on the trellis installation. All of the vines were in full bud-break by now, and I had to be extremely careful not to knock any buds off when lifting the trellis wire into place.

That evening, I asked Ron to use his team to finish up the railing installation. Though I had hoped to complete the project myself, the creation of the custom newel posts had just taken too long; with our deadline just ten days away, I could not risk incomplete railings. Early the next morning, I met with Vernon and Tim to explain my design before heading into the office. Late that night, after a long day of pre-show meetings, emails, and phone calls, I visited the house to check out their progress. I was thrilled to see not only the quality of their work, but the success of the style. While the carpenters were working on the railing, the electricians had installed the two ceiling fans in the tasting room. Given that the peak of the ceiling is twenty-eight feet up, it must have been quite a challenge. As soon as they were turned on, however, the temperature in the huge space quickly evened out, as the hot air trapped in the upper reaches of the ceiling began to circulate throughout the room. The last day of April slowly faded to night, and with just eight more working days left before the deadline, I was starting to feel a glimmer of hope.

Tuesday, May 1st was a flurry of activity. Tom was in the catwalk installing more Bloodwood, while Vernon and Tim continued on the catwalk railings. The electricians were working downstairs, and Trevor was outside digging drainage trenches for the winery. I was moving from project to project, answering questions, giving sound bites for the television crew, cleaning up construction debris, and going through checklists. The Tops of the Town crew arrived to deliver the new countertop. The new pieces sitting on top of the cabinets made a huge difference in the look of the tasting bar. Late in the afternoon, after the crews took off for the day, I made my way out to the vineyard to install tensioners on the trellis catch wires, devices that control how much tension are applied to the wires. Too much tension and the trellis can experience too much strain; too little tension and the weight of the canopy can make the wires sag, allowing the vines to droop and create unwelcome shade in the fruiting zone. As daylight faded, I pulled my truck up and turned on the headlights to keep working in the dark, heading home to the rental late that night. The following day while Shannon and I were at the office, the Hawes crew finished up the grading and installed the base layer and top layer of gravel to create the customer parking lot next to the winery.

Thursday, May 3rd, our new lawn was installed. The crew swept the entire landscape with a huge nylon brush roller attached to front of a skid steer; then they sprayed on a mixture of seed, water, fertilizer and mulch, which is colored green, so that you at least feel like you have real grass in place. Not only is this step important in quickly establishing a new lawn to prevent erosion from the freshly created slopes, it is also a key requirement for the final inspection. While the landscape crew was working their way across the construction site, Vernon and Tim completed the loft railings while Tom and Lance continued installing the catwalk Bloodwood. On the main level, Darren installed several sheets of thin plywood to the front of the bar. This was a requirement for the final inspection, since the bar had electrical wires running throughout.

Friday, May 4th was a beautiful spring day, with every crew working furiously toward the completion of the house. Outside, the landscape crew was finishing up the hydroseeding process while Trevor excavated a drainage creek from a culvert pipe underneath

Sagle Road down into our pond. This would help the saturated meadow adjoining the vineyard to drain, now that the spring rains were subsiding. Vernon and Tim spent several hours installing the main staircase railings, and when they were done, I was amazed at how fantastic all the complex joints looked. Tom and Lance completed the last of the catwalk flooring, and after a quick meeting, we decided to schedule their return for the end of May, since the flooring in the main tasting bar area was not a requirement for the occupancy permit. I installed shower doors, painted trim, and installed shelving in the audiovisual closet. With a major show just a week away, my email inbox was bristling with activity, and I was answering inquiries and taking calls from the bustling job site. Darren was working through his punch list, and installed the new ducting that I had purchased for the range hood, along with a dozen other small tasks that were all required for the final inspection. Ron was down at the county building and secured our zoning permit, another big hurdle that was a relief to overcome.

The countertop crew arrived right after lunch to begin the installation of the big curved top, now affectionately known as the "candy cane," due to its shape. Given its enormous length, it would not be possible to glue it together then lift it in place; it essentially had to be assembled right on top of the cabinets, where it would stay. The crew took the time to create temporary braces and gluing blocks, which would then be used by the large number of clamps that were required to properly secure each of the joints. I had to remove one of the kitchen cabinets so that they could reach underneath to install the clamps, but it would be simple to reinstall it later. The entire countertop installation took about six hours, and after all the scraping and sanding was done, the seams were absolutely invisible. To ensure the top was working properly, we set out a twelve-pack of beer, which quickly disappeared.

After the crew left and I began my nightly process of taking pictures for the blog, it occurred to me that the top two floors of the house, the catwalk and the music loft, were completely finished. I stood there on the catwalk looking around, thinking there must be something left to do. Could it be possible that we had reached this mini-milestone? I went up into the music loft and looked out over the catwalk, admiring the beautiful Bloodwood flooring and the well-crafted railings. All the electrical outlets, switches, and fixtures were in place, as were the windowpanes and hardware in the dormers. For years, I had envisioned standing up in this loft looking out over the floors below, and now here I was.

Saturday, May 5th was a long hard day, but full of progress. I began early with yet another quick tiling job and caulked the master suite shower before heading out into the vineyard to install four more rows of tensioners. After completing that, I had to assemble a new spot sprayer, which I used to tow behind our old riding mower and spray herbicide underneath the vines to keep the weeds down. I had just enough daylight left to apply the herbicide to one acre, and decided to call it day and head home. Early the next morning I was in the vineyard, applying the herbicide to the remaining two acres, then back in the house to grout. The final inspection just two days away, and it was time to do my own inspection, going from top to bottom, checking for stray tools, spare parts, or anything that did not need to be left out prior to the inspection. It took several hours of scouring the house, scraping floors, and sweeping up before I was satisfied that I had done all I could to make it ready. Although the Hawes crew had a few more items on their punch list to complete the following day, it seemed to me that we had a really solid chance of passing the final inspection on Tuesday.

The following day, Ron called me at the office to inform me that we had received our gas and plumbing inspections, which are pre-requisites to having the final inspection. With those in place, we were cleared to schedule the final the following morning. Shannon and I hugged each other in her office, knowing we were so close to the finish line. Later that evening, I went out to the vineyard to fill up the big sprayer for the first fungicide application of the season. Once the sprayer was filled and the chemicals mixed, I moved the tractor into position, flipped the switches, and... nothing. I had planned my evening spray with just enough time to get it finished before 10:00

P.M., my cutoff time so that I do not annoy the neighbors with the noise. It took me forty-five minutes of tinkering with the sprayer to finally find a blown fuse in the control panel. I dejectedly returned home to pack for my trip the next afternoon.

Tuesday, May 8th was a very surreal day. Shannon had taken the day off of work to be on the job site, in case there were any last minute decisions that needed to be made. I awoke very early to finish packing for my drive to New Jersey, and then got out to the vineyard by 7:00 A.M. to complete the vineyard spray that had gone awry the night before.

As soon as the spraying was done, I stopped into the house, where Ron was awaiting the county inspector. Knowing there was nothing more I could do, I thanked him with a big hug and wished him luck. Spending a few minutes with Shannon, we held each other, secure in the realization that we had done all we could. It was now out of our hands, and we would soon find out whether or not we, and our whole hard-working crew, had gotten it done. I gave a few sound bites to the television crew, removed my microphone, and drove away.

Several hours later, as I was driving up the New Jersey Turnpike, Shannon called me to give me the wonderful news: we had just passed our final inspection, and Ron had received our occupancy permit from the county. It was 3:30 P.M., the day before our construction loan expired, and ninety minutes before the office closed, he faxed a copy over to our mortgage company so they could begin the loan conversion process and schedule us for our closing. Although the house was now legal for occupation, it was definitely not move-in ready. It still looked like a construction site, with dusty floors, piles of flooring boxes awaiting installation, several downstairs rooms just primed or bare drywall, and not a single piece of furniture in sight. We could have cared less, however, for we had achieved something that most people considered neither rational nor possible.

I longed to be with her and the boys to celebrate this moment together, and we cried on the phone as the anxiety washed away and the realization set in that the pressure of the construction phase was really over. We could now take the rest of our lives to finish the house if we needed to; there were no more deadlines. We hung up and I continued my journey into New Jersey, to the hotel where our show would soon load in. Immediately upon arrival, I made my way to the ballroom to begin what would turn out to be a very long night, working well past midnight to complete the audiovisual setup and guiding the team on the finalization of the client's presentations. I was in a daze, trying to stay focused on the event while still in shock that the house was livable. To be honest, I was glad I had a production to throw myself into to keep my mind occupied. Without that, I would likely have been sitting in the rental shack in stunned disbelief, trying to make sense of how far we had come, and all that yet lay ahead. There were, however, a few brief moments through that long night when there was a break in the action, and in those moments I found myself, for the first time in a very long while, incredibly at peace.

We had done it.

CHAPTER 27

"Housewarming Party"

T
he next two days were typical corporate event production mayhem, working twenty-hour days on a few hours of sleep. As soon as the final session concluded on Friday, I was out the door and headed home, eager to see Shannon and the boys. It would be a momentous evening for us, our first night sleeping in the new house, and we were so excited. I hit very little traffic on the drive home, and was at the rental shack before dark.

After tossing our spare mattress in the back of the truck along with a few blankets, we hurried over to the house. I just dropped the mattress on the floor in the spare bedroom, and we all cuddled up in bed together. The boys thought the carpeted room was great fun, and rolled around together giggling. Shannon and I just watched them play, both of us utterly content. No phones, no televisions, no laptops, no diversions of any kind—just two little boys being silly on the floor of our new home was, to us, the greatest show on earth. Sunday, May 13th, was not only Mother's Day, but also Shannon's thirty-third birthday. She said she could not have wished for anything more.

Once we had the occupancy permit, everyone agreed we needed a break from the construction. It was resolved that there would be no projects of any kind underway for at least a month in order to allow Shannon and me to recuperate. Our minds, bodies, and emotions had taken a real beating over the preceding fifteen months. We were looking forward to some much-needed family time, unencumbered by the pressures of homebuilding.

One reality that would not be deferred, however, was the conversion of the construction loan into a mortgage. Our lender had set our closing date for early June, meaning our first mortgage payment would be due July 1st. We knew we had to be completely moved out of the rental shack by June 30th to avoid double paying on the rental and the new home. We also knew that the television producers were anxious to wrap filming; they were pressuring us to set a date for a housewarming party where they could interview friends and family, as well as get footage of the finished home in action. As we were also extremely burned out on our television obligation as well, Shannon and I discussed various options for doing a small party in a week or so, just to appease the producers and complete the filming. However, we had grown so close to the field crews that we knew we had to find a little more strength and create something special for them, as well as for the viewers who would someday enjoy the series.

With that in mind, we resolved to throw a major party to celebrate Tristan's second birthday and our housewarming. Penciling in the date for July 21st gave us ten weeks to move out of the rental and finish up many of the interior cosmetic projects that remained in the new home. Now that we were completely focused on work with no remaining vacation time available, that only left us nights and weekends to move and work on the house. In addition, the vineyard was in full swing and in need of constant attention as we prepared for our first commercial harvest just under four months away.

The next two weeks of May were delightful, and we settled into a routine of getting the boys to daycare, heading into the office and back again, with the evenings spent either casually packing boxes in the rental or tending to the vineyard. We spent the weeknights in the rental so that we could begin the moving process. We had resolved to get plenty of sleep, after so many miserable months of deprivation. As if they were tuned into our plan, both Duncan and Tristan cooperated by sleeping through the night, and we all began to feel human again.

Memorial Day weekend was spent with friends and family in a vacation rental on the shore of Deep Creek Lake in Maryland. After over a year of missing nearly every family gathering, it was wonderful to reconnect and let the kids enjoy each other's company, and let the adults enjoy some time in our boat cruising around the lake. In so many ways, Shannon and I felt like we were emerging from a very dark place, like a fog was lifting in our lives, and the whole world seemed completely renewed and brighter. I think we had completely underestimated the toll that the construction process would take upon us. I suppose that is true of anyone who embarks upon a project such as ours. Still, at the time I could not decide if the process had made us mentally more resilient or more fragile, more adventurous or more risk-averse. It was too soon to tell.

The first week of June, the Conestoga crew returned to finish up the winery. They spent a day roughing-in the floor drains and installing the gravel, and the following day pouring the slab. Shannon, the boys and I had spent each weekend sleeping in the house, and on Saturday, June 9th, I decided it was time to get back into construction mode.

Looking back on those first few weekends sleeping in the house, we realized we rarely went upstairs into the timber frame. To this day, we are still not sure why that was, but as best as we can figure out, we considered the basement the living quarters and the upstairs the tasting room. Maybe it was because we had grown so accustomed to living in a cramped space, we felt more at home in the basement. Maybe since there was still so much unfinished work to do, and the winery was not likely to open for years, it just felt odd being in that big space. Whatever the case, on that morning, I resolved to cook breakfast using our new stoves in the tasting bar, and we brought the boys up to play in front of the big picture windows. Shannon and I laughed when we realized we had been staying in the house for nearly a month and had never had breakfast on the main level.

The television crew arrived shortly thereafter, and it was great to be reunited with everyone after the four-week break. The crew captured a few hours of me painting before heading home, and by late afternoon I had to put down the tools and head out to the vineyard for a fungicide application. Jim MacKenzie, our local Helena Chemical rep, was proving to be a trusted resource in recommending various treatments as I progressed through the season. It was great to have him swing by once in a while to walk the vineyard with me and discuss various spray strategies for the myriad of problems we faced with viticulture in Virginia. Due to the paint fumes, we spent that night back in the rental shack, Tristan enjoying playing hide and seek amidst the dozens of boxes that we were packing up. I spent Sunday back in the house painting, while Shannon stayed at the rental packing boxes, tending Duncan and chasing Tristan. That night, I took over a load from the rental and dropped everything in the winery. Having that big open space made the move go really quickly, and we decided to not rent a moving truck. We would just use our pickup truck to take one load at a time over to the house.

We spent the rest of June enjoying our semi-normal routine of working long days in the office, Shannon spending the evenings packing boxes, while I gathered them up and over to the house when I was not spraying the vines. The vines were all in really great shape, with no mildew or rot present, and the shoots all well-tended and securely placed in the catch wires. Shoot-positioning, spraying, and mowing both the vineyard and our new lawn were taking dozens of hours I had hoped to devote to packing and moving. The vineyard had to be my priority, however, and once again we called upon our mothers to help Shannon with the boys and the packing.

Sunday, July 1st, was our last day in the rental, and the television crew was on hand to film the action. We knew that this would be an emotional day, as we both choked up a few times reminiscing about the house. Making the last round trip to the new house, we returned to the shack for what would be our last load. Once the trucks were loaded, we decided to take one last walkthrough of the little rental that had been our home for nearly three years. As we visited each room, memories flooded back, and it was all we could do to hold back the tears. Standing in the middle of Tristan's room, however, there was nothing we could do to stop them, and we were both overwhelmed as we thought back to the day we brought our first baby back to this very room. We held each other and whispered our favorite memories back and forth, oblivious to the television camera capturing every moment. Looking through the kitchen to the bedroom where we brought Duncan home, we cried and even laughed a little when we recalled those long sleepless nights with that poor anxious baby and his upset tummy, somehow managing through the frenetic pace of the construction project. Although neither boy would have any memory of this place, it had played an important role in our family story and would forever hold a very special place in our hearts. Setting our keys on the counter, we glanced over our shoulders, gave it one last look, and we all drove away.

Arriving at the house, we quickly unloaded the last of the boxes. We had a celebration toast and then everyone went their separate ways for the evening, while Shannon and I got the boys settled in for the night. The realization set in quickly that now this truly was our home. The good news was that we were no longer paying rent for the shack, but the not-so-good news was that our first mortgage payment was due. The following day, we sent off our first payment for nearly $7,500. We were both pretty nauseous as Shannon dropped the envelope in the mailbox.

The next few weeks leading up to the housewarming party flew quickly by, as we were incredibly busy in the office during the week, and spending nights and weekends working in the house. I spent the morning of July 4th installing a water softener and iron filter. Our well water had a very high iron content, which was not only already staining our new fixtures, but Shannon hated for washing babies. The weekend of the 7th and 8th was spent with custom vanity and tiling in the master suite, while Shannon was busy unpacking and getting the house in order. We did take a nice long break for lunch and enjoyed our first family picnic together. Shannon had picked up a little wading pool for the boys to splash around in, and made sandwiches for us all. She had also picked up the cutest (and possibly most ridiculous) green swimsuit and floppy hat for Duncan I had ever seen.

Along with all of the ongoing sweat equity projects was the nev-er-ending ongoing task list in the vineyard. Taking a tip from Doug,

I placed a call to a local crew chief who brought out several guys to help with hedging the vines, pulling leaves away from the fruiting zone, and shoot positioning. This was a huge help and freed me up to continue working in the house, as well as keeping the vineyard sprayed and mowed. Given that we were having the party in a few weeks, I wanted the vineyard in top form for everyone that would be taking a walk through. Several of our guests had not seen the place since the wedding, and were in for a real shock at the progress that had been made in just over three years.

All of the extra effort in the vineyard was paying off; the fruit was disease-free, and I was able to fend off the marauding hordes of Japanese beetles, mites, aphids, leafhoppers, deer, rabbits, and raccoons, as well as the threat of powdery mildew, downy mildew, black rot, and phomopsis, just to name a few. The crew taught me additional tips about dropping fruit to ensure that clusters of grapes were not piled up on top of one another, as well as ensuring that any single cane was not carrying too much yield. I was beginning to see with my own eyes that fine wine is grown in a vineyard, not made in a lab, and the attention to detail in keeping a vine in balance was fascinating. After working for several hours alongside them, I could begin to feel whether or not a particular vine was in balance; you can just sense it. Although the fruit still had not developed any sugars or flavors yet, they assured me that our site, trellis configuration, and varietal selection were all well designed, and that the fruit was looking superb for this time of the season.

Two days before the big party dawned hot and sunny, and although it was going to be a typically humid Virginia weekend, there was no chance of rain in the forecast. Shannon had taken the next two days off of work in order to make the mad dash of final preparations, and had several friends and family come out to assist as well. With ten people sleeping at our place over the weekend, the spare bedroom needed to be painted. Shannon's cousin Allison and my sister Rebecca were put to work painting it, while our mothers were busy tending to linens, shopping, and decorations. Sean and Lori from High Noon had flown out from Colorado to oversee the final shoot, and Pam,

George, and Bill were on hand to film the pre-party preparations. Tom and Lance were on hand, working feverishly to finish up the Bloodwood on the main level, but it soon became apparent that they would only be able to complete half the floor; the remainder would be bare subfloor for the party, and it did not bother us in the least.

The day before the party, the large inflatable bounce house we had rented for the kids to play in arrived and was set up behind the house. Tristan's eyes nearly fell out of his head when I inflated it for the first time, and he scurried right up inside as soon as it was ready. It was a long but immensely fun day. One way or the other, the party was the next day, and given the number of loved ones that would be attending, it would be impossible to have a bad time.

We awoke the next morning, and after a big breakfast, made ready to greet our first guests. It was incredibly important to Shannon and I that we include all the crew in the festivities, and after discussing it with Ron and Tony, they thought it best to essentially have two events that day. The first would be an open house for all of the crew who worked on the house, and later in the afternoon was for friends and family. That way the subcontractors could enjoy some time touring the house without being overrun by family members.

The crew started to arrive around 10:00 A.M., and we were thrilled that several members of the Lancaster County Timber Frame team made the trip down from Pennsylvania. They even brought Tristan a gift for his second birthday, a beautiful wooden wagon. As the other subs wandered in and enjoyed coffee and pastries, they began to introduce themselves to each other. We learned from several of the crew that this was the first time they had ever been invited to a housewarming party; most of the time they performed their tasks and never actually got to see the finished home. It was wonderful to see the pride in their eyes. Working side-by-side on many occasions with them, I think the crew appreciated the effort and commitment Shannon and I put into the project. As they gathered on the front porch for a group picture, the television crew captured every moment—each handshake, each hug, each smiling face illustrated what was in everyone's heart. This was a special place.

We said our goodbyes to each of the crew, knowing that we would see most of them again someday, as they promised to stop in for a glass of wine. After taking a quick break for lunch, I greeted our first musician arriving for set up, a classical guitarist. We thought it would be a nice touch to put the music loft to good use during the afternoon party, so I took him upstairs to show him the setup. He was completely in awe, having never seen anything like it in over two decades of being a professional musician. As I dialed in the sound system and slowly brought up his guitar volume, the acoustics of the room and the sound of the wood all came together in perfect harmony. All of that extra work and expense were worth it in an instant.

Everyone started arriving around 2:00 P.M., and then the real fun began. It was hysterical seeing the television crew randomly pulling people aside for interviews. Shannon and I had been doing it for fifteen months and did not give it a second thought, but seeing people put on camera for the first time made us realize that we were now seasoned television veterans. They all took it in stride, and eavesdropping into some of the interviews, we were both really humbled by people's reactions. We had been so caught up in the process that we did not really stop to think about it from an outsider's perspective. At one point, Shannon's brother Steve grabbed George's camera and the tables were turned as I interviewed George for a change.

The afternoon was a whirlwind of laughter, tears, hugs, storytelling, television shots, live music, good wine, house tours, vineyard tours, bounce house silliness, and birthday cake. Over sixty friends and family members attended, many of them having flown in from around the country to participate. Pam put down her audio gear for a while and enjoyed herself helping out in the kitchen. One of the most enjoyable aspects of the party was the people's amazing reaction to our wine. We had set out the last remaining bottles of the Viognier we had made for Christmas presents alongside some big-name brands, and sure enough, our wine was disappearing rapidly to high praises and more than a few people's apparent surprise. I had not really thought about it at the time, but in retrospect, I suppose it would have been rather embarrassing to have spent years of our lives blabbing about starting a winery, spending over a million dollars on a home and vineyard, and then pouring undrinkable plonk at the housewarming party.

By early evening, the moment of truth had arrived: my welcome speech and housewarming toast. I knew there was no way I was going to be able to get through any kind of speech without completely breaking down, but the television producers were pushing hard for one, and it seemed like everyone in attendance was as well. George pulled me aside, and as we tested my microphone, I told him, "Do not miss this shot, this is only going to happen once." He smiled at me and said he was not worried about missing the shot; he was worried about being able to see through his tears.

We called everyone into the tasting bar, and when they were gathered and the wine had been poured, Shannon and I took our places behind the bar. I was shaking and she knew I was an emotional mess, and she stood by me, holding me tightly. I do not really remember everything I said, but I do recall there was not a dry eye in the place. I thanked our parents, who were all there, I thanked our siblings and our friends who had given so much love, encouragement, and support. I thanked the television producers and the construction crew, and true to his word, George was barely holding it together (Pam was a complete basket case), but that camera never wavered, a mere four feet from my face. I thanked Shannon and our boys, whose unyielding love and confidence had carried me through so many trying times over the past years. Calling for a toast, I watched as everyone raised their glasses, and in my wavering voice announced, "Welcome to Notaviva Vineyards."

The cheering was deafening, and as Shannon and I held each other, the energy in the room was overwhelming. Shannon quickly reminded me of one more thing I had forgotten to do, and I told George to roll the camera again. I announced to everyone that we had permanent markers available, and that we wanted them all to sign the front of the tasting bar. Since it was still unfinished and would eventually be skinned over with a thin layer of veneer, which meant that each one of those signatures and well wishes would forever be attached to our tasting bar.

Over the next couple of hours, people made their way to the bar to congratulate us and write down some of the most inspirational thoughts we have ever read. We simply had not realized how much everyone was rooting for us, and how much we had touched each and every one of them throughout this entire endeavor. I learned that day that many of them would stay up late on Sunday nights, waiting to read my blog posts to see how the project was coming along. They had lived these past few years right alongside of us, hoping and praying that no matter what we faced, we would find a way. Whether we fully appreciated their confidence during those years—and I do not think we did—their faith kept us motivated during the many times we lost sight of the dream; their encouraging words steered us back onto the path.

As the night approached, the guests began to leave, and although it had seemed like the party had just started, it had actually been a very long day. Though Shannon and I had thought we were completely cried out, more tears came when it was time to say our final goodbye to Pam, George, Bill, Sean, and Lori. I am not sure if we even got any words out, and after fifteen months together, I do not believe any would have sufficed. More than anyone else, they had witnessed firsthand the toils, the challenges, and the obstacles that we endured.

Without a doubt, everyone had a wonderful time and had fallen in love with the house. That part of our dream—creating a magical place for family gatherings—had come true beyond our wildest expectations.

Now it was time to settle down and focus on our boys, focus on our careers, and maybe find some peace. For maybe six weeks, anyhow, because our first commercial grape harvest was fast approaching and we had neither the equipment to make wine, nor a functional winery in which to make it, nor the expertise to use either of them even if we did. Worse than all of those issues, however, was the fact that in a few short months, our whole world was going to completely implode, and the dream was going to come crashing to an end.

CHAPTER 28

"First Harvest"

Discussing our winemaking plight with Doug the first week of August, we quickly arrived at our only real option: outsourcing all of the winemaking tasks for our first year. This is known as a "custom crush" arrangement, whereby a licensed winery receives another winery's grapes, processes the fruit and makes the wine, then later sells it back to the first winery. Doug had come out to walk the vineyard with us, and was very impressed with the quality of the fruit. Warning us that there were still a few weeks ahead of potential challenges like hail, excessive rain, and late season molds and mildews, he also advised us that our first harvest had excellent potential if we stayed the course.

Tapping into the local network of winery start-ups, Doug suggested we hire Ben Renshaw to make our tank-fermented Viognier over at nearby Sunset Hills, where he was winemaker. At that time, Sunset Hills was a very small operation located in a large workshop behind the home of proprietors Mike and Diane Canney. Mike was a serial entrepreneur who had grown and sold several technology companies and now owned a race team. The winery was in a room adjacent to space for one of his racecars. We hit it off with Ben right away; his outgoing personality and can-do attitude were very uplifting, and after tasting some of his wines, we knew our fruit would be in good hands.

We did have to provide Sunset Hills with some supplies for our wine, and so had to dip into what was left of our savings to purchase a $6,000 tank, which would be installed at Sunset Hills. We also needed another $1,000 to purchase harvest lugs, which are used in the vineyard for picking the fruit. I also bought a couple of critical pieces of testing equipment, a refractometer and a pH meter, which I began using twice weekly to measure the chemistry of the grapes as they began to ripen.

Doug offered to make our Cabernet Franc for us at his winery, and we would need more equipment for that process. Again dipping into our savings, we bought two MacroBin fermenting bins, and several barrels second-hand from large wineries in California. We quickly learned the economics of wine barrels; a brand new French oak barrel can easily cost $1,200, whereas a "gently used" one can be purchased for about $250. In our dilapidated financial state, that was a pretty simple decision. All in all, between new equipment, harvest labor, and winemaking consultative services, we would end up spending about $14,000 in August and September just to get our bulk wine made. Bottling expenses (bottles, labels, corks, capsules, labor, and rental gear) would be a completely different expense the following year.

In addition to all of the winemaking operation and logistics planning, there was also the ongoing vineyard maintenance; spraying and mowing were essential late in the season, to ensure the quality of the fruit as harvest approached. Shannon and I were busy navigating the complex world of winery license applications, first at the federal level and then at the state level. The stacks of paperwork that needed to be completed were astounding, but taking one form at a time, we tackled the process over a period of several weeks. I recall sitting in my room at the Opryland hotel in Nashville, bleary-eyed the day after completing a major week-long event, working on permit forms for the Alcohol and Tobacco Tax and Trade Bureau. I had them spread all over the bed in various sections while I was checking and double-checking every field. Given the number of wineries that were popping up all over the country during that time, the application approval process was going from a few weeks to a few months. As it turned out, even if we did have the equipment and winery that September, we would not have been able to make wine anyhow, since we were not licensed.

Checking my degrees Brix and acid levels throughout August, it began to appear that our harvest would happen sometime around the 10th of September. As I learned that year, harvest is absolutely the most nerve-wracking phase of viticulture, due to the myriad of interrelated variables that go into making a harvest decision. Not only are you measuring fruit ripening parameters (sugar, acidity, and most importantly, flavors), but you also have to be watching the weather, reserving the crew, ensuring that you have access to a crush pad, and ensuring that all the winery equipment is cleaned, tested, and well-running. As I was measuring the fruit, I also had to make my first pre-harvest spray decision. There is a window of time, known as the pre-harvest interval (PHI), which is the number of days from your last treatment until you can legally pick the fruit. During this time, the residue from the last spray application dissipates to a level safe for human consumption. However, at that level, there is no longer any residue left on the grapes to combat the molds, mildews, and insects for which the spray was applied. Getting the timing right on the last spray is absolutely critical. Spray it too late and you could overrun your ideal harvest time because you are not yet out of the PHI; spray it too early and your fruit could start to rot while it continues to ripen. Spray it just right and you could find a thunderstorm pounding your vineyard on harvest day anyhow, or a broken tractor, or you cannot find the crew because they are at another vineyard, or a dozen other potential complications.

Complicating the entire process was the fact that different varietals all ripen at different times. White grapes typically ripen a month before red grapes, young vines ripen before old vines, and some hybrid grapes can ripen extremely early. I am positive I was not the first novice grape-grower who was wishing for a crystal ball in the weeks approaching his harvest.

So on Thursday night, August 23rd, I rolled the dice and put an application of Pristine on the Viognier, which has a fourteen-day PHI. That would allow us to harvest any time after September 6th; Shannon would have to make the harvest decision, since I would be out of town most of that week at an event. When I left on Sunday afternoon, September 2nd, the forecast called for a perfect week of bright sunshine and warm temperatures, ideal for a run-up to harvest. While I was away, Shannon took samples from the vineyard and emailed me the measurements. Everything was falling into place, and on Tuesday we made the decision to harvest the Viognier on Friday morning. I flew home Thursday and went straight out to the vineyard to set lugs out in the rows and get ready for our big day the following morning.

I awoke early at 4:00 A.M. to have a big breakfast, make coffee for the crew, and head out to the vineyard by 5:00 A.M. to continue distributing the lugs. Walking up and down the rows, I could not help but admire the perfect clusters of fruit. Vineyards are mystical, magical places on harvest morning, and I was completely at peace alone with the fruit before the crew arrived. Inside, Shannon was tending the boys until my mom arrived at 6:00 A.M. to take over, allowing Shannon to head out into the vineyard. Family farming, everyone pitching in—another part of the dream was coming to fruition. When Shannon arrived, we took a moment to look over the vines and up at the house, the big windows reflecting the colors of the sunrise. We knew that Tristan would be pressed up against the glass looking out over the meadow, curious about the cars heading down to the vineyard gate and all the bustling activity.

The crew arrived and went to work immediately. I had never actually seen a seasoned crew pick grapes, and I was instantly amazed. Intense, focused, and efficient, they moved quickly through the rows, filling lugs and tucking them underneath the vines to stay out of the sun. I began loading the filled lugs into my pickup truck to transport them the few miles over to Sunset Hills, where I unloaded them into the air-conditioned storage room.

By lunchtime the picking was completed, and we enjoyed lunch with the crew up at the house. It took another couple of hours of making runs in the pickup to transfer everything over to Sunset Hills, and we had to borrow a few of their lugs, since our yield came in heavier than we anticipated. I only had enough lugs for about three thousand pounds of grapes and we actually ended up with two tons, with negligible amounts of rot.

The following morning we jumped out of bed, eager to get over to Sunset Hills for our first professional grape crush. After the infamous kitchen incident the previous year, we were anxious to see how intelligent beings manage to get the juice out of a grape without destroying a kitchen floor. Shannon's mom arrived to watch the boys, and we were off.

When we arrived the crew was already there, cleaning and sterilizing the crusher/de-stemmer, press, tank, pump, hoses—pretty much anything that would be coming into contact with the juice. We dove right in with the scrub brushes and got to work with the preparations, knowing full well that we were probably more in the way than actually contributing, but it was our fruit and we were definitely going to get dirty. Ben was orchestrating all of the activity, and the atmosphere was incredibly enjoyable. He was very easy-going, answering dozens of our questions and guiding us through the process. We shared a similar mindset of "show someone how to do it, then walk away until they ask for help." He showed us the proper operation of the equipment, the process flow, and the chemistry involved in keeping the juice fresh. It was all so new and exciting to us, and the morning flew by.

Sunset Hills owned a one-ton press, but Ben decided that rather than overfilling the machine for two runs, he would rather do three smaller runs to achieve a more efficient pressing and prevent the possibility of overstuffing the second press run. With each press cycle taking about two hours to fill, press, unload, and clean, we worked continuously until mid-afternoon, then began the long job of cleaning up. We were amazed at what a huge mess our small yield of two tons had made; I could only imagine what it must be like at large wineries with tens, hundreds, or thousands of tons of grapes to process. As exhilarating as it was, it was also very daunting, contemplating the finances that would be required to purchase all of our own equipment in the years ahead.

My mom stopped by to check out the process and all of the equipment in the winery. She really enjoyed tasting the sweet Viognier juice from the tasting valve on the tank. Having never tried fresh juice from a winegrape, her reaction was the same as everyone's: "I cannot believe how sweet this is!" Most everyone is accustomed to the sugar level of a table grape, which is typically around 14-15 degrees Brix, whereas a winegrape is typically around 21-22 degrees Brix, sometimes much higher. Imagine taking a tall glass of store-bought grape juice, pouring a glass, and then dissolving two heaping tablespoons of sugar in it. That is about how sweet winegrape juice is at harvest.

After a full day on the crush pad, our tank was about half full with around 310 gallons of delicious juice. Ben was very happy with the chemistry of the juice, and although he added a typical amount of potassium metabisulfite during the crush process, he indicated that he would not need to adjust any of the other parameters through either chaptalization to increase the sugar or acidulation to increase the titratable acidity. We had grown great fruit, had a successful first crush, and had a tank of spectacular Viognier juice. Now it was up to Ben to turn it into wine.

With our first commercial harvest of Viognier safely in the tank, it was time to make a decision on our Cabernet Franc harvest date. As soon as I got home that afternoon, I went right out to the vineyard to sample the fruit, and realized that we might be ready for harvest in as little as two weeks. Exhausted as I was, I knew I had to load up the sprayer and put down an application of Pristine to ensure that we would be outside the PHI when it came time to pick. Although I had anticipated picking the Cabernet Franc in October, we had learned that younger vines ripen sooner, and it was obvious we were picking sometime at the end of September.

Our colleagues at work were very curious to hear about our harvest experience, and it was a lot of fun sharing the stories with the team before our Monday meeting. With two more big events coming up in the weeks ahead, we both knew we would be swamped with work tasks and were relieved that the Cabernet Franc had received its last spray. It was now a waiting game. By September 19th, I made the decision to harvest on Sunday the 23rd, but in looking at the forecast, it appeared that a large storm would be coming through.

Talking it over with Doug, we decided to harvest a day earlier, and the schedule was set.

Since we were now seasoned farmers (with whole one crush under our belts), the preparations for our second harvest went much more smoothly than for the Viognier. I had decided to rent a cargo van to transport the fruit so I could keep it cool while awaiting the transfer to Fabbioli Cellars, about forty minutes from our place. As soon as we filled the van, I took off for Doug's place, while Shannon continued to work with the crew and fill the back of our pickup. Once that was full, she drove to Doug's as well, and we passed each other on the road as I made my way back for the last of the fruit. We blew kisses to each other as we passed; we were as silly as two newlyweds, but we both cherished that moment. Tired, dirty, and sore, we were making it happen together.

Doug had harvested his Cabernet Franc that morning as well, and when I arrived with our final load of fruit, they were almost done crushing his grapes. Since he and his wife Colleen already had a host of volunteers on hand for his crush, and we had brought several of our own, the crush pad was bustling with activity. Shannon, her mom, brother, Geno, and I all pitched in with the hand sorting of Doug's fruit in preparation for processing our own. It was essentially a process where we used a gravity-flow setup, with the crusher/de-stemmer positioned high above the MacroBin, and as the fruit and juice came out the bottom of the machine, it came down a slide before dropping into the fermentation bin. We took turns standing alongside the slide removing stems, leaves, and the occasional insect, all known as "material other than grapes" or simply MOG.

Since this was my first time using hand sorting at crush, I was also eager to taste as much as I could. I had read extensively that hand sorting fruit enabled removal of much of the stem material, which could contribute very bitter tannic and vegetative flavors to the finished wine. I figured what better way to validate that theory than by popping a few stems in my mouth and grinding them up between my teeth. As I expected they tasted horrible, but the experience was valuable and I continued tasting the juice, the skins, and the seeds, just as a training exercise. I was very curious about every aspect of winemaking, and was not afraid to taste anything.

By late afternoon, we were nearing completion of our nearly three tons of beautiful Cabernet Franc, and on the horizon we could see storm clouds moving in. We were so grateful to Doug and his friends and family for welcoming us as we all shared the day together. I could not help but stare into our two completed fermentation bins that were now under Doug's watchful eye, soon to become a fine Virginia Cabernet Franc that would find itself proven on the international stage.

The whole experience that day was a perfect example of the spirit of the nascent Virginia wine industry. It was our interpretation of the "garagistes" movement of independent winemakers, creating small lot, limited-production wines crafted in makeshift wineries with second-rate equipment. Like many of our wine industry colleagues, Doug and Colleen lived on their farm raising their children, and their crush pad was on their back patio, with storage in their basement as well as a couple of buried sea containers acting as a makeshift cave. It was the picture of quintessential pioneering Virginians: farmers working together, helping each other, waking up early, enjoying the crisp morning air, grateful for the earth and its bounty, reveling in the physical soreness and the emotional joy and the success of a beautiful harvest.

The entire experience was beautiful, it was authentic, and we were perfectly in love.

CHAPTER 29

"Happy Holidays"

Now that we had spent thousands of dollars on equipment and labor, completed our first harvest, and engaged a couple of winemaking consultants to produce our wine for us, it occurred to us that we ought to begin thinking about a plan to possibly sell it someday. At this point in the evolution of Notaviva Vineyards, we had yet to create an actual business plan of our own. There was no well-researched document of competitive analyses, economic forecasts, profit and loss projections—none of that existed. We had downloaded a few example winery business plans, glanced through them out of curiosity, and almost fainted at the startup costs and projected timeline to razor-thin profitability. Shannon had wanted to raise babies on a farm, and I was just trying to impress the girl who captured my heart. The notion of running a viable business that could sustain itself through cyclical seasonal revenue swings, while buoying itself through occasional poor harvests, just seemed like a lot of unpleasant math that was going to spoil the romance. All that profit and loss nonsense would have to wait while we made preparations for our first real Thanksgiving and Christmas in our new home.

Since we did have an increasing number of inquiries coming into our Notaviva website, as well as several articles in local and regional newspapers about the upcoming television show, I felt we needed to rebuild our website with our new branding that I had been developing over the past several months. By mid-October, I had launched the new site, complete with an online clothing store. In addition, I created new business cards for Shannon and me, now that we were continually networking with people, building brand awareness for the winery. I found the brand identity creation process fascinating and rewarding, and building websites was by now second nature to me. At work, I was becoming more involved in the creative aspects, not just the execution of the technical production. The culmination of these experiences would soon change the course of our lives.

The weekend of October 20th and 21st was spent (much to my chagrin) with more tiling preparation. We had decided to invite our extended families to our first Thanksgiving, and Shannon was hopeful that I would be able to finish all the flooring before the guests arrived. Tom and Lance had long since completed all the Bloodwood; now the only sections remaining were the slate tile that I was going to install in the foyer and around the tasting bar. Tristan was very curious about all of my tools and the construction materials, and kept himself entertained by scattering flooring screws around the room while Duncan cheered him on from his playpen. Although Tristan's assistance did not speed the project along, there were a few priceless photos taken and I enjoyed every second of it. When not in his playpen or high chair, Duncan was learning to walk around the tasting room, and what would someday be a wine tasting bar was, for now, just a very expensive children's playroom.

The night before Thanksgiving, I finished the entire area, and then set up all of the tables, chairs, and place settings for the following day. Realizing that we had no interior photos for the website yet, I spent some time photographing the decorated setup to use in our upcoming marketing initiatives. Early the next morning after the turkeys went into the ovens, I mopped up all the residual dust, and finished only about an hour before our family began to arrive.

The house looked gorgeous decorated for the day, and several family members were on hand who had not had the opportunity to visit during the housewarming party that summer. Although many of them had been following the blog during the entire process, it was still overwhelming to see their reactions when they first came through the door. Tristan thought having everyone over was just the greatest thing ever. He enjoyed running around visiting with everyone, as did Duncan, who crawled and toddled his way through the crowd, proudly showing off all six of his happy little teeth.

By mid-afternoon it was time for dinner, and as we gathered together in front of the big picture windows overlooking the vineyard, a calm settled over the group. I asked my mom if she would like to say the blessing, and she accepted gratefully. After saying grace, she spent a moment thanking everyone for making the trip, acknowledged those who could not attend and those who had passed, and lastly thanked Shannon and me for building such a beautiful home where we could all gather to celebrate. For some reason, that caught me completely off guard; it had never occurred to me that someone would want to thank us for building our place. It was just what we felt we were supposed to do with our lives, in no small part due to the influence of those people gathered there, as well as the ones honored by the star window. Having everyone there just felt natural.

After dinner, we spent hours telling stories about the construction; now that we were several months beyond the completion of the project, hearing the stories was both hysterical and heart wrenching. At times I could not believe what we had put ourselves through, and there were several moments when recounting a tale that some people simply would not believe me. With each retelling of the events of the previous two years and the realization of how deeply our story seemed to touch people, I found myself starting to wonder about the release of the television series, now slated for the following summer. Would it convey the same depth of authenticity, or just be another shallow reality series flop? Being in the creative agency business, it was definitely starting to nag at me that we had absolutely no input into the format of the series. If it was terrible, we were going to look like complete charlatans.

Early December was incredibly busy at the office, as I prepared for a January trip down to Mexico City to produce an all-hands simulcast, streamed live from three cities. Two other large productions coming up after the first of the year were also keeping the team busy heading into the busy holiday season. Everyone was looking forward to blowing off a little steam at the company holiday party in a few weeks.

We awoke Christmas Eve and enjoyed sitting by the tree sipping coffee, watching the boys play together. Watching them, I began to think back to my childhood Christmases shared with Jim. Memories came flooding back, and I could not help but smile, watching Duncan hold on to Tristan for support as he walked around the room. Quickly getting my camera, I snapped one of my all-time favorite photos, a picture of the boys in front of the picture window looking at each other. The settings on the camera just right, the shot is their two silhouettes, Duncan looking up at his big brother. I hope they treasure that photo their whole lives.

We spent that evening at Shannon's mom's place, enjoying a wonderful dinner together before letting the boys tear through their presents. Tristan made short work of his wrapping paper, while Duncan was a bit more hesitant at first, a little taken aback by all the commotion. After Tristan showed him the ropes, however, he soon followed suit.

Our first Christmas in our new home was everything we could have wished for. Tristan was up before dawn, brimming with anticipation to see what Santa had brought during the night. His excitement soon woke Duncan, and I got the video camera ready to film the big moment. Christmas morning is magical with any small children, but to be there beneath the star window in that beautiful timber frame home was almost too much to handle. It was hard to grasp that a year earlier we were sitting in the rental shack in front of our last-minute tree with just a few lights, while this very room sat frozen, dark, and lonely.

I was completely choked up when I saw Tristan's face light up as he rounded the corner and saw all the beautiful presents. Too big to wrap, their toy rock star keyboard and their mini-coaster with riding car were obviously the first presents to draw their attention. Before Shannon and I even realized what was happening, Tristan was on the little car and zooming down the twelve-foot track. Shannon amused herself by putting a fuzzy reindeer diaper on Duncan, complete with antlers and a bright red nose, and we laughed hysterically as he crawled around with it on. Duncan, no longer suffering from his wrapping paper insecurities, enjoyed the morning immensely. By the time my mom arrived later that morning, the first round of presents was complete, soon to be followed by many more. My family began to arrive after lunch, and we continued to open gifts, take dozens and dozens of photos and videos, and eat and eat.

As the year drew to a close and I reflected on all that had happened, the burden of our ninety-minute commute to Rockville, coupled with the extensive travelling required in my role, had finally taken their toll. Throughout the construction process, I had kept myself going on the promise that as soon as it was over, I would be able to spend so much more time with my boys. As it turned out, most days during the week they were still asleep when I left in the morning and already in their pajamas when I returned home at night.

We returned to work the first week of January 2008 while beginning to evaluate our other career options. It was simple math to figure out that our enormous monthly mortgage required professional salaries to stay afloat, and given that Notaviva's permit applications were still with the TTB, opening the tasting room did not seem like an option. I began to reach out to former colleagues in the market research industry, and learned that the former CEO of Greenfield Online, Dean Wiltse, was now running a company in nearby Dulles, Virginia. Among the many résumés I sent out over the next few weeks, one went to his new company, Vovici. I was surprised to hear back from him right away; though they did not have an opening at that time, he promised to keep me in mind, as they were in a rapid expansion mode.

The second week of January I was on a plane to Mexico City, and though I had been there before, it was still shocking to see the expanse of the city at night, its lights stretching off into the distance. The next morning during load-in, I experienced one of the worst back injuries I have ever had in my decades as an audio engineer and live event professional. There are few things worse than sustaining a serious injury in a foreign country, and I have been in hospitals in Canada, Ireland, and Spain, as well as a few visits in the United States. Although I badly needed some medical attention, the schedule of the simulcast and the likelihood of a long wait at a hospital meant that I was going to have to get through that evening's rehearsals, the next day's simulcast, and the following day's flight home with nothing more than an ice pack and a few anti-inflammatories.

One of the few bright spots that January was a visit over to Sunset Hills to meet with Ben and check on our wine. The moment we walked into the winery our moods lifted, and we were so excited to meet our wine for the first time. Using the tasting valve on the tank, Ben poured each of us a small bit and I was fascinated to see how cloudy it was prior to its upcoming filtering and fining processes. The aromas were superb, and Ben had no qualms about telling us that, even though there were two other Viogniers in nearby tanks for other wineries, ours was spectacular—truly a step above. Ben indicated that he had used the same strain of yeast on each of the other wines; we tasted each of them ourselves, and though perhaps biased, we could clearly see what he meant. Much more than just a splendid bouquet, our wine also had a wonderful mouthfeel, well-balanced acidity, and citrusy pink grapefruit flavors. Ben felt it best to get the wine into the bottle quickly, and had arranged a bottling day for February 15th. Since our permits were not yet processed (which was becoming cause for concern), we would not be able to label the bottles; they would be bottled as "shiners" with no labels affixed. That did save us from having to rush a label design as well as printing, which often can take weeks to complete. I was grateful that Ben would take care of ordering the corks, capsules, and labels for us.

The other bright spot that January was Duncan's first birthday, and as with every family event, it turned into a big party. Shannon and Shayna decided to have a dual party for both Duncan and our niece Makenzie, who was turning two. Dozens of friends and family turned out, and the pile of presents was nearly as big as the pile we'd had under the tree just a few weeks earlier. Nothing works as well for squashing new house anxieties like hosting a big children's party. Crumbs, icing, diapers, crayons, and all manner of "customizations" truly make a house a home.

Having learned my lesson with the disastrous Valentine's Day plan the previous year, I opted for a simple, quiet dinner at home with Shannon and the boys. Given that our first bottling was happening the following day, it definitely seemed like the most sensible option. When we awoke the next morning, we were incredibly excited to see the bottling process. As with the majority of small Virginia wineries, we would be using a mobile bottling line, which was housed in a large tow-behind trailer. The truck simply pulled up to the winery, connected to the tanks of prepared wine, and went into action. We learned that sterilization is the most critical aspect of preparing the bottling line, and watching the team run pressurized steam through every piece of equipment was fascinating. One dirty piece of gear can destroy an entire run, and this phase of preparation takes time and diligence.

Once the line was prepared, Ben had determined that, due to the tank order, our wine would be the first one bottled. As he connected the hose to our tank, the bottling crew was already in action dumping the bottles from the boxes onto the conveyor belts, where they would automatically be drawn into the equipment. When the bottling team gave the signal, Ben opened the valve on the tank, and we watched as the wine was pumped into the filling machine. It seemed that the whole truck sprang to life as the bottles were fed into the equipment, upturned and rinsed, then drained and flushed with a short burst of nitrogen. After sparging, the bottles were filled and leveled, the cork was pressed into place, and then the capsule hit with a quick burst of compressed air before being tightened by a spinning machine. Since we were not applying labels, the bare bottles returned from the end of the equipment line down a conveyor belt back to the outside of the truck. Shannon and I were trembling with excitement as the first bottle made its way to the end of the belt, and as the crew handed us that bottle, everyone congratulated us on the special moment. Ben was standing by with our camera to get the picture: Shannon and I standing amidst the pile of boxes and equipment, holding our first bottle. It was a moment we will remember forever.

The following Monday would prove to be our last day with the company. That evening, several of our colleagues reached out through their personal emails to wish us well and assure us they would be watching the show and would visit as soon as the winery was open. Though both Shannon and I had already been seeking new career alternatives, very few opportunities had emerged, and nothing had yet become a viable option.

With no savings left after building the house, funding the harvest, and bottling our wine, we were without any financial cushion save some money in our retirement accounts. Our checking account had less than two months' worth of expenses in it. We were now unemployed with no source of income and over $10,000 a month in bills, plus two toddlers to support. The United States had gone into a recession only two months earlier in December 2007 due to the Great Financial Crisis, which would eventually lead to the Great Recession. Companies were no longer hiring, and housing prices were falling, as were investment portfolio valuations and consumer confidence. The entire world was in an economic tailspin. To top it all off, we had a reality television show that would be on the air in a few months, putting our faces, our names, and our dream house on national television. It appeared to be a mathematical certainty that by the time the show aired, there would be a foreclosure sign hanging in the front yard. Our beautiful dream had seemingly overnight turned into a disaster worse than either of us could have ever imagined.

It seemed there was no way out this time; it would soon be all over.

PART THREE
Believe

CHAPTER 30
"Two Leaps of Faith"

There are moments in everyone's life when you are tested—truly, deeply, and cruelly tested. Not just faced with a difficult choice, like having to select the lesser of two evils, but really questioning the meaning of your entire life's journey up to that point. Many have referred to these moments as crossroads, where the path behind you seems clear, while the path ahead lies shrouded in mystery. To the left and right you find alternatives, less adventurous options much safer than the road ahead, though not fulfilling your passion as the original destination might have. On Wednesday, February 20, 2008, just two days after our corporate careers ended, Shannon and I got in our truck, hit the gas, and sped off straight ahead into the unknown.

We had spent that Tuesday in a daze, alternating between anxiety attacks and outright panic attacks. The financial calculations were beyond bleak; there was simply no way to support our huge mortgage and our boys without finding new jobs, fast. We spent hours combing career websites, looking for opportunities and sending résumés with little hope.

Wednesday dawned grey and dreary, and we decided it best to keep the boys engaged in their normal routine. We enjoyed breakfast together, prepared our coffees in travel mugs, got them dressed, and dropped them off at daycare. Then we did what comes naturally to both of us: we hit the road. Although I had spent over thirty years in Loudoun County, there were still large rural areas I had never explored. We decided to clear our heads and hope to be inspired by the surrounding landscapes. We drove for a couple hours, intentionally turning down roads we had never visited, for no reason other than to just be there, together in the moment.

Listening to the news each morning was not helping our outlook in the least. Anyone who remembers this period in American life will recall dismal job outlooks and foreclosure signs hanging everywhere. We began discussing how we were going to launch the Notaviva Vineyards tasting room in the months ahead, as we knew it needed to be operational before the television series aired in order to capitalize on that incredible marketing opportunity. As we proceeded through the checklist of startup marketing initiatives we would need, a realization began to set in.

For several years, I had been managing our winery website, and had also created our logo, brand identity, and first label designs. All that had been done on an old laptop with a web coding application and some graphic design software. I had all the tools I needed to start building websites and brand identities for other small businesses as well. Since we'd had no luck at all with our résumé submissions, we figured we had little to lose in setting up a new small business focused on creative media design and development. The more we drove and the more we talked, the more excited we became that this could actually be a real opportunity.

Arriving home for lunch, I quickly got on my laptop and began doing research, trying to figure out what we were going to call this new company. I was looking into descriptive terms for the core of our brand identity, a one stop shop for creative media. I knew I could program anything on the web, from simple sites to complex database applications. Although my graphic design skills were rudimentary, I knew I could challenge myself to become a master of those tools, learning art direction along the way. I knew I could write a script and produce a video, and though I had never actually edited anything besides our wedding video, I had every confidence I could figure that out as well. Producing events was something that both Shannon and I had been doing for over a decade, both on this continent and others, so that was a no-brainer. In addition, I knew I could write creatively, whether marketing copy or scripts, and that Shannon could pick apart a consulting contract like a classical music critic at the eighth grade variety show. Regardless of the challenges, creative media was our universe, and I believed with all my heart that we could pull it off if we could just stay afloat long enough.

The idea of "we do it all" really resonated with me, and as I got deeper into my research I kept coming across a communications technique known as "meshing," leveraging an experiential network to enable simultaneous integrated media delivery through multiple channels. In other words, businesses need to consider all possible channels when crafting their marketing message and strategic initiatives. By having all those skills under one roof, we would make it easy for businesses to have a single point of contact for all of their creative media needs.

During dinner I told Shannon about the concept, and she agreed it really conveyed our capabilities. By the time dinner was over, we had decided on the name Mesh Multimedia. I purchased Mesh Multimedia.com right away, secured a web-hosting package, and then went to an online business startup site to fill out the forms for a Virginia LLC. We opted to create the business as a women-owned entity; Shannon was a 51% member and I a 49% member. By midnight I had designed our first logo and built a five-page static website, all while sitting at my old laptop, perched upon Shannon's sewing machine desk inside what was supposed to have been a nursery adjoining our master bedroom. That four-foot by eight-foot closet was now the office of Mesh Multimedia, LLC.

Each of the next two mornings after dropping the boys off at daycare, Shannon and I set off in the truck again to find some answers along the back roads of Loudoun County. Excited that we had created a new opportunity for ourselves, the reality of our finances was ever-present on our minds. Knowing that it could take our new creative agency years to generate the kind of revenue we needed to simply survive, we knew that our situation was still incredibly bleak. Arriving home each afternoon frustrated and depressed, we did our best to put those thoughts aside for the sake of the boys. As we had already placed ourselves on a financial lockdown, that weekend was spent at home, playing with the boys and trying to keep a positive outlook. As bad as things were, we could always find solace in their hugs, and no matter what lay ahead of us, we were all healthy and incredibly thankful that we had each other.

Monday, February 20th again found us back in our mobile conference room after the day care drop-off, coffee in hand, our minds working furiously as we drew inspiration from the rolling hills and scenic vistas. Although we continued brainstorming how we could quickly market our creative agency to build some business, we always slipped back into the financial crisis discussion. We were in the same quandary as many small businesses; we had no money to allocate for marketing, so had few options for creating new client leads to create new business to fund new marketing initiatives. No matter how many times we ran through our account balances, the result was always the same. It began to occur to me, however, that perhaps our biggest asset was not in any bank, but was sitting empty every weekend on top of a hill with a beautiful view overlooking a vineyard. It dawned on us that maybe the house could save the house.

Shannon had mentioned to me that her brother was interested in bringing out some Georgetown University alumni on Sunday for an informal gathering. Suddenly, it all came together; I turned to Shannon and said, "Let's open the tasting room on Sunday. Why not let those Georgetown people come on out for their party?" She looked at me and said, "Well, then let's open on Saturday." We realized that although there was still an enormous amount of finishing work to do in the tasting room, we could get it looking done enough. The only missing piece was the wine.

We pulled over to the side of the road and called Doug. I hit him with the punchline right away: "Doug, we want to open our tasting room in five days, and you need to help us figure out a legal way to do it." Doug had gotten so used to our wild ideas, he did not seem rattled in the least. He quickly mentioned the notion of a "permanent remote" solution, which is a mechanism of Virginia ABC law that allows a farm winery to conduct retail operations at an offsite location. This is how wineries conduct tastings at festivals. Doug told us to get over to his place so we could figure out a plan. I hit the gas and off we went.

When we arrived, Doug explained that each winery is allowed to have up to four concurrent remotes that could last either a day or for an extended period of time. He would be able to enable an ABC license on our property, and we would sell Fabbioli wines. He also explained that we could have patrons taste our Viognier, but we would not be allowed to sell them a bottle. We all felt that it would be beneficial for brand awareness, and decided to add our Viognier to the tasting lineup. We would use Doug's credit card slips; he would then run the cards and pay us just the same as if we were festival employees. The plan sounded solid, everything was legal, Doug was thrilled to have another outlet for his wine, and we had solved our beverage dilemma. As we were leaving, Shannon called her brother and told him that he could invite over a few friends.

On the way home, we quickly put together our task list for the week, which, upon first glance, seemed pretty much impossible. We needed seating, tables, glassware, signage, and checkout supplies, in addition to a finished and usable tasting bar. As soon as we got home I got to work updating our website, then began designing a few pieces of signage. We figured we would place a few signs at various intersections out on the main road, which over the past couple years had turned into one of Loudoun County's two main wine alleys. We would also need some parking directions and a main entrance sign. I worked well into the night on the art files, which I took to the printer the next morning. I also collated the several dozen email addresses we had been collecting from curious passersby and family, and sent out a short newsletter announcing our soft launch that coming Saturday. Shannon got on the phone with Doug again to sort out what we would need in terms of checkout and tasting bar supplies. Tasting sheets, pencils, corkscrews, cleaning supplies, citric acid for the dishwashers; the list kept growing.

The next morning, I created a plan for finishing the tasting bar. It was still exactly as we had left it at the housewarming party, a 2" x 6" curved skeleton framework, covered by a thin sheet of plywood adorned with the signatures of family and friends. I needed to create a structural plywood top, which would support a flagstone tile finish and trim edging. I also needed to skin the outside with a knotty pine veneer to match the trim, as well as install several Douglas fir supports designed to complement the timber frame.

I had most of the tile material left over from the flooring installation. The pine veneer was challenging, but I found a supplier online who could ship for arrival late the following day. I headed out to the supply store for some sturdy oak plywood, which would be the curved structural top, and began construction by midafternoon. Shannon spent the day running errands, and returned home with a "festival box" from Doug, containing most of the supplies typically used for checkout at a festival as well as several cases of wine. She also brought his tasting sheets, which I used as a guide to create and print our own Notaviva-branded ones. In the end, we decided to pour our Notaviva tank-fermented Viognier, Ben's "LoCo Vino" off-dry white blend, and four of Doug's wines. It was Tuesday night, four days until opening.

I spent a cold day Wednesday outside with the tile saw for the tasting bar's flagstone top, and finished up just as the pine veneer was delivered. I installed the supports and started the veneer on Thursday, and on Friday, the day before opening, I finished the bar veneer and a few pieces of trim. I was out of time, and would not be able to grout the bar top, nor install any kind of toe kick, but as we had hoped, the bar was done enough and was able to hold up a wine glass just fine. I drove over to the printers to pick up the signs. We only had a couple hours left before we had to pick the boys up from daycare, so we quickly went to the local big box store to pick up four card tables and sixteen folding chairs—very swanky stuff.

After enjoying dinner together, Shannon played with the boys while I began cleaning up my tools and moving them back out to the winery. Once the boys were asleep, Shannon joined me for the final cleanup; after vacuuming and mopping, the place really looked nice.

We awoke on Saturday, March 1st with just a few tasks left unfinished before we were ready to open, chief of which was placing the signage at strategic places on the main road. Shamelessly, I placed a "Now Open" sign in nearby Hillsboro, at the intersection where Doukénie had also placed a sign. Later that day, their staff was gracious enough to call over and see how we were doing, as each of them had noticed our sign and wanted to congratulate us on our opening.

Arriving home to a big breakfast Shannon had made to celebrate the day, I began to reflect on the enormity of the situation. Just a week earlier, we had been riddled with panic attacks about our bleak situation, had made yet another huge leap of faith in deciding to open the tasting room with exactly zero experience, and here we were. It was daunting to say the least, but invigorating nonetheless. As noon approached, I stood behind the bar, wondering if anyone was even going to show up; in true Virginia wine country fashion, I did not have to wait long. About 12:15 P.M. a car pulled into the parking lot. Shannon and I looked at each other and we both just froze. It suddenly dawned on me that I had never conducted a wine tasting before. In fact, I had never even set foot behind a wine tasting bar in my life. I looked at Shannon and asked, "What the hell am I supposed to say to these people?" to which she replied, "Just be yourself, and you have about two minutes to figure it out."

Our first customers turned out to be the sweetest middle-aged couple we could have hoped for, and they were so taken with the timber frame I could barely get a word in edgewise. It turned out they had known about the filming of our HGTV show, and were on their way to Doukénie when they saw our sign. Thus our first customers were actually pirated from Doukénie, so I made them promise to head straight back there, which they had intended to do anyway. They were Viognier lovers, and based their wine country visits around wineries that had a Viognier in their portfolio. They were incredibly complementary when they tasted our wine, and although disappointed that they could not buy a bottle, promised to be back in a few months when our licenses were in place. They bought a bottle of Fabbioli's, in spite of my bumbling through the tasting—just like that, we made our first sale. I could not have gotten luckier, and Shannon was so excited while we chatted with them. They wished us luck, took a few pictures of the tasting room, and promised to watch the show when it aired. It was such a whirlwind; I regret to this day not getting their names.

We were off and running, and as our first couple was leaving, another came in. Now that I was a seasoned wine industry veteran, I was ready for these folks; though I would not say it was an aficiona-do-worthy tasting, I had them laughing throughout their entire visit. They also loved the Viognier and wished they could have bought a bottle, but were just as happy to buy one of Ben's LoCo Vinos instead. As they were leaving, they said something that Shannon and I have used to define the Notaviva Vineyards tasting room experience to this day: "You all are so fun!" Five little words, yet they had such huge implications. On both of my first two tastings, we had achieved the exact vibe we had envisioned on all those long trips back and forth to Connecticut. There was no wine snob atmosphere, no condescension, nothing of the sort. We had a semi-finished tasting bar, super cheap furniture, and neither couple could have cared less. We had great wine and casual conversation; we just talked to them like friends, because we were genuinely excited and appreciative that they took the time to visit, and that meant everything to us. We also introduced them to the boys, and they were stunned to learn that they were standing in our kitchen, and that our bedrooms were downstairs. Within one hour of opening our doors, our tasting room customer experience was set in stone.

The rest of the day was a blur, as a dozen or so other guests made their way out to enjoy a tasting, and all of them added their names to our email list. Shannon had picked up cheese and crackers that we made available for purchase, and a few people shared a bottle with these snacks at a card table in front of the picture windows. They looked as content as if they were sitting at the finest winery in all of Europe. On that cold winter day, we learned one of our most important lessons: it is the people who make the experience memorable. We knew we would never be the most extravagant, the most elegant, nor the largest, but we could always strive to be the friendliest and the most fun winery someone had ever visited.

The following day we had a few couples come by, as well as the Georgetown group, who hung out for several hours up in the catwalk. It flew quickly by as we regaled people with stories from the television shoots and the construction project. As the last guest left late that afternoon, Shannon and I enjoyed a bottle of our Viognier with dinner and toasted to the week behind us and the wonderful years ahead of us.

Monday, March 3rd, after we dropped the boys off at daycare, we were on the road again for another planning session. We spent hours driving the back roads, evaluating the weekend: the things that went well, the lessons that we learned, the people that we met. Even though we had a few dozen people visit, and even though they had all enjoyed and purchased wine, our profit was about $200. Although we had no illusions that we were somehow going to make big money through our ramshackle opening, we now had real receipts, expenses, and projections that we could use to assess our opportunity. In no time at all, it was clear that although opening the tasting room was the right move in terms of building marketing buzz, it was going to do little in terms of actually supporting our mortgage and family.

In two weeks, we had gone from salaried executives to owning and operating two woefully underfunded small businesses. If we got really lucky and it never rained on weekends ever again, our winery would be able to generate enough revenue to pay the utilities and buy groceries—that was about it. Our creative agency had an asset valuation (one old laptop) less than the desk it was sitting on, a client roster of exactly zero companies, and a pipeline of exactly zero dollars.

When Roger called that evening to ask how we were doing after the weekend winery launch, Shannon simply fibbed and said, "Everything is great!" to avoid giving him a panic attack, which telling him the truth would have undoubtedly caused. Parents worry anyway, and

Roger is a very intelligent guy; I do not think he bought her story in the least. That night, much like his grandson Duncan did in the months after he was born, I am sure he went to bed with an upset stomach and a worried look on his face.

CHAPTER 31
"The Grand Opening"

In a strange twist of fate, the house threw itself a lifeline. After completing our tax returns, it turned out we were due a sizeable refund because of the mortgage interest and points we had paid during the closing the previous summer. When I showed Shannon the estimated refund in the software, I thought she was going to faint. We were actually going to be able to live in our house for at least another three months before we got tossed out onto Sagle Road.

A few days later, we made our way up to Lancaster, Pennsylvania for the annual Wineries Unlimited industry conference. For us, those kinds of shows can be pretty depressing—walking around the expo floor, looking at all the shiny equipment, knowing that we may as well be walking around an exotic car show. Still, you need to have an eye on the future, and we found inspiration looking at the tools and equipment that real wineries were using. While we were there, we stopped into the TTB booth to ask about the delays in our permit approval. We learned that the agent assigned to our project had been out of the office for nearly two months on personal medical leave. They were visibly concerned that we had not been notified of the situation, and promised to follow up when they got back to the office. Sure enough, our application was reassigned to another agent the following Monday; after a quick phone call to get caught up, we were assured that all of our paperwork was in order and that we should receive our approval in about a week.

Now that spring was fast approaching, our morning meetings had gotten quite short, if they happened at all. Shannon was busy working in the tasting room, sanding and painting the main stairway and tending to other interior touch-ups. I was busy working outside on landscaping, working my way through several huge burn piles that were remnants of the construction project. We both worked at pruning the vineyard in preparation for the upcoming season.

On March 26th, we hosted our first Loudoun Winegrowers Association (LWGA) meeting to introduce ourselves to the many members of the winery community we had not yet met. Nearly forty people turned out to see the house, attend the meeting, and visit with friends and colleagues afterwards. It was wonderful for us to finally put faces with the names we had heard about for years now, and everyone was incredibly friendly and complimentary about the timber frame. One of the growers was on the board of the performing arts center at nearby Franklin Park, and during my welcome, I mentioned that we had just formed Mesh Multimedia. She approached me afterwards, indicating that the arts center was looking for a new website, and we agreed to meet the following day to discuss the project. A critical synergy between Notaviva Vineyards and Mesh Multimedia began that has continued to this day.

In early April, Shannon and I were featured in the *Washington Business Journal* article, "Virginia Gradually Builds a Reputation as One of the Nation's Leading Wine Regions." As a die-hard web analytics enthusiast, I was amazed to see the spike in traffic to our website after the article came out. In addition, we saw a sizeable lift in traffic to the Mesh website due to the links at the bottom of the Notaviva page. A few inquiries came in, and a few proposals went out. Small jobs mostly, but still enough to create some excitement and positive energy.

Our approval from the TTB had finally come in, and now it was time to begin the application process with the state of Virginia. Thankfully, much of the application was the same as with the federal process, though there were a few additions, including public posting on the front of the house as well as in local newspapers. I got to work on that right away, since completing the Virginia process was the final step in getting our farm winery license, which we would need in order to bottle and sell our own wines. So much was happening all of a sudden that we had to place a call to Doug's vineyard crew to come over and help us finish our pruning. Shannon and I had completed nearly half of the entire vineyard by ourselves, but now the demands of marketing and running both businesses were actually starting to keep us busy. Doug also advised that it was time to start thinking about blending our Cabernet Franc and figuring out what else we wanted to sell, so we set up a meeting at his winery for April 21st.

In my opinion, the blending process is the point in a wine's life-cycle where it goes from being a technical endeavor to an artistic one. It was this realization that eventually led me to change my title from "winemaker" to "wine composer." This is where the soul and personality of a wine is revealed for the very first time. It can be a very challenging and humbling process, and requires discipline, intense focus, and copious note taking to conduct properly. Our first blending exercise was an incredibly eye-opening experience, definitely one of the moments where we realized how little we actually knew about the mysteries of winemaking.

Doug's assistant Ryan was on hand to help, and having different perspectives and opinions on each blend was very enlightening. For Shannon and me, the process was very much akin to mixing music, and I was particularly amazed at the differences that even the most subtle adjustment could make in a wine blend. I found myself thinking back to the hundreds of times the slightest touch of a console fader was all that was required to balance a rhythm section and a lead vocalist. I was also reminded of how often in pro audio the right answer to a mixing challenge was to bring one instrument down in order to open up the spectrum for another. Mixing music is not always about pushing faders; more often than not, it is about pulling faders or shaping a tonality to "make room" in the mix. Although I had just sat down at my first blending experience, I knew in an instant I had nearly twenty years of perspective behind me.

The blending table starts off looking like the desk in a chemistry lab, with graduated cylinders, Erlenmeyer flasks, pipets, pH meters, and other assorted test gear. The most important piece of equipment is the spit bucket, which is essential if you want to keep your wits about you and make solid judgments. The process begins with an inventory of each of the wines available and their available amounts. Experience plays a key role in starting down the right path, and this is where working with a seasoned consultant is critical.

We began by tasting our Cabernet Franc, samples of which Doug had pulled from the barrels that morning. We also individually tasted some Petit Verdot, Tannat, and Tinto Cão that Doug had made some small batches of to use as blending wines. Doug suggested that we make an educated guess as to where a starting point might be; he suggested we begin with an 80% Cab Franc/10% Tannat/10% Petit Verdot blend. I figured that with 80% Cab Franc, the blended wine would pretty much taste just like the varietal Cab Franc; it was not even close. Shannon and I were amazed how completely different the blend was, yet how we could still pick out the distinct characteristics of the two smaller blended wines as well. We took our notes, then Doug changed the blend to 90%/7.5%/2.5% and we all took more notes. With the second pass, we all seemed to agree that the wine took on a truer Cabernet Franc varietal characteristic: ground black pepper and a hint of dried tobacco leaves. There are no right answers and there are no wrong answers when blending a wine, there are just different answers. To us, it was the exact same realizations gleaned after years of mixing music. A mix that I thought was "perfect" might sound thin to bass players, wimpy to a drummer, keyboard-heavy to a guitar player, or "too much band" to a vocalist. The key is to find the best middle ground that keeps most of the people happy most of the time, but more importantly than anything, to follow your instincts.

After only our second blend, we decided that we wanted our Cabernet Franc blend to exhibit those varietal characteristics, and determined that it would be 90% of the blend. Now we were entering the fine-tuning stages, adjusting the percentages of the other two wines in different directions to see where they might fit. Next up was the removal of the Tannat altogether, and we took notes on a 90% Cab Franc/10% Petit Verdot blend; it only took a second for us to agree that something was missing. I asked Doug to create a 90% Cab Franc/9% Petit Verdot/1% Tannat blend. That 1% of the Tannat absolutely brought the wine to life, even more from a bouquet perspective than on the palate. Ryan remarked that the moment was like walking through the woods on a crisp October day, dragging your foot through a pile of leaves to reveal the heady scent of the earth mixed with the spicy complexity of the leaves. That subtle touch of Tannat was the soul of the wine, and our "Cantabile" Cabernet Franc was born. I chose the name "Cantabile" as it is a musical term meaning graceful and full of expression. I felt that wine really captured the prevailing notion of Virginia wine being an old world style, similar to European wines, in stark contrast to the new world wines of Australia, New Zealand, and California.

We moved to blend two other wines, a dry Chambourcin and a Tinto Cão dessert wine inspired by Doug's popular Raspberry Merlot. These two wines would be purchased in bulk from Doug, then bottled with our label on them, an arrangement very typical of new wineries. This has an impact on the verbiage that is placed on the actual wine label, but it turned out our customers could have cared less; they just liked the wines and experience. I had not yet named these wines, but had a concept inspired by our recent homebuilding experience. The day was a success, and we were very excited to get the wines into the bottle.

We were contacted by the Virginia ABC the very next day, and were thrilled when our agent indicated he could set up a meeting with us in just two days. Meeting with Dallas "Burnie" Gaskill was amazing; his experience and knowledge were vast, and although I peppered him with numerous neophyte questions, he took the time to answer each one carefully. He talked me through each aspect of the inspection, and was glad that I had prepared our winery and equipment for his visit. We established camaraderie right away, and as he was preparing to leave, he said, "If you are not sure about how to abide by a law or a rule, just call me first." He said the ABC would much rather help people stay in compliance, rather than have to chase them down after a law has been broken. We have heeded that advice, and through the dozens of phone calls, we have avoided many of the pitfalls that have gotten other wineries into serious (and expensive) trouble. Crafting and serving alcoholic beverages is a monumental responsibility, not only to the patrons, but to your staff, your business, and most importantly, to your community.

Now that we were officially a Virginia farm winery, we could get moving on label designs and approval processes, and set a date for a grand opening. The producers at High Noon had emailed to tell us that the *Dream House* series would premiere the morning of Saturday, July 5th, so we decided to have our official grand opening the previous weekend. It was the first week of May, and the house was abuzz with activity. We were working on label designs, ordering supplies for the upcoming bottling at Fabbioli Cellars, and also trying to figure out how we could come up with more wine to sell. Doug suggested we reach out to Breaux Vineyards to see if they had any bulk wine to sell, so I contacted their winemaker, Dave Collins. Dave indicated that they had some availability, and suggested I come over to taste some of their inventory.

It was a full circle moment for Shannon and me, since Breaux was the spot where we had our romantic whim of founding our own winery. As we discussed our plans with Dave, we noted we had a dry, un-oaked Viognier, two dry reds, and a dessert wine. It seemed to me that we needed an off dry white to complete our portfolio, in part because Ben's "LoCo Vino" continued to be a hit in our tasting room, and also because Dave indicated that Breaux's "Chere Marie" semi-sweet white was a top-seller during the summer months. We began tasting through the wines, and felt it was one of those decisions we could not get wrong. All the wines were well-made; it was just a matter of picking a style and getting the residual sugar in balance with the acidity. We chose a tank-fermented Chardonnay, and rather than match the "Chere Marie" 2% residual sugar, we felt that a lower 1% complemented the acidity without being cloying. I mentioned that it would be interesting to have just a slight touch of oak in the wine, and Dave said he could add a few oak spirals to the tank, to create a slight hint of oak aroma and flavor to the stainless steel wine. We now had our fifth Notaviva Vineyards wine, and this Chardonnay would be the first in the construction-inspired wine series I had finally named. The "Dream" Chardonnay, "Build" Chambourcin, and "Believe" Tinto Cão would each feature a before, during, and after photograph of the tasting room during each phase of construction. Our total production that year was just over 500 cases.

We were also researching area bands to find some great local talent to feature on opening weekend. We came across Chelsea Lee, a young singer-songwriter who was selling out venues in the area. Chelsea would be our first act, opening up for Furnace Mountain, a traditional Appalachian ensemble of incredibly talented musicians. Having the diversity of an indie-rock singer-songwriter opening for a traditional regional act was the perfect complement to our tasting room vibe. For Sunday, we opted for a classical guitarist to soften the mood and create a more peaceful vibe.

Mesh had also begun to gain momentum. We had recently met with several members of Loudoun County's Department of Economic Development (DED), who were incredibly supportive of our recent winery soft launch and also very intrigued by the fact that we were now running both a rural business and a creative agency. The team extended Shannon and me an invitation to their upcoming VIP reception at the National Conference Center just a few weeks away, so we could network with other business leaders in the county.

We scheduled a meeting with the DED's technology sector manager, Buddy Rizer, who paid us a visit the first week of May. During that conversation we learned that he was previously the program director at DC-101, my absolute favorite local rock radio station, and we instantly had a connection through our love of music and sharing of "backstage" stories.

Buddy inquired about our capabilities at Mesh, and was interested in having us create a welcome video for the VIP event. The piece was to be an extension of a marketing campaign they had been working on, featuring a montage of prominent business leaders. I assured him that we had vast experience in video production and would extend them a deep discount on the editing in exchange for sponsorship recognition at the event. He was excited that such a professional looking video would greet the guests as they entered. What I somehow neglected to mention was that I personally had never edited a single video in my life (other than my wedding photo montage), nor did I own any video editing software or a machine on which to run it. Somehow Shannon held herself together while listening to this conversation, and when Buddy left, calmly inquired exactly how I thought I was going to pull this off. "No problem," I told her, and got her blessing to use our personal credit card to go online and buy an iMac from the Apple refurbished computer store and a copy of Final Cut Express HD.

The computer and software were set to arrive on Monday, May 5th, and the event was Saturday, May 17th; I had twelve days to learn how to use a Mac (I had never actually owned one) as well as the video editing software. Other than a few minor distractions like spraying the vineyard every ten days, designing marketing materials for Notaviva, coding a few client websites, meeting with the DED team to collect media and prepare the storyboards, bottling wines, and working in the tasting bar, I figured there would be plenty of time to digest a few dozen hours of tutorials to get that video delivered. I bought a folding banquet table, and relocated my office from the master suite closet to the spare bedroom. As I disappeared into a production black hole, Shannon had the boys, the house, the bills, and now the staff to deal with, as we had enlisted some family and friends to help out in the tasting room on weekends. I lost count of the hours and late nights learning about video editing, compression codecs, rendering engines, and workflow, but somehow I actually managed to pull it off with a few days to spare.

The video was incredibly well-received during the event, and DED would use it for years on the screen in their lobby in the Loudoun government building. We were a bit shocked at how many people knew who we were and were familiar with our story. People were curious about the television show and about the wine industry, and we had a wonderful time visiting and networking with such an amazing diversity of business owners. After we picked up the boys from my mom's place and returned home late that night, we were still talking about all the conversations we'd had and people we'd met. Although our bank accounts were still suffering and sliding backwards, there was very positive energy surrounding both businesses, and it was up to us to capitalize on that momentum.

Now that all of our wine was getting bottled, I had to turn my attention to building a temporary temperature-controlled space where we could store it. The winery building was just a metal shell with a concrete slab, unsuitable for storing wine. Since we had no money to hire a contractor, I was going to have to do all the work myself; we hit the credit card again to order lumber, drywall, and materials for a case storage room in the back of the winery. It took me about three days to frame and drywall the room, which was designed with a ceiling that would eventually become the floor of a mezzanine level. The worst part of the construction was donning a full-body protective suit and facemask to install the insulation. Of course, that day it was in the high nineties, so by the time I had insulated the walls, I thought I was going to pass out.

As I was insulating the ceiling, my foot slipped off the joist and I went straight down through the ceiling drywall until my hip crashed into a joist. It took me nearly an hour to gather my senses enough to climb down the ladder and make my way up the house. Shannon wanted to rush me to the emergency room, but I did not think my hip was broken. The swelling continued to grow, and I could not walk for another two days. During that time, the electric company came out and ran power from the street to the winery, hooked up our meter box, and installed a GFI plug in the storage room. After I limped down to the winery, all I had to do was plug in the two small air conditioning units that I had pre-installed, and the room was complete (with the exception of the hole in the ceiling where the insulation was hanging through).

We had decided to take advantage of the early June slowdown to visit Roger and Bev in Indianapolis. I was miserable sitting in the truck for the eleven-hour trip, but made the best of it. In addition to my hip, the rest of my joints continued to trouble me with stiffness and pain, no matter how much rest I tried to get. The first day in Indianapolis, Shannon told me I was going to see a doctor no matter what I thought, and made me an appointment. The swelling on my hip had grown so large it created a visible lump in my running shorts; after an X-ray, I learned that nothing was broken, and the lump was a hematoma that I would likely have for the rest of the summer. We enjoyed a wonderful vacation, and by the time we drove home, we were excitedly making plans for the winery's grand opening a few weeks away.

June 12th was our fourth wedding anniversary, and as we cuddled with the boys in bed that morning, we tried to take stock of what had transpired over the previous four years. So much had happened; it was hard to take it all in. We finally got up and went about our day, and when I came in for lunch, Shannon had just gone out to check the mail. She came in with an envelope from the Virginia State Fair. She quickly opened it and screamed, "You will not believe it!" The letter was congratulations from the State Fair wine competition, letting us know our Viognier had won a gold ribbon. Our first wine, our first competition, and we had received a top honor. The letter listed all the winners, and we were stunned to see our name amongst the finest and most storied wineries in the state. It was a wonderful anniversary present.

The next two weeks flew by as we continued our preparations for the grand opening. The vineyard was in full swing and in need of constant attention, from leaf pulling to shoot positioning to spraying. The biggest task was the construction of the side deck. Now that we would be attracting larger crowds and possibly people needing assistance coming up the front stairs, we knew we would need a ramp to get in the tasting bar. It took about four days to dig and pour the footers, place and level the support posts, install the ledger board and joists, then install the decking. Even though I ran out of time and would have to install the railings later, at least the deck was in place with a temporary ramp installed. I spent an afternoon building two picnic tables that we set outside the boys' rooms overlooking the pond. Those and a few of our old patio furniture sets would have to do for customer seating.

Saturday, June 28th dawned bright and sunny, perfect for our big day. Both of our mothers arrived early to help with set up and watch the boys, while Shannon and I hurried about with final preparations. Shannon's brother Steve, our friend Tracy Krohn, and my cousin Beth Smith were on hand to help out with the wine pouring. Due to two more local newspaper articles, one in the *Loudoun Times Mirror* and another in the *Washington Post*, the word had spread that a new winery was opening with two highly regarded local music acts. Guests started arriving right as we opened the doors at 11:00 A.M., and by noon the parking lot was packed.

When the bands arrived for sound check, they were simply amazed at the unique nature of the music loft. They had never seen anything like it, much less the professional audiovisual equipment we had installed. Set up went quickly, and both bands were fascinated by our backgrounds in live sound. It did not take long for them to understand that this was not just another "play in the corner" gig. Even better than the musician's reaction was the reaction of the guests when the bands started playing. They were not accustomed to seeing that kind of talent in such an informal winery setting. Chelsea had teamed up with her collaborator, local favorite Todd Wright. The two of them kicked off the day with a set of originals from Chelsea's debut EP, and the moment they began playing, it was safe to say the bar had been raised for live music in the Virginia wine industry.

Our Viognier was drawing rave reviews at the bar, as were all of our other wines. Not only were people enjoying their tastings, but they were also buying wines by the glass and by the bottle to sit and enjoy the music. Once Chelsea and Todd finished up, I took a break from the tasting bar and raced upstairs to set up Furnace Mountain. They were so easy to work with, incredibly talented, and in no time at all, we had sound checked. As I went back to the bar, several of the customers stopped me to compliment us on the building, the music, and the wines. It almost seemed like people were shocked that the wines were so good; I think they half-expected the wine to be terrible since we had just opened our doors. It was rewarding to hear the compliments.

As Furnace Mountain blazed through raucous arrangements of traditional Appalachian music, their infectious spirit resonated throughout the tasting room. People were tapping their feet, enjoying the music, enjoying the wine, enjoying the whole atmosphere. Tristan and Duncan came up to the tasting bar to say hello to the guests, and people enjoyed meeting the boys while Shannon and I poured and regaled them with stories from the construction and television production. It was all very magical, and even though there was no fancy furniture or opulent décor, nobody cared. We were all having the time of our lives, surrounded by friends, family, customers, wine, and music.

That evening, after the guests had left and we had swept up the day's debris, we gathered around the bar to open a few celebratory bottles and recount the stories of the day. Since we had been open for a few months by now, most of the operational processes had been sorted out, and there had been no major incidents to contend with throughout the day. Tristan and Duncan were now in their pajamas running around the tasting room, wondering why all the people had disappeared and if they would be returning. We explained to them that those people were Mommy and Papa's customers, and that they had come to our house to buy the wine that we made. Duncan snatched a cookie, and Tristan asked, "Will they come back someday?"

Since we had just unveiled a completely unique perspective on the world of wine, and had spent the day telling customers that wine should be paired with music, Mommy and Papa were actually wondering the same thing.

CHAPTER 32
"Learning to Make Wine"

Three days before our grand opening, I had received an email from Dean Wiltse, the CEO of Vovici, reaching out to see if I might be interested in a position that had just been created. I responded that Shannon and I had launched the winery as well as a fledgling creative agency, and I was pretty busy already. Dean, knowing well my ability to multi-task and handle tough assignments, thought I should come in anyway. The Tuesday after Notaviva Vineyard's grand opening, I was sitting in his office in nearby Dulles, Virginia.

We spent some time catching up, me filling him in on the years since I had left Greenfield, and he filling me in on how Vovici was formed by the acquisition of two companies: one with a software solution, the other with a large customer base. Dean was looking for someone who could navigate the grey areas of the enterprise software world. He needed someone who could be conversant with customers to understand their custom requirements, a sales team who wanted to win a deal regardless of whether or not it could be built, a marketing team trying to figure out why the product offerings changed with every deal, and a development team who had to actually implement and support the custom solution. I knew only a nutcase would take that job, and so did Dean; that was why he wrote me.

After figuring out that Dean was really trying to rein in the custom jobs that had gone awry and subsequently turned into big expensive messes, I was intrigued. As I counted up the hours in the day and the days in the week, however, I realized that a forty-hour per week office job with a commute would essentially end my involvement with both Notaviva and Mesh. We were really hitting our stride with both, and to turn away now did not seem to make sense.

As we discussed my reservations, Dean became intrigued by my video production capabilities with Mesh, and asked if I was able to do software demos. The marketing team had just been given a budget to create several new product demos, and the previous ones had turned out terribly. I, of course, responded, "Certainly, I could create a software demo unlike anything you have ever seen." Dean had realized that I probably was not going to walk away from our two new small businesses, but he also had enough faith in me to realize that there was still an opportunity here. He urged me to consider all the options, and as I was leaving simply said, "Put together a proposal for the videos, and then figure out what kind of employment scenario makes sense and send it over—I'll take a look at it and see what the other executives think."

Shannon, who had always liked and respected Dean, pounced on me as soon as I got home. As I relayed the details of the conversation, she knew that we had an opportunity to restore a bit of stability to our lives. Although I was worried about being able to devote enough time to her and the boys, much less the two small businesses, she did have a point; some stability did sound very attractive. The question of whether or not I would respond to Dean with an employment scenario was settled instantly, however, when I informed her that part of any employment package would be comprehensive health insurance. The conversation was over; the fact that we could have baby number three if I took this job was the deciding factor.

That night, I sent Dean a letter outlining my thoughts for a thirty-hour per week engagement as director of professional services, with a corresponding salary and full benefits. In exchange for only having to be in the office one full day a week, I would agree to a seven-day per week availability clause. In addition, I sent a separate proposal for the creation of six software demo videos, the sum of which was larger than all of the projects we had worked on up to that point. Two days later, my employment agreement was approved, with a starting date of that coming Monday, July 7th. I was also connected with the marketing team and we scheduled a meeting to discuss our video proposal, which they commented was extremely competitive. Shannon was elated, and as soon as I faxed off my signed employment agreement, she called the midwives to schedule an appointment for a checkup.

We were also putting together our production plan for the upcoming harvest. We had made the commitment to produce as much of our own wine as possible, though without a refrigeration system, our tank-fermented Viognier would have to be produced elsewhere. Mark and Vicki Fedor of nearby North Gate Vineyard agreed to take our tank and install it into their winery so they could produce our Viognier for us. In the summer of 2008, a few years prior to building their new beautiful facility, their tank farm was still located in their garage; they had just enough room to squeeze in our tank. We had met the Fedors several years earlier at one of the first Loudoun Wine-growers Association meetings we had attended. Simply put, they are two of the kindest, smartest, most sincere people we have ever had the pleasure of knowing, in the wine industry or anywhere else. Their passion and abilities for winemaking, love of music and family, and their backgrounds in computer science made us fast friends.

Knowing that our tank would live at North Gate for the year, we still had to figure out how to produce the rest of our wines. Looking at the inventory depletion rates we were seeing in the tasting room, the 500 cases we had produced in 2007 were barely going to make it to the end of the year before being sold out. We put together a production plan targeted at 1,200 cases. Winery production plans are actually pretty simple to put together; you basically target how much finished wine you want to produce, then work backwards from there. For example, 1,200 cases are 14,400 750mL bottles of wine, roughly 2,853 gallons. Accounting for a 10% production loss from juice to wine (from settling, racking, filtering, etc.), you need to start with about 3,170 gallons of juice. The loss is usually lower, but the higher value is useful for estimation purposes. Assuming 150 gallons of juice per ton (varietal and equipment dependent), we would need to crush just over 21 tons of fruit in the upcoming season. In addition to our anticipated 12 tons, we had secured grape contracts with three other local growers to provide the rest of the fruit.

Once you have those numbers, you calculate how many gallons of storage you need, for fermentation as well as transfer and storage. The concept of transfer and storage is incredibly important, as having a single tank really does you no good—you always need at least one extra, usually more than that, depending on how complex your blends are going to be. If you have one tank containing a fermented wine, you need somewhere to go when you are racking off the lees or filtering or fining. Then you clean out the gooey tank and it becomes your transfer tank.

Doug suggested that we ferment our white wines in barrels, to avoid having to invest in multiple tanks and the refrigeration system for a couple of years until we built up the capital to invest in that equipment. The major issue with wine fermentation is temperature control. Fermentation is an exothermic reaction, which gives off a lot of heat, thus the required refrigeration jackets on the back of our stainless steel tank. By fermenting in barrels, however, the smaller amount of liquid would allow the ambient temperature of the winery to keep the temperature of the fermenting wine at a reasonable level. An unrefrigerated tank with hundreds or thousands of gallons of juice could easily reach temperatures well over 100 degrees, ruining the wine for certain. Juice fermenting in a barrel stays about five degrees over ambient temperature, or in our storage room, about sixty-four degrees.

Given our limited space (still just the single cold storage room in the back of the winery) and limited funds, this really seemed like our only option. We purchased thirty used barrels from Doug, who each year coordinates a deal with a barrel shipping company in California. Whereas a new French oak barrel can cost upwards of $1,200, a second or third-fill barrel can be purchased for around $250, which is a significant savings for a startup winery. Once our barrels arrived, along with the racks used to stack them, I moved them into the cold storage room. Since they would not be used for several months, they would have to be treated by burning small discs of sulfur inside of them, creating a noxious gas that kills any microbes within. I was doing my best to process all of this information and was increasingly grateful for my AP chemistry class in high school, as well as my year of chemistry at Virginia Tech.

By mid-July, everything had settled into a reasonable groove. I was adapting to my new role, though my thirty-hour per week job was more like forty. As expected, I found myself on conference calls and proposal reviews at all hours of the day and evening, while working on Mesh web projects and learning new video tools and techniques late into the night. Shannon was busy running the tasting room, which was now open on Thursdays and Fridays as well as the weekend. Although I was not able to be in the bar during the week, I still joined Shannon each weekend to conduct wine tastings and visit with customers. Many were curious when the HGTV show was going to air; we had just learned that the premiere had been delayed. They simply wanted to air a show about a winery in the fall, and we all soon learned that was the best decision they could ever have made.

Shannon and I awoke at 2:00 A.M. on Wednesday, July 23rd, to a torrential thunderstorm and the unmistakable sound of hail pelting the windows. I knew without a doubt that I was not going to enjoy my morning walk through the vineyard. Sure enough, when day broke, I was looking at berries that had been cracked open by the hail, leaving them to rot in the hot morning sun. I estimated we lost about 10% to 15% of our crop that night from the damage. Now those clusters would have to be hand-sorted (or just not picked at all) at harvest, depending on the extent of the damage. Worse, there was now sugary juice from the damaged berries leaking all over the rest of the fruit, which would be much more exposed to molds and mildews. I contacted Jim MacKenzie, our representative at Helena Chemicals, and he advised I purchase some Oxidate, which I would need to spray that night to eradicate any live molds or mildews prior to my next preventative spray. Since I had conference calls to make, Shannon headed down to the Helena warehouse.

Just a few weeks later, we were hammered by an even more severe hailstorm. On the afternoon of Thursday, August 14th, Shannon and I watched helplessly from the tasting room as hail piled up against the glass doors. By the time it was over, the pellets of hail were several inches deep where they had collected against the house. As quickly as it began, the storm dissipated and the sun shone hotly over the vineyard. The damage was far more extensive than after the previous storm. The canopy looked like someone had blown it apart with a shotgun. We had easily just lost another 25% of our crop in about ten minutes. The stark realization hit that no matter how hard we tried, nor how well we planned, the winery business at its core is farming, and we would forever be at the mercy of the environment.

I again reached out to Jim as well as Ben Renshaw for advice. They both were worried that such canopy damage might slow the ripening of the fruit and suggested I apply a foliar fertilizer to spur new growth and hopefully ensure complete ripening of the remaining fruit. With four applications of Oxidate to eradicate the molds and mildews, plus another application of Megafol, I made five complete spray passes in four days, a personal best I hope never to beat.

Earlier in August, we became the first Loudoun winery to create a presence on MySpace, engaging in social media very early on to complement my blogging activities. Wine country marketing initiatives were being launched at a furious pace, and the highly anticipated debut of the official www.VirginiaWine.org was well received by everyone in the industry. Numerous other Virginia wine blogs were popping up all over the state, and many of the authors had made the trip to visit our tasting room as word of the upcoming television series premiere spread.

On September 8th, the *Loudoun Times Mirror* ran a feature story about the HGTV series, and the volume of web traffic, emails, and phone calls skyrocketed. It seemed the whole area was excited about seeing the show, and the delay in moving the series premiere to the fall was making more and more sense. As more and more customers visited each weekend, we continued to promote the series from within the tasting room. Two days later, the Viognier hit 21.0 Brix and I started making calls to the crew to line up possible harvest days. Since we would spend a day picking fruit and crush the following day, I would need to rent a refrigerated truck for overnight storage and transportation of the fruit to the Fedor's winery. I was incredibly lucky locating a rental; not many truck rental places carry refrigerated trucks, and those who do rarely have them during the busy harvest season. As I tasted the fruit, looked at the weather forecast, considered the crew availability, checked the availability of the refrigerated truck, and coordinated the processing of our Viognier on the Fedor's crush pad, everything seemed to converge on September 18th. I inked the day, locked everything in, and spent the next week having panic attacks over weather forecasts.

Doug came by for my last pre-harvest training meeting on September 14th, just as I completed my last Viognier spray. We walked the vineyard together, tasted the fruit, talked through the production and gear plan, reviewed the proper operation of some new gear, and checked fermentation supplies. He felt I was as ready as I was going to be. He was obviously worried that I was stretched way too thin with the multiple job responsibilities, but by now had enough faith and confidence to know that Shannon and I would figure it out somehow. We wished each other luck, and I promised to give him a call if I got in a bind.

As always, I found it hard to sleep on harvest morning and was up well before my alarm went off at 6:00 A.M. My third harvest, and first as a professional winemaker, found me uncharacteristically at peace as I walked the rows before the crew arrived. There is such solace in the moments before a harvest, a oneness with the earth that cannot be adequately described. It is a feeling that can only be experienced by those who have spent an entire year preparing for that day and bear the scars within and without.

The day was long and arduous, made even more so by the remnants of the hailstorm and damaged fruit. As we attempted to sort the damaged clusters, we fell further and further behind our schedule;

by early afternoon, I had to call around for reinforcements. I found another crew, and upon their arrival, calculating what we had picked, we knew that to finish we would have to abandon the sorting in the field and pick everything, just to get it in the truck. The decision was mine and I was fine with it, as even the damaged clusters were free of rot (due to my spray regimen). By sundown, the last of the lugs was placed in the truck, and by my calculations, we had nearly six tons of Viognier. With the refrigeration turned down, the fruit was well on its way to an overnight chill, ready to be processed early the next morning.

I arrived at North Gate by 7:00 A.M. and found Mark already up and prepping the gear. Soon afterwards, the crew arrived and began moving lugs from the back of the truck onto the crush pad, and Shannon arrived after dropping the boys off at daycare. Mark and Vicki had a one-ton press, so we calculated six press runs at about an hour and forty-five minutes per run. Mark and Vicki had been making wine for nearly ten years at their winery and previously at Corcoran, and ran an efficient and enjoyable crush pad. They truly enjoy the magic of the winemaking process and never stop smiling, even when something is not going as planned. The day passed quickly by, and although when cleanup was finished it was nearly dark and everyone was sore and tired, we all felt very, very alive.

The plan for our newly processed juice was for it to cold-settle overnight, to allow any sediment to settle to the bottom. Mark would then rack over to our tank to begin fermentation, and I would take the remainder back in a few barrels for fermentation at Notaviva. Rather than split the wine equally, Mark preferred to fill our tank nearly to the top to minimize any air contact later in the winter; I was able to fill four barrels with juice. I had no idea at the time what I was going to call my barrel Viognier, but the tank Viognier would be called "Vincerò," inspired by the last line of Puccini's "Nessun Dorma" aria. The piece ends in the upper range of the tenor, and as much as I love heavy metal, rock, jazz, and other forms of music, this piece moves me so deeply. Vincerò – I will win.

When I arrived home I unloaded the barrels, moved them into the winery, and began the process of rehydrating my yeast. We still had not installed running water in the winery, so I had to work in the kitchen sink. I had downloaded a series of best practices documents on the proper steps for rehydration to ensure a healthy yeast population. I found this to be one of the keys to any production process: have it all figured out ahead of time (along with as many contingencies as you can imagine) because you will be too tired to think straight when the time comes to execute the plan. This was certainly true in live event production, and particularly true during the winemaking process. Since I had my equations and formulae all programmed into Excel, it was a simple matter of measuring out the yeast nutrients, monitoring the time and temperature, rehydrating the yeast, and then pitching it into the four barrels. It is an incredible process, watching the yeast spring back to life, and the aromas are heady and complex.

As soon as I cleaned the gear, I checked my email and read an industry-wide email from Chris Pearmund, a pioneer in the Virginia industry. His winery had pressed more juice than their tanks could hold, and he was selling bulk juice in sixty-gallon drums. I put a hold on two of the drums and hopped in the truck. Five hours and a big check later, I was back at the winery, where I pumped the two drums into two additional barrels, pitched the yeast, and headed back inside to work on videos until well after midnight.

Early the next week we were back at North Gate, processing four tons of Chardonnay that we had purchased. Everybody pitched in for a very long day on the crush pad, working well into the night to finish up the final press run. The following evening, after the juice had settled, I arrived with ten barrels, which we filled nearly to the top. When I returned home, I unloaded the barrels, stacked them two-high with the tractor forks, and rolled them into the cold storage room. Following the same process as the Viognier, albeit with a different strain of yeast, I prepared and pitched the yeast into the barrels while enjoying the amazing aromas that the actively fermenting Viognier barrels were releasing. Although wineries can be very dangerous places in terms of suffocation, the intensity of the aromas is unlike anything I have ever experienced.

As I was finishing cleaning up, Quentin pulled up with a pickup truck full of lugs. He asked if I was interested in a ton of Chambourcin, and I said absolutely. He had a guy in the truck with him, so the three of us quickly cleaned out and sterilized a fermentation bin and the crusher/de-stemmer, and in less than an hour had processed the fruit. I ran back up to the kitchen, rehydrated more yeast, pitched it into the Chambourcin, cleaned the gear, and went inside for a shower. Now I knew why Doug had encouraged me to buy extra supplies... you never know what will happen during harvest!

The rest of September was absolutely frenetic. Two more newspaper articles appeared about the upcoming HGTV show in the *Frederick News Post* and the *Washington Business Journal*, and the emails and phone calls were relentless. The tasting room was packed every weekend; we had to hire a couple part-time employees and a bar-back to help with the customers. We hosted our first wedding, and I was being asked to give winemaker and vineyard tours to corporate groups. We continued to push the music envelope as well, bringing live Irish musicians and live electric blues. Our barrel-fermented wines were being tended with the appropriately timed additions of fermentation nutrients, and the Cabernet Franc and Petit Verdot still needed spray applications as they continued to ripen in the vineyard. Mesh landed a series of big website projects, and I had to spend three days commuting to Rockville to take a series of project management courses for my corporate job. To cap off the month, we learned that Notaviva Vineyards was a finalist in the rural category of the Loudoun Chamber of Commerce Small Business Awards, and I was a finalist in the Entrepreneur of the Year category. I am pretty sure that Shannon was feeding and caring for the children; someone must have been, because it surely was not me.

We entered October and things got totally out of control. The first day of the month, there were two more press mentions in the *Washington Post Loudoun Extra* and *Virginia Business* magazine. With only three days to go until the series premiere, it seemed every call or email was an inquiry about the show and if we would be open that day. The show was scheduled to air at 7:00 A.M. on Saturday morning, October 4th. As we tried to go to sleep that Friday night, we checked and double-checked the DVR to ensure that the show was going to be recorded in the off chance we slept through it, but we both knew we would not be able to sleep at all. It was an odd mix of excitement and anxiety.

At 6:59 A.M., the last of the late night infomercials faded to black, and we both held our breath as the first episode of the *Dream House* series "Meet the Mackeys" hit the airwaves. The show opens with a voiceover summary of the story, talking about our backgrounds and the immensity of the project ahead. Seventeen seconds into the first episode, I am seen slamming a drill through a wall because I was so mad at the electricians, which caused me to breathe a sigh of relief; maybe there would be some reality in this reality television show after all.

We watched the show, and when it was finished, rewound it and watched it again. It is hard to convey how odd it is to see yourself on the screen, and it was probably even more so for us, because we were both so used to being part of the production team, where seeing oneself on screen was considered taboo. Now here we were, putting our hopes and dreams and fears and failures out there for the whole world to see. After watching the show for a second time, the boys joined us for a second breakfast, and the phone calls from friends and family members started pouring in. Everyone was blown away by how great a job the editing team had done with the footage, and how authentic we came across on camera. Of course, everyone had been watching the other *Dream House* series over the course of the previous two years since we had been selected for the show, and so of course they all proclaimed, "Yours is the best!" Having only seen one of eight episodes, I thought it was a bit premature to declare such a victory; I was simply glad no one told us we looked ridiculous.

There was no traffic jam that day at the winery, though there was a huge increase in email inquiries through the website, interestingly, many of them from the West Coast, asking if we shipped our wine to California. Californians know their wine, and are always seeking something new. A few people stopped in to congratulate us, and we enjoyed telling them about the filming process and dropping a few teasers for the upcoming episodes.

Two days later, Shannon and I were getting dirty in the winery, completing our first pressing of the Chambourcin. We borrowed a small bladder press from Mark and Vicki and in a few hours had completed the job and cleaned up the gear. The following day, after the sediment had settled out, I racked it into a few barrels and rolled them into storage to age over the winter. As I was finishing up, Shannon ran into the winery to tell me that another email had gone out with fruit for sale, this time from Chrysalis Vineyards in Middleburg, Virginia. They had a higher yield in their vineyards, and had run out of tank space in the winery. Quickly reaching out to Jenni McCloud, we tried to work out a harvest date; she offered to have her crew pick the fruit for me, but they would not be able to schedule that for a few days. Checking the weather, there was a serious storm on the way, and I did not want the fruit to be diluted from the rains. Jenni indicated that if I could organize my own crew, I would be welcome to pick the fruit myself the following morning. I got a twenty-four foot truck, and called Seve and found out he and a few guys would be available the following day.

When we arrived at Jenni's vineyard, we were astonished at how steep the slope was. Situated high atop the Blue Ridge Mountains, the property was both stunning and intimidating. The thought of carrying several tons of fruit up that hill by hand was daunting. We saw the Chrysalis crew moving back and forth with the tractors harvesting a different block, and when we asked if there was any other equipment we could use, their winemaker sadly informed us no. My crew looked at me, hoping that I would just walk away from this disaster. I asked Seve to tell the guys I would be paying them time and a half for the extra labor. Parking the truck as close to the vineyard block as I could safely maneuver it, we simply put our heads down and got to work.

Getting back to Notaviva with our haul, our winery still did not have a concrete crush pad. If we had the large fermentation bins outside, we would not have been able to move them into the winery. My solution was to position the bin just inside the rollup door where I could move it around with the pallet jack, and put the crusher de-stemmer inside the rear of the box truck. We rigged a playground slide up so that the fruit slid down from inside the truck into the bin, while the crew stood on footstools on either side of the slide picking out jacks. Any professional winemaker seeing that setup would have probably doubled over with laughter. I loved it.

Just as we finished crushing the last of the fruit, the rain began, and we had to clean all the gear while getting soaked by a cold October storm. When the gear was stored and the crew gone, I limped into the house with the intention of taking a four-hour long hot shower. That was not to be, however, as Shannon had been checking my email throughout the afternoon and told me I had a high-priority proposal to review for a client in Germany. While I showered, she made dinner and a pot of coffee, and after eating I got back to work.

We had been trying out different events in the tasting room, trying to draw in customers. We had approached the dean of the school of music at Shenandoah University about finding talented students looking for live gigs. He connected us with a young lady who functioned as a booking agent for a lot of students, and we ended up having a jazz pianist playing every Friday evening. In addition, we were having live music every Saturday and Sunday as well, everything from jazz to blues to classical to folk to Irish to flamenco. The idea of a winery as a performance venue was new to everyone, but the artists loved being able to promote their appearances at a winery to their mailing lists and their nascent social media channels. It did not take long for these musicians to approach other wineries in the area about bookings, and before long, our wine region had become a legitimate live entertainment circuit.

On October 14th, we brought in the last of our fruit, the Cabernet Franc. After having survived each of the previous harvest and crush pad adventures, the Cab Franc was actually a pleasant experience. We had learned how to organize the processing, and since I didn't have a big truck to move the fruit, I rented some scaffolding to raise the crusher so we could use the sorting slide again. We organized everything so that the processing had a very efficient workflow. Although the work was still hard, the mood was light and everyone was enjoying the beautiful fall day. After cleanup, we made short work of a case of beer, exchanging stories from the season. My Spanish is actually somewhat passable from all my years in Miami and being on the road with Julio Iglesias, thus I'm able to enjoy the conversations with the crew. They are so hard working and so dedicated, and I could tell that they really appreciated my efforts in continually trying to improve our process.

As great as the feelings of anticipation are at the beginning of the harvest season, so too are the feelings of sadness at the end. You think back on the pruning, training, spraying, mowing, and measuring, as well as the hailstorms that nearly robbed you of everything; it all comes rushing back, and you find yourself completely at peace. It is a deep, joyful peace, knowing that you have connected with the land, and have begun the process of creating something unique and special. It never mattered to us that we did not own fancy equipment, and that we had to work ten times as hard to make up for our inexperience and lack of tools. The only thing that mattered was that we had completed our first harvest season at our new winery, with our boys excitedly seeing all the activity, tasting the fruit, and watching the crew operate the equipment. It was such a big adventure for all of us, and we were forging our own path the only way we knew how—with hard work, tenacity, and love.

When I went inside to clean up, I checked all three of my email accounts and realized I had several dozen responses to write. I simply shut the lid of my laptop, turned off my phone, took a shower, and went upstairs to enjoy dinner with my family while we gazed out through our picture windows at our completely picked and stunningly beautiful vineyard. Two beautiful boys, an incredible home, working our own land, reveling in our bountiful harvest; it was one of those moments that made Shannon and me almost dizzy, as we dreamed of the harvest dinners we were going to have for many years to come. As we stared silently into each other's eyes, we knew there was only one thing that could make next year's celebration even more special. We put the boys to bed early, retreated to our bedroom, and made baby number three.

CHAPTER 33

"Agricultural Small Business of the Year"

A s one of Loudoun's newest wineries, we were excited to be a part of Loudoun's Farm Color Tour the weekend of October 18th and 19th. The tour is an event created by the county's Department of Economic Development, and encourages thousands of visitors to visit our farms and learn about the various products that are raised and grown locally. Farm to table had begun just a few years earlier, and buzzwords and phrases such as "locavore," "slow food," and "food miles" were now appearing on magazine covers. Even though many of Loudoun's restaurants had always sourced some supplies locally, customers were now in the know and were beginning to seek them out. The Loudoun Farm Color Tour was having a huge impact in advancing those ideals to a wider audience.

Saturday morning dawned bright and clear, with crisp fall temperatures and perfectly timed colors. My dad drove his fully restored 1941 Ford coupe out and parked it on the lawn right in front of the tasting bar. We partnered with one of the area fresh flower farms, and they had set up a stand on the front porch. The live music began in the early afternoon, and it was a wonderful experience seeing families coming out to enjoy the wine, the music, and the scenery.

We were busy at the bar all day, pouring wine and regaling people with stories from the television production. I had to break away by mid-afternoon to tend to punch down in the winery. Punch down is when you re-integrate the grape skins with the fermenting juice. As the yeast is consuming the sugar in the must, it produces alcohol and carbon dioxide, and the release of the gas pushes the grape skins up to the top of the bin, where they form a cap. If left untouched, the cap can dry out and become infected with all manner of microbial nastiness. The tool used for punching down looks like a huge potato masher, and you stand over the bin and push small sections of the cap down into the must. It is a fascinating process, though it can be incredibly dangerous. Early on in the fermentation, the cap can be very tough to punch through. You are leaning over the bin, and as you punch through the cap, you release huge amounts of carbon dioxide. You are breathing harder from the exertion, and there is less oxygen to be found. Most people have no idea that suffocation is a real danger in winemaking; every year winery workers are tragically killed, either becoming trapped while cleaning a large tank or passing out then drowning in a fermenting bin.

The weather stayed beautiful all weekend, and the farm tour was a great success. Sales were strong, though it had now become obvious that we had a serious inventory problem approaching. We had hoped to make it through December with our current stock, but with the October rush, we were not sure we were going to even make it that long.

It is easy to get caught up in the romance of harvest season in wine country, much as Shannon and I had done years earlier at Breaux. We now enjoyed watching couples share special moments at our place. It is very rewarding knowing that your hard work is so appreciated by guests, and that they are creating their own moments that they will cherish forever. Earlier that month, we even had the opportunity to help one of our customers get engaged, creating a custom wine label and orchestrating the proposal.

Since our work with Loudoun's DED earlier in the year for the VIP reception, we had come to be well acquainted with everyone in the department. That afternoon, Dorri Morin, the communications manager for the county, paid me a visit with her good friend Mary Porter, founder of the Curiosity Zone, a small business focused on connecting fun science to actual learning. What I thought was just an innocent wine tasting turned out to be a carefully calculated recruiting operation. They had come to get me to apply to the county's Economic Development Commission, a public/private partnership responsible for promoting Loudoun's economic development. They figured with my background, I would be perfect as a voice for small business, technology, and rural economic development. Try as I might, I was unable to fend them off, and eventually found myself (quite literally) backed into a corner with two very driven, very intelligent ladies pointing loaded wineglasses at my head. To escape this very precarious situation, I promised to fill out the application and send it in by the deadline, just a few weeks away.

As October faded into November, it was time again to focus on winemaking tasks. Now that the red fermentations were complete, I needed to press the wine off of the skins. We were able to press all of the Petit Verdot and Tinto Cão in one day, then the following day we pressed the remaining Cabernet Franc. After the sediment settled for a couple days, the clarified wine was racked into barrels to age for several months before bottling the following summer. As this was my first time actually pressing red grapes, I was amazed at the aromatic intensity of the pomace (remnants of the grape skins and seeds after pressing), and found myself digging my hands into the mess and holding it to my nose, inhaling its beauty. It is yet another of the many special moments a winemaker gets to share with his or her wine that those who have not experienced it will never understand.

We awoke on Thursday, November 6th with butterflies in our stomachs. That night was the Loudoun Chamber of Commerce Small Business Awards, and although we had not given it much thought through the rush of harvest, the realization had now set in that we were going to be recognized in front of the Loudoun business community. The thought of actually winning had not crossed our minds, so I was not going to bother putting together any form of acceptance speech. Shannon had taken a pregnancy test the day before, and learned that we were going to have a third baby; that was really all we could talk about.

Part of being a finalist in the award show was having the opportunity to create a brief video vignette about your company. I had reached out to the chamber and asked if we could produce our own vignette. They were happy to allow us that opportunity, so I created two high-impact motion graphics trailers in After Effects (one for each category) and sent them off to the production company.

We had purchased a table at the ceremony and invited some friends and family members to join us. Given the inquisitive nature of my family, I knew they were going to be all over Shannon when they realized she was not drinking that evening; there would be no hiding the fact that we were pregnant again.

Our babysitter arrived, and we were off to the National Conference Center to enjoy a rare night out. As I had suspected, it took all of one round of drinks for Shannon to be called out. My cousin's wife Beth, my sister-in-law Shayna, and my friend Tracy picked up on the fact that Shannon passed on a glass of wine and were practically in her lap assailing her with questions.

"Why aren't you drinking?"

"What's going on, sister?"

"I bet you're pregnant!"

"Smell her hair—is she pregnant?"

Shannon folded under the inquisition, so right there in the lobby of the conference center, she informed our family we were expecting. Of course, my mother was elated, as were the other hens. They began clucking around the expectant mother as I went off to do some networking, my departure wholly unnoticed in the light of Shannon's glow.

An hour later, the xylophone chimes alerted everyone that dinner was about to begin, so we made our way to our table. We tried our best to just enjoy the event as honorees, but as professional event producers, our minds constantly wandered through all the ways we could turn this award show into a first-rate event. As the dinner plates were cleared, Tony Howard, president and CEO of the chamber, took the stage. Hosts introduced each category, and then announced the four finalists. As each was announced, their video vignette would play while they walked to the stage; I was glad we'd produced our own, given the mediocre production value of all the others.

Once all the finalists had been named, it was time to announce the winners in each category. At that point I really began to get nervous. After watching the other three finalist videos in our category, it began to occur to me that we might actually have a chance of winning. I was wholly unprepared to say anything reasonably intelligent if I were to suddenly find myself standing on stage behind the podium in front of Loudoun's small business community.

As the agricultural category approached, Shannon and I held hands under the table. I remember seeing the envelope being carried onto the stage by the previous year's small rural business honoree. Slowly, she opened the envelope, "And the winner of this year's agricultural small business of the year is..." She pulled out the card, and as soon as I saw the look on her face I knew we had won, because I knew she had absolutely no idea how to pronounce our name. She sort of quickly glanced over her shoulder for help, then she said, "Not...A...Um...." It was impossible to hear anything else after that over the roar that erupted from our table. Our people are not afraid of making a spectacle of themselves, and did so in grand fashion at that moment.

Shannon and I stood, laughing in disbelief, and made our way to the stage. How was this possible? Just a few months into the launch of our business, we had been nominated, vetted, and selected by our peers in the community to receive this honor. Climbing the stairs to the stage, Tony shook my hand and whispered to me, "Great videos, by the way." After receiving our award and being photographed with the hosts, it was my turn to take the podium. I graciously offered the moment to Shannon, who responded with a quick laugh and whispered a sweet, "Forget it."

I had no notes to take from my jacket pocket, no prepared remarks, and so as I looked out over the audience, I simply spoke from the heart. I thanked the teams from the Department of Economic Development as well as the Chamber of Commerce. I thanked Doug,

Mark and Vicki, and all of our friends in the wine industry. I thanked our friends and family for all of their support and faith in our endeavors. Finally, I thanked Shannon, Tristan, and Duncan, and being lost in the excitement of the moment, also thanked baby number three. Behind me, I heard Tony whisper to Shannon, "Did he just announce to a ballroom of strangers that you are pregnant?" to which Shannon replied, "I'm pretty sure he just did."

We returned to our table, congratulated by dozens of people—some we knew, most we did not—as we made our way through the crowd. Hugs and kisses were shared all around as we tried to settle back into our seats to enjoy the rest of the event.

Afterwards, dozens more people approached our table with congratulations. Many offered kind words about the television show and the incredible buzz building about both Notaviva Vineyards and Mesh Multimedia. As the commotion subsided and people began to make their ways out the door, we said our goodbyes to our family and friends and walked hand in hand out to our truck. Driving home, we replayed all of our conversations, basking in the positive energy we had received from that amazing community of small business owners. It truly was a night we will never forget.

The next day was spent in the winery, filling barrels. As usual, a task that I had estimated would take about four hours ended up taking ten, and by dinnertime I was a wet, exhausted mess. A hot shower helped loosen up my stiff joints, which were still taking a beating. In addition to my joint issues, I was starting to have frequent dizzy spells, which I attributed to my non-stop pace, and I resolved to take it easy, now that the barrels were filled and tucked safely away in the winery for the winter.

Saturday, November 8th, we were awake early as usual to catch the latest episode of the television show, aptly named "The Pressure is Mounting," which documented the challenges we experienced during the final two months leading up to receiving our occupancy permit. These later episodes of the show were becoming increasingly difficult to watch; having to relive that pressure and stress was very unsettling.

Traffic in the tasting room was slowing down a bit now that we were coming to the end of the season, but we were still hosting live music from Friday through Sunday and enjoying a solid stream of people. The continual press coverage about the television show, as well as the coverage from the small business awards, was keeping public interest high. Now that winemaking chores had subsided, the middle of the week was just focused on Vovici and Mesh tasks, so I was working much more reasonable seventy-hour weeks. Although there was still a large vineyard project ahead before the ground froze, it was nice to be away from it for a while.

On Friday, November 21st, the day before the final HGTV episode, I received notification that I had been selected for the Loudoun Economic Development Commission. After a three-month recruitment period, eleven members were selected from thirty-nine applicants. As I read the names of the other new members, I was amazed to see the diversity in careers and backgrounds, and became even more excited about the opportunity to become engaged in public service with such a talented group of colleagues.

The following morning, as we prepared to watch the final episode of *Dream House*, we were filled with a mix of emotions. It seemed like the airing of this last episode would finally close this chapter in our lives. The years of toiling through the construction of the house and winery, and the promise of airing our story for viewers across the country, was now coming to a close. We wondered if anyone out there across America really cared about what we were doing. We knew that the viewership was solid, and from what we heard from High Noon, ours was the highest rated *Dream House* series of all, yet still we wondered if anyone would be moved or motivated by what we went through. The answer to that question would be revealed in just a few hours.

The last episode documented the last ditch efforts to get the inspection permit, moving out of the rental house, and the housewarming party. It brought back so many terrible and wonderful memories all at once. By the time it was over we were both crying, holding Tristan and Duncan between us. High Noon had done such a wonderful job of capturing our story, and we were so sad to see the series come to an end. As we learned throughout the day, so were a lot of people.

As soon as we opened our doors later that morning, we were greeted by a group of people who had watched the entire series and came by to congratulate us. While we stood at the bar talking about the show, another gentleman came in and silently approached the bar. I welcomed him, and inquired how he had heard about us. Nonchalantly, he replied, "You were the number one search term on the Google Zeitgeist this morning." I thought he was kidding. Moving quickly to my computer, I went to the website to see for myself. The Google Zeitgeist was a rolling list of the top 100 search terms, updated every fifteen minutes. Apparently that morning around 8:00 A.M., the number one search term in the entire United States was "Notaviva Vineyards." To put that in perspective, the other search terms on the list were major college football games and pop music princesses. Several other people visited during the day who had also seen us listed on the Zeitgeist. In the days before the explosion of social media, making that list was about the coolest thing any small business could hope to attain.

After the tasting bar closed, I checked our emails and was astounded to see a flood of well wishes from across the country. Earlier, I had wondered if anyone had really cared about what we were doing; now I knew the answer was a resounding yes. The kindness of people whom we knew we would likely never meet was so incredibly humbling; we had obviously touched them very deeply. Many promised to visit someday; many asked if they could have wine shipped around the country. Most, however, just wanted to take a moment to thank us for putting it all out there for them to watch. Our goal of inspiring people to follow their own dreams had been achieved, and basking in the warmth of those messages, we knew it was all worth it. The challenges and frustrations involved in filming the television show were forgotten, and our dream of proving to people that you can achieve anything had truly come to fruition.

As 2008 began to wind down, we had one major task to complete before the ground froze: the marking of three more acres of vines to be planted in April. I had read an article by the renowned viticulturist Dr. Richard Smart, where he indicated that Virginia would do well to look to Eastern Europe to discover new varietals. Wanting to explore new winemaking opportunities, as well as create some differentiation from our competition, I began researching the vines of Hungary, Croatia, and Slovakia. I came across the famous red wine blend known as Egri Bikavér or "Bull's Blood," whose major blending component was Kékfrankos. I dug deeper and learned that Kékfrankos was actually the Austrian grape Blaufränkisch. Although I was more than a bit worried about Virginia's troublesome humidity, as Blaufränkisch is sensitive to both downy and powdery mildew, I decided to forge ahead. I placed an order with the vine nursery for an acre each of Blaufränkisch, Petit Verdot, and Sauvignon Blanc.

I had been marking out the rows in the back half of the vineyard, placing the bamboo stakes and painting guide marks in the grass. On December 20th, we began sub-soiling the rows to open up the earth, so it could lie fallow over the winter. I found it very interesting how different these three acres were in terms of soil composition and rock content from the front three acres. Although they were adjoining, it was like working in a different field, and our soil tests confirmed my suspicions. Where the front block of the vineyard is comprised of richer soil, the rear block is comprised of much more clay, with a tough layer of shale just below the surface. Using the sub-soil implement on the back of the tractor was proving to be a very rough ride. At one point the implement got stuck under a huge shale shelf, and just snapped in half. The tractor leaped into the air as the four-inch steel bar broke with a deafening crack, and I would have gone face-first into the windshield if I hadn't been wearing my seatbelt. Luckily, my assistant Ryan was standing clear and was not hit by any of the flying metal pieces. We were both lucky not to have been seriously injured.

The following morning I was at Tractor Supply, buying a new implement to finish the job. The next morning, the local farm supply company delivered our lime and fertilizer, which we spent the day spreading over the newly cut rows. As we looked out over the completed project, we were glad to have emerged unscathed from the process, and even happier that we were truly done for the year.

Now that the winery and vineyard tasks were finally complete, our depleted wine inventory and our physical, mental, and emotional exhaustion required us to decide on whether to stay open over the winter or take a much-needed break. The decision was not an easy one. On the heels of the television show's success and subsequent marketing opportunities, we were worried that we might kill our momentum. However, we had to be realistic about our product availability; we did not want to bottle any of the new wines before they were truly ready. More importantly, we needed to regroup as a family and as a married couple, shut the world away for a while, spend time with our boys, and let Shannon nest for a few months.

We knew in our hearts the best thing for all of us was to close down until Valentine's Day weekend, when we would reopen to the surge of traffic that accompanies that very busy season in wine country. Eight weeks away from the winery business would allow me to focus on Vovici and Mesh, allow both of us to begin brainstorming new Notaviva initiatives for the year ahead, and allow Shannon to focus on the baby and the boys. I decided to move my Mesh equipment up into the music loft. Although it was exposed to the public, I needed the dedicated space, and enjoyed the quiet nights alone working in the timber frame, knowing that Shannon and the boys were safe and sound down below.

The four of us spent Christmas morning together before Shannon's mom and brother joined us around lunchtime, and my family soon thereafter. As much as we loved the hustle and bustle of the weekend tasting room crowd, it was wonderful to be able to just enjoy the company of our loved ones. Late that night, after everyone had left, we lay awake in bed, taking stock of the all that had transpired over the previous twelve months, and it seemed almost impossible. We had left corporate America, launched two small businesses, nearly went bankrupt, found a consulting job, become pregnant, won the small business award, completed our first harvest as winemakers, and prepared the vineyard for an expansion; it did not even seem possible that so much could happen in a single year. Against all odds, we were still afloat; through sheer determination and hard work, we had found a way to stay the course. Though the future was still so uncertain, we felt we had been through the worst that life could throw at us and had somehow prevailed. There could only be brighter days ahead.

We were so very wrong.

CHAPTER 34
"Open for Business (Again)"

"It's a boy!"

Shannon and I just laughed when the ultrasound technician showed us the gender of baby number three. Oh well, our beautiful girl's name would have to wait until baby number four, whom we had resolved would be the last, no matter what. Meeting him for the first time was a wonderful moment; he was in perfect health and the pregnancy was going along incredibly well. It was time to head back to the drawing board to come up with a boy's name, so we got to work on a cold night just a few days after Duncan's second birthday party in early January 2009.

We knew we were going to stick with names of Scotch-Irish origin, and also wanted the three brothers to share something unique. As we looked at the first two boys' names, we realized that both first names ended with "-an" and both middle names ended with "-or," completely by coincidence; Tristan Connor and Duncan Gregor. Going back to our original list, we knew that we liked the name Ronan and the middle name Tyler; once we saw the spelling similarity with his brothers, we simply changed the letters. We settled on Ronan Tylor Mackey and then promptly polished off two pints of ice cream to seal the deal.

The following day, January 13th, we left for a trip to Florida to visit Shannon's family. We took the long way through Blacksburg, Virginia, home of Virginia Tech, where I would be attending a two-day intensive winemaking laboratory course conducted by Dr. Bruce Zoecklein. The seminar covered topics ranging from analysis techniques to fault determination, with hands-on lab work every step of the way. Recognized and respected as an industry thought leader, Bruce took us through the study with an amazing degree of intensity. Though I knew it would be some years until we could afford any sophisticated laboratory equipment for our operation, the lessons learned (and horrible aromas that we endured) laid a proper groundwork for future study.

Since we were now operating an actual winery, we were expected to submit our first TTB report by January 15th in order to file our first excise tax payment. I had brought along my winemaking records from the previous fall, as well as all of our purchase orders and register reports. A purchase order is a monthly report of the amount of wine that physically moves from the winery to the retail outlet, namely the tasting bar. Each month, we are required to submit that report to Virginia ABC and pay the corresponding tax. The summation of those reports then gets calculated for the federal report. I figured it could not be too difficult to fill out two forms with some wine volumes on it to arrive at a tax figure, so instead of getting it done before we left, I planned to complete it after the first day's lab work.

Arriving back at the hotel, we put the boys to sleep and I began work on my TTB report. Three hours later at midnight, cowering in the face of a very irritated wife, I acknowledged that perhaps I should have done some work on the tax form in the days leading up to our departure. At 1:00 A.M., as I was still going around in circles making calculations on the most cryptic tax form in the galaxy, Shannon informed me that she was going to bed; I, in fact, would not be doing any such thing, since our report had to be postmarked the following day. Convinced that if the envelope were not stamped by 5:00 P.M., the TTB would be waiting for us upon our return from Florida to carry off the children and deposit me in Leavenworth, Shannon made it clear that failure was not an option. Although I doubted that the TTB would be that offended about our $200 excise tax (we qualify for a small producer discount), I decided that perhaps it was best if I just got it done. Finally turning in at 3:00 A.M., I got a few hours of sleep before day two of class. Although groggy from sleep deprivation, the sensory experiment on sulfur off-odors was enough to shock my system into a state of high alert.

After class that night, we hopped in the truck and headed south for Florida, where we spent the next ten days. I brought along my iMac so I could keep working on Mesh client sites, as well as my Vovici laptop so I could stay on top of those projects as well. We spent the days together taking the boys to play in the sand and visiting the nearby sea turtle rescue at the Loggerhead Marinelife Center. In the evenings I would retreat to my computers, while Shannon and the boys spent time with Roger and Bev. The week flew by all too rapidly, and through tearful goodbyes, we began our trek back north. On the way up the road, we stopped overnight in Orlando. Although we did not have the money for the expensive park admissions, we took the boys to Downtown Disney for an afternoon of looking through the shops. Our ruse worked; when we got home, the boys told their wide-eyed cousins that they had visited Disney World.

February began with a host of marketing and legislative initiatives. I had been approached by the county's tourism bureau and asked to participate in a regional co-promotion event with Destination DC, the city's tourism organization. We traveled to New York City to pair Loudoun wines with food prepared by D.C.'s finest chefs. The event was a two-day affair: a dinner at the Astor Center, followed by lunch the next afternoon at a five-star posh restaurant. Each course was paired with a particular wine, and our "Cantabile" Cabernet Franc was available during the pre-dinner reception with hors d'oeuvres. I found myself hobnobbing with restaurant critics, wine writers, and travel bloggers, all asking the same question: "Virginia makes wine?" The following day I was seated at a table with tourism emissaries from Hong Kong and Shanghai, as well as the New York correspondent for the *London Times*. They were asking the same question, but by the time both events were finished, not only did everyone know that Virginia made wine, but that we made great wine and had a tourism infrastructure in place worth recognizing. A few days later, the magazine *Travel Agent Central* printed an article about the event, and identified our Cabernet Franc as "particularly memorable."

That evening, on the train back to Washington, I was moving through the quiet car and happened to notice one of my TruSecure colleagues, Curtis Donato. Tapping him on the shoulder to say hello, he jumped up and we hugged and laughed to a chorus of "shhs" from the other passengers. We chatted for a few minutes to get caught up, and I learned that he was on his way back from a meeting with his new employers, Evidence Exchange, an eDiscovery firm in Manhattan. They were just beginning a website redesign, so I gave Curtis my card and asked them to get in touch. As the years went by and the engagement grew, we became close friends with the company's founders, Michael Prounis and Myron Eagle. Proud of the work we created for them, our dinner outings in Washington, D.C. and New York City will forever be some of our most cherished memories, and we can only aspire as entrepreneurs to exemplify the kind of integrity they have demonstrated.

I arrived home in time to catch a four-hour nap, only to awaken again at 4:00 A.M. to drive down to Richmond for a day of wine industry lobbying. Each year, the Virginia Wine Marketing Board arranges a "Wine and Vine" day during the General Assembly session. I thought it would be interesting to observe firsthand how the process worked, as well as have the opportunity to personally meet some of our state legislators. I arrived early, parked, walked to the marketing board office where we were to meet, and was admittedly disappointed at the turnout. For some reason, I had thought there would be a passionate throng of winery owners eager to shake hands with our elected officials. Perhaps a dozen of us made the effort that day, so with wine in hand, we made our way up to the offices to hand out bottles. We were each assigned a subset of legislators, and spent the morning squeezing our way through the crowds of people standing outside the offices, waiting their turn to spend a brief moment arguing their cause with an official.

Each meeting lasted perhaps a minute, and the wine board had coached us on what to say. "Hello, my name is Stephen Mackey, owner of Notaviva Vineyards in Northern Virginia and I would like to thank you for your continued support of the Virginia wine industry. Please accept this bottle from one of my colleagues as a token of our appreciation." Most of the time I was met with a very polite handshake and genuine interest, though one gentleman asked, "Aren't you a little young to own a winery?" and another one asked— I believe in all seriousness— "Virginia makes wine...?"

I arrived home that evening exhausted from my whirlwind trips, but thrilled to be "part of the process." I figured if someone with my inexperience, limited means, and busy workload could make the effort to take action, then why not everybody? My first experience seeing the General Assembly in action, coupled with my recent acceptance on the Economic Development Commission, had fanned the flame that had always existed in me to become involved in the community. My youthful exuberance would soon be tempered by the reality of "the system," delivered by a first-hand understanding of what really greases the wheels of the local political machine.

On February 12th, we received a letter congratulating us on a silver medal in the Virginia Governor's Cup wine competition for our Cabernet Franc. Two days later, we opened the tasting bar again for Valentine's Day to a swarm of happy customers who had been anxiously awaiting our return to the scene. Local favorite Emma Bailey, accompanied by her father Rob, provided the live music, and it was wonderful to see the timber frame come back to life with all the happy couples and disgruntled single folks. Rob, a true English gentleman and superb musician, convinced me to join him and Emma for a few songs, so I grabbed my guitar and ascended the stairs. Emma propped open her song list, Rob told me the chord progressions, and off we went. Although I was pretty rusty from an insufficient (nonexistent) practice regimen, we fumbled through a few tunes to the delight of our guests.

That night we hosted our first live jazz dinner, with the Seth Fromal Trio performing in the loft and a catered meal provided by one of the local restaurants, Savoir Fare in nearby Round Hill. We had known the owner and executive chef, Joanie Wolford, since she had catered our wedding in 2004. Shannon and I were everywhere, chatting with guests, pouring wine, clearing plates, and ringing up purchases. It was after 11:00 P.M. when the crew finished cleanup and the catering truck pulled away. Shannon and I enjoyed a glass of wine together with some leftover desserts, and wondered where the hell our winter break had disappeared.

Shannon and I signed up for the "Responsible Sellers and Servers: Virginia's Program" (RSVP), intended to inform people in the alcoholic beverage industry of the necessary information and techniques required to sell alcoholic beverages in a safe, responsible manner. We were shocked at some of the stories that the ABC agents regaled us with during the daylong class. Basically 95% of their infractions come from 5% of their licensees, and the stories of stupidity were beyond belief. They had dozens of tales about high school kids walking into a bar (with their class shirt on nonetheless), able to buy mixed drinks without presenting any form of identification. Watching these kinds of sting operations through the window, the agents would then calmly walk in and shut the place down. Not only is the licensee (e.g. the bar owner) liable for the infraction, but the person who served the alcohol is also personally liable for breaking the law. To this day, we have paid for all of our staff to take the necessary courses to protect our patrons, our staff, and our business.

Early March was busy with the normal complement of small family farm winery chores: hiring new staff for the spring, getting bottling supplies ordered and delivered, preparing the vineyard for the upcoming planting, and potty training a two-year old. In addition, the Mesh client roster continued to grow with a large number of web development projects, though things at Vovici were starting to come unraveled. There was a murmur through the ranks that all was not well with the balance sheet, and I knew without asking that if there were going to be reductions, I would be the first one shown the door.

On March 6th, we bottled the first run of our "Calor" white wine blend at Tarara winery in Leesburg. Tarara's winemaker, Jordan Harris, a very talented young winemaker originally from Canada, had a great relationship with a Canadian bottling truck and had retained them to make a trip into the states. We had purchased about 100 cases of bulk Tarara wine, which I had blended with Jordan. The wine was 45% steel-fermented Chardonnay blended with 45% steel-fermented Sauvignon Blanc and 10% barrel-fermented Pinot Gris with 1% residual sugar. "Calor" was the name of my first post-college tour as Julio Iglesias' carpenter and drum technician. Shannon and I wanted to create a wine that incorporated our backgrounds in South Florida, and "Calor," as used in the lyric to the album's title track, means passionate attraction. On the back label, I decided the wine was great with Latin jazz and "best paired with hot sax."

The following day we bottled another new wine, our "Celtico" Chambourcin, which we had purchased in bulk from Doug. Since Fabbioli Cellars is just a short drive away from Tarara, Doug had coordinated with Jordan to have the Canadian truck move over to his place so he could bottle his wines as well. This day, as with the previous one, I pitched in to help bottle everyone's wines; after a long day at Doug's, I loaded our two new wines onto a rental truck and transported them home. No rest for the weary, however, and back at Notaviva I had dinner and some coffee and got to work on client websites, knowing tomorrow would be another long day in a bottling truck.

On March 8th, we bottled our "Vincerò" Viognier at North Gate. Now that I was actually becoming adept at filming and producing videos, I took the opportunity to create a behind-the-scenes bottling piece. As multimedia producers and early adopters of technology, we had long had Facebook, Twitter, and YouTube accounts, so I took advantage of posting the bottling video on our blog. Customers loved seeing what happens inside the bottling truck, and we had a lot of curious people asking about Mesh capabilities after seeing that video. We were thrilled that the bond between the two companies continued to foster opportunities for both. By the time we were finished bottling and I had transported the wine back to Notaviva and packed it in the winery, I was completely exhausted and the pain in my joints was almost unbearable. I knew I needed some rest, but there was just so much to be done.

The next morning as I dragged myself into Vovici, my earlier fears were confirmed. I was summoned to the vice president's office and informed that I and several of my colleagues were being let go due to a downsizing initiative. That was tough news, as although both Notaviva Vineyards and Mesh Multimedia were keeping me busy, that steady paycheck was going to be sorely missed, as was our healthcare. Essentially a consultant, there was no large severance package that was going to get us through the next few months; email account was locked, laptop turned in, last paycheck would be mailed. Shannon took the news in stride, immediately researching the healthcare options that were provided by the human resources team.

Though we knew things were going to get very tight, we were now disappointed in the decision we had made several weeks earlier to finance the vineyard expansion. While I was employed at Vovici, we had qualified for a line of credit, which we had used to secure the vineyard stock and trellis installation. Violating the number one rule we learned several years before at a conference—do not go into debt to grow your winery—now we had a huge vineyard bill to cover. We were back to the entrepreneurial rollercoaster ride of sell, work, bill, wait, with a baby due in just over three months. March had come in like a lion and was going out like a Tyrannosaurus Rex.

April began with some great press coverage, both for Notaviva as well as the Virginia wine industry. CNN ran a story on the state's growth as a wine region, which was a huge morale boost for everyone across the state. Although the piece focused mostly on the Charlottesville region (stoking the competitive spirit between them and our Northern Virginia wineries), it was still amazing to see the hard work of our colleagues recognized at that level. On the heels of that story, Shannon and I were featured in the Loudoun Extra section of the *Washington Post*. They interviewed us by phone and had one of their photographers come out to take some pictures, and we appeared on the cover as well as in the online version. We were thrilled to see the huge jump in web traffic following the story.

Activity in the tasting room was back in full swing, and so were our efforts to drive our wine and music pairing brand identity. We continued to pursue partnerships with area music schools, including Shepherd University and the Shenandoah Conservatory. Through the Shenandoah connection, we were able to host the world-renowned Audubon Quartet for a private concert of Shenandoah supporters. Seeing talent of that level performing live in our tasting room was a thrill, and their patrons thoroughly enjoyed the music, the wine, and our hospitality.

On April 28th, we began planting the final three acres available within the existing deer fence perimeter. All the work done the previous fall had the site in fairly decent shape, though the tough, rocky soil that destroyed the sub-soiling tool was going to make hand planting the vines with shovels (instead of the tree planter) a miserable experience. Though we had hired enough crew to get the job done in a day, it ended up taking nearly two and a half days and quite a few broken shovel handles. The crew worked diligently regardless of the adversity, and as soon as the young vines were installed, they began working on the grow tubes. To save money, I decided I would put off installing the trellis until the following year, figuring the young vines would have plenty of support with just the bamboo stakes and grow tubes to get established.

With May upon us, we knew we were in serious financial trouble again, though we were starting to lose count of the number of times we had been in serious financial trouble. The loss of my consulting job was apparent as all the bills from bottling and the new vineyard installation hit at once. Tens of thousands of dollars in bottles, labels, corks, capsules, vines, trellis, and labor all arrived in about a three-week span. Pregnant women love a stack of bills $40,000 larger than the current bank balance. Not even ice cream can remedy that sort of predicament.

We considered taking emergency funds out of our retirement accounts, but realized that would be a very slippery slope; once we started doing that, we would likely wipe out everything in short order. Defaulting on the mortgage was definitely not an option, but everything else was on the table. I suggested that we sell the boat; the reality was that we had neither the time nor money to ever enjoy any time on it. Sitting in the parking lot doing nothing was a complete waste of space and resources, so we made the difficult decision to put our wedding present on the market.

Watching the buyer drive away with our "Manihi Pearl," I felt like a complete failure. Although the check in my hand and the line of credit we had secured would get us through this rough spot without dipping into our retirement accounts, I could not help but wonder how long we could keep going like this, living on the edge. I wanted so badly to give Shannon some peace of mind and financial security, so we could just focus on our babies without the daily stress of worrying about how we were going to cover our bills. In times like those, it was easy to lose sight of the dream, to get washed away by the anxiety that comes with no security, only the dreamer's promise of a brighter tomorrow. When you are in that moment, it takes an extraordinary amount of courage, discipline, and resolve to continue moving ahead, trying to muster what may be your last shred of self-confidence. Once again, as I had done so many times before, I picked myself up, brushed off the dust, and got back to work.

We hosted a very unique Mother's Day experience, with a local mobile spa joining us for the day to treat our guests to treatment packages. The event turned out to be a lot of fun, with several dozen ladies enjoying the relaxing mobile spa. The masseuse offered Shannon a complimentary massage and pedicure, which she gladly accepted, not being able to recall the last time she had any sort of maintenance work done. After that, the spa staff and our Notaviva staff all had a good laugh at my reaction when they offered me a complimentary pedicure as well. Suffice to say, the word "no" actually did, at some point, appear among the long list of expletives I was uttering. I could only imagine the reaction from my friends if they caught a glimpse of a photo of me sipping wine whilst enjoying a pedicure. Man card gone.

The next event we tried to pull off was an absolute failure. Seeing as how Saturdays were our biggest day of the week, we wanted to plan something really unique for the upcoming Memorial Day weekend.

We thought it would be fun to appeal to sports fans, having never seen that done at a winery, so we contracted with the Washington Redskins to have two cheerleaders come out on Saturday afternoon to sign autographs and talk to fans. As we have since learned, three-day weekends find Sunday being the busiest day, and Memorial Day Saturday has continued to be somewhat of a bust. We had seven people turn out to meet the ladies, six of whom were family. Uncle Hank—my mom's cousin and my godfather—and his wife Debbie (who had read at our wedding), and their daughter Jessie's family were on hand, along with one other guy. Uncle Hank, who had been confined to a wheelchair since the late 1970s and who was a die-hard Redskins fan, thoroughly enjoyed meeting the cheerleaders, in one of those rare situations when someone might actually appreciate being seated for a conversation with a standing cheerleader. The ladies were gracious and fun, even in the face of a total disaster. Oh well, you win some, you lose some, but it was a win for me, as my dear Uncle Hank was very thankful for the autographs our $1,200 Redskinette bill provided.

Over the next few weeks, when our friends and family asked us about what had happened the boat, we lied and told them we figured we were not going to be able to use it enough to warrant the expense, and besides, the boys were too young to really enjoy it anyway. The truth was we had to hock our beloved wedding present to cover May's mortgage payment and buy groceries.

CHAPTER 35
"Almost Goodbye"

With Ronan's due date approaching in early July, we began making preparations for his arrival. We had asked Debbie to help us paint his room, since it would be the first time we could actually prepare a nursery, as the other two boys came home to the rental shack. Shannon and I decided on a knights, castles, and dragons theme for his room, so I applied a base coat of light blue to the top half of the walls, and a light green to the bottom half and Debbie took it from there. She hand painted the most amazing mural, with a fantasy castle right above the crib, and a meandering path adorned with trees, flowers, and caricatures of our three dogs, Tamra, Gypsie, and Chewie. Refusing payment of any kind, Debbie bartered her skills for a sleepover, dinner and breakfast, and a couple cases of wine.

Even though we had technically opened our tasting room the previous March, our official grand opening had been at the end of June 2008, which we considered to be the launch of our business. As our one-year anniversary approached, we wanted to create a unique event to commemorate the occasion. I came up with the idea of a wine and music pairing experiment, which we would call the "Notaviva Experience." I created playlists of music, ten thirty-second clips of music from a wide variety of genres, which we would present to people while they conducted a blind tasting of several of our wines. They would know nothing about the wine, simply if it was white or red, which they could discern from looking in the glass. I created a rating sheet, which they would use to rank each track's suitability with the wine they were drinking, along a scale of zero to ten. I also added a favorite selection, which they were to use in case any of the tracks were a tie.

As soon as we announced the event at the end of May, interest was high and ticket sales went well. We knew it was going to be the last project we would take on prior to Ronan's arrival, and as the evening of June 27th approached, I was beginning to get very nervous. The people we told about the event, however, seemed genuinely excited about the opportunity to explore something wholly unique, putting our theories to the test that the music you are listening to can impact your sensory perception of wine.

As the tasting room filled up for the inaugural event, we had hors d'oeuvres, gourmet cheeses, fresh breads, and desserts on hand to greet the guests. When the time came, I ascended the stairs up to the music loft, where I was to introduce the event and then play the music. After a brief discussion of the cognitive neuroscience—known as crossmodal correspondence—believed to play a role in this phenomenon, we began. It was amazing to see how quickly people dropped their heads, studying the wine and focusing on the music.

We proceeded through five wines, and at the end of the evening, we had a show of hands to indicate which tracks people voted as their favorite with each wine. Attendees' jaws dropped open when we determined nearly 70% of them voted for a Latin jazz music track paired best with wine one, our "Calor," meant to be paired Latin jazz. As I read the text from the label, the room erupted in applause; the entire crowd understood and appreciated that, without question, wine and music DO have an impact on one another. To experience that firsthand was a memorable moment for everyone in the room, but certainly for Shannon and me. To see the happy faces, and bask in that moment of understanding when a group of people overcame their doubts about an untried methodology and opened their minds to a new way of thinking, was very special indeed.

With that success behind us, it was now time for a total focus on the safe arrival of our third baby boy. All the ultrasounds and pregnancy examinations had gone exceedingly well, and now it was just a waiting game for another week or so. We did schedule two extra sonograms due to Shannon's unusually large size, though both went well and Ronan was clearly in good health. However, in the days that followed the anniversary event, Shannon was getting increasingly uncomfortable due to the onset of some worrisome pains that she had not experienced during the previous two pregnancies. Paula Senner, the midwife who had delivered Tristan and Duncan, started seeing her every other day. As we approached his due date and the pain and discomfort increased, Paula made the decision to induce Shannon on July 6th.

On the evening of the 5th, I took Tristan and Duncan over to my mom's house. As I prepared to leave, I asked the boys if they were excited about meeting their new baby brother; Tristan jumped up and down laughing, saying he could not wait. Duncan, at just two and a half years old, certainly did not fully grasp what was about to happen, but jumped up and down in excitement anyway, to be like his brother.

By 7:30 A.M. the next morning, we were on the road to the Birthing Inn, after taking a few posterity photos of Shannon's belly. Paula was already there waiting for us, and within a few minutes of checking in, Shannon was in the telemetry room, changing into her gown. Paula stopped in to review the plans again, and she administered the Pitocin to induce labor. As expected, it began to take effect right away, and by 10:00 A.M. Shannon was experiencing regular, evenly spaced contractions. We spent the morning and early afternoon much as we had with Tristan and Duncan's labor, walking the halls and "dancing" through the contractions, giddy with excitement to meet our new baby.

By 5:00 P.M., not even the tub was giving Shannon much relief, so Paula decided to give her another exam. After an hour on her side, we knew she was well into transition, so Paula decided to elevate the bed. I continued to be amazed at how many different techniques midwives have at their disposal as they work to mitigate pain and discomfort. After only a half hour in the sitting position, it was now time for Shannon to push. I was at Shannon's side holding her leg back, while the nurse was on the other side doing the same. Even with two deliveries behind me, the intensity of the screams, the encouragement of the midwife, and the sheer beauty of the moment were an absolute sensory overload. I was overcome with such a deep respect and boundless love for Shannon's commitment to our boys.

Ronan Tylor Mackey was delivered at 7:05 P.M., and was the most vocal of our three boys right from the start. The moment he was out, Shannon was immediately relieved, again asking, "Is it really over?" I hugged her and kissed her, congratulating her on another perfect delivery. She fell back with equal measures of relief and exhaustion as the nurses snatched up the baby to begin the weights and measures process. Shannon's mom came in to give her a hug and see her new grandson. Paula began preparations for the final part of the process, the delivery of the placenta, which she wanted to complete before handing the baby back to Shannon. The placental expulsion would begin soon thereafter, and in those moments, our entire world would be turned upside down.

A few moments later, I could tell by the look on Paula's face that something was not right. I had stood by Shannon's side for the expulsion of the two previous placentas, and she had gotten through it with just a bit of wincing and the occasional expletive. The shrieks I was now hearing were not only worrying me, but Paula as well as the nurses, who were sharing nervous sideways glances. Blood was everywhere; I had never seen anything like it with Tristan or Duncan, the bed was covered. Shannon finally could not take anymore, and began screaming, "Paula, stop! Paula, stop!" What Paula said next will ring in my ears for the rest of my life; she looked at the nurse and said, "Get Doctor Smith now, and prepare his gown and gloves."

The nurse turned and ran out of the room, and I glanced across the bed at Shannon's mom and in a panic just said, "Get out." She was pale, also fully aware that her daughter was in serious trouble and that this delivery had just gone off the rails. She whispered, "I love you" to Shannon as she turned to leave, dodging nurses on her way out the door. As it turned out, the nursing staff was right in the middle of a shift change, and there were double the typical number of staff in the Birthing Inn. Although our room was a flurry of activity, I was in a heightened state of awareness, seeing everything in slow motion—Paula doing her best to stem the blood flow, Shannon getting paler by the moment, nurses hurriedly cleaning Ronan and preparing to move him to the nursery. There were more nurses helping Paula get into her gown and gloves, and still others getting Dr. Smith's gown and gloves ready.

Dr. Steven Smith walked in not even a minute later, and amid the madness of the delivery room, he appeared cool, confident, and level-headed. He leaned over to Paula, who quickly gave him her assessment of the situation. I leaned over and kissed Shannon and promised her everything was going to be alright. Two of the nurses took me by the hands, looked me in the eyes, and told me I had to go look after my baby boy now; Shannon was going into surgery. They were trying to determine if I was in shock, and confident that I was not going to pass out, they began wheeling Ronan out, wrapped up in a blanket with a hat on, completely at peace and sound asleep. As they moved past me, I paused at the door to listen as Dr. Smith explained to Shannon that she was bleeding to death, and that she was in a life-threatening situation; he was taking her into emergency surgery to save her life. He said her placenta was not releasing from the uterus, and they needed to operate immediately. Depending on what they found, there was the very real possibility that they would have to perform an emergency hysterectomy. I was looking back at Shannon's face as he told her, and when she heard the word "hysterectomy," she began frantically shouting through her tears, "No! Oh my God no! No, please, NO!" She was so pale from the blood loss, I was sure she was in shock and going to pass out any moment.

That was the last I saw her before they took her into the operating room. The nurses pulled me out into the hallway and again calmly told me, "Your baby boy needs you now, you must come with us to the nursery so we can take care of Shannon." In a daze, I followed them into the nursery.

I sat there with Ronan for what seemed like an eternity, whispering to him that he was a good boy, and that his mommy loved him and he was going to see her very soon. It was like floating in a dream; there I was in a nursery filled with at least a dozen newborns, and not a single one of them was making a sound. They were all sleeping quietly; beautiful babies snuggled warmly in their hats and blankets, somehow sensing that all was not right in the world. For an hour and a half, we stayed there together, until the nurse who had been with us all day came in to say that Shannon was still in surgery, and she did not have any updates. She was heading home, but wanted to stop in to say goodbye. I hugged her and she smiled at Ronan and the other babies before she slipped quietly away.

I knew Shannon had just become Paula's one in a million emergency delivery (as she would later phrase it), yet I never let the thought of losing her into my mind, not one single time. I set my mind with an unwavering resolve that Shannon would make it through this, and we would all be together again very soon.

About two and a half hours later, a nurse came in and said that Shannon was out of surgery and that Paula wanted to give me an update on her condition. Slowly I got up, told Ronan I would be right back, and followed the nurse. We made our way out into the lobby of the Birthing Inn; Paula was there, along with Shannon's mom and Jim and Shayna. Paula held my hand and said that although Shannon had lost a lot of blood, they were giving her transfusions to restore her. The bleeding had just been too severe; Dr. Smith had made the difficult decision to remove her uterus. They also noticed a large cyst on her right ovary, and made the decision to remove that as well.

All I remember of that moment is a sensation of falling; as everything faded to black, I remember seeing Shayna's hands covering her mouth, her eyes wide with fear. I can only liken the experience to the days when I was a pole vaulter on our high school's track team; the sensation was the exact same as the moment a pole breaks and you find yourself spinning through the air, unsure of which way is up and how or when you are going to come crashing back to earth. Thankfully, Paula was holding on to my hands, so I did not fall directly backward; I just kind of sunk to the ground, where I blacked out for a few brief seconds. When I began to regain my senses, they helped me into a chair. Shayna was still frozen with the same expression on her face, too in shock to even let the tears flow, Jim steadying her as much as himself. Sue was crying and trying to gather herself. Although in shock, we were all relieved that Shannon had survived a life-threatening emergency, though she was definitely not out of danger. Paula sat down beside me, crying as well, and I knew this was incredibly painful for her. Through the years, she had grown to love Shannon, and even though her experience and training had prepared her for the technical aspects of what had just transpired, no amount of training would have ever been able to prepare her heart for a blow of that magnitude.

Paula held my hand and again whispered to me, asking if I understood what she had told me, if I was processing everything. I nodded that I did, and then asked her not to tell Shannon until I could be there with her. I did not want her to be alone or scared when she got the news. Paula promised she would not, and then told me she had to get back to the operating room. They would soon be finished dressing her incision while waiting for her to come out of the anesthesia before they transported her over to the adjoining hospital. She wanted me to come with her, so she could put me in a room, ready when Shannon came out of the operating room. Slowly getting to my feet, I hugged Sue and told her she had to call Roger to tell him the news. Jim and Shayna were to relay the news to my family; we hugged together for a moment before Paula led me back into the Birthing Inn, where she found me an empty room whose doorway looked down the hallway where Shannon would soon be brought out.

It was another thirty minutes before I heard the doors swing open and saw the foot of the gurney coming out, pushed by Paula and another nurse. Slowly, I moved forward into the doorframe as the gurney inched closer; as they made a wide left turn, I caught sight of Shannon's face, and our eyes met. She took my breath away, and in my entire life I have never seen anything so perfectly beautiful, yet so frighteningly frail. It seemed as if she was a dream come to life, a work of art crafted of the finest handspun glass, stunning to behold, though the lightest touch might cause to shatter, never to take form again.

Though she was still heavily sedated she recognized me instantly, and as the gurney moved past my room, she looked up at me and whispered, "No more babies. I'm sorry." I was stunned, and before I could even fully focus on Paula, she was already apologizing, saying, "I had no choice, she made me tell her. I had no choice, you have to believe me." We made our way out of the Birthing Inn to the recovery rooms of the hospital.

When we arrived in recovery, Paula conferred with the nurse on staff, and then introduced me. They told me that she would be here at least an hour to ensure she was fully recovering from the anesthesia, and then they would change her incision dressings and move her into a room. Paula got me situated in the waiting room.

I just sat in that room, unmoving, for an hour, staring at the floor. Although Shannon was the only patient in there, protocol prevented me from remaining with her until her dressings were changed and she was ready to be moved away. As I sat there, I wondered how Ronan was faring. I wondered how my mother and sister had taken the news; I wished I could have been the one to tell them. Actually, I wished there was nothing to tell. I wished that Shannon and I were lying together in a warm post-partum room, with Ronan sleeping contentedly on her chest. For the first time since these events began unfolding, I cried, and it took me a long time to pull myself together. Activity outside the waiting room brought me back to my senses, and as I peeked through the door, I could see that they were finally getting Shannon ready to move into a room.

Paula appeared again to check that Shannon had made it into her room, and as Shannon was semi-lucid, she leaned down and kissed her on her forehead. Taking me aside, Paula asked if we could bring Ronan up, just so she could see him to help lift her spirits. I agreed instantly and we told Shannon we would be right back, and she told me to hurry; she did not want to be left alone. Paula and I hustled back over to the Birthing Inn to get Ronan, and when we entered the nursery, the nurse on duty asked if I wanted to hold him. I simply responded, "No, thank you, his mommy will be the first one to hold him when she is feeling better." We wheeled him over to the hospital, into the elevator and up to Shannon's room. Though she was still too weak to hold him, Paula picked him up and laid him on her chest so she could see his perfect little face. Knowing Shannon so well, I took his hat off so she could smell the top of his head, and she brightened as she kissed his forehead and whispered, "Mommy loves you."

Paula got Ronan back into the bassinette, and before she made her way back to the Birthing Inn, told me she would wait for me to return to my room, as I would not be able to spend the night with Shannon. About that time, the nurse asked Shannon if she could bring her anything, and Shannon asked for some food, saying she was incredibly hungry. The nurse shook her head and told us, "No food for you for another twelve hours." I was incredulous; after all she had just been through, now they were going to make her starve? As if on cue, Dr. Smith came into the room to check on Shannon and heard the tail end of my objections. When he told the nurse to get Shannon some dinner, she gave him the same response; he cut her off mid-sentence. Fifteen minutes later, a hot plate of food arrived.

Saying goodnight to Dr. Smith, I fed Shannon some dinner, and as she began to fade to sleep, I kissed her goodnight and made my way back to the Birthing Inn. Paula had just come to check on me, and thankfully had thought to bring me a turkey sandwich, some chips, and a soda. We hugged and cried, and she promised to come by the next day. I finished off my food in the blink of an eye, walked over to the nursery to see Ronan through the window, and then returned to my room. I fell asleep on top of the bed with both my shoes and the lights on; somehow, when I awoke the next day both were off, and I was tucked under several blankets with my glasses safely on the nightstand.

By the time I made it back over to the hospital, Shannon had already awoken and eaten some breakfast. By 11:30 A.M., Shannon was in her post-partum room, starting to get some color back in her face, and very eager to see her baby boy. About fifteen minutes later they wheeled him in, and with tears of joy drifting down her cheeks, she held him for the first time on her own.

We had some family members visit before Paula came in around 4:00 P.M. A very emotional time for everyone, she and Shannon hugged in silence for a while before Paula snatched Ronan out of his bassinette. Although everyone had been through a nightmarish experience, there was, in fact, a perfectly healthy baby boy to cuddle. Paula asked me if I had held Ronan yet, and I realized that I had not. Finally I sat down, and she handed Ronan over to me. He was sleeping soundly, and I just looked down at him, reliving the previous evening as we sat together in the nursery awaiting the news on Shannon. Even years later as I look at him sleeping, I am still transported back to that moment.

Through the years, we have been amazed at the level of misunderstanding surrounding the field of midwifery. From the moment Shannon selected Loudoun Community Midwives for Tristan's birth, we have experienced diverse reactions from people, from amused to condescending to downright offensive. Simply put, midwives are not "witches in the woods," as some have mistakenly opined, but rather an industry of highly talented, highly trained, and supremely focused individuals, who are as equally adept with modern technology as they are with millennia-old birthing techniques. Their vast expertise, coupled with their respect for a family's birthing plan (whether natural or assisted childbirth), is inspiring. Paula and Shannon are now forever bonded through the tragedy they shared; yet, before Paula found herself assisting Dr. Smith in the operating room, she successfully caught three Mackey boys after healthy pregnancies and successful deliveries. For the rest of our lives, when Shannon or I are asked by young couples we meet about childbirth options, our first response will always be, "Call a midwife."

After Paula's visit, Shannon was exhausted and worried about Tristan and Duncan. Though I did not want to leave her, she insisted that I go over to Mom's place and pay them a visit. She assured me she was going to be sound asleep any minute, so I picked up some milkshakes and made my way. The boys were ecstatic to see the milkshakes, and I suppose happy to see me as well. By this point, I was cried out and still in a state of disbelief, but more than that, I did not want Tristan and Duncan to think that anything was wrong; I held myself together and sat down to play with them for a while.

On the morning of July 9th, now knowing that we still had a couple more days in the Birthing Inn while Shannon recovered, I decided to make a trip home to get my computer. I had not planned on being out of touch for so long, and figured I would have some clients looking for me. I'm not sure what the nurse on duty thought when she saw me carrying an iMac down the hallway, but in short order, I was set up in the room tending to emails. At this point, the news of Shannon's ordeal was really only known to a close circle of family and friends; Shannon asked me to send out an email to our extended family and friends and give them the full account of all that had transpired. That was incredibly difficult to write, though I cannot imagine how hard it must have been for the people close to us to read. The responses were instantaneous, thoughtful, emotional, and moving.

That evening, Mom brought the boys over to the Birthing Inn to finally meet their baby brother. Mom, who had obviously been champing at the bit waiting to get her hands on her new grandson, had been a real trooper tending to the boys at home. After Tristan and Duncan got a peek at Ronan, I put a DVD in the computer and they watched a movie while Mom held the baby. Shannon, who had finished her transfusions days earlier, was finally beginning to look like herself. Though still easily exhausted, her color was back, and although there was deep sadness behind her eyes, she was delighted to see Tristan and Duncan, and they her. After the boys left with Mom and Shannon fell asleep, I stayed up working on a few client projects, beginning to worry how we were going to manage Shannon's recovery once we got home. Although we had both managed to get some rest over the past couple days, I was starting to experience frequent dizzy spells, and was beginning to suspect that something was really wrong with me. I resolved to get in to see a doctor as soon as Shannon was back on her feet.

Shannon was discharged the next day, and although she was able to get up and slowly move around, the doctors made it clear that she was to stay in bed for at least another week. Steps were out of the question, so I knew we were going to have to rearrange our entire living quarters to ensure I could work downstairs while keeping the boys occupied. Mom agreed to keep Tristan and Duncan for another day to allow Shannon to get settled. We set her up with Ronan in our bedroom, while I set up a temporary office in the spare bedroom, along with a small television and DVD player. This would allow me to work on Mesh projects (with headphones on to drown out the cartoons) while Tristan and Duncan watched movies and played in Tristan's room. Shannon was able to nurse and change Ronan, and the two of them got on a pretty reasonable sleep schedule right away. Thank goodness he was not as fussy of a baby as Duncan; having a newborn with a bad belly would have been really hard to deal with in our current situation. I would make dinner upstairs and bring meals down so we could all sort of eat together, the older boys and I in the playroom, looking through the door at Shannon in our bed, Ronan sleeping soundly beside her in the bassinette.

I was finding it difficult to focus on client projects with two small boys tearing in and out of the room with all manner of toys and games. I figured it would be best to just spend the time with the boys while they were awake, and focus on my work in the evenings and late into the night. My dizzy spells were almost unbearable, and I was having trouble even focusing on my computer screen. Nearing midnight on July 12th, it all came crashing down. While trying to finish up a web design for a new client, I felt nauseous and faint. I began to feel a weird tingling in my hands, and when I looked down at them, I saw that my hands and feet were all completely white, devoid of any blood flow. As I sat there staring at my worsening condition, I began to shake, at first somewhat mildly, then suddenly in violent spasms. Knowing that I was in real trouble, I tried to get up, but fell out of my chair from the dizziness. Slowly regaining my sense of balance, I was able to make my way down the hall into our bedroom, where I knew I had to wake Shannon. I remember the look on her face when she saw me; she was terrified. I could barely speak; I was shivering and shaking uncontrollably. I somehow muttered that

I was freezing and needed to warm up, so she helped me move into the bathroom and turned on a hot shower. I got in and sat down, trying to regain some body heat. Shannon was crying and asking me, "What do you need me to do? Do you want me to call 911?" I told her not yet; I needed to get my blood sugar back up, so she went into the kitchenette and brought me a jug of orange juice. I tried to swallow some, but was spilling most of it all over the place. Shannon held the jug, and I finally was able to get some juice down. Slowly, I could feel my blood sugar rising and could see some color coming back into my extremities. Once I could hold the jug myself, I continued to drink until I felt I could stand again. By now it was nearly 2:00 A.M., and Ronan was stirring to nurse; I assured Shannon that I was not going anywhere, and that she needed to deal with the baby.

After another thirty minutes in the hot shower, I felt I could stand up. Ronan had fallen back asleep and Shannon wanted to help me, but there was no way I was going to risk falling and having her try to catch me, popping out belly staples in the process. I was able to get on my feet, dry off, get dressed in several layers of sweat clothes, and make my way upstairs to get something solid to eat. I was completely drained, and it took all my energy just to get upstairs and make a sandwich. Shannon was beside herself, worried that I was going to pass out and fall down the stairs, but I was able to get back downstairs, where she helped me get into the spare bed.

A few hours later, our general practitioner's office agreed to see me right away once I told them the details of my early morning episode. Meeting with the doctor, I told him of all the symptoms I had been experiencing over the past months. Right away, he knew he wanted to test me for Lyme disease, so I moved into the next office where the nurse drew the required number of vials. He indicated it would be a few days until he had the results back, but given how things had gone for me the night before, he advised that I needed to get plenty of rest. When he asked if I had been under any unusual stress lately, I told him of Shannon's ordeal; he just stared at me, dumbfounded.

The rest of that week was a sleep-deprived, dizzy, nauseous blur, though thankfully family and friends were reaching out to offer help with pretty much anything, from making dinners and watching the boys to mowing the lawn. Sadly, no one reached out offering to help build websites, edit videos, or design logos, so I continued to tackle those tasks to the peaceful, soothing sounds of a two-and-a-half year old and a four year old horsing around all day long. I was able to get some design and development time in while they watched a movie here and there, and most of my clients were flexible with their deliverables in the few instances I had to tell them what was really happening behind the scenes.

Just over a week later, I was diagnosed with Lyme disease. They inquired if I had any idea when I might have contracted it, as it was clear I had an advanced case. I racked my brain, trying to remember when I could have been exposed, and just could not figure it out. They called in a prescription for a six-week course of Doxycycline, but were worried that my infection might be too severe and might require more advanced treatments; time would tell. As it turned out, I went through two six-week rounds of Doxycycline with no success. My general practitioner then referred me to an infectious disease specialist, who was very reassuring, and promised me that I was treatable and that he was going to rid me of the Lyme disease. The issue was that the disease had progressed very deeply into my soft tissue, thus my dizziness and cognition issues were beginning to show, in addition to the very typical joint pain. He prescribed two six-week rounds of Ceftin, and six months after being diagnosed I was finally cured. It was not until the writing of this book some years later, while sifting through the thousands of photos and blog entries I had kept, that the incident with the deer tick came back to me. Such a simple yet inexcusable oversight, and I now believe my joint issues and persistent fatigue will continue to plague me for the rest of my life.

Our follow-up meeting with Dr. Smith was very emotional; how do you begin to thank the person who saved your life, or your wife's? It was a difficult conversation, as he mentioned several times that Shannon probably would have died. As we spoke, we learned how fortunate we were that he happened to be the OB-GYN on staff that evening. During his residency, he'd had the opportunity to assist on several emergency hysterectomies, and during his career he had performed fourteen of them. He assured us he had done everything in his power to save her uterus, but that the damage was too great and the blood loss too severe; he had to make the call when he did.

Even though her staples were out, Shannon was still prohibited from lifting anything heavier than Ronan. Steps were also out of the question for another month, though she was getting around the downstairs pretty well, and was able to make it upstairs by walking around the house up a gentle slope and up the few steps to the front door. We got through the next couple of weeks without ever speaking about the finality of what had happened. I was not going to bring it up, figuring Shannon would let me know when she was ready to talk about it. One day, she approached me and asked if we could get away, find a rental cabin somewhere with the baby, and finally talk about what had happened. I knew we needed to talk, to confide in each other about how terrifying the situation had been, and to ensure that we would be stronger as a couple for having lived through that ordeal. Shannon was worried about our oldest dog, Tamra, who at well over seventeen years of age, had been very lethargic the past few weeks. The cabin was not pet friendly, so we figured she would be alright with the dog sitter for two days until our return.

Prior to leaving on our getaway, we had learned the lab results from the examination of Shannon's uterus. It was determined she had a placenta accreta, where the placenta attaches abnormally to the inside of the uterus. Essentially, after Ronan was born, as her body was trying to expel the placenta, it was pulling the uterus out with it, causing the excruciating pain and severe bleeding. The cause will forever be unknown, and to us it simply does not matter. There is no one to blame.

We found a small cabin about two hours away, in beautiful Luray, Virginia in the Shenandoah Valley. After dropping Tristan and Duncan off at Mom's, we slowly made our way down the scenic Skyline Drive, stopping off at a few overlooks to take some photos. We stopped at a small country store to buy a few groceries, and once we arrived at the cabin, spent the afternoon relaxing and talking about new opportunities with both Notaviva Vineyards and Mesh Multimedia. I knew she would bring the subject up when she was ready, and she did later that evening.

We talked for hours, trying to make sense of all that had befallen us over the past several weeks. In our hearts, we both knew the hours of conversation were just a prelude to the one question that was on both our minds: were we done having children? Would we ever consider alternative methods of childbirth? Technically, Shannon still had one perfectly good ovary that was producing eggs. For me, the answer was clear and something I had thought about a lot over the past few weeks; it was no. Fate had sent us a message to simply be thankful for the three beautiful boys we had, and for our continued time together. We were both in total agreement that we were very lucky to still have each other and all the wonderful adventures that lay ahead of us as a family.

We also both agreed that Notaviva Vineyards and Mesh Multimedia needed to move ahead. Though the dream was to found a vineyard, our fledgling multimedia development company was really starting to come into its own, with a growing list of larger and larger clients. It was now clear we had not given its potential proper consideration. We talked late into the night, starting to dream again about a brighter future now that our recent nightmare was fading to memory. Shannon nursed Ronan and we fell asleep in each other's arms, hiding deep in the woods, far away from the rest of the world.

The next morning, we enjoyed a big breakfast together before packing up and returning home. As soon as we pulled up, I realized something was wrong; only two dogs ran out to greet us. Opening the door to the mudroom where the dogs slept, I found Tamra lying in a puddle of urine, unable to get up, her tongue hanging out of her mouth, barely able to hold her head up to look at me. I heard Shannon coming in behind me and I stopped her before she entered the room, telling her about Tamra's condition and that she needed to make her decision. It was Tamra's time to go. She immediately burst into tears, not wanting to accept the reality that she knew had been close at hand for weeks. I cleaned Tamra up, wrapped her up in her favorite blanket, and brought her out into our bedroom, where I laid her upon the bed so Shannon could say goodbye. While Shannon held her, I called the veterinarian's office, telling them we had an emergency and we would be in right away.

When I arrived at the veterinarian's office, they took us into one of their back rooms with a nice dog bed on the floor. They explained the procedure to me, and after I had signed the form, they began. The first shot would just put her into a deeply relaxed state, and then the second shot would stop her heart. As the first shot took effect, she tried to lick her nose, but was too weak to completely shut her mouth again. So there we lay on the floor, I on the hard linoleum and Tamra on her comfortable doggie bed, sticking her tongue out at me for all eternity.

Life is so fragile, and we typically go through each day giving very little thought to what a precious gift life upon this Earth really is. Shannon's ordeal strengthened us as individuals and as a married couple in ways that we are still discovering. I have lost count of the number of times in the tasting room people have asked us, "Why did you stop at three boys? Didn't you want to try for a little girl?" Those questions are like a knife through the heart, and though we put on a brave face—for I do not believe anyone would ever intentionally ask that question if they knew what we had gone through—it will always hurt, and it hurts deeply.

As early as our first date, Shannon and I had thought it would be wonderful to have a little girl. We had such a keenly shared vision of what she, our little Ailyn Skye Mackey, would have been like. Chasing puppies through our meadow, in cowgirl boots and a dirty sundress, equal parts tomboy and little lady. She would have loved fishing with her big brothers, gardening with her mommy, and falling asleep in her papa's arms late at night, camping under starry skies and the beauty of our infinite universe. I can see her pretty smile, and sense her bold spirit. I do not allow myself to dwell on these feelings of loss, and instead brighten with utter contentment and pride when I think of Tristan, Duncan, and Ronan. Shannon and I are so grateful for our three healthy, bright boys, and will never take a single day with them for granted. We think of the many families that have yet to bring a child into their lives, and know we are among the fortunate. Whenever we see a St. Jude's commercial, or meet a child with developmental disabilities, we well up with emotion and our hearts go out to those families; we admire their strength and courage. Our lives revolve around these boys, and we will spend the rest of our days cherishing them, teaching them how to live life to the fullest, how to thrive in an ever-changing society, how to respect others, and how to care for the Earth and all its bounty.

Yet as I write these words and reflect on these times, the pain we shared and all the lessons we learned, I know in my heart I will wonder about her for the rest of my life. To this day, in those rare moments I spend alone in our meadow, I still find myself gently blowing kisses into the wind.

CHAPTER 36
"Third Harvest"

While helping Shannon through her recovery and dealing with the impact of my Lyme disease, I somehow managed to stay on top of my vineyard tasks. The spray regimen, hedging, and mowing all took an enormous effort to maintain, yet I knew that we would need a great harvest to continue expanding our production. Our 2007 harvest yielded 500 cases, 2008 saw 1,200 cases, and I was planning on producing 1,800 cases in the months ahead.

Now that Shannon was somewhat back on her feet and able to oversee the tasting room operations, I turned my attention to a few much-needed winery improvements. Our spring bottling runs had filled up our small storage room in our otherwise un-insulated winery. With the upcoming harvest, I would have to get the rest of the winery ready to receive fruit and safely store barrels over the winter. Up to that point in mid-August, we had been enjoying a relatively mild summer, but as soon as I embarked upon a construction project the temperatures skyrocketed, and we ended up working in an oven for two weeks.

The primary task was to leverage the interior height of the building to its fullest advantage. With a sixteen-foot high ceiling, the winery allowed the roof of the storage room to function as the deck of a mezzanine level. The plan for the next several days was to extend this mezzanine level out toward the front of the winery, install flooring, then move all of our non-winery personal storage up and away from the production floor. This would then allow the future development of an office on the third level, with stairs ascending from the mezzanine.

Determined to do the work ourselves, I ordered a flatbed full of lumber, and the following day it was deposited on the gravel in front of the winery. The large pile of support posts, joists, and plywood decking attracted the attention of the boys, who immediately climbed atop and declared it conquered.

Over the next several days, my assistant Quentin and I suffered in the miserable heat, installing the support posts, headers, joists, and flooring. The project came together well, with Shannon and the boys stopping in to bring cookies, check progress, and ensure we were drinking enough water. After the decking was in place, it was time to install my first set of stairs, a carpentry task I had always wanted to try. Calculating the rise and run of the staircase, learning how to use a speed square, then cutting the stringers was an interesting challenge, and certainly furthered my experience as a carpenter.

When the insulation team arrived, I could tell right away they were seasoned professionals. Quentin and I had already moved everything away from the walls to give them ample space to maneuver, and they quickly went about covering our gear and personal effects to protect everything from the overspray. After they had carted in ladders and run their spray gun hoses, they donned full-body protective gear and respirators and began the process. The liquid foam exits the applicator at several hundred degrees, and the curing process is an exothermic reaction. Add the oppressive August heat, and the temperature inside the building was soon over 140 degrees. I went inside to take a few pictures for the blog, and did not last more than five minutes in there. I had never experienced anything like it, and the application technicians were not enjoying the experience either. Though they had gotten an early start that morning, by 1:00 P.M., they had to quit for the day. Starting early again the following day, the process was complete by noon, after which they packed up their equipment and were hopefully headed to someone's pool.

On September 2nd, the fall issue of the *Virginia Wine Gazette* was released with a feature story on Notaviva Vineyards. Though Shannon and I were featured on the cover of the Summer 2009 issue, our article came out just in time to generate additional interest for the busy fall season. Virginians are ardent supporters of our wine industry, and any mention in a wine-centric publication always yielded a noticeable increase in tasting room traffic.

Two days after, we were back outside, continuing our work on the side deck, though thankfully not in such sweltering heat. We dug the footers for a handicapped access ramp, and one turned out to be located right on top of a rain drainage pipe, necessitating the relocation of the pipe. I just shook my head; we could not even dig a few holes without having some sort of drama ensue, but given what we had experienced over the previous two months, it was not worth getting excited about. Even though we were not required by the county to install a ramp, we did; we just felt like it was the proper thing to do.

Tuesday, September 8th was Tristan's first day of preschool, and both Shannon and I were emotional basket cases. We all got up early, and I made a big breakfast for everyone while Shannon checked and re-checked Tristan's backpack for supplies and proper labeling. Arriving at the Round Hill Community Center, we took several photos of Tristan and Duncan outside, inside—pretty much everywhere. Tristan was unfazed by all the commotion, and Duncan enjoyed playing with all the new toys. However, when it was time to go, poor Duncan did not understand why we were leaving his big brother behind, and fell into tears as we made our way to the car. We must have looked at the clock a hundred times throughout the day until it was time to go pick him up. Seeing his face light up when we all walked into the classroom was a very special moment, and we beamed when his teacher, Ms. Kim, told us how well he had done that day.

On Monday, September 14th, we harvested our Viognier, and as in the previous year, Mark and Vicki offered to produce our tank-fermented "Vincerò" while we would produce the barrel-fermented "Ottantotto." Since I was still experiencing a lot of joint stiffness and fatigue, my brother offered to come over and help me load the fruit into the refrigerated truck I had rented as I gathered it from the vineyard rows. Moving nine tons of fruit from the loader of the tractor and stacking it inside the truck makes for a very long day, and it was great to have Jim on hand to help out. As is everyone during their first experience working with our vineyard crew, he was both amazed and impressed at their work ethic and persistence.

The quality of the Viognier fruit was magnificent, bursting with amazing flavors of ripe apricot and pink grapefruit. Mark and Vicki were thrilled to have such great juice to work with. Crush day was long and tiring, but as always, very rewarding and exciting. Two days later when the juice had settled, I arrived with my barrels to receive my portion after we had racked off the sediment and filled our stainless steel tank. We filled eight barrels before the settling tank was empty. Arriving back at the winery, I used the tractor forks to lift the barrel racks into the winery, organized the production floor, and began pitching the yeast. Although it was only my second year making wine, I had learned so much the previous harvest through bone-headed mistakes that this time around I was far more organized, documented, and efficient.

The previous year, as I was learning about yeast nutrients and fermentation best practices, I began to realize how much of an advantage I had living fifty yards away from the winery. So much of fermentation management is about timing. Winemaking could never be thought of as a nine-to-five job, and on many occasions I have found myself heading out to the winery at midnight. One particularly crucial aspect of a healthy fermentation is the addition of a blended complex yeast nutrient right at the end of the lag phase, which occurs directly after inoculation. This is where the yeast is becoming acclimated to its new environment. Although there are a myriad of factors that can affect the timing of this phase, it is generally considered to be between six and twelve hours. Winemakers who pitch yeast late on a Friday night need to be at work early on Saturday morning without fail, because any undue stress to the yeast during initial fermentation can trigger long-lasting and sometimes unrecoverable negative consequences in the finished wine.

The other impact of adding nutrients to an active fermentation is the risk of a blowout, which I found out the hard way during the 2008 harvest. The second addition of yeast nutrients occurs at one-third-sugar depletion, which is measured on a hydrometer. So if your starting Brix is twenty-one, then you would be at one-third-sugar depletion at fourteen Brix. The previous year, I diligently measured the Brix over the first few days, not wanting to miss this critical addition. When the time arrived, I measured out the exact amount, dissolved it in some warm water, and unceremoniously poured it through a funnel into a barrel full of actively fermenting Chardonnay. Within seconds, the rapid addition of that large amount of nutrients triggered a reaction in the barrel, which suddenly began foaming uncontrollably. The foamy wine shot up out of the barrel's bung hole nearly a foot high, then spilled all over the winery. I would not be making that mistake again—actually, yes I would, and quite a few more times.

Like the previous year, we also bought Chardonnay from the same grower who supplied the Fedors, so we spent the day working the crush pad, returning in a couple days to retrieve our portion of the juice. Rather than segment the fruit into different tanks, Mark just put everything into one large tank for settling. When I arrived to pump the juice into my barrels, he calculated how much of the settled juice came from the grapes we had purchased, filled my barrels, and racked the rest into another tank for his fermentation. Though we both started with the exact same juice, it was fascinating to taste the differences in the finished wine the following year. Theirs was a dry tank-fermented style, and ours was an off-dry barrel-fermented style. This acknowledgement of how different winemaker's styles impact the finished wine is an element of winemaking I discuss to this day with our customers.

Since we had committed to scaling our production up to 1,800 cases, I had also secured several tons of Vidal Blanc from a grower a couple hours' drive south in the Shenandoah Valley. The challenge with buying fruit from growers some distance away is the need to provide the harvest lugs for their crew to pick the fruit. For example, if a harvest is planned for a Thursday morning, then the lugs have to be delivered the previous day to allow the crew to distribute them amongst the rows. Thus, the day before harvest, I had to load all of our lugs into a rental truck, drive them two and a half hours south to the vineyard, unload them by myself, and then drive home.

Upon arriving home, I would check the ongoing fermentations, shower, and head to my Mesh workstation to work on client projects. The next day, I would awaken early to get a jump on my Mesh projects before having to leave again to pick up the fruit. Arriving at the vineyard by mid-afternoon, I would inevitably have to wait with the other truck drivers, who were arriving to pick up their fruit as well. Several hours later, the fruit would be weighed and lifted into my truck, where I would use the pallet jack to roll the stacks of fruit into place, secure the load with upright pallets and load straps, and head for home.

As it turned out, we were able to process our Vidal Blanc over at Tarara. Jordan had also purchased fruit from the same vineyard, so we agreed that I would transport his lugs down to the vineyard to save him the time and expense, and in exchange we would use their gear to process our fruit. Our tiny press would not have been able to process that many tons of fruit, so the deal worked out well for everybody, and I learned a lot about winemaking working with Jordan that day. You may read as many books as you like about making wine, and knowing theory is a wonderful basis for learning, but until you are pulling hose, adding chemicals, cleaning gear, and getting stung by bees on a bustling crush pad, you really know nothing at all about getting it done.

Amidst harvesting our white grapes throughout the month of September, we were busily preparing for our first folk music festival, which was scheduled for Saturday, October 10th. We were promoting the event through social media channels, distributing posters all around the county, and encouraging all the bands to do likewise. The tasting room was packed each weekend with customers enjoying the wine and music, Shannon was steadily regaining her strength and enjoyed being back in action, and I had my hands full making wine and growing Mesh. The boys loved meeting customer's kids, making new friends and inviting them out to their playground.

On September 26th, we took our own crew over to a vineyard in nearby Waterford to pick several tons of Chambourcin. Progress was slow as it was our grower's first substantial harvest, and it took more time than expected to transport the picked fruit out of the vineyard to the truck. The fruit was in excellent shape, however, and it has always been my mantra to suffer through whatever challenges may present themselves, as long as the fruit (and ultimately the wine) are of the highest quality. Since it took so long to pick, I postponed the crush until the following day to ensure we were not out on the crush pad until well past midnight. The following day, following advice from several other winemakers who also make Chambourcin, I added the higher end of the suggested range of pectic enzymes to the must. Pectic enzymes essentially perform the reverse function of adding pectin to jelly. Where pectin causes the jelly to gel, pectic enzymes break down pectin, allowing the must and subsequently the juice to clarify. Chambourcin is notorious for clogging filters later in the production process, and several other winemakers who'd had long nights filtering Chambourcin and fruit wines encouraged me to not be shy when adding the enzymes.

Saturday, October 10th, the day of our first music festival, dawned dreary and drizzly. I had spent the previous day building an eight-foot by sixteen-foot stage in the picnic area adjoining the tasting room, which would be able to accommodate the six bands we had in the lineup. Advance ticket sales were slow, typical of an inaugural event, and I was worried that we had a total washout on our hands. No matter, we were about to enjoy some spectacular folk music, even if it turned out to just be the bands, my family, my crew, and Brooksie.

Todd Brooks, known to many as Brooksie, is a friend of mine from middle school and an avid musician as well as a fellow gear junkie. He truly is a cartoon character come to life. As Loudoun County's only homegrown winemaker, I have a lot of people from the neighborhood who have stopped by through the years. The summer after Notaviva opened, Todd paid us a visit to check the place out. I inquired as to his musical pursuits, and learned he owned a nice PA system, did some DJ work on the side (he owns a landscaping and snow plowing business), and still played both acoustic and electric guitar. Several months later when we began hosting open mic nights, Todd would swing by and play for a bit, and I encouraged him to really pursue his music. We began booking him at Notaviva, and thus began the birth of a legend. He is now one of the busiest musicians on the wine country circuit, and my sincere apologies to every winery and brewery owner who has had to shoo Todd out at the end of the night.

Todd had also come to realize that he had spent a lot of money on expensive audio equipment, and really had no idea how to use it to its fullest capabilities. He had the basics down pretty well, but was very interested in learning more advanced mixing techniques. When he learned about our upcoming folk festival, we decided to swap usage of his PA in exchange for some audio lessons. Todd arrived early, as excited as a kid on Christmas morning, eager to set up the gear and listen to the music, holding an enormous cup in each hand. When I asked about the cups, he responded, "One is my sweet tea, the other is my spit cup." You just have to love him.

The lineup consisted of six local acts: Jake and the Burtones, the Polka Dots, Stoney Creek Bluegrass Band, Andrew McKnight, the Woodshedders, and Steve DeVries. It never actually rained that morning, but the two opening acts played under damp, grey skies. In addition to the music, we had also invited some local artisans to set up under their canopies in the front yard. Our neighbor down the street, Big Mike, had a fledgling barbeque smoker business and was happily set up at the bottom of the hill. Everything was ready—now we just needed some people to show up.

And show up they did. I would not go so far as to describe our first foray into music festivals a runaway success, but we made enough in tickets and wine sales to cover the bands and crew. The music was great, it was the first folk festival hosted at a Loudoun winery, people loved the wine, and everyone had a good time. The parking lot was full and all the extra cars were parked across the meadow adjoining the vineyard. We had put free tickets in all the neighbors' mailboxes, and several showed up to enjoy the bands. Many of our avid customers were on hand, some with their families, and it was wonderful to see the kids enjoying the music and the rural setting. Although I was busy setting up and mixing the bands, and Shannon was dealing with the ticket booth and the tasting bar, we did share a few moments together to just stop and look around at all the activity.

With the festival behind us, I turned my attention back to wine-making and creative digital media pursuits. Four days later, we harvested our Cabernet Franc, and after the recent Chambourcin harvest, our crush pad setup was honed and efficient. The fruit was picked and at the winery by early afternoon, and after a nice lunch with the crew, we processed the fruit well into the evening. After the gear was cleaned and everyone departed, I rehydrated and pitched my yeast. Another winemaking technique that I had learned the previous year (but not fully appreciated at the time) was the usage of different strains of yeast. Each one of the large fermentation bins that we use for our red wines holds about one and a half tons of fruit, thus our Cabernet Franc was distributed across three bins. I selected different yeast for each bin, and when fermentation was complete, I pressed the must into three different containers to keep them separate. A few days later, I racked the settled wine into barrels and labeled them accordingly, so I could track the development of the various wines by yeast type through the winter. The differences were striking, and although each was clearly Cabernet Franc, the strains of yeast each imparted their own unique characteristics on the resultant wines. The beauty of this methodology comes to fruition when the wines are blended back together, adding complexity and interest to the finished wine. Not only are wine blends comprised of different kinds of fruit, but within each blending wine there may be various kinds of yeast and barrels selections combined to craft the winemaker's final vision.

Another interesting lesson I learned earlier in the year happened when Doug was visiting to check up on my progress. As we were discussing plans for bottling, I asked him, "What makes a wine a 'reserve' wine?" He explained that the word technically does not mean anything from a TTB labeling standpoint, however most people understand it to mean a wine of some special quality that the winemaker reserves either to age for a longer period of time or to bottle separately and sell at a premium. I mentioned to him I thought I might have something special going on with my Petit Verdot; he looked at me rather dubiously, but agreed to have a taste. Cleaning off the wine thief, I pulled a couple of samples, and upon trying the wine, Doug was very impressed. When I asked him if I should age it for another year, he encouraged me to do so. Although it was only two barrels, the wine was spectacular, and I later bottled it as a 100% Petit Verdot named "Johann," in honor of Johann Sebastian Bach.

Now that we had planted the Blaufränkisch, which would be inspired by Mozart, and had a Bach wine, I felt it was time to create a wine for Ludwig van Beethoven. It had to be big, bold, and complex, like the man and his music. Our grower in Waterford also had some Cabernet Sauvignon planted, and so we had a contract on that fruit. Planning on making the Beethoven wine as a Meritage, I also had a contract on one ton of Merlot from Breaux Vineyards, which I would use in the blend.

The challenge in growing Cabernet Sauvignon in Virginia is letting the fruit hang late into the season to ensure it has achieved a proper level of ripening. Growers and winemakers are typically at odds over when to harvest. The growers sense the onset of colder temperatures, late autumn storms, and the onset of rot. Winemakers are walking the rows, tasting the fruit, and telling the grower it is not ready yet. These situations can test even the best of relationships, and we found ourselves doing our best to assure our grower that we needed to wait just a few more days to let the fruit mature. In the end, it worked out perfectly; we experienced a nice run of warm, windy days leading up to our harvest. No sooner was the fruit fermenting in the bins than the weather turned ugly, and we were in for a stretch of cold, rainy days. The weather soon broke, and we experienced gorgeous weather the first weekend in November. Wine enthusiasts were out in force, and we set our new tasting room record with two hundred sixty tastings. Right in the middle of the madness, we had yet another brave lad drop to his knee and propose to his girlfriend amidst the cheers of our customers and staff.

By now our Cabernet Sauvignon was fermenting in the safety of the winery, as was the Merlot. After fermentation was complete, I let the wines sit on the skins for another week to ensure maximum extraction while starting the malolactic fermentation, then we pressed, settled, and racked everything into barrels. By the time Thanksgiving arrived, all the crush pad gear had been cleaned and stored, the wines were in the barrels, and the entire winery was being heated by two small space heaters due to the efficiency of the spray foam insulation.

The pace of life slowed down to just running two small businesses and raising three small boys. We settled happily into the spirit of the holiday season, and the significance of simply being able to sit together as a family in front of a tree, surrounded by the warmth of our beautiful timber frame home, was not lost of either of us. We had come through the most terrifying experience of our lives, pulled off a great season, and had proven something to ourselves in the process. Shannon was superb at managing our family and our businesses, training and mentoring staff, tracking the alcohol and sales reports, navigating the asinine insurance policies and premiums, hosting corporate outings and planning events, and dealing with the complexity of personal and business cash flows, all while raising three babies under a roof that was invaded by thousands of total strangers each year. Although we had neither fancy equipment nor an elaborate winery, we now knew beyond the shadow of a doubt that I could make wine. Not just any wine, but great wines that could impress even the most jaded wine snob, who at the beginning of a tasting would growl, "I do not drink Virginia wines," only to find themselves later leaving with half a case. In addition to proving myself as a winemaker, I had also proven myself as a developer, producer, and designer, and was increasingly proud of my growing portfolio.

As we sat there holding each other, gazing dreamily at the tree and watching the boys play, something happened most unexpectedly.

Like the faintest whisper in the woods on a cold windy night, barely perceptible over the dry rustling leaves, it was something we sensed rather than saw or heard. It was the return of hope. In that moment, we discovered a renewed confidence in ourselves, a restoration of spirit strengthened by enduring the challenges of the past two years. We allowed ourselves to move beyond the fear that had held us so tightly in its grasp, and once again dreamed of brighter days to come while a star-shaped moonbeam drifted slowly across the room.

CHAPTER 37
"Crooked Run"

In January 2009, I attended my first meeting of the Loudoun County Economic Development Commission as a Group C member with full voting rights for a one-year term. Looking around the room at the host of talented business leaders, experienced men and women from a diverse array of industries large and small, I found myself wondering, "What the hell were they thinking when they asked me to be here?" These people were actual grownups, running businesses with real balance sheets and everything. I resolved during that first meeting that I would immediately educate myself on the challenges Loudoun faced, so that I would be prepared to intelligently participate in the activities of the EDC. I felt then, as I do today, that public service is a duty to be taken seriously, and would involve real sacrifice and effort.

I had been selected (after an application, interview, and review process) due to my unique background and current situation running two small businesses, one in agriculture and the other in digital media. The review committee figured I could bring relevant insight into the issues facing the burgeoning wine industry, contribute to the marketing and business retention committee, as well as champion the needs of small business owners. Although two-thirds of Loudoun's land mass is rural, Doug was the only other agribusiness member in the thirty-five-member commission. As chairman of the Rural Economic Development Council, Doug was a Group A member in the EDC by virtue of his role on the REDC. In a reciprocal arrangement, the EDC also had a seat on the REDC.

I spent the year becoming acquainted with my fellow commissioners while attending the monthly EDC meetings, monthly MBRC meetings, and networking events. After a few months, as I began to gain an understanding of current issues and the players involved, I would raise my hand at meetings and attempt to contribute to the dialogue. After some embarrassing freshman attempts, stammering out a few meek sentences from behind bright red cheeks, I realized that my colleagues were very interested in my perspectives; as my confidence grew, they acknowledged that I was becoming well versed in the politics of the day. As both a member of the business community and as a parent of three young boys, I had a keen sense of responsibility for our efforts. Amid growing two businesses, raising three children, helping my wife recover from a near-death experience, all while enduring and recovering from Lyme disease, I felt I had displayed appropriate levels of commitment and initiative during my first year on the EDC, and so did the membership committee. They asked me to return to the commission as a Group B member for a three-year term, beginning January 1, 2010. Given the exposure I had received to issues such as workforce development, zoning applications, economic development, transportation, and taxation, I knew that continuing to serve on the commission would not only allow me to contribute to the direction of the county, but also advance my business acumen.

Throughout 2009, I had also been actively participating in the Loudoun Wineries Association (LWA), attending meetings and bringing the concerns of the group to the attention of the EDC and MBRC. The head of Visit Loudoun was on the MBRC with me, and it gave us an additional opportunity to exchange ideas. Leading up to the elections that fall, several members had approached me and asked if I would be interested in running for president. Though I had never led an organization like the LWA, I felt strongly about the role of the association in the community and agreed to run. In the week before the election, I hand-delivered a letter to every winery in the county asking for their support, and I won the election by a very narrow margin. Among the many issues I intended to further during my two-year tenure as president were the need for collaboration with other county organizations such as the EDC and Loudoun Chamber, and the need for educational opportunities for winery and vineyard staff within Loudoun County. Presiding over my first LWA meeting a month later at Notaviva Vineyards, we formed education, marketing, and legislative committees.

At the January 2010 EDC meeting, incoming Chairman John Wood, CEO of the Telos Corporation, asked me if I would be the EDC's representative to the REDC. My nomination was put to a vote and I was unanimously elected. Now in addition to the monthly EDC and MBRC meetings, I would have to attend the monthly REDC meetings as well as preside over the LWA, both the organization and the legislative committee. In between meetings, I found myself staying up late, reading to stay abreast of current news articles and completing commission paperwork. Doug, an avid supporter and defender of the rural economy, would occasionally ask me over along with a few other agribusiness owners to brainstorm solutions for the issues continually facing small rural business owners. The Loudoun Chamber of Commerce had approached me about being on their board as well, and my three-year term began a week later.

Throughout 2010, both Notaviva Vineyards and Mesh Multimedia continued to grow, and the summer was blisteringly hot and dry. As the house was now over three years old, the navy blue stain had faded to a light grey, and needed to be re-applied. I had reached out to the same company that had done the work during construction, and received a bid for $12,000. That was completely out of our budget, so I bought several dozen gallons of stain and rented a giant articulated lift so I could do the job myself. Spending eight days in the stifling heat, at times forty feet in the air climbing out of the bucket onto the roof to stain the dormers, I spent a lot of time thinking about the plight of small family farms in Northern Virginia. So much sweat equity goes into running a farm, keeping equipment running and maintaining structures; how was I going to afford to keep this place looking good when I was too old (or wise) to dangle out of a lift?

Harvest hit us like a freight train that year, with me now being pulled in so many different directions. Along with all of my public service activities, I was also an assistant coach for Tristan's flag football team, the fearsome Panthers. Coaching was something I had always wanted to do, and enjoyed tremendously. I have such fond memories of soccer, football, and high school track, training with Ed "Coach Z" Zuraw during the summer and riding around in his old blue van, pole vault poles strapped to the top, empty pizza boxes strewn about, listing to Maynard Ferguson's "Pagliacci" at deafening sound levels. Coaches can have such a positive impact on young people's lives, and I have always found it reprehensible to see parents yelling obscenities at a little league coach who is so giving of their time. I knew I would value my time with the kids tremendously, though I soon learned that helping to teach kindergartners the basics of playing football is unquestionably where the phrase "herding cats" originated. The days were busy with Mesh projects and winemaking, while the evenings were busy with practices, games, meetings, and networking events. It was all a blur, but we were meeting so many new and interesting people, the boys were making friends, and the tasting room was busier than ever.

In late 2010, the REDC was addressing one of the most divisive issues presently facing the county. The Chesapeake Bay Protection Ordinance (CBPO) was a proposed water-quality measure that had environmentalists facing off against developers and the business community. The ordinance would mandate the establishment of 100-foot buffer zones adjacent to perennial streams and wetlands, and would require permits and fees to build on land near waterways. At their September 21st meeting, the Loudoun Board of Supervisors postponed action on the ordinance pending additional review and revision by community stakeholder groups. Farmers, developers, business owners, and local government leaders strongly opposed adoption of the ordinance.

As the REDC members deliberated the issue, it was clear that much more information and research would have to be conducted to come to a consensus. The challenge for the farming community, particularly those who raised livestock, was the tradeoff of maintaining a healthy environment versus the high costs of fencing and restrictions on fertilizers. The REDC would be required to be present at the forthcoming stakeholder meetings, scheduled for early December; we resolved to send a representative abstaining from all votes, since we had been unable to arrive at a majority position on the issue. The representative, however, took it upon himself to vote on behalf of the REDC according to his personal agenda. When I learned of his actions, I requested an emergency meeting of the council to select a new representative who would fairly and accurately convey our concerns, while honoring the group's decision to abstain from the voting. The group, who appreciated my ardor over the misrepresentation, appointed me as the new representative. I had now inherited two three-hour long meetings each week in the three weeks leading up to Christmas, along with hundreds of pages of proposals, commentary, legalese, and scientific research to digest.

I was also pursuing new educational opportunities on behalf of the LWA. In early November, I had taken it upon myself to reach out to key faculty at Northern Virginia Community College (NVCC) who offered a horticulture technology program. Our neighbors to the south at Piedmont Community College had recently launched a program in viticulture and enology, and searching their course catalog, I noticed that many respected area winemakers were listed as instructors. Given Loudoun's rise as a respected wine region, we had a unique opportunity to take the lead in creating an educational partnership. My inquiry was met with enthusiasm; the dialogue opened between the wine industry and NVCC to pursue an initial offering through the non-credit workforce division and gradually work towards a credited program. I organized the first ever roundtable with Virginia ABC, Loudoun Sheriff's Department, and the LWA to discuss safety at the wineries and to help open communications channels. I also pulled together the first dual meeting of the LWA and the Loudoun Wine Growers Association (LWGA).

One highlight of that busy holiday season was our first wine pouring in Washington, D.C. We had been selected by the Choral Arts Society's Young Patrons to pour our wines after the Belgian Midwinter holiday concert. Shannon had to navigate the intricacies of legally getting our wine into the city, which was to be poured at Rivers restaurant in the Watergate, next the John F. Kennedy Center for the Performing Arts. For a small farm winery that paired its wine with music, this was a real milestone for us. We would be on hand at the restaurant to pour our wines and chat with the attendees, and in return we would receive complimentary tickets to the event, dinner at the restaurant, and exposure for our wines to a new crowd of arts supporters with a lot of disposable income. We refer to events like that as "date nights," and though I was worried they would have a negative reaction to Virginia wine, those fears were unfounded, as all the wine we had brought was gone halfway through the reception.

By winter of 2011, we were also expanding our sales channels to include local restaurants and wine stores. Established in 2008, the Virginia Winery Distribution Company (VWDC) is a non-profit, non-stock corporation created by the Virginia Department of Agriculture and Consumer Services (VDACS) to provide wholesale wine distribution services for Virginia farm wineries. The VWDC allows us to legally self-distribute our wine to area retailers, and then provides a mechanism for payment. Essentially, we deliver the wine, the retailer writes a check to the VWDC and signs several copies of the purchase order, Shannon sends off the check and paperwork, and we get paid the following month. The formation of the VWDC was the result of legislation passed after a U.S. district court invalidated Virginia's distribution laws, forcing small farm wineries to use a three-tier distribution system. Many wineries felt the impact of this decision immediately, as we are too small to merit the interest of large distributors. The solution to this problem was to allow small farm wineries to self-distribute up to three thousand cases of their own wine to stores and restaurants through the state agriculture department. When people would ask us how we determined our distribution radius, we would tell them it was the distance Shannon could travel to and from after preschool drop-off and before pickup.

On June 7th, 2011, at our monthly REDC meeting, we had a guest presenter. Kelli Grim was on hand to request the support of the REDC for local farmers Sam and Uta Brown of Crooked Run Orchard in their fight against the Town of Purcellville. Crooked Run was a large pick-your-own orchard located on the eastern end of the town, comprised of two large tracts of land. These two tracts touched at a corner; one was inside the town limits and the other was outside. The town intended to build a road right between the parcels, and when the Browns would not sell their land, the town condemned it and took it anyway. Over twenty thousand people visited the farm each year, picking fresh apples, peaches, blackberries, plums, gooseberries, pears, pumpkins, cherries (sour and sweet), and assorted vegetables. The situation for the Browns had gone from bad to worse, and now they were reaching out to the community to ask for support. Kelli gave a brief overview of the history of the Browns' battle with the town, and passed out a thick packet of papers containing maps, correspondence, and information on Virginia's eminent domain laws. I took a packet, chatted briefly with Kelli before she left, and assured her I would take the time to read the materials thoroughly.

A few nights later, after the boys had gone to bed, I began reading. Staying up late into the night, I became more incredulous and incensed with each page I turned. The facts surrounding the Crooked Run case could fill an entire book all on their own, but suffice to say it is a classic story of David versus Goliath, farmers versus developers. A small family farm, run by an aging married couple with absolutely no interest in selling their land, had a portion of their farm annexed through a "quick-take" condemnation process. The goal of this condemnation was to allow the town to complete their Southern Collector Road, inducing more commercial development on the adjoining properties. A short documentary, "Dividing Crooked Run," is available online, and provides a brief overview of the situation as well as footage of Mayor Bob Lazaro and the town council taking the very unusual step of holding both a public hearing and a vote on the condemnation during the same session. The more I fumed over the situation, the more I knew I had to get involved.

The next day, Shannon and I decided we were driving over to introduce ourselves to Sam and Uta right then. I could not just send off yet another concerned citizen email to a mayor and town council who had proven they could care less about public input. Shannon agreed that the only way to help these people would be to escalate public awareness of their plight, to fight the battle in the court of public opinion. We drove straight to Crooked Run, pulled up to the house, walked up to the kitchen door, and knocked.

The look on Uta's face when she answered the door and I started talking was one of surprise. She invited us into the kitchen to have a seat, while Sam tended the bacon sizzling in the skillet. I began again, this time properly introducing Shannon and myself, and started asking questions about the information I had received from Kelli. Both Uta and Sam were wonders of information retention; they could recite dates, names, and dollar amounts from the entire progression of their battle with the town, going back over a decade to the time when they first tried to purchase the land from Sam's father and subsequently his brother. At the end of that first meeting, Sam and Uta were convinced that we were genuinely passionate about farming, had a faithful love of the land, and were willing to go the distance— win or lose—to help them in their efforts to save their land. We resolved to apply for a remote winery license, which would allow us to conduct wine tastings on site at Crooked Run on the weekends. We also decided to use Crooked Run blackberries to blend with our upcoming dessert wine, and demonstrate by our actions which side of the fight we were on.

I sent a letter challenging the mayor and town council to meet us on site at Crooked Run Sunday, July 17th, to appear on camera and provide public statements about their rationale for the quick-take condemnation. In the letter, I listed all the public officials (both local and state), local business leaders, newspapers, and wine industry colleagues with whom I had shared my correspondence. Though I made it clear I was acting on my own accord without any formal involvement from the various organizations in which I served, I also made it clear that I would be championing Crooked Run's plight at all upcoming meetings.

Knowing full well that none of Purcellville's elected leaders would show that morning (nor did any even bother to respond), I was more interested in seeing how many other interested parties would attend. George Patterson, who had filmed the HGTV show, was on hand with his camera, and I would be interviewing anyone who had something to say. We began the morning with a walkthrough of the property hosted by Sam, who gave us the centuries-old history of the land while he pointed out the fencing and stakes where the town had seized the land and informed him he would be trespassing if he were to pass. Several local wine and political bloggers were on hand, as were two journalists, all asking questions and taking notes for their readership. The most difficult part of the morning was the interview with Uta, who broke down in tears as she tried to recount her dreams of preserving her land for future generations. After we filmed the interviews and b-roll for our video project, we also filmed the construction activity across the street, where the adjacent Cole Farm had been bulldozed to make way for a shopping center. Several months earlier, the construction crew destroyed a significant portion of the original barn and silo that was to be incorporated into the new development. The local conspiracy theorist bloggers and town historians were up in arms over that situation. Though the offending contractors were let go, and no public officials were ever actually accused of any wrongdoing, it was a portent of things to come.

A few days after our taping at Crooked Run, I had an appointment with an orthopaedic surgeon to examine my right knee. I had injured it a few weeks previously; kneeling while spreading mulch in the front yard, I had turned and twisted in an awkward direction. I suddenly felt a great pressure in my knee, and before I could stop, heard a nauseating crunching sound and experienced a searing pain. After two weeks of limping around, I realized that I needed to see a specialist. An MRI confirmed my fears; I had torn my meniscus and would need to undergo arthroscopic surgery in a few weeks to repair the damage. Returning home from my appointment, I was met by Janet Clarke, a candidate for the Loudoun Board of Supervisors in the coming election, and James "Doc" Wiley, a member of the Purcellville Town Council. We had allowed Janet to use Notaviva for her campaign launch party in April, though we never officially endorsed her candidacy. In a newsletter we received from her campaign, she was running on a platform to respect property rights, help protect our agricultural community and preserve historic properties, and create more transparency, openness, and accountability in government.

They had arrived unannounced, with Janet hoping to have Doc explain "both sides of the Crooked Run story," since he had such a long history with the town. As we walked up the hill from the parking lot to the tasting room, Janet advised me she was worried about my reputation, since I had sided so strongly with the Browns. That this woman thought she could somehow influence me by playing on my concerns about what she and the rest of her ilk thought of me was laughable. Having spent ten years touring the world, rubbing elbows with music and television stars, to enjoying successful careers in online market research and digital media, to founding two small businesses at the worst possible time in recent history, I was way beyond caring what the local politicos and their legions of mindless sycophants thought of me.

I listened politely while Doc tried to present his version of events to justify the actions of the town. Unmoved, I responded to his every statement with informed data points and insights contrary to each position he tried to take. When the meeting ended, I thanked them for their time. A few days later, while picking blackberries at Crooked Run, I told Sam about the incident. He was infuriated, and stormed out of the field to tell Uta what had happened. Not an hour later my cell phone rang, and Valerie Joyner, publisher of the *Blue Ridge Leader* was on the line, incredulous at the tale Uta had relayed to her. She wanted to interview me for an article right away, but I convinced her to let me try my hand at writing an editorial for the upcoming September issue. The article, which was written as I lay in bed recovering from knee surgery, detailed the meeting and was entitled "Are They Dead Yet?"

During the September town council meeting, Doc Wiley insinuated I misrepresented myself in the article. Having recounted the story exactly as it had unfolded, I was livid. When it came time for the October town council meeting, I decided to attend and take advantage of the public input time to demand an apology. As I tore into Wiley, he just sat there motionless, unable to offer any kind of response. The local paper reporting on the confrontation depicted a scene right out of a movie, and the local Boy Scout troop in attendance was riveted, suddenly believing that local politics might actually be pretty cool. No way was I going to allow such an affront go unaddressed. If someone wants to show up at my home unannounced, debate me unintelligently on an issue, then misrepresent me to the press after I hold true to my views and values, then you better believe I will be in your face, publicly, without hesitation, and with no concern "for my reputation."

The response to my article was unbelievable, and the number of Purcellville townspeople who made it a point to visit Notaviva in the weeks that followed was inspiring. I heard over and over again how people had just been watching from the sidelines as Crooked Run was continually beaten down by their elected representatives. Most had thought it would all work out in the end, and then when the Browns lost their land, people were embarrassed that their inaction might have played a part. I believe that in many ways, our involvement gave people the courage and inspiration to shake off their contentment with the status quo. Nonetheless, after receiving significant funding from the development community, Janet Clarke won the election over incumbent Jim Burton as our district's new supervisor.

The first half of harvest season 2011 was an exercise in misery, futility, and aggravation due to continual rainfall in the weeks leading up to our Viognier harvest. Our fruit was getting more and more diluted as the rain kept pouring into the vineyard. By the time we picked our Viognier, the berries had swollen so much that many of them were breaking open and beginning to rot. Yet with so much water weight, we were now twenty percent above our typical yield.

Though the flavors of the fruit were fantastic, the sugar levels had been diluted to an unacceptable level. The Viognier, as well as the first red harvest (local Chambourcin from Waterford), required chaptalization—adding sugar to unfermented grape must in order to increase the alcohol content after fermentation. It was actually pretty funny heading to the local membership warehouse club; it looked like I was hosting a meeting of the LWA in the bulk sugar aisle. We actually heard from several other winery owners that they just cut their Viognier off in the vineyard and dropped it on the ground, figuring it would be too hard to make good wine in those miserable conditions with such compromised fruit. As it turned out, all the extra effort it took to make our Viognier that season paid off, and in August 2013, our "Ottantotto" barrel-fermented Viognier became one of our first two international gold medals at the Indianapolis International Wine Competition.

After my September article was published and the local blogosphere had their run, the political activity surrounding Crooked Run had quieted down significantly. On the few days when it was not raining, we had a team member over at the farm conducting wine tastings. By Christmas, we had agreed to sell Sam's handmade wreaths at the tasting room, and the front porch looked beautiful adorned with the fresh pine. As gifts to our staff that year, I had created several dozen votive holders from wine barrel staves. We took one over to Sam and Uta as a Christmas present, and we left it inside the front porch door with a card that the boys had drawn. Uta called Shannon later that evening, worried and needing assurance that I had harmed no trees in the making of her gift. Shannon got her calmed down and promised that the stave came from a barrel that was no longer in production, and that the gift was created in the spirit of reusing existing materials. Uta huffed something about, "Stephen should leave his barrels alone, they were pretty the way they were," and then thanked Shannon and the boys for her hand-drawn card, and wished us love for a wonderful Christmas. I was glad the boys did not get fussed at as well for using non-recycled card materials, which clearly Shannon and I would have to be more careful about in the future.

Late in the evening of January 3rd, 2012, I received a frantic phone call from Kelli Grim, who had just left the first meeting of the new Loudoun Board of Supervisors. "You're off the EDC! You're off the EDC!" she ranted; she was so furious, I could barely make out what she was saying. Once I got her calmed down, she informed me that during the meeting of the board, when the new slate of EDC members were presented for confirmation, Janet Clarke (who had been voted vice chairman) had motioned to take the unusual step to vote on my name individually. Her rationale had been that the EDC wanted to have a positive approach with the community, with the towns, with the businesses, and that she didn't think that people who hold themselves contrary to that position should be allowed to serve. Shannon, who had barely been able to keep her cool during the mudslinging of the past few months, was completely enraged at this turn of events. The next morning, a flood of emails and phone calls came in from community supporters, all infuriated that this was how Janet had chosen to begin her term.

I, on the other hand, had quickly realized that my name was not supposed to have been on the ballot in the first place. I was serving a three-year term; my name was not to appear on the slate until 2013. I placed a call to the head of the EDC nominating committee who had prepared the list of nominees two months prior. He assured me that my name had not been on the list when it left the EDC's nominating committee. Somewhere along the chain, someone added it.

When the truth was revealed that my term was not to end for another year, the four board members who voted along with Janet had to face the embarrassment of being aligned with her on an act of sheer retribution. At the next EDC meeting, I sat down directly across the room from her so I could just stare at her. When Chairman York entered the room, having suffered the embarrassment of this debacle unfolding on his watch, he came right over and sat down beside me in a show of support, his glare across the room speaking volumes. Doug, who was attending the meeting merely to say goodbye, had decided to not continue with the EDC in order to focus on the REDC. He was presented with a plaque for his service, and after shaking hands at the front of the room, walked by my seat and gave me a pat on the back. When the meeting adjourned, Supervisor Ralph Buona approached me, shook my hand and apologized on behalf of the citizens of Loudoun County, and thanked me for my continued public service. Some months later, Ken Reid, who actually had voted with Janet, approached me at a networking event and offered his apologies as well. After the dust had settled and Ken had begun his work on the board, he was continually hearing my name and the contributions I was making. I suppose at some point he realized he had made a bad choice, and I sincerely thanked him for the courtesy he had shown in offering an apology.

As I have already written, the intricate details of the myriad events surrounding our involvement in the condemnation of the Crooked Run Orchard could fill a book all on their own. I have perhaps recounted ten percent of the story here, and though I could have taken the bitter road to point fingers and list out each affront, that is not my aim. I bring these events to light not to place blame on any of the participants, but rather to encourage others to get involved in local, state, and federal politics. If you are truly passionate about an issue, then it is absolutely unacceptable to simply sit at home and gripe at the television, or post inflammatory comments on an elected representative's social media page. You must physically get out, attend events and meetings, and make your views known. Meet people face to face, teach them, and learn from them. The success of our democratic form of government will be based on its constituents' active participation, not on what we see, read, and hear on media outlets. If you are not living it firsthand, then you are not really contributing.

In the months and years that followed our engagement in the Crooked Run issue, a few realities came to light that I feel bear mentioning. To colleagues on the various commissions, I became known as a hothead. As one close friend eventually confided in me, "People in the political circles are saying that Stephen Mackey is really good at pulling other people's pants down in a crowded room." I actually do not have a problem with that depiction; it is rather accurate. To the hundreds of people who took the time to visit Notaviva Vineyards, and who have written, called, and introduced themselves even years later, I was a cult hero. I was someone they could believe in, someone who felt so strongly about an issue and was wholly unafraid to publicly voice his views without "worrying about his reputation." The way I see it, if you are telling the truth and speaking passionately about issues you believe in while trying to make a positive impact on the world, you should be confident about your actions and cast off the irrelevant commentary made by those with less integrity.

I left the field after the first inning of my political endeavors to focus on my family and raise my boys through their fleeting early years. I can only offer these words of encouragement to anyone pondering public service: it is an honor and a privilege to live in a country where it is your right and duty to take action and voice your opinion in a democratic process. If you are worried that your voice is too small, or that your vote does not matter, think again. Think rather of our men and women in uniform; it is likely that someone you know has a family member serving in the Armed Forces. Are you prepared to tell their mother or father, son or daughter— who are getting shot at every day to preserve your right to free speech— that you were not comfortable attending a public input session because you were too tired from work or you had other plans?

Serving your community in any aspect, whether as an elected official, member of a commission, or speaker at a public input session, will enrich your life. Gaining valuable life experience and meeting like-minded people is not such a bad thing. You will not come out on the winning side of every issue, but it is the continued evolution of ideologies and dialogue that make the democratic process so fulfilling. As with all aspects of life, most of the time you learn more by losing than you do by winning.

The pain and humiliation that Sam and Uta endured in their brave fight to save their land showed an inner strength and courage that I have rarely witnessed. Shannon and I have found them to be such an inspiration. When the Southern Collector Road opened on June 28, 2013, Sam and Uta were forbidden from standing on certain sections of the road during the dedication ceremony. They watched through the fence as state and local dignitaries congratulated each other and declared the road open. A few months later, the Virginia state police pulled Sam over and gave him a warning for driving his tractor too slowly as he tried to make his way over to his rear field to tend his crops. Now when we take the boys to visit Uta, she leads us on a hike down to the large culvert where Crooked Run Creek runs under the roadway. She pauses to point out the various forms of plant life to the boys, explaining which are edible and how each plays an important part in the creek's ecosystem. She loves watching the boys splashing in the cool water and turning over rocks to look for crayfish, while enlightening Shannon and me about some South American medicinal herbs she wants to plant the following spring, or the fascinating flavor profiles of carrot varieties. As the sun begins to set, we round up the three muddy children and make our way back up to the old farmhouse; Uta makes sure we each pick up crumpled trash from the side of the Southern Collector Road. Though this piece of her beloved farm was taken from her, she so deeply loves the land that she makes us pick up every piece, carelessly discarded from the passing cars as they hurry by on their way to the bustling shopping center across the street, in search of fresh produce.

CHAPTER 38

"Living Off the Land"

Growing up in a small suburban community, I had never been exposed to hunting as a child. No one in my family hunted, none of my friends had any camo gear, and it was not until Coach Z took our high school pole-vaulting trio of Ken, his son Eddie, and me to a campground with a firing range that I ever shot anything more powerful than a BB rifle. Though I found I was a decent shot with a .22 rifle, I had some years earlier resolved that I would never shoot another animal, after a misguided shot with my cousin's BB rifle took the life of an unsuspecting bird perched on a tree limb. I was devastated by the incident and had trouble sleeping for some time.

Reunited with Coach Z some years earlier, he had been hunting our farmland even while Shannon and I were living in Connecticut. We shared a passion for the woods, and once Shannon and I were living in the timber frame, he brought over a .30-30 deer rifle and encouraged me to go out with him into the rear field and sight in the scope. Intrigued but still unable to wrap my head around actually pulling the trigger with an animal in front of me, I agreed to the target practice, and we spent about an hour, first on the proper handling of the rifle, how to load it, and then firing techniques. As with the little .22 twenty years earlier, I proved to be a natural, placing a tight grouping in the center of the target. After Coach Z was confident I was no longer a danger to anyone, he agreed to let me keep the rifle at our place, in case I ever did decide to hunt. That fall he called me a few times to see if I had any time available to go out, but one thing or another always prevented me from joining.

In the fall of 2010, we had taken the boys to Indianapolis to visit Roger and Bev for Halloween. We all dressed up like *Star Wars* characters, The night before we left Indianapolis for home, we passed a hunting supply store that was having a sale and decided to pull in to see what they had. Though I still had reservations about hunting, Shannon and I had been talking extensively about wanting to learn more about living off of our land. As with every other pursuit we had pondered, there would really only be one way to truly find out. She had been purchasing homesteading magazines and doing a lot of reading about innovative gardening techniques, and these magazines were full of interesting stories about families who provided their meals entirely from their own property. Hunting, fishing, gardening, canning, and preserving were now continual topics of conversation, rekindled from our earliest days together dreaming about our future.

My childhood friend Ty Eanes had recently retired from the Navy as a Master Chief, and we had the honor of hosting his "coming ashore" ceremony in our tasting room. To this day, hosting that fine group of dedicated servicemen and women, along with an admiral, no less, has been one of the highlights of our winery journey. While stationed in Tennessee, Ty had taken up hunting, and was looking forward to teaching his sons Zack and Stewart as they settled down in Northern Virginia.

All roads had converged on the fact that I would be trying my hand at whitetail deer hunting when the season opened in late November. Armed with my loaner rifle and clearance rack camouflage garb, Ty and I found ourselves talking about hunting all the time. I had resolved myself to pulling the trigger, though the prospect of field dressing a deer still hung heavily over my head. I was able to find a wealth of videos online about the proper techniques recommended for field dressing, and I treated the subject with a great deal of respect. The date was set; my first hunt was to be Saturday, November 13th, 2010.

The weekend before, Ty and I scouted the rear field and woods for trails and rubs, the abrasions caused by bucks when they rub their foreheads and antlers against the base of a tree. Coach Z had built two tree stands, one at the tree line overlooking the rear field, and another in a copse near the center of the field, adjacent to where the wedding reception tent had stood over six years earlier. As the meadow had not been mowed since, it had grown a significant amount of briar patches and small trees; the entire area crisscrossed with deer trails. In addition to the two handmade tree stands, Ty had installed another tree stand in the woods just behind the wedding site.

Sunrise was predicted for 6:51 A.M., and according to Virginia law, you may fire one half hour before sunrise (and one half hour after sunset). Ty wanted us to be in our respective tree stands an hour earlier, to ensure our scent and noise had faded. I would take the stand in the middle of the field, and he would be in his stand behind the wedding site. Though Ty had never shot a big buck, the signs were all over the field that there was significant recent activity. By now, I was so excited about just getting out into the woods in the crisp pre-dawn air that I was not even thinking about hunting. Donning my cheap one-piece camo suit over several layers of sweat clothes, I figured my body heat would be plenty warm enough to keep my hands and feet comfortable. That naïve notion would soon be discarded.

Weapons and gear were inspected and we were out the front door into the twenty-four degree weather before 5:00 A.M. Walking silently to the rear field, we stayed together right until I veered off the last few dozen yards towards my stand, while Ty continued down the hill into the woods. As I had studied and practiced in the daylight, I tied my gear to a haul line, climbed into the tree stand, and pulled up the rifle and backpack. I got situated into my seated position, donned my camouflage hood, organized my binoculars and water bottle, chambered a round and placed the rifle in the half cock safety position.

My first impression was of the eerie silence that enveloped me. As I had studied, humans entering a nocturnal environment set off an alarm amongst all the other creatures that are typically active. Everything goes completely quiet, and this in turn becomes a warning sign to any deer that may be moving into an area. If a deer senses an unusual quiet as it moves in a particular direction, it will stealthily change course to circumvent the area of concern; thus the guidance to get into the tree stands far enough in advance to allow restoration of the natural order of the myriad creatures surrounding me.

My second impression was a sense of an awakening of something deep inside me, a feeling I had never felt before. Though I had long questioned whether or not I would actually be able to take the life of an animal, now that I was, in fact, a predator, I felt my internal conflict quickly fading, being replaced with a heightened awareness of my environment. Suddenly, all of my senses were on high alert; my sense of hearing quickly able to discern the direction and distance of any sound, my sight adjusting to the dim light, while my sense of smell could detect the amazing array of scents emanating from the meadow as they floated by in the light wind. I felt completely alive, and knew that hunting would hold something special for me for the rest of my life, regardless of whether I saw a single deer. A few moments later, I need not have worried about that either.

He appeared like a ghost on the hill in front of me, about one hundred yards away. One second that hill was empty, and when my eyes returned to that spot after a quick scan of the area to my right, he was there, appearing as if from thin air. The adrenaline rush that accompanies a moment like that is impossible to describe; it is something that only hunters can understand. Suddenly, you can hear your heart pounding in your ears, your senses go into overdrive, and everything becomes reduced to a singular focus—the target in front of you. All those years of telling myself I could not pull the trigger on an animal were gone, and there was not a millisecond of hesitation as my thumb instinctively cocked the hammer back into the firing position. The buck began moving down the hill to my right, headed towards the wedding site, moving in and out of underbrush where at times I would lose sight of him for seconds at a time. I was watching him with my naked eye and calculating his path to find a spot where I could take the shot. He never stopped moving, and as he neared the edge of my firing lane, I knew I only had a second to fire before he would be in the safety zone between Ty and me, where I would not be able to shoot. As he disappeared behind the last small group of cedars in my range, I put my eye to the scope, and as he reappeared from behind the trees, I fired.

The round hit him perfectly; he lurched forward a few strides, stumbled, and fell. I was trembling from the adrenaline rush, with the sound of the rifle shot still ringing in my ears. We waited for a few minutes, and when I saw Ty's bright orange vest moving through the trees, I got out of my tree stand and walked down the hill. When I arrived at the buck, he was just staring at me, half-stunned, half-laughing, and asked, "Do you have any idea what you've just shot?" I replied, "I'm pretty sure I shot a deer with some horns on top." He rolled his eyes and said, "Those are called antlers, you idiot, and you just shot an eight-point buck less than an hour into your first hunt."

Still trembling from the excitement, the reality of what had just happened had now hit home, and I stood over this magnificent animal whose life I had just taken. I thought about what that would mean for Shannon and me for a few moments. I went to get my pickup truck in order to transport the deer, and then we field dressed it.

Having watched numerous videos on the process of field dressing a deer definitely made it easier than I imagine it would have been had I merely read a book with pictures. There are techniques and certainly an order of operation involved that ensure the meat is protected from any taint. Without getting too graphic, and being sensitive to those who may have difficulty with this subject, suffice to say my first attempt at cleaning a deer went exceedingly well, in part due to my research, but largely because Ty was on hand to walk me through the steps. Once the deer was properly dressed, I decided to hang it in the winery by its antlers until I had time to transport it to the processing facility in nearby Burkittsville, Maryland.

My first visit to the deer processing shop was very enlightening. One of the busiest in our region, there must have been over four dozen skinned deer hanging in the cold room, and several hundred more in various phases of processing or freezing. When I arrived, I informed one of the butchers this was my first deer, and that I would appreciate any guidance. He was very friendly, and actually took a few minutes to walk me through each of the stations, explaining as we went how I was to complete my order form. As I filled out my order (you actually get to specify the kinds of cuts you prefer, and how you want your ground meat prepared), it was fascinating to watch the workers moving quickly about. These men were highly skilled professionals whose talents with the blade were amazing.

A few days later, I returned to retrieve my now packaged and frozen meat, each piece carefully wrapped and labeled. Shannon and I had decided our first foray into eating venison would be a crock-pot of chili. As soon as I had stored the meat in the freezer, I thawed our first pack of ground venison and prepared the ingredients in the crock-pot. Browning the lean venison in a bit of olive oil, there was simply no fat to drain. As the crock-pot worked its magic and the wondrous aromas filled the tasting room through the afternoon, a wonderful sense of fulfillment began to wash over me. Here we were, on the verge of serving our first meal from wild game harvested from our land. It was invigorating, but also comforting, knowing with one hundred percent certainty that we were serving organic, hormone-free meat to our boys and ourselves. By now I had done extensive research on the nutritional advantages of venison, and was confident we were making a sound decision.

"Spectacular" is how I would describe that first venison dish, and essentially every meal that has followed since. One of our favorite recipes is a venison roast with rosemary new potatoes, drizzled in Cabernet Franc morel mushroom gravy, accompanied by fresh garden vegetables and followed by a spiced apple compote, each course accompanied by a Notaviva Vineyards wine. You would pay well over $100 a plate for a meal like that at a fine restaurant, and now we can make that dinner with ingredients grown in our backyard. Sadly, olive trees will not survive in Virginia, otherwise we would be making our own olive oil by now, and we have not found a salt deposit yet, therefore we will have to keep purchasing those items. In both cases, we enjoy seeking out the most obscure, authentic, and locally sourced products we can find. If you want to elevate your culinary prowess, take my advice and start by using better ingredients.

A few months later in March of 2011, while Shannon was away in Florida attending her aunt's funeral, I decided to surprise her with a gift of six baby chicks. Shannon and I had been talking for years about taking the plunge into raising livestock, but with our busy schedules, had worried that we would not be able to devote the proper amount of time to the endeavor. Still, with one news story after another, books like *The Omnivore's Dilemma*, as well as independent films and documentaries such as *Food, Inc.* illustrating the grim realities of the industrialized food system, we knew we could no longer accept our inaction. Early Saturday morning on the 12th, I took the boys over to the local Southern States to begin yet another new chapter in our lives.

I had done quite a bit of reading the night before, and had a pretty good idea of the basic equipment we would need to get started. When I walked in, I told the young lady behind the counter what I was getting myself into, and she was happy to help out. As Tristan and Duncan explored the store, I kept Ronan on my shoulders with one hand, picking out gear with the other. When it finally came time to get the chicks, I let Tristan and Duncan pick them out, the store clerk dropped them in a box, and away we went with the new additions to our family. Arriving home, I quickly got the chicks inside to keep them warm, and placed the small galvanized tub on the floor of the boys' bathroom. Covering the bottom with pine shavings and filling both water and food dishes, I transferred the chicks to their new temporary home until I could build a proper henhouse outside. I had planned to keep the chicks a secret, but when we called Shannon later that day, the boys erupted in a flurry of squealing, "Mommy, we got baby chicks!" When I could finally get the phone back, she asked me what on earth was going on, so I had to spill the beans. Needless to say, she could not wait to get home and get her hands on those babies.

Over the course of the next few days, as Shannon became more and more enraptured by the thought of having a flock to tend as well as a limitless supply of fresh eggs, she decided that six chickens was not going to be enough. Why settle for six hens when you can have twelve?

And why settle for twelve hens when you can have eighteen? Why not sell a few dozen to our tasting room visitors to introduce them to farm-fresh eggs? Suddenly we had been propelled to the realm of hobbyist livestock farmers, with Araucanas, Rhode Island reds, Leghorn whites, and Sussex chicks. What was to be a small box with a wire-protected run now scaled up to a walk-in henhouse with perches, laying boxes, and a large pen complete with wire mesh roof and sides buried a foot deep in the ground to keep out all manner of predators. The henhouse took several days to construct, and when it was complete, I was satisfied that we were giving our flock a fine place to start their lives. We were ecstatic to get the poults out of the bathroom, as the mess from their molting feathers had become intolerable.

We settled into a semi-manageable routine of caring for the growing birds for a few weeks, until Shannon happened to meet Patrick Ryan, a friend of ours who used to work for the Loudoun County government. Patrick had since left his job to focus on his own hobby farm in Taylorstown. He was thrilled to learn of our foray into livestock, and mentioned to Shannon that one great idea for keeping away predators would be to have a couple of hogs next to the chicken coop—perhaps even a breeding pair that could produce offspring for sale and slaughter.

Immediately she called me to tell me about Patrick's idea, and I could hear him in the background encouraging us to consider it. If I knew next to nothing about raising hens, then I knew absolutely zero about raising a breeding pair of hogs; figuring there was only one way to learn, I agreed to purchase a breeding pair of hogs from Patrick.

A few weeks later, we arrived at Patrick's place to pick up our first piglet, an American Guinea hog who we named Magnus after Shannon's great-grandfather. American Guinea hogs are known as a heritage breed, and ours came with a complete set of paperwork documenting his origins. This breed of hog is solid black, with an exceptionally calm and friendly temperament making them well suited for small sustainable family farms. Guinea hogs possess very desirable gourmet-quality flavor characteristics, and though we had no intention of slaughtering our breeding pair, we were now planning on selling their offspring as well as slaughtering some for our own use. That would prove to be an incredibly difficult bridge to cross.

Magnus took to his new pen right away, which wrapped around the henhouse and was bordered by our property fence. The first few days were a nightmare of fixing fences, as that little bugger could squeeze his way under, around, or through just about anything. I was glad to finally have him soundly penned in—or so I thought, until Ada came along. She was our second piglet (named after Shannon's great-grandmother), and if Magnus was somewhat troublesome, she was just plain naughty (and adventurous).

It turned out that Roger was in town for a week while Bev was traveling with some friends, and got to experience Patrick's farm first-hand when he accompanied Shannon and the boys to pick up Ada. Tromping through the mud, meeting several dozen piglets, as well as turkeys, chickens and rabbits, I can only imagine what he must have been thinking about our latest pursuit. After we had the piglets settled, stocked up on food for them and the chickens, and showed our staff how to feed and water all the critters, we headed down to the Natural Bridge in southwest Virginia for a brief camping trip. The boys were so excited to set camp and begin exploring; even at their young age, they were well on their way to becoming avid outdoorsmen. We enjoyed visiting the bridge, hiking the trails, visiting the butterfly center, and playing around the campground. Sitting by the fire chatting, watching the boys play with their toys in the dirt was such a peaceful and welcome respite from our typically hectic pace. To this day, we have managed to make time for at least one camping trip every year.

On our way back home, we had decided to take the opportunity to visit Polyface Farms, self-described as "America's premier non-industrial food production oasis." Shannon had learned of Polyface, having seen it referenced in several of the books she had read recently, as well as in a myriad of homesteading magazines. When I suggested we swing through on our way home, she about did a back flip. Driving the back roads of Virginia's Shenandoah Valley on our way to Polyface, we found it amazing that many of the finest chefs from Washington,

D.C. and Northern Virginia drive several hours down here to source meat for their restaurants.

Once we had parked, we made our way to the store to chat with the clerk about the best way to learn about the farm. There were no tours, and the entire farm is camera-accessible, which means there are no trade secrets and no locked doors behind which any manner of improper food handling might be occurring. After giving us a brief overview and a general layout of the farm, we began wandering the various fields where they continually cycled their livestock. It was shocking to see firsthand how their farming practices allowed the land to naturally heal itself, by moving small mobile chicken pens across a paddock over a period of weeks. You can stand there and see the pens, and just to their left, patches of burned out turf from the chicken droppings where the pen had sat the previous week. Immediately adjacent to that, where the pen was two weeks prior, the grass has started to return, and as you keep looking to the left, each subsequent patch from previous weeks is in a further state of restoration, until there is simply no trace of the pen having ever passed that way.

As it turned out, we happened to arrive on a day when the Polyface team was processing chickens, and we had the opportunity to observe the chickens quickly moving through the various stations. From bleeding to scalding, to plucking, to eviscerating, to packing, it just took several minutes to prepare a bird for the store. In fact, there were a few chefs that were apparently wise to the Polyface schedule, who were on hand awaiting the fresh poultry. Given the treatment of chickens we had seen in *Food, Inc.* versus what we had just experienced on this amazing farm, our perspective on food had been forever changed.

A few months later while watering the chickens, Shannon was overjoyed to find our first egg sitting in one of the nesting boxes. We had read that the first few eggs should be discarded (though have since learned that is not accurate), so she dropped it into the pen for Ada. By now, we had begun letting the chickens out of their pen during the day, allowing them to free range around the farm. Although it was pretty irritating discovering they enjoyed scratching up all the mulch around the tasting room in search of tasty bugs, I realized there was no point in trying to keep them out. Soon after we saw that first egg, the other hens began laying as well, and in another week or so, we had begun collecting the eggs and storing them in our refrigerator. I will never forget the first Saturday morning that I made scrambled eggs for breakfast. When I cracked open the first egg and dropped it into the bowl, I was stunned by the color of the yolk. Its dark orange color was unlike anything I had ever seen in the store-bought eggs to which we had become accustomed. You would do well to conduct an Internet search for "homegrown versus store-bought eggs" and look at the various pictures to see the difference for yourself. Beyond the obvious color differences, the intensity of the flavors was immediately apparent. Coupled with the fact that I always add a random selection of fresh herbs from my herb garden to my scrambled eggs, that morning's breakfast was memorable indeed. That was a true turning point for us, as not only were our egg-based dishes noticeably improved, but so was any recipe that called for eggs. To this day, as Shannon and I have had the opportunity to travel for client engagements and stay at some of the finest hotels in New York City, Washington, D.C., and around the world, there is no comparison at breakfast to the eggs from our little henhouse.

Since we had been taken so deeply with our hobby farming exploits, we figured it would be fun to share our experiences with our customers. That year for Father's Day, we encouraged guests to bring their poles, and held a fishing derby in the hopes that families who had no access to a pond could enjoy spending the day together. We had several dozen families participate, and our boys (by now avid fishermen themselves) had a wonderful time catching bluegill and the occasional largemouth bass. Guests also had the opportunity to walk over and see our new piglets, busily rooting around the pen in search of fresh forage.

Harvest of 2011 was memorable in so many ways. While in the process of healing from my knee surgery and dealing with the fallout from our Crooked Run involvement, we had finally saved enough money to pour a proper crush pad in front of the winery.

This allowed us to process our white grapes at our place and bottle our wines at our winery, rather than having to transport bulk wine all over the place. Tristan was playing flag football again, and I was enjoying being assistant coach. Tristan had also joined Cub Scouts, and I volunteered to be the assistant den leader for our Tigers Cub den. As an assistant coach, an assistant den leader, commissioner for the EDC, councilman for the REDC, treasurer for the Virginia Wine Council, re-elected president of the LWA, board member for the Loudoun Chamber, wine composer for Notaviva Vineyards, and creative director for Mesh Multimedia, I felt just a bit overcommitted, but at least I was having fresh eggs for breakfast.

To help keep our pig food costs down, Shannon had been taking empty five-gallon buckets to Savoir Fare. On the nights they were open, the kitchen staff would put scraps into the buckets for us to pick up. Our piglets were eating rather well, to say the least. At some point, Shannon and Joanie decided that since Shannon was making so many trips over, she might as well bring some eggs along with her in addition to the wine deliveries. All of our area farm-to-table restaurants list the name of the farm under the selection, and it was very fulfilling to see the Savoir Fare menu list Crème Brûlée on the dessert menu with "Eggs from Notaviva Vineyards" in parentheses below. We felt that this, in addition to having our "Vincerò" stainless tank-fermented Viognier on the wine list, sent a very positive message to both Joanie's customers and ours, that we were both making a concerted effort to create sustainable and valuable collaboration.

The pigs and chickens all weathered the cold winter without issue, and by mid-March of 2012, Shannon was pretty sure that Ada was pregnant. On the morning of Saturday, March 24th, Shannon came bursting through the door into the kitchen, out of breath from sprinting up the hill and yelling excitedly, "We have piglets! We have piglets!" It took her a minute to settle down and relay that she could see five for sure, but was worried that a sixth had not survived. I was going to have to crawl inside the pigpen and find out for sure. We walked back down the hill and peered inside the pigpen, where Ada was lying on her side, contentedly nursing her farrow. Shannon figured she would only come out for some food, so she dropped a huge pile of restaurant scraps outside the pen, and when Ada came out, we blocked her off with a hog panel. I crawled in to see the piglets, and sadly confirmed that there was a dead one lying in the corner. I removed it, and then Shannon went in to snatch them up while Ada was finishing her breakfast.

As if having five baby piglets that morning was not enough, that day we were also hosting a puppy adoption at the tasting room. The Appalachian Great Pyrenees Rescue organization had approached us about using our front porch as a place to put their puppy cage, and we thought it would be fun to have them out. I had secretly been thinking about getting another dog to keep Gypsie company, so I was just going to wait and see if Shannon brought it up. AGPR arrived with four little pups, two white ones, a brown one, and another brown one with white paws and a black snout. Later that day, Shannon was looking at me and I knew what she was thinking, so I just said, "Pick one." As Shannon leaned over into the pen and selected the brown one with white and black markings, we became the happy owners of a Leonberger/Great Pyrenees puppy. Not even two weeks later in early April, we picked up six ducklings at Southern States to round out the farm, now totaling twenty-eight chickens, two pigs, five piglets, six ducklings, and two dogs. Later that month, we hosted a Cub Scout meeting at our place so the boys could meet all the animals, and the other parents—though happy to see their sons enjoying the farm—looked at us like we had lost our minds.

Though the boys' chores entailed gathering the eggs, the task of maintaining the animals fell primarily to Shannon. She loved tending them. I had put in a large garden for her, and throughout the summer she became quite the hardy homesteader. Although I would occasionally make the runs over to Savoir Fare to retrieve the food buckets, pick up food from the farm store, and feed and water the animals, she had found her passion and worked diligently at it. When it came time to make the decision whether or not to slaughter any of the hogs for our table or just sell them off, it would be her choice and hers alone. After several days of introspection, she decided to follow through with our original plan of butchering two, selling one and keeping two. We reached out to Patrick again, who had told us all along he wanted to be there to help us with the process when we felt we were ready.

I will omit the graphic details of butchering hogs, but suffice to say December 22, 2012 was a very difficult day for Shannon. Although she was committed to her decision, she felt she could not be there for the actual death of the animal. Though she stayed some distance from the pen, when she heard the gunshot ring out across the farm, she wept for some time. After we had scalded the carcass, scraped the hair off, and eviscerated it, Shannon was able to rejoin us as Patrick instructed us on how to create the various cuts. He had brought along a French charcuterie book that we followed, which gave all of us a wonderful reference for how to properly section the animal. We packaged and labeled the first hog for Shannon and I, and the second was split for Ty as a thank you for helping and the chef at Savoir Fare, who was beyond thrilled to be getting such a fine animal for his upcoming holiday party at his home. Though Shannon was still emotional about the events of the day, she did feel a small sense of reward when the chef handed her a check for the meat and thanked her for a job well done. We had decided to keep the boys away from the crush pad until the very end of the butchering process, but when we were nearly finished, we let them come out and watch us making the final few cuts. It was important to us that they understood from a very early age where food comes from.

For Christmas that year, Shannon's mom bought us a smoker, and I began researching the various methods and recipes for curing meats. We decided our first attempt at smoking our own meats would be with bacon. I removed the skin from the pork belly and cured it with a mixture of curing salts and maple syrup. After several days, the bacon was ready to be smoked, and when it was complete, I let it cool to room temperature, then wrapped it and refrigerated it over-night. The next morning I sliced it into very thick cuts, each at least a quarter of an inch, and placed them in a pan. As the aromas from the smoky maple bacon filled the house, we shared with the boys where it had come from. Though they had previously been aware we ate venison from deer I had killed, this was different, in that they knew this animal. I was very proud of their reactions; they were sad for the animal, respectful of its journey, yet not overly emotional or melodramatic. Shannon had also crossed a bridge of her own. Her efforts over the past several months were now going to provide a wholesome, locally sourced meal for her children, by her own hand. When it was finished cooking, the bacon, as with the eggs, vegetables, venison, and everything else we had produced ourselves, was astonishingly delicious and re-set our understanding of what food can taste like when it is properly raised or grown.

As with all of our pursuits, our efforts to live off of our land have been full of wonderful successes and miserable failures. At one point, a fox wiped out our entire flock of chickens and ducks in a matter of days; that was terribly hard on Shannon and the boys, who found chicken carcasses strewn about the yard. We have had entire gardens fail from bugs, disease, deer, or drought. Through it all, we have simply kept at it, trying new techniques, doing more research, working longer hours. It is important to us to teach these lessons, not only to our boys, but to customers who inquire at the bar about our farming pursuits. Farming has brought us immense joy and a deep respect for the Earth and its fragile ecosystems, and we feel it is critically important to share that knowledge with people who do not have such ready access to the land. Urban dwellers, geographically isolated from their food sources, are at such a disadvantage when it comes to understanding and appreciating the delicate balance of various ecosystems. Learning about environmental issues in a newspaper or on television simply does not compare with walking the land where an animal forages, where you can gain a real respect for the undeniable fact that we as human beings are truly stewards of the land. Make no mistake, you are not what you eat, you are what you eat eats.

When people ask me about our decisions to hunt and farm, I often reflect on my favorite hunting memory, on a frigid December day with not a deer in sight. While walking out to the tree stand, I was caught in a blizzard so thick I could barely find my way along the trail. Knowing it was supposed to snow, I had brought along a blanket, and as I settled into my tree stand, I pulled the blanket over me, completely shielding me from the heavy snowfall. Two hours later, when the storm finally subsided, I slowly lowered the blanket and gazed around at the stunning beauty of the forest, adorned with the freshly fallen snow. The moment is memorable for me not only because I was completely at peace, but also because I felt at one with the Earth—utterly connected and personally whole. The feeling is indescribable—one can only experience it for oneself—however that sense of connectedness is also what Shannon and I feel when we serve a meal plated with ingredients sourced from our land.

I truly wish that everyone in the world could have the opportunity to take a day away from the hustle and bustle of their modern life to walk into the woods with me at night, to feel the crisp pre-dawn air on their faces, to share the exhilaration of hearing the sounds of the forest come to life around us, to awaken a long forgotten inner sense of awareness. I wish everyone in the world could join Shannon one afternoon in the garden to pick fresh vegetables for the evening salad, and smell the aromas of the herbs, produce, and meats as they blend in the pan and fill the room with anticipation. It saddens me to know that the demands of modern life are pulling the vast majority of people in the other direction, further away from the source of their food, insulated from the grim realities of its procurement through industrialized food systems. I know in my heart that the world would be a better place if more people had the access, ability, and patience to source their own food. Without hesitation, we believe that we are, and believe that our children will be as well. We have become intimately familiar with the circle of life, and in doing so, have gained a deep and abiding respect for the Earth, mankind's place upon it, and the darkening future for both.

CHAPTER 39
"Powhatan School"

O n September 7, 2010, Shannon, my mom, and I sat waiting with Tristan for the school bus to arrive, which would carry him away to his first day of kindergarten. As for all parents sending their oldest child off to school on their first bus ride, we were experiencing a powerful mix of emotions; pride, joy, apprehension, and love. The twenty-minute bus ride would take him to nearby Hillsboro Elementary, one of Loudoun County's older elementary schools, which had opened to students in 1966. Shannon and I had attended back to school night a few weeks prior, and though we found Tristan's teacher to be a bit stuffy, we figured everyone has their style.

One of the stark realities of Loudoun's education system is the disparity between the older schools in the western rural communities and the modern schools built in recent years across the newly minted suburbs in the eastern part of the county. In the five years preceding Tristan's entry into kindergarten, Loudoun County had appeared either first or second atop the list of wealthiest counties in America. The county school board had previously considered closing the school, but the public outcry from the local community pressured the decision makers to keep it open, seemingly content to value convenience and quaintness over quality of education. Although we had known for years that the decision to raise our family in this rural corner of Loudoun might someday have an impact on the boys' education, we were resolved to mitigate the situation through our continued participation in school activities.

Right away, Shannon signed up to be a classroom volunteer, which meant that for a couple of hours one morning each week, she would head into school to help out with any tasks that the teacher may need. From reading books to the students, to cutting out shapes for art projects, to helping straighten up the room, she found herself assigned all sorts of tasks. She quickly became friends with the teaching assistant, a delightful woman who was both passionate about teaching and genuinely cared for the children; the relationship with Tristan's teacher never warmed. Though we were concerned about such a negative personality teaching small children, the minimal size of the school meant there was only a single class for each grade, kindergarten through fifth, so moving to a different teacher was not an option. Further, due to the size of our school and the small size of Lincoln Elementary about twenty minutes to the south, the county had made the decision to split the principal's time between these two schools. With a part-time principal only on site half the day, we felt like we had very little recourse to address our concerns.

One morning in the winter of 2011, Shannon had a meeting, so I took her place as classroom volunteer. When I entered the office to sign in, I was met with an indifferent stare from the administrator, who waved me through to the classroom. I got my list of tasks from Tristan's teacher, and began cutting out leaf shapes from colored paper. That morning the class had a visitor, a forester who was teaching them about the different shapes from various tree leaves. One little boy, whom I had met on a few other occasions and had found to be very bright and inquisitive, blurted out a question about one of the leaves. Instantly, the teacher, who was seated close by, reached over and smacked him on top of the head. I was stunned, not sure if I could have possibly just seen that. The poor little boy put his head down, more embarrassed than injured from the incident, and sat quietly for a few minutes before his curiosity got the best of him. Again without thinking to raise his hand, he asked a question of the forester. Another slap to the head—now I was certain I was not seeing things. The forester looked at me; we made eye contact and shook our heads at what we had just seen. Now, at this point I was thinking to myself, "Touch my kid, lady, and I will tear your arm off and beat you with it." I could see the little boy now had tears welling up in his eyes, but before either the forester or I could figure out how to react, the teacher decided to end the presentation early to move the kids into another activity. On my way out of the school, I stopped into the office to report the incident to the principal, who of course was not on site.

As soon as I got home, I told Shannon what had happened; she knew the little boy very well and was mortified that such a sweet child had been treated that way. When Tristan got home that afternoon, we quizzed him about his teacher; had she ever spanked or hit him in any way? He repeatedly told us that she had never hit him (lucky for that woman), but he eventually confided in us that he was terrified of her. We decided right then that we were going to explore options for moving him out of that school, even if it meant driving him across the county.

Over the next several days, Shannon researched options for transferring students to different schools within the county. At that time—and it is my understanding this has since changed—you needed a justifiable reason to request enrollment in a different school. As we looked at the various rationales, we realized that daycare would be a legitimate reason to apply at Round Hill Elementary for the following year. Tom and Beth Smith, in whose basement I had lived so many years prior, had relocated to the small town of Round Hill, and their two middle sons Dalton and Riley both attended. We had several discussions with Tom and Beth, and worked out an arrangement where we would drive Tristan to school in the morning, and he would then ride the bus home to the Smith house to spend a few hours in the afternoon. This would allow Shannon to squeeze in a bit more time for work before having to go get Tristan. With our daycare plan in place, all we could do was submit our application and wait for a response, which we expected by mid-summer.

Without knowing for sure whether or not Round Hill would have a spot (acceptance was based on year-to-year availability on a first-come-first-serve basis), we mentioned nothing to the Hillsboro teaching staff in case our application was rejected. Though we found the rest of the teachers to be absolutely delightful, one bad apple had definitely spoiled the bunch from our perspective. Worse, we had learned that due to a potential reduction in enrollment, Hillsboro was considering combined classes; if it worked out as proposed, Tristan would be entering a combined first and second grade class. We found ourselves residents of the wealthiest county in the country, paying an enormous amount of property taxes for education, and our children were facing combined classes circa the early 1900s, while schools twenty miles to the east were being wired with fiber optic Internet connectivity.

We received word in mid-July that a spot had opened up at Round Hill and that Tristan would be able to attend on the daycare provision. Tom and Beth were very excited, as we would now be able to send Duncan to the same preschool as their daughter Addison, while Ronan could attend the other preschool a few blocks away. It would mean, however, an enormous amount of driving on Shannon's part. Each morning she would have to drive twenty minutes to drop off all three boys at their respective schools, before returning home to tackle Notaviva office work for a few hours. At lunchtime she would have to drive back to Round Hill, pick up Ronan at his preschool, then Duncan at his preschool, then head home again for a few hours so hopefully one or both boys could take a nap. Later each afternoon, she would have to make the third trip back to retrieve Tristan from the Smith house, where he would be playing with his cousins. Now with all three boys, she would swing by the restaurant to pick up the pig scraps and return home again.

Though that was her typical worst case scenario with respect to shuttling kids around, once we settled into the school year, Shannon and Beth would work out different schedules some days depending on who was going which direction, or who had an appointment where, or any number of variables. Depending on my schedule with harvest, video shoots, or client meetings, some days I would do drop-off or pickup, allowing Shannon to focus on her tasks. Other days, depending on whether or not Tristan and I had football practice or Cub Scouts, we would both have to make the trip, swap kids from one vehicle to the other, run errands, deliver wine to local restaurants, and try our best to create some manner of driving efficiencies.

All that of course was layered on top of harvest duties, special events at the winery, association meetings, and the few rare occasions we were actually able to attend a family function. The harsh reality was that no matter what kind of routine we would try to settle into, it was potentially going to change every single year for the next eight years, depending on whether or not Round Hill had space for all three of our boys. Each year we would be faced with the possibility of having one, two, or all three boys bounced between one school or the other, depending on whether or not a family moved to town with a child their age, effectively bumping them out of class. Worst of all would be the impact on the boys and their relationships with their friends and classmates. It was a very challenging scenario, but given the vast improvement in the quality of the school Tristan was now in, it was one we were prepared to deal with for the foreseeable future.

Winter of 2012 turned to spring, and it was time to evaluate our options for the following year. Thankfully, the kindergarten teacher with whom we'd had such a negative experience had moved on to another school (why she did not get a job as a prison guard is beyond me), and the new kindergarten teacher had been widely praised by many of our neighbors. With Duncan entering kindergarten, we were giving serious consideration to dispensing with the back and forth driving nightmare we had endured throughout the school year, and returning both boys back to Hillsboro Elementary. Still, we felt it prudent to keep our options open, and filled out the transfer paperwork for both boys, Duncan heading into kindergarten and Tristan heading into second grade.

One morning in late May, after I had dropped Tristan off at school, I took the other two boys to our favorite local country store, Hill High Orchard, as I still had about twenty minutes before their preschools opened. We loved to visit Hill High, a country store that had been around for over sixty years. The boys enjoyed talking to the three old farmers who sat in the corner ruminating about the issues of the day. Hot coffee, breakfast sandwiches, and the local color were always a fine way to start the day. During one of Roger's visits, we had taken him with us to Hill High after school drop-off, and that particular morning, he happened to be wearing a Harvard polo shirt. While chatting with the farmer trio, Roger made a comment to which they responded, "Oh, go on, Harvard!" It was a classic scene that could only play out in an old country store during a conversation between a Harvard graduate and three crusty (and very bemused) old farmers discussing the politics of the day.

This particular morning the store was not yet open, so I sat dejected in the parking lot for a while, wistfully thinking of a hot coffee while the boys wondered if the fresh cookies were still baking. With the store still closed, my time had expired, and it was time to head to preschool. As I was preparing to leave, a school bus pulled into the parking lot and parked next to me. I thought it odd that we had been coming to this store for several years and I had never noticed a school bus; what was it doing here? As I watched several children hop out of waiting cars and head to the bus, I saw the name of the school on the side—The Powhatan School. Having never heard of it, I pulled out my phone and did a quick Internet search. When the website appeared, I learned the school was located about thirty minutes away in the small town of Boyce, in Clarke County just to our west. The pictures of the school were very unassuming—beautiful yet quaint, well-kept yet inviting—with wonderful photos of a diverse group of children. I sent Shannon a text, asking her if she had ever seen this bus, and then sent her the link to the school. Thinking little of it, I pulled out and made my way over to the boys' preschools, not knowing at the time that chance encounter and a simple text would change all of our lives forever.

When I arrived home, Shannon met me at the door asking, "Did you look at their website? It's beautiful! It reminds me of my school!" From the moment she had received my text she was entranced. Shannon and her brother had both attended private school, the Benjamin School in North Palm Beach, Florida. I had come up through Loudoun's public school system and remember believing as a child that all kids who attended private school wore ascots in gym, rode ponies to class, and had "Esq." after their names (before I even knew what that abbreviation meant). That without ever even actually knowing anyone who attended private school, as that just did not happen in our neighborhood.

After I got her settled down enough to talk, she recounted how she had been immediately moved by the similarities in the two schools, Powhatan and Benjamin. Not just the photos of the campus, but the curriculum and philosophy, one aspect being the Nature-Enhanced Approach to Learning (NEAL), where they bring the students out into the natural world, as well as bring the outdoors in. There was a mindset here that was very appealing, and a message that resonated with both of us. She asked me if we could visit; I gave her a sideways glance and reminded her that we were just barely keeping our heads above water, living month-to-month, running two small businesses. She pressed on, and I agreed that the school looked amazing. Math is math, however, and when I took a look at the tuition page, I just looked at her and said, "There is just no way we can swing this." We talked about it constantly the rest of the day, and by that evening had resolved to fill out the inquiry form on the website. Although we were in no financial position to seriously consider enrolling the boys, the reality of the back-and-forth rollercoaster ride we were facing over the next several years was enough to push us down the path; maybe at some point in the future, we could afford to make it happen.

The next day, Mike Hatfield, the director of admissions, called me to say he had received our form. When he inquired as to the ages of our boys, I responded we had two, one entering kindergarten and another entering second grade. I remember the excitement in his voice when he told me they had one remaining spot in each of those grades, and he asked if we could meet him the next morning for a tour of the campus.

On Thursday, May 31, 2012, we drove onto the campus of the Powhatan School for the first time. Having never set foot on the grounds of a private school, I had no idea what to expect, and was immediately taken with the atmosphere. As we approached the administration building, Shannon spotted a bell hanging under a beautiful vine-covered pergola, almost an exact replica of the one at her school. We parked, entered the administration building, signed in, and chatted briefly with the delightful receptionist. Mike had been waiting for us, and after introductions, we began our tour.

Although I remember vividly the details of that first visit, I also recall a sensation of floating, as if the entire experience was part of a dream. We started our tour in the two kindergarten classes, and while Mike explained the various aspects of the curriculum to Shannon, I just kind of listened and drifted off as I watched the student-teacher interactions. This late in the year, there were numerous class projects taped to the walls, and I was beyond impressed at the work of these children. I recall various adjectives sticking in my mind—creative, engaging, nurturing, challenging, authentic, caring. Though I had approached this whole topic of private school with much trepidation, I had been transformed by simply entering a classroom.

Over the next two hours, we explored the school. Art, music, sports, technology, and world languages were integrated into each grade level. More than anything, I remember being impressed by the character of the students. Though we arrived in each class unscheduled, we were greeted both by teachers and students in a truly genial manner. There was an aura of respect and warmth everywhere; more importantly, there was an air of positive energy all around us that we had simply never experienced before. By now Shannon was brimming with excitement, and I was walking around in a daze.

When the tour was complete, Mike thanked us for our time and excused himself to his office, encouraging us to find a quiet spot to sit and discuss what we had each taken away from the tour. We wandered over to the playground and sat on a bench under an old tree. We sat in silence for a few minutes, each lost in our own thoughts. When our eyes met I knew exactly what she was thinking; she simply said, "I love it." I responded, "I love it too, but we did not plan for this." We sat there for over an hour, discussing the atmosphere of this incredible place, the challenges we were facing potentially changing schools every year, and the reality of not having stable incomes sufficient to cover the costs of tuition. Through that whole discussion, we kept coming back to the single most important question: "What is best for the boys?" By now, we both were convinced and in total agreement that enrolling them in Powhatan would be an absolutely enriching and rewarding experience for them on every level. But how on earth were we going to pay for this?

"Pull it out of our retirement accounts." It was my suggestion, though I know Shannon was already thinking about it. It was financially foolish, and something that every advisor in the world cautions against. Sitting on that bench, we decided to withdraw Tristan and Duncan's tuitions from our retirement accounts. Though we had not made a single contribution since leaving corporate America, our accounts had managed to maintain much of their value throughout the recession. Without giving it a second thought, Shannon agreed, and we sat again in silence for a while. Finally, I asked her, "Did we just agree to put our children in private school?" to which she responded, "Yes."

We knew it was impulsive, we knew it was a risk, but we knew in our hearts that no matter what it took to make this a reality for our children, we were committed and we would be up to the task. Having weathered so much together, we knew this was the start of a new chapter, one that would be rife with challenges. We figured we had a year to put a plan in place that would allow us to generate new business, whether in Notaviva or Mesh or both, that would enable us to create a financial plan and ensure we could cover the boys' tuition. We also discussed the very real possibility that no matter how hard we were willing to work, the world around us was still in an economic downturn and the numbers might just not add up. What then? Would we be willing to shut down the winery and go back to full-time salaried positions to make this happen? Did this dream just replace the original one for our family, or could they both come to fruition? Only time would tell, and as we walked hand-in-hand from the playground to the parking lot, we were completely at peace. The panic would set in later.

Our applications were accepted, and both boys passed their assessments with flying colors. Everything was in place for the first day of school, which was set for Monday, August 27th. A few days prior, on the 23rd, we had attended the new parents' gathering, where we had the opportunity to meet their new teachers as well as many of the other parents. With a student to teacher ratio of twelve-to-one, and only two classes per grade, the school fosters a very close community.

The weather cooperated, and our first day at Powhatan was bright and clear. Ronan was as excited as his big brothers to participate in their first drop-off. Both Tristan and Duncan looked handsome in their school-mandated unbranded plain-colored golf shirts and blue khaki shorts. The energy from the students, teachers, faculty, and parents was palpable, and as Shannon helped each of the boys into their classrooms, I took dozens of pictures. As we drove away, we were both in tears, knowing that we were doing everything we could to give our boys the best start possible in life. We knew it would be a long road ahead; working extra-long hours in both businesses to bring in additional revenue, sacrificing equipment upgrades in the winery, putting off improvements to the tasting room and landscape, and foregoing personal interests in order to make the finances work. All of those things would be there waiting for us in a few years, once the boys were well on their way. In the years since we made the decision to enroll our boys in the Powhatan School, all our lives have been enriched by the relationships we have forged; the boys with their teachers and classmates, Shannon and I with the teachers, faculty, and parents. It is a joy to be a part of that community.

Admirably, the community around Hillsboro Elementary worked tirelessly to improve the state of education for their children, and on June 24, 2015, the Loudoun County School Board voted eight-to-one to approve the creation of the Hillsboro Charter Academy. The school is creating a brand-new curriculum that will span the disciplines of science, technology, engineering, arts, and mathematics, and will be run by a non-profit organization funded through grants, private donations, and the public school system. Although we have continued at Powhatan, we continue to be friendly with many of these families through scouting, sports, and community events, and applaud the evolution of the Hillsboro school and the commitment of those who made it happen. Their work is proof that parental involvement, sacrifice, and hard work still matter, and we are proud to call them friends.

What I believe we all share, beyond our deep and abiding love for our children, is our strong belief that a great nation is built on the foundation of strong families and robust, active communities. If you look back through time, most great civilizations that crumbled essentially eroded from within. As I look around today at what passes for popular culture, I am shocked at the decline in morality that has emerged. I know every generation says that; my grandparents said it to my parents, they said it to me. How can this be a positive trend, and where does it end?

I attribute many of our current societal woes to the degradation of the American family, and though I am building a business in the digital media space, I do worry a lot about the impact electronic devices are having on our ability to communicate face-to-face. We see it at the winery every weekend: a group of people gathered around a picnic table overlooking our scenic vineyard and mountains, their heads down, focused on their mobile devices, without any form of conversation taking place whatsoever. Talking to another person—real communication with somebody—is a complex blend of body language, verbal inflection, pace, tone, and mutual respect. It is important to realize that these are skills that must be fostered early in childhood. Rest assured, there would never be an electronic device at our family dinner table, and the results speak for themselves. I have lost count of the number of times total strangers have approached us in public, whether in a restaurant or at an event, and complimented us on how well behaved our three boys have been that evening.

Children are our most precious resource. The care, nurturing, and education of our future leaders and citizens must be a primary focus for America to remain competitive in a global digital economy with increasingly challenging environmental concerns. In the face of incredible technological advances and innovations that my generation considered science fiction, we must not lose our ability to not only remain human, but to strive for excellence as humans. We must reverse the current destructive trend of entitlement in our children, and restore a sense of accountability and work ethic. These take effort, require failure, and are hard-won through persistence and tenacity; handouts do not build character. To forge real and lasting relationships, to argue passionately and fairly about topics of interest, to find common ground and compromise, to work hard and live creative fulfilling lives—these are the values critical to authentic human communication, and cannot be achieved through an email or a text. Learning these skills begins in the home and must be augmented in the classroom.

Regardless of whether your child is home-schooled or attends a public or private institution, I believe the key to determining whether or not a child has a successful educational experience begins with a fundamentally sound home life and interested, engaged parents who are materially participating in the activities of the school. Though they are hardworking, committed, talented, and passionate, teachers simply cannot—nor should they be expected to—educate and simultaneously raise our children in silos. It is our right as parents—in fact, I believe it is our duty as Americans—to be actively contributing to our schools and our communities. Get involved in school functions, join a committee, go on a field trip, do anything you can to help out. Not only will you be rewarded with the personal fulfillment of seeing your child's successes and failures firsthand—for we must agree that both are important in their growth—but you will also build real relationships with your school, from the teachers to the faculty to the other parents. It is undeniable that America is faced with countless threats both from abroad and from within, and that we must be increasingly vigilant and committed to defend our freedoms. Yet as we look to strengthen our borders and support our allies, let us not do so with our gaze so affixed on the horizon that we fail to see the foundation crumbling beneath our feet.

CHAPTER 40
"The Entrepreneurs"

The classic definition of an entrepreneur is one who assumes the risk of business, but I've never subscribed to that. I've always felt that a true entrepreneur is one who assumes the responsibility of a business. I am driven by that sense of accountability, which at times can be very inspiring, but can also be very humbling. I don't believe in the phrase, 'It's just business.' Everything I do, whether in my business or my personal life, is a reflection of my true self. Regardless of the outcome, facing any challenge without the utmost passion is the greatest failure. Thomas Jefferson once said, 'The harder I work, the more luck I seem to have.' When Shannon and I reflect over the past ten years and the mountains we have climbed, building three businesses and raising a family, we cherish the many special moments that we've shared together. As we look ahead to the future, there's such excitement knowing we have so many more great memories to create together. That restlessness, that drive, that need to explore, that is what I feel is the true spirit of an entrepreneur.

These words are mine, transcribed from our 2012 finalist video in the Entrepreneur of the Year category of the Loudoun Chamber of Commerce Small Business Awards. In an unprecedented turn of events, Notaviva Vineyards was a finalist in the rural category, Mesh Multimedia was a finalist in the technology category, and I was a finalist in the entrepreneur category. No one had ever been named a finalist in three separate categories. My biggest worry in having to go to the stage three times over the course of the evening to accept finalist awards was who would run the video switcher. Not only were we expected to appear on stage three times (more if we actually won in one of the categories), but we had also begun producing the show the previous year. I was operating the video switcher, while calling the show (technical director) and cueing video playback and graphics; Shannon was mixing the show as audio engineer. We would have to play our finalist video, tear off our headsets, get out of the tech booth, make our way through the audience, accept the award onstage, and hustle back to the tech booth to quickly continue executing the show's technical elements. How on earth did we get ourselves into this predicament?

An interesting phenomenon had occurred by the winter of 2010; I was becoming a practiced public speaker. Now that both Notaviva and Mesh were becoming widely known throughout Loudoun, we were being sought out for interviews and appearances. Most people found it fascinating to learn our story and discover that we had one foot in the wine industry and the other in digital media, and many began asking how the two businesses complemented each other. I would give presentations to local business groups on leveraging social media for rural businesses, proper web design, and mobile technologies. Though my formal public speaking training was limited to one high school class, I had become adept at speaking to large groups at the tasting room. Notaviva was now a destination for corporate groups, who insisted on having the winemaker do a presentation. I would coordinate with the company's event planner on the business goals at hand and tailor my presentation to the appropriate theme based on the real-world experiences we had during our startup. Attendees loved hearing my tales from the trenches, and as the size of the groups grew, so did my confidence. From stuttering through my first tasting for two people just two years prior, I had found my stride. Shannon was amazed at my ability to be a chameleon and change my tone, vernacular, and storyline based on my sense of what was resonating with any given audience. Some wanted to laugh, some wanted to cry, some wanted to stare with their mouths agape, but all wanted to be entertained. After nearly two decades of being the person backstage, I was now increasingly finding myself center stage.

I was approached by Gary Hornbaker and Kellie Boles from the Loudoun Department of Economic Development to speak at the upcoming Forum for Rural Innovation about social media and how it can be leveraged for rural businesses. I was excited about the opportunity, and though two hundred people was a larger crowd, I knew the only way to improve was to continue tackling new challenges. In addition, Gary, Kellie, and I had a shared vision about delivering actionable tactics to the audience. Rather than just standing before them saying, "You could do this, or you could do that," I was going to stand before them and say, "Do this thing tomorrow, and do this thing next week."

Determined to send people home with a concise to-do list, I spent a couple days before the March 19th, 2010 event creating a comprehensive screen-by-screen tutorial on various social media initiatives. Knowing full well that I would have to blaze through my presentation in order to get through all the material, I was also committed to sharing my presentation with the event organizers so they could disseminate it to any attendees who wished to have my playbook on hand as a reference. The night before the event, the butterflies in my stomach were having a full-on riot. I settled into a restless sleep until the phone rang right around midnight.

Shannon jumped when the phone rang, saw from the caller ID that it was my mother; both of us knew that a call from her at that time could only be terrible news. I could hear her crying as Shannon passed the phone across the bed, and as I said hello, she said, "Uncle Hank died." It was as if a white-hot bolt of lightning had torn through my heart.

He and I had become incredibly close through our shared love of music. He taught me my first guitar chords, and we would sing a few old ditties together. In 1995, he had a little Christmas party at his place, so I went over a few times before the party so we could learn a few songs. Hank, the bandleader, would sing and play acoustic guitar, while his friend Mike Cantwell played some lead guitar and I borrowed a bass. That was the first iteration of the Thirsty Camel Band. I would phone Hank from around the world during my travels, and I could hear him light up each time I described my latest European or South American roadie tale. "You're living my dream, Steve," he would say each time. In the mid-1990s, I enjoyed recording Hank's songwriting demos; he was a great writer, and I believe to this day Debbie is still probably finding misplaced lyrics written in little notebooks squirreled away through the house.

I was devastated, but could not stop thinking about Debbie. She and Hank's marriage was wondrous to behold; there have never been better friends or deeper soulmates. Many years earlier, when Shannon and I learned we would share a wedding anniversary with Hank and Debbie, we took it as a sign that our marriage was destined to last an eternity.

Shannon held me long into the night as I just sobbed; the tears just kept coming until there were finally none left to shed. By now it was nearly dawn, and there was no way I was going to give any kind of presentation to anyone that morning. Shannon began looking through emails to try and find someone's cell phone so we could cancel, until I told her to stop.

One of Uncle Hank's favorite sayings was, "The show must go on." I knew in my heart he would have never wanted me, or anyone, to miss a gig, no matter how insignificant, on his behalf. I asked Shannon if she thought I should try and pull it off; she just responded, "Do what your heart tells you." Years of experience with executing shows through misery, sickness, and pain kicked in. Later that morning, through puffy eyes and with a hoarse voice, I delivered the top-rated seminar of the conference and was subsequently asked back the following year.

A few days later, I had to deliver Uncle Hank's eulogy, after my dad phoned the day before saying he simply could not do it. I began by quoting one of Hank's favorite lyrics, "Forever Young" by Bob Dylan. It was the song Hank would sing at the end of every party, to wish friends and family well until the next time we could all gather together. He was one-of-a-kind, and I know he loved me like a son;

he told me so. To this day, I keep little trinkets around to keep his memory close—guitar picks, cassette tapes, ball caps, and photos. Ask any entrepreneur about his or her assortment of talismans; you will be amazed at what keeps each of us going when times get tough.

Now that I was re-engaging in the event production side of things, though sometimes as a public speaker and not an event producer, it was weighing on me heavily that Loudoun's premier awards banquet, the Small Business Awards, was presented in such a modest manner. In 2009, as the winners of the previous year's agricultural small business of the year, I had the pleasure of opening the envelope in our category and reading the winner's name. Once again sitting through a very low-budget production, I knew that this show had the potential to be something very special for Loudoun's small business community.

In early 2011 and now a board member, Shannon and I decided we should approach Tony Howard, president and CEO, about offering up our services. Although he had not been thrilled with the production value, he assumed that doing a larger award show would be out of the chamber's budget. I asked him what the current budget was—around $7,000. I told him I could take that money and use it to bring in some scenic design, as well as some rock show sound and lights, and that Mesh Multimedia would do all of the video production (thirty-six one-minute vignettes) as an in-kind sponsorship. When I described the set design I had in mind, he agreed to take it to the committee for approval, and shortly thereafter we were locked in as the official multimedia sponsor for the awards banquet.

The challenge was that it always happened the first week of November, which meant that the videos would have to be filmed in early October. The filming took two complete days in the chamber conference room, one interview after another. The final two weeks leading up to the event would be completely consumed by editing. Of course, this would all be happening right at the tail end of harvest season, coinciding with football, Cub Scouts, and school events. Raise hand, overcommit, dig out; everything was going typically as planned.

Our production of the Loudoun Chamber Small Business Awards that fall of 2011 was a resounding success. Although by the time show day arrived I was an exhausted mess from eight twelve-hours days of editing video by myself, we managed to pull off a flawless production. I had talked Brooksie into helping me out with the audio; he thought it would be cool to see his PA used for something other than drunk people dancing in shiny clothes and, as always, was interested in learning more about system setup and tuning. Though it took us all day to load-in and set up the stage, lights, sound, and scenic into the National Conference Center, we managed to get one rehearsal in before doors opened to the public. Dozens of people who had been to the show previously came up to the tech booth afterwards to congratulate us on the production. Though for us it seemed like a giglet compared to some of the shows we had produced in the past, we had a great time meeting and interviewing the finalists from all the categories. The happy looks on their faces when they took the stage with loud music bumps and moving lighting was all the reward we needed. Tony made it a point to thank us for the great introduction, the pre-recorded voiceover booming through the room saying, "Ladies and gentlemen, please welcome the Loudoun County Chamber of Commerce President and CEO, Tony Howard!" I hit the cue for the loud, energetic music and Shannon pushed up the faders and Tony took the stage. Just like a real award show.

A month after the success of the 2011 awards show, the Loudoun Industrial Development Authority approached us about producing a video on Loudoun's burgeoning data center industry. They felt they needed to create a two-part piece, one segment focused on exactly what a data center was, and the second part focused on why they are beneficial for Loudoun. We won that job not only for our video production capabilities, but also because of our background in technology management. The fact that I had worked for an Internet security firm that had built its own in-house data center, and that I had run a programming group in India, and that we both had worked at AOL gave the IDA the confidence to know we were going to get the story straight. It was to be our first green screen production, high tech and high impact, and it was to be premiered in less than a month at a technology council seminar. Everyone who was anyone in the region's data center businesses would be on hand, and we were expected to deliver.

Buddy Rizer, assistant director of the DED, along with several key executives from data center companies and accomplished consultants, had agreed to be interviewed for the piece. As producer, I knew I had my work cut out for me. Immersing myself as I always do in the topic at hand, I quickly assimilated current trends, topics, and technologies, so that by the day of filming, I felt confident in my mastery of the subject matter. We must have made an impression on our interviewees, as some months later Pete Stevenson, CEO of Latisys, had his marketing team engage us to produce their corporate video. On the 29th when the video was premiered, Mesh Multimedia became a household name in data center alley.

By early summer, Notaviva was getting weekly (if not daily) inquiries about contributing wine to this or that charity event. Virginia ABC law prevented us from donating wine, though many of our colleagues who were known for operating in the grey areas were happy to do so. We were happy to give gift certificates for group tastings, vineyard tours, winemaker presentations, and any other item that could be valuable for a local charity silent auction. Mesh was active with non-profits as well, donating either free or deeply discounted websites to area organizations. We have definitely found community outreach to be just as valuable for your business as it is for your soul. Given two equally competent business proposals, customers will prefer to do business with people they consider honest, contributing members of society whose heart and heads are in the right place.

All of these storylines converged in mid-summer of 2012, when we received our nomination letters and response forms in the mail from the chamber, which I filled out and submitted. When we later learned we had been named finalists in three categories, we were stunned.

The day before the awards banquet, which would take place on November 9th, I had to reach out and ask Danielle Kabban, the chamber's event manager, for the list of winners. We needed to know who the winners were so I could complete my show reel, the PowerPoint containing the slides we put on screen when each name was read. It was my understanding that maybe only five people on the Chamber staff had access to that list, and when Danielle emailed the list, she wrote a simple "Congrats!" in the body of her message. I opened the document, and sure enough, there was my name: Loudoun County's 2012 Entrepreneur of the Year, Stephen Mackey. My head felt faint and I had to sit back in my chair and close my eyes for a few minutes to let the realization sink in. For Shannon and I, there would be no anxious moment holding our breath as the envelope was opened on stage. For us, the anxious moment began right then, as I would have to tell her, and we would have to keep this an absolute secret right up until the moment the envelope was opened the following night. When I gathered my wits together, I found her downstairs and told her the news; she was as shocked as I had been, and we just quietly held each other for a few minutes, hoping to make sense of what this recognition meant. There was no time for that yet; we had a show to produce and I still had several videos to finish editing before packing up all the gear late that night for transportation to the National Conference Center the following day.

Having built the show the year before, the load-in went much more smoothly and we were able to have an actual rehearsal with the hosts. As part of our sponsorship package, we received a complimentary table for ten and had several friends and family on hand for the event, including my mother and Roger, who had flown in from Indianapolis for the week. Out in the lobby where finalists had the opportunity to set up a table display, I had positioned two large flat screen televisions side-by-side. One played a loop of Notaviva Vineyards video and photomontages, and the other played through the various Mesh Multimedia demo reels. The screens were enormous and mounted atop silver truss stands; they made quite the impression as attendees walked by.

Our table guests were nervous wrecks, figuring that since we were finalists in three categories, we had to be taking home at least one trophy. I lied and told everyone we still had no idea who the winners were. After dinner was over the show began, and we progressed smoothly through the various categories, playing all the new finalist videos. The entrepreneur category was the second to last envelope of the night, and I could see everyone at our table watching us nervously. The guest host read, "And the winner is..." while tearing open the envelope, "Stephen Mackey." The ballroom erupted in applause, and I had to start my own music bump while Shannon pushed up the fader on the audio board. I slowly took off my headset, leaned over and kissed Shannon and said, "I love you." She said, "I love you too, baby, I am so proud of you," and I said, "Be proud of us."

Walking through the audience, I was so moved by the encouragement and well wishes of our fellow small business owners and their families. I could see it in their faces that they were as happy for us, as were our friends and families. I could see my mom crying tears of joy as I ascended the few stairs to the stage to accept the award. Pausing for a picture with Tony and the hosts, I returned to the podium and took my notes from the pocket of the Prince Charlie Jacket (a formal Scottish coat) that I had decided to wear with my wedding kilt. Thankful that I actually had a day to prepare what I was going to say, I had thought a lot about what that moment would mean for Shannon and I as entrepreneurs, parents, and as a couple. Though many in the audience knew us, there were just as many whom we had never met before. Standing before them as the Entrepreneur of the Year, I knew I wanted to make a positive impression on this accomplished group of people. I wanted them to know that Stephen and Shannon Mackey were truly grateful to be receiving this honor.

I began by thanking our parents, who had always encouraged and supported us through every endeavor. I thanked our family and friends, whose constant faith in us motivated us in so many ways. I thanked our team members from both businesses for their efforts and commitment, and actually spoke in Spanish when I thanked our vineyard crew, much to the delight of the audience members. I thanked our colleagues in the wine industry, for their support, guidance and camaraderie. As I had done in 2008, I thanked the chamber for its tireless work on behalf of the Loudoun business community, as well as the DED and Visit Loudoun and all of the organizations that support the infrastructure in which we had been able to thrive. With over nine thousand small businesses in Loudoun County, I wanted them to know their efforts in educating, nurturing, and supporting our companies while promoting our products and services meant that a little piece of that award was theirs to share.

When it came time to thank Shannon, I remember the room was absolutely quiet. It took me a moment to gather my thoughts, and let the wave of emotion pass over me until I could speak. Through tears, I thanked her—my friend, my partner, my wife, my world. I could hear others in the audience becoming emotional as I spoke. When I finished, the applause was just as loud as when we had been announced, and as I made my way back to the tech booth, I could see many still wiping their eyes.

A moment later the show was again underway, and the envelope was opened announcing Catoctin Creek Distillery as the Small Business of the Year. We cheered loudly and turned up the music as husband-and-wife team Scott and Becky Harris took the stage, Scott resplendent in his kilt. It was a proud moment indeed to have the two biggest awards of the night presented to rural businesses. After the show ended, the line of friends and colleagues coming by the tech booth was amazing, and we enjoyed spending a few minutes exchanging hugs and taking pictures. We were invited to several post-event parties, but sadly had to decline, as now we had a show to load-out. It is true that the show must go on, but the show must also go out. As all the other award winners left to begin their celebrations, we went back to work.

We will cherish that night forever, for reasons special to us that many people may not understand. Being recognized in that way by our business community was fulfilling for the simple fact that we never set out to win anything. We simply charted a course into the unknown and forged ahead in the face of numerous challenges, doing our best along the way to learn from our mistakes, of which there have been many. We have no regrets, because we have never inten-tionally or maliciously harmed anyone. There have been numerous lessons learned, and some hurt very deeply, from the times when our inexperience as business owners has had a negative impact on others. From being late on payments to vendors, to not providing proper guidance to employees, to learning how to deal with disgruntled customers, there have been so many embarrassing failures that they could fill a memoir of their own. In retrospect, they were necessary for professional as well as personal growth, and it is the doomed entrepreneur who cannot acknowledge his or her mistakes and move forward with a new resolve in a positive direction (after paying late fees and writing apology letters, of course).

The future is a bright, wide-open horizon of unlimited possibilities and exciting opportunities. Though we have had several people inquire about franchise opportunities, there was a time when we swore we would never open up Notaviva Vineyards to outside investment; we now feel that topic is open for discussion. Dr. Bruce Zoecklein was once asked at a seminar, "Which Virginia wineries are for sale?" He chuckled and replied, "All of them!" A winery brand fundamentally paired with music has far more potential than our limited capital could possibly support. When you stop to consider that the Hard Rock Café started as a single American style diner in London, you have to wonder how a music-themed winery would fare in various locations around the globe. Pairing the terroir of local wines with the soul of local music is a concept that we have proven beyond the shadow of a doubt resonates with customers. How do we take this idea to the next level? What could we do with real funding and a larger team of talented visionaries? We shall see.

Our three boys have already found their entrepreneurial calling, selling vegetables from the garden in the tasting room, as well as handmade wine charms and macramé bracelets. At their young ages, they have already learned valuable lessons about pricing materials, calculating labor costs, and finding the right price point for a finished item. Perhaps most importantly, they have also learned that even if you are a cute seven-year old, sometimes people are simply not interested in your product and are not going to part with $2, or they may think that your product is not quite up to their quality level. The lesson learned? Make better products. Learning to deal with that aspect of business is valuable for entrepreneurs of any age; sadly, some people never figure that out.

I began this memoir in January of 2010 at the behest of customers (who always seemed to want more details after I had completed a tasting) and write these last passages in the days after Christmas of 2015. So much has changed since the fall of 2012. In the spring of 2013, Mesh won two Telly Awards for our "Valor" video (which we produced at no charge for our county's first responders), and in the summer we rebranded Mesh Multimedia as Mesh Omnimedia as we expanded our service offering. That fall, I was selected by AmaWaterways to be the first Virginia winemaker to host a European river cruise, and two years later when we sailed on the AmaSonata for the "Melodies of the Danube" trip, our "Vierzig" Blaufränkisch became the first Virginia wine ever poured on such an excursion. In the fall of 2014, Mesh was again nominated as the technology small business of the year, and this time we won.

Active as parents at Powhatan, in winter of 2015 we were contacted by Susan Scarborough, the head of the school, to see if we knew of anyone who may be seeking employment, as the school was looking for a director of technology. After reading the job description, we realized that no one person could handle the wide range of responsibilities to take the school forward with the myriad new STEM initiatives that the board had directed. Shannon applied for the job anyway, since we felt it would be a unique opportunity to teach at the same school our boys were attending. We began a several-month long dialogue about having Powhatan partner with Mesh in an agency of record model, an incredibly innovative solution for a small independent school of Powhatan's size. This past summer we took the reins for every technology initiative at the school, and this fall Shannon became the school's technology teacher and program manager. Though it was a big adjustment for us both as business owners and as a family, it has been so rewarding to be such an integral part of the school, and I relish the days when I am there working alongside her, the five of us all working and learning together on the same beautiful campus.

As for me, I hope I have earned the right to be called a good Virginian, proven worthy through hard work, love of family, home and country. I am hopeful the completion of this memoir and the honest depiction of our story will fulfill the repayment of my debt, that responsibility which was entrusted to me when I was fortunate to receive the gift, now that I finally understand what it means. Perhaps someday soon, I will begin to feel the burden lighten, this weight I have carried for so long finally lifted from my persona. I would relish the ability to relax, to rediscover my love of music composition, or perhaps to just sit under a tree with my mind free of worry. I believe I have done my utmost to devote my talents with passion and zeal to each and every challenge I have ever faced. I believe I have honored those who have fought to preserve America's freedoms, as well as those who will never be fortunate enough to have the opportunities with which I have been blessed. I believe Shannon and I seized upon the idea of what the American dream was conceived to be, and committed ourselves to creating a place where others could foster their own dreams and start their own magical journeys. I believe our small parcel of the Earth is better for our efforts, as are the thousands upon thousands of people who have taken the time to visit. I am thankful for everyone who helped us along the way, for the hundreds of mentors, colleagues, friends, and family who believed in us. I am sorry for the mistakes I have made along the way and the people who may have been hurt, and though I know in my heart that every one of those failures occurred with no ill intent, I will never forget the lessons; that is my pledge. I continue to be afraid, though I will never accept fear. I continue to fail, though I will never accept failure.

Most importantly of all, I have loved, and have been unashamed to express that love in a world where such outward displays of emotion are tragically diminishing each day. Our modern societies possess the intelligence and technologies to right our many wrongs; let us not allow ourselves to grow colder and more callous, missing our fleeting opportunity to do so. As I have learned on my journey and have been blessed to experience firsthand, love is the only sweat equity that lasts. It is the gift, and it is our responsibility to pass it along to our future generations, for without it, they will not succeed.

That is what I choose to believe, that is what I want to believe, and after everything Shannon and I have been through together, it is all I can believe.

To be continued...

SPECIAL THANKS TO THE FOLLOWING:

- The Past, Present, and Future Crew of Notaviva Vineyards
- The Past, Present, and Future Crew of Mesh Omnimedia
- Wine Industry
    » Paul Breaux, Jen Breaux, and Chris Blosser at Breaux Vineyards
    » Dave Collins
    » Doug Fabbioli & Colleen Berg at Fabbioli Cellars
    » Mark & Vicki Fedor at North Gate Vineyard
    » Jordan & Jen Harris at Tarara Winery
    » Clyde & Terri Housel at Hiddencroft Vineyard
    » The Late Jim MacKenzie at Helena Chemical
    » Ben & Connie Renshaw at 8 Chains North Vineyard
    » The Loudoun Wineries Association
    » The Loudoun Wine Growers Association
    » The Virginia Wine Council
    » The Virginia Wineries Association
    » The Virginia Wine Board Marketing Office
- Beta Readers
    » Beth Hodge
    » Paula Kidwell
    » Kaitlin Manocchio
    » Elizabeth Ricketts
    » Allison Robelia

- **Business Community**
  - » Loudoun Chamber of Commerce
  - » Loudoun Department of Economic Development
  - » Visit Loudoun
- **Susan Scarborough, Dr. Kevin Hessberg, and our entire extended family at the Powhatan School**
- **Contributors**
  - » Shauna Ploeger of Photography Du Jour for the rear cover photo
  - » Rodney Gibbons for the wedding reception photo
  - » Lauren Kanne, our editor, for her diligence, patience, and creativity.
- **A very special thanks to Naren Aryal and the team at Mascot Books**

Have a book idea?
Contact us at:

info@mascotbooks.com | www.mascotbooks.com